Hebrews 12.1–13 portrays the suffering of the community to which it is addressed by means of two images: an athletic contest, and God's fatherly discipline. N. Clayton Croy provides a thorough exploration of the theme of suffering in the Jewish and Greco-Roman traditions, and surveys the different interpretations of this passage which have been offered by Christian writers over the centuries. He argues that the concept of "training" unites the passage, which presents Jesus as the supreme athlete, an agonistic exemplar for those running the race. This section of Hebrews also supports a non-punitive understanding of discipline, in which God's children undergo a positive process of education. The educative notion of *paideia* combines with images of athletic training to establish a call to faithful endurance rather than repentance. This book concludes with several theological reflections on the relationship between sin, suffering, and eschatology. A wide-ranging bibliography allows the interested reader to pursue questions further.

SOCIETY FOR NEW TESTAMENT STUDIES

MONOGRAPH SERIES

General editor: Richard Bauckham

98

ENDURANCE IN SUFFERING

Endurance in suffering

Hebrews 12:1–13 in its rhetorical, religious,
and philosophical context

N. CLAYTON CROY

Columbia Theological Seminary

PUBLISHED BY THE PRESS SYNDICATE OF THE UNIVERSITY OF CAMBRIDGE
The Pitt Building, Trumpington Street, Cambridge CB2 1RP, United Kingdom

CAMBRIDGE UNIVERSITY PRESS
The Edinburgh Building, Cambridge CB2 2RU, United Kingdom
40 West 20th Street, New York, NY 10011–4211, USA
10 Stamford Road, Oakleigh, Melbourne 3166, Australia

First published 1998

Printed in the United Kingdom at the University Press, Cambridge

Typeset in Times and Greek New Hellenic [AO]

A catalogue record for this book is available from the British Library

Library of Congress cataloguing in publication data

Croy, N. Clayton.
    Endurance in suffering: Hebrews 12.1–13 in its
rhetorical, religious, and philosophical context / N. Clayton Croy.
        p. cm. – (Society for New Testament studies monograph series;
98)
    Includes bibliographical references.
    ISBN 0 521 59305 0 (hardback)
    1. Bible. N.T. Hebrews – Criticism, interpretation, etc.
I. Title. II. Series: Monograph series (Society for New Testament
Studies); 98.
BS2775.2.C77 1997
227′.8706 – dc21 97-6079 CIP

ISBN 0 521 59305 0 hardback

CONTENTS

Acknowledgments   *page* viii
List of abbreviations   ix

1 Introduction, retrospect, and prospect   1
2 Athletes and exemplars   37
3 Punitive and non-punitive suffering   77
4 Endurance in suffering: Interpreting Hebrews
   12.1–13   162
5 Summary, conclusions, and theses   215

Bibliography   225
Index of ancient texts   237
Index of topics   248

ACKNOWLEDGMENTS

This monograph is a revised version of a dissertation written for Emory University in 1995. Several persons helped inspire, shape, and improve this work. In the fall of 1989 Professor Fred B. Craddock initiated me into the scholarly examination of Hebrews in a seminar at Emory. A paper on Hebrews 12.1–3 written for that seminar would sprout into a proposal some years later. In 1993–5, under the guiding hand and meticulous attention of my adviser Professor Carl R. Holladay, the proposal took shape, was approved, and grew into something resembling the present work. Thanks are due to the members of my dissertation committee, Professors Luke T. Johnson, Hendrickus Boers, Fred B. Craddock, John H. Hayes, and Peter Bing, for their many helpful suggestions and corrections.

I thank the editor of the series, Dr. Margaret Thrall, and the anonymous reader for their gracious acceptance of the work and their constructive comments. Everyone with whom I have dealt at Cambridge University Press has been responsive, capable, and pleasant. In particular, I wish to thank my editor Ruth Parr, production manager Ann Rex, and especially my copy-editor, Virginia Catmur. Their assistance has greatly facilitated a process that was new and somewhat bewildering to a first-time author. Finally, neither this monograph nor the degree accompanying it would have been possible without the material and emotional support of my wife, Marty, during a long period of graduate study. I did not realize at the outset how suitable the title "Endurance in Suffering" would be as a description of those years of research and writing. Marty encouraged and sustained me through them, and I thank her.

ABBREVIATIONS

ABD	*Anchor Bible Dictionary*
ANRW	*Aufstieg und Niedergang der römischen Welt*
BAGD	Bauer, *A Greek–English Lexicon*, ed. Arndt, Gingrich, and Danker
BDF	Blass and Debrunner, *Greek Grammar of the New Testament*, trans. and ed. Funk
CBQ	*Catholic Biblical Quarterly*
CBQMS	*Catholic Biblical Quarterly Monograph Series*
EJMI	Kraft and Nickelsburg, eds., *Early Judaism and its Modern Interpreters*
ET	English Translation
JBL	*Journal of Biblical Literature*
JSNT	*Journal for the Study of the New Testament*
JSOT	*Journal for the Study of the Old Testament*
JTS	*Journal of Theological Studies*
KJV	King James Version
LCL	Loeb Classical Library
LSJ	Liddell and Scott, *A Greek–English Lexicon*, ed. Jones and McKenzie
NEB	New English Version
Nestle[26]	*Novum Testamentum Graece*, 26th edn.
NIV	New International Version
NRSV	New Revised Standard Version
OCD	*Oxford Classical Dictionary*
OTP	*Old Testament Pseudepigrapha*, ed. Charlesworth
PG	*Patrologia Graeca*
PL	*Patrologia Latina*
RAH	*Rhetorica ad Herennium*
RSV	Revised Standard Version
TDNT	*Theological Dictionary of the New Testament*

TEV	Today's English Version
UBS	United Bible Societies
UBS[3]	*Greek New Testament*, 3rd edn.
UBS[4]	*Greek New Testament*, 4th edn.

1

INTRODUCTION, RETROSPECT, AND PROSPECT

1.1 Introduction

Few human experiences are quite so universal as suffering. Its forms and its causes are diverse. Because of its prominence and persistence in human experience, religious traditions (and sometimes philosophy) have given considerable attention to suffering, whether to lament its existence, explain its origin, ascribe some purpose to it, rally forces to alleviate it, or simply to encourage those who face it. Jewish and Christian traditions have done all of the above.

This study focuses on a specific NT passage which addresses the problem of suffering: Hebrews 12.1–13. The text is enclosed by athletic imagery and unified by a common paraenetic aim. The author likens the life of faith to a race, an ἀγών, a process of rigorous discipline, and he[1] urges his readers to endure their struggles and not to be faint-hearted. There are, nevertheless, two distinct sections in the passage: verses 1–3 and 4–13.[2] The first of these issues a call to the readers to "run with endurance," surrounded by the great cloud of witnesses enumerated in chapter 11 and looking to the example of Jesus, who suffered hostility and death. The second section contains a similar exhortation to endure, this time substantiated by an understanding of suffering as divine παιδεία. In short, the author offers the readers two means of encouragement: the supreme paradigm of

---

[1] I will use masculine pronouns in referring to the unknown author of the epistle. In light of the masculine participle in the first person statement of 11.32, this seems justified. Nevertheless, conjectures have been made about female authorship. See J. M. Ford, "The Mother of Jesus and the Authorship of the Epistle to the Hebrews," *Bible Today*, 82 (1975) 683-94; R. Hoppin, *Priscilla, Author of the Epistle to the Hebrews and Other Essays* (New York: Exposition, 1969).

[2] Some disagreement exists about the end of the pericope. Nestle[26] makes a paragraph break after vs.11; UBS[3] divides the text after vs. 13. The latter is preferable in view of the *inclusio* produced by the athletic imagery of vss. 1–2 and 12–13. Most recent commentators favor this division.

endurance in suffering and a view of suffering as divinely purposeful and personally beneficial.

Using this division of the text, scholars have identified two broad streams of tradition as part of the formative milieu of Hebrews 12.1–13: the martyrological tradition exemplified in 4 Maccabees as the milieu of verses 1–3, and the Jewish wisdom tradition such as is represented in Job, Proverbs, and Sirach as the milieu of verses 4–13. This identification is surely valid; the influence of these two traditions is unmistakable. Nevertheless, my own reading of Hebrews 12.1–13 has led me to ask if other dynamics are more influential. Several observations in particular underlie this reappraisal.

First, while the author of Hebrews does indeed draw upon the Jewish wisdom tradition in verses 5–6 (Prov. 3.11–12), his exposition of that passage is selective. Certain features of the passage are developed; others are ignored. This is in keeping with the author's practice of appropriating OT texts often on the basis of a small number of key words. In Hebrews 12.4–13 the concept of παιδεία and the father/son image are clearly the chief concerns of the author. Παιδεία and παιδεύω each occur once in the citation; along with their cognates, the words occur six more times in the exposition. Ὑιός occurs twice in the citation; υἱός and πατήρ occur three times each in the exposition. The more punitive terms in the citation, ἐλέγχω and μαστιγόω, are not appropriated in the exposition. The central term, παιδεία, is notoriously diverse in signification, and the author may very well be exploiting this diversity in his appropriation of Proverbs 3.11–12.

Secondly, the Jewish wisdom tradition often viewed suffering as divine "discipline": in Hebrew texts, *musar*, in Greek texts, παιδεία. This discipline sometimes presupposed culpability on the part of those disciplined, a waywardness of some kind for which they were being punished. But this was not invariably so, and it does not seem to be the case in Hebrews 12.1–13. The epistle addresses a community that was experiencing adversity from an external source: reproaches, trials, imprisonment, and the despoliation of their property (see especially 10.32–4). The immediate causes of this suffering are unnamed persons and/or institutions in the readers' social environment, and although their hardship could be understood as having its ultimate cause in some moral wrongdoing, there is no indication that the author of Hebrews has this in mind.

Thirdly, the athletic imagery of the passage (occurring not just in verses 1–2, but also 4, 11, 12, and 13) favors a non-punitive understanding of παιδεία. Sinners face punishments; athletes face struggles and challenges. Both plights can be conceived in terms of "discipline," punitive discipline for the former, non-punitive discipline for the latter. Since παιδεία can be understood in either sense, the concentration of athletic language may indicate that a non-punitive sense of παιδεία is foremost in the author's mind. Moreover, the particular way in which the athletic imagery is used in verses 1–3 favors a non-martyrological emphasis, even while it appropriates some language from martyrological texts. The call is to faithful endurance, not death. Even the example of Jesus, which could certainly be portrayed as martyr-like, is used to highlight his endurance of shame and hostility. The exegetical crux in verse 2 regarding whether Jesus renounced joy or pursued it also enters in here. The latter interpretation, which I deem far more likely, contributes to a picture of an athlete's exertion toward a goal, rather than the martyr's sacrifice.

Lastly, the list of exemplars in chapter 11, especially with Jesus as the culmination in 12.1–3, lionizes not persons who have endured punishment for sin, but those who have endured (undeserved) hardship, privation, and mistreatment. If the readers of the epistle were suffering God's punishment, they would not have a sense of solidarity with the luminaries of Israel's past as the author has described them. Similarly, the list in chapter 11, while certainly including martyrs (vss. 35–8), primarily highlights those who have remained faithful in difficult times. The forward-looking, or promissory, emphasis of chapter 11 is strong. Again, the call is to endure, not to die.

The two categories that I used above are crucial for this study: punitive and non-punitive. Their meaning should now be clear. These categories will serve as a heuristic device, especially in chapter 3 below, to frame alternate interpretations of Hebrews 12.1–13. I will use them to speak both of two different ways of understanding suffering and of two different types of "discipline" (παιδεία). The latter category, "non-punitive," being a category of negation, is admittedly a "catch-all" grouping, but this sacrifice of precision is compensated by the simplicity gained. The categories have not been chosen to organize a comprehensive, nuanced study of ancient views of suffering, but rather with a view to interpreting Hebrews 12.1–13. If the meaning of παιδεία in this text can be shown to be non-punitive, it will then be necessary to distinguish positively and more precisely the nature and aim of this παιδεία.

This study, in a nutshell, will be an investigation of the rhetorical, religious, and philosophical background of Hebrews 12.1–13 and its two images of suffering. I will be especially concerned to investigate the relevance of *non*-Jewish traditions of the meaning of suffering. Greco-Roman comparative texts have generally been neglected in the history of research, as the following survey will show.[3] Yet they hold the promise of contributing significantly to the interpretation of the passage. In general, the survey will show that Hebrews has been the locus of intense scholarly and homiletical interest, and, with reference to 12.1–13 in particular, a lively arena of debate.

1.2   Retrospect: the history of research

The scholarly investigation of the Epistle to the Hebrews is vast. An adequate treatment of its history would require a sizeable monograph.[4] Here I will only attempt to sketch the more significant contributions to the interpretation of Hebrews 12.1–13, with special attention to two major concerns of this study: the concept of παιδεία and the use of Jesus as an exemplar. The latter will entail a survey of the shifting interpretation of the phrase ἀντὶ τῆς χαρᾶς (12.2). This

---

[3] The terms "comparative text" and "parallel" are used somewhat loosely in scholarship today. Sometimes there seems to be a distinction of quantity, a parallel referring to a text containing an individual word or phrase, whereas a comparative text refers to a similar story or juxtaposition of ideas. This distinction seems to be implied by Abraham J. Malherbe, "Hellenistic Moralists and the New Testament," *ANRW*, II.26.1, (New York: Walter de Gruyter, 1992) 267–333, especially 277–8. Elsewhere there seems to be a distinction of kind; a different version of the same story is a "parallel" (as in Gospel parallels), whereas a comparative text is a different but analogous story. Since the central passage in this study is non-narrative, the latter distinction is not applicable. As for the former distinction, current practice has not established it. I will use the terms interchangeably although I have a slight preference for "comparative text." On the use and abuse of parallels, see the celebrated article by Samuel Sandmel, "Parallelomania," *JBL*, 81 (1962) 1–13.

[4] The early period is covered in Rowan A. Greer, *The Captain of our Salvation. A Study in the Patristic Exegesis of Hebrews* (Tübingen: Mohr, 1973), and E. Riggenbach, *Historische Studien zum Hebräerbrief: Die ältesten lateinischen Kommentare zum Hebräerbrief* (Leipzig: A. Deichert, 1907). Sixteenth-century research is the topic of K. Hagen's *Hebrews Commenting from Erasmus to Bèze* (Tübingen: Mohr, 1981). Most of the twentieth century is treated in two essays by E. Grässer, *Aufbruch und Verheissung: Gesammelte Aufsätze zum Hebräerbrief* (Berlin: Walter de Gruyter, 1992) 1–99, 265–94. See also the essay and extensive bibliography by Philip E. Hughes, "The Epistle to the Hebrews," 351–70 in Eldon Jay Epp and George W. MacRae, eds., *The New Testament and its Modern Interpreters* (Atlanta: Scholars Press, 1989). Further bibliography can be found in the recent commentaries by Harold Attridge, Paul Ellingworth, Hans-Friedrich Weiss, and William L. Lane.

short phrase has been the focal point of a remarkable debate over the centuries.

On the one hand this text is admittedly *not* among the most celebrated passages of the epistle. The history of research has dwelt on topics such as the enigmatic figure of Melchizedek, the ideas of perfection, priesthood, and covenant, the epistle's copious use of the OT, its Christology, and the question of authorship. Prior to the twentieth century there are scarcely any topical monographs or essays on παιδεία, suffering, or athletic imagery in Hebrews. Therefore, most comments on 12.1–13 are found in the context of early homilies or in commentaries covering the entire epistle. Accordingly, these sources form the bulk of the material in the following history of research.[5]

On the other hand, one should not think that this passage is inconsequential, a sort of epistolary backwater. On the contrary, it not only contains several of the recurring features of the epistle (an OT citation, an allusion to Psalm 110, an *a fortiori* argument, and a reference to the historical Jesus), but it also seems to express supremely the letter's paraenetic aim: to reinvigorate the flagging faith of the readers.

The first literary use of the Epistle to the Hebrews is 1 Clement, probably written in the last decade of the first century.[6] Possible allusions to Hebrews 12.1–13, however, are few and obscure. First Clement 19.2 contains the exhortation ἐπαναδράμωμεν ἐπὶ τὸν σκοπόν (Let us run to the goal) which faintly resembles Hebrews 12.1.[7] In 1 Clement 56.4 a series of OT citations includes Proverbs 3.12. This appropriation of Proverbs offers an interesting comparison with the use of the same text in Hebrews 12.5–6 (a comparison that will be taken up later), but it does not constitute an interpretation of Hebrews.[8]

Among the earliest commentaries on Hebrews was that of Origen

---

[5] I have made use of the chronologically arranged bibliography of H.-F. Weiss, *Der Brief an die Hebräer* (Göttingen: Vanderhoeck & Ruprecht, 1991) 12–15.

[6] Although 1 Clement's dependence on Hebrews has been disputed, a convincing case is made by Harold W. Attridge, *The Epistle to the Hebrews* (Philadelphia: Fortress, 1989) 6–7 and n. 52.

[7] See also 1 Clement 63.1: ἐπὶ τὸν προκείμενον ἡμῖν ... σκοπὸν ... καταντήσωμεν (Let us gain the goal set before us). Translations of patristic, medieval, and modern commentators are mine unless otherwise indicated.

[8] The same is probably true of Tertullian's remark (*De Patientia 11: PL* 1.1378) "'Those whom I love,' he says, 'I chasten.'" Whether Tertullian has in mind here Prov. 3.11, Heb. 12.5, or even Rev. 3.19, is hard to determine.

(*ca.* 185–254). Regrettably, the loss of Origen's writings is extensive; his commentary on Hebrews (as with 275 of his 291 works!) is not extant, surviving only in small fragments of catenae, Biblical manuscripts, and later quotations.[9] Some of Origen's thoughts on Hebrews survive, however, in scattered portions of his other works.

In *Exhortatio ad Martyrium* 37 (*PG* 11.612 BC) Origen quotes Hebrews 12.2c and likens the humiliation and exaltation of Christ to that of Christ's followers: "And those who imitate him 'despising the shame' will 'sit' with him and reign with him in heaven." Origen clearly views Christ's experience as paradigmatic for the church, but whereas he highlights Jesus' exaltation as a pattern for the believer, the author of Hebrews does this with Jesus' endurance.[10]

The notion of divine correction is treated by Origen in *Selecta in Exodum* (*PG* 12.293 A). He cites Proverbs 3.11 as well as Psalm 89.32–3 to assert that the Lord's "rod" is an instrument of divine mercy, visited on those whom God regards as sons (and daughters). Chastisement is a sign of God's love for the people of God. The general tradition here and the specific use of Proverbs 3.11 are shared by Hebrews, but there is no explicit appropriation of the text of Hebrews. Moreover, "Origen tends to disassociate the passage from any specific reference to persecution and applies it more generally to God's disciplinary rule of His people."[11] The author of Hebrews, on the other hand, applies Proverbs 3.11–12 precisely to a situation of persecution.

Finally, Origen once explicitly cites Hebrews 12.11. In *Homily* 27 he comments on Numbers 33.8 and the Israelite camp at the bitter waters: "When you hear this word 'bitternesses,' do not be frightened or terrified. 'For the moment all discipline seems painful rather than pleasant; later it yields the peaceful fruit of righteousness to those who have been trained by it.' "[12] Here we find the common reflection that life's bitter experiences are necessary discipline prescribed by God for our benefit. The reference is not specifically to persecution, but presumably could include it.

The first extant homilies on Hebrews are those of John Chrysostom

[9] Johannes Quasten, *Patrology* (Westminster, MD: Christian Classics, 1986) II, 51.
[10] In addition to *Patrologia Graeca*, a critical edition of Origen is available in Paul Koetschau, *Die Griechischen Christlichen Schriftsteller der Ersten Drei Jahrhunderte, Origenes, Erster Band* (Leipzig: J. C. Hinrichs'sche, 1899) 34.
[11] Greer, *Captain of our Salvation*, 30. The same is true of Origen's citation of Prov. 3.11 in *De Principiis* 3.12.
[12] Translation from Greer, *Captain of our Salvation*, 30–1.

(*ca.* 347–407). Homilies 28–30 are a rambling commentary on the last few verses of Hebrews 11 through about the middle of chapter 12. The commentary proceeds verse by verse, interrogating the text, clarifying expressions, frequently citing Gospel and Pauline texts, and offering detailed "application" sometimes having little connection with Hebrews. For my purposes it will suffice to cite Chrysostom's remarks on Hebrews 12.11.[13]

The words τοῖς δι' αὐτῆς γεγυμνασμένοις from Hebrews 12.11 are quoted, and then, in typical fashion, Chrysostom asks "Τί ἐστι;" (What does this mean?) He answers, "Τοῖς ἀνασχομένοις ἐπὶ πολὺ καὶ καρτερήσασιν." (To those who have endured for a long time and been steadfast.) Then comes a succinct but perceptive statement: ἄρα γυμνασία ἐστὶν ἡ παιδεία. (Discipline is, therefore, exercise.) In a simple predication, Chrysostom observes that the discipline of which Hebrews speaks is a kind of training. The following clauses reinforce this: τὸν ἀθλητὴν ἰσχυρὸν ἐργαζομένη, καὶ ἀκαταγώνιστον ἐν τοῖς ἀγῶσι, καὶ ἄμαχον ἐν τοῖς πολέμοις (... making the athlete strong, and unconquerable in contests, and invincible in battles). Chrysostom conceives of παιδεία as a disciplined regimen which prepares a person for life's contests. In doing so he makes an explicit link between παιδεία and the athletic imagery of the passage, a link which has too seldom been appreciated.

A few additional figures from the fifth to sixth centuries made minor contributions to the patristic exegesis of Hebrews. In most cases, however, the works of these preachers and expositors are only extant in fragments, and their comments are often limited to minor lexical matters, paraphrases of the text, and interpretations of individual clauses. Since these commentaries are sparse, and there are no noteworthy interpretations of παιδεία, I will postpone discussion of them until the detailed exegesis of chapter 4.[14]

Apart from Chrysostom, the only early church leader producing

---

[13] *PG* 63.209.

[14] The persons involved are the following: Severian (d. *ca.* 408), bishop of Gabala; Theodore of Mopsuestia (d. 428), whose commentary on Hebrews survives in fragments; Cyril of Alexandria (d. *ca.* 444), whose commentary is now extant only in catenae; and Cassiodorus (485–580), Italian statesman and monastic scholar, whose *Complexiones in Epistolas Apostolorum* includes scattered remarks on Hebrews. Their works can be found in the standard collections and/or in Karl Staab, *Pauluskommentare aus der griechischen Kirche* (Münster, 1933). The references are: Severian (Staab, *Pauluskommentare*, 345–51), Theodore (*PG* 66.952-68, and Staab, *Pauluskommentare*, 200–12), Cyril (*PG* 74.953–1006), and Cassiodorus (*PL* 70.1357–61).

extensive commentary on Hebrews was Theodoret of Cyrus (*ca.* 393–466), the last great theologian of Antioch. His commentary on Hebrews extends to about sixty full columns of Greek in the standard edition.[15] Theodoret saw the special significance of Jesus' example for Christians. Whereas the exemplars of chapter 11 are called "the archetypes of godliness," in Jesus the author of Hebrews adduces "the greatest archetype" (12.2). Another point made by Theodoret, found repeatedly in patristic commentaries, is the voluntary nature of Jesus' suffering. Regarding the problematic phrase ἀντὶ τῆς προκειμένης αὐτῷ χαρᾶς (vs. 2), Theodoret asserts that the cross was not inevitable: ἠδύνατο ... μὴ παθεῖν, εἴπερ τοῦτο ἠθέλησεν ([Jesus] was able not to suffer, if in fact he had wanted this). Presumably Jesus might have chosen to continue his earthly life and forgo suffering. An alternate way of construing ἀντί yields, as we shall see, a very different interpretation.

Between the expositors of the fifth and sixth centuries and the turn of the millennium, the work of one particular exegete is worthy of mention. Saint John of Damascus (*ca.* 675–749), whom the modern Orthodox churches consider the last of the "Fathers," produced a collection of notes on Hebrews.[16] Two of his comments on our passage are typical of patristic exegesis. First, he interprets ἀντί in verse 2 as implying that Christ's suffering was not compulsory: Ἐξῆν αὐτῷ μηδὲν παθεῖν, εἴπερ ἠβούλετο. Ὁ δὲ ἀντὶ τούτου σταυρὸν ὑπέμεινε, μηδεμίαν ἔχων ἀνάγκην τοῦ σταυρωθῆναι. (It was possible for him to suffer nothing, if in fact he had so wished. Instead of this he endured a cross, though having no need at all to be crucified.) Secondly, he adopts the "gymnastic" interpretation of παιδεία, quoting verbatim, but not acknowledging, the exposition of Chrysostom in reference to γεγυμνασμένοις (vs. 11).

In the tenth and eleventh centuries we find Oecumenius and Theophylactus respectively. Oecumenius, bishop of Trikka, composed a substantial commentary on Hebrews, nearly ninety full columns of Greek in the standard edition.[17] Theophylactus, bishop of Ochrida, also wrote a lengthy exposition, extending beyond 100 columns.[18]

Oecumenius, as Theodoret before him, calls attention to the primacy of Christ's example. When the biblical writer moves from the cloud of witnesses to the author and finisher of faith, he comes to τὸ κεφάλαιον τῆς παρακλήσεως ... τὸν Χριστόν (the main point of the

---

[15] *PG* 82.674–786.   [16] *PG* 95. 929–98.   [17] *PG* 119.281–456.
[18] *PG* 125.185–404.

exhortation ... Christ). Both Oecumenius and Theophylactus stress the voluntary nature of Christ's suffering.[19] The latter wrote, Ἐξῆν γὰρ αὐτῷ μὴ παθεῖν, μὴ ἀποθανεῖν (For it was possible for him not to suffer, not to die). Oecumenius gives the positive alternative: Ἐξῆν αὐτῷ ... μετὰ δόξης καὶ χαρᾶς διάγειν (It was possible for him to go through life with glory and joy). Both expositors cite John 10.18, Ἐξουσίαν ἔχω θεῖναι τὴν ψυχήν μου, as a confirmation in the Lord's own words. Such readiness to interpret Hebrews by reference to a Gospel text is typical of patristic exegesis, but, of course, problematic.[20]

Regarding the meaning of παιδεία, Oecumenius offers an exposition which contains some inner tension, but perhaps no more than the text itself possesses. In the exposition of verses 5–10, by necessity Oecumenius uses the imagery of parental discipline. But even here there is a tendency to move away from the punitive tone of Proverbs 3.11–12. After Oecumenius quotes Ὅν γὰρ ἀγαπᾷ Κύριος, παιδεύει (12.6a) his exposition continues: Οὐδεὶς γὰρ δύναται δεῖξαι δίκαιον χωρὶς θλίψεως ἐπειδὴ στενή ἐστι καὶ τεθλιμμένη ἡ εἰς τὴν ζωὴν ὁδός. Τοιγαροῦν καὶ ὑμᾶς εἰς παιδείαν καλεῖ ὁ θεός, οὐκ εἰς κόλασιν. (For no one can point to a person [who has become] righteous apart from affliction, since the way to life is narrow and hard. Therefore, God calls you also to discipline, not to punishment.) These three clauses give an indication of Oecumenius' interpretation of Hebrews 12.5–10. First, θλίψις is viewed as the means of παιδεία. The readers are experiencing θλίψις, affliction or hardship, and its (potential) result is to render a person δίκαιος. The second clause, an allusion to Matthew 7.14, corroborates this. Παιδεία is understood as the incidental affliction that befalls one who pursues the Christian ζωή.[21] The final clause makes this explicit: God is calling you to a process of παιδεία, not κόλασις.[22] In this last sentence Oecumenius clearly lifts phrases from the two parts of Hebrews 12.1–13. Τοιγαροῦν καὶ ὑμᾶς comes from verse 1 (with the pronoun changed to second person); εἰς παιδείαν comes from verse 7. These subtle echoes show that Oecumenius viewed the passage as a unified call to the training or discipline that inheres in affliction.

---

[19] They are probably dependent on Chrysostom who makes the same argument and also adduces John 10.18 (*PG* 63.193–4).
[20] One might just as easily appeal to Rev. 13.8 to show the inevitability of the cross.
[21] Theodoret also cites Matt. 7.14 in his brief comment on vs. 11 (*PG* 82.773).
[22] Κόλασις is often used of divine punishment in Jewish, Christian, and pagan writers. See BAGD, 441.

Theophylactus' exposition of verses 5–10 similarly underscores the role of θλίψις in παιδεία. In an echo of Oecumenius he writes Ἀδύνατον γὰρ εὑρεῖν τινα τῶν ἀγαπωμένων τῷ Κυρίῳ χωρὶς θλίψεων (For it is impossible to find a person among those loved by the Lord who has not experienced affliction). Later in a paraphrase of Hebrews 12.8 he substitutes θλίψεις for παιδεία: Εἰ μὲν γὰρ ἐκτὸς θλίψεων ἦτε, ἐφαίνεσθε ἂν ὅτι νόθοι ἐστὲ καὶ οὐχ υἱοί (For if you were without afflictions, it would appear that you are illegitimate and not sons). Anticipating an objection, Theophylactus admits that bandits and thieves are punished, but he distinguishes their punishment from that of sons. The whipping of sons (μαστίγωσις) should be understood as education (παίδευσις), not as payment for evil (κακίας ἔκτισις). Although "whipping" is strongly punitive and the choice of a different word might have lessened the tension in his exposition, Theophylactus clearly regards the aim and presupposition of the "whipping" of sons as quite different from those of the punishment of malefactors.

A second place in which both Oecumenius and Theophylactus interpret παιδεία is in their exposition of verse 11. Both men seize upon the athletic imagery latent in γεγυμνασμένοις. Theophylactus' comment recalls Chrysostom: Ὅρα δὲ ὅτι γυμνασίαν καλεῖ τήν παιδείαν, ῥωννύσυσαν τοὺς πιστούς, καὶ οἷόν τινας ἀθλητάς, καὶ εὐτονωτέρους ποιοῦσαν. Τί οὖν ἀποφεύγετε τὴν ἐνισχύουσαν τὰς ψυχὰς ὑμῶν; (Now see that [the author of Hebrews] calls discipline an exercise, one that strengthens the faithful, as if they were athletes, and makes them more vigorous. Why then do you flee from the [discipline] that strengthens your souls?) Oecumenius pens a terse but evocative sentence: Γυμνάζει ἄρα ἡ παιδεία πρὸς ἀρετὴν καὶ ἀλείφει (Therefore, discipline trains [a person] for virtue and anoints). Anointing seems to intrude awkwardly here, but it serves the athletic image.[23] Ἀρετή in conjunction with γυμνάζει may evoke the manly, physical qualities of the Homeric epics, but it more likely serves as a Hellenistic equivalent of Hebrews' ἁγιότης (12.10) and δικαιοσύνη (12.11). In summary, both commentators understand παιδεία as including an element of formative discipline, training, or exercise. The faithful who patiently undergo God's παιδεία will be strengthened thereby.

A few trends emerge from this survey of the first millennium

---

[23] For references to anointing in preparation for exercise as well as metaphorical uses, see LSJ, 62.

of exposition. First, the example of Christ's endurance in Hebrews 12.1–3 was seen as the climax of chapter 11 and the supreme motivation for Christian endurance. Second, 12.2 was understood to imply that Jesus' passion was not a necessity. He had joy within his grasp, but in lieu of it (ἀντί) he voluntarily endured the cross. Third, the readers' suffering was interpreted as God's discipline, but this was distinguished in nature and in purpose from the retributive punishment of wrongdoers; it was παιδεία, not κόλασις. Lastly, παιδεία was strongly linked, even equated with γυμνασία by several early commentators. The divine discipline of verses 4–11 was associated with the athletic imagery in verses 1–4 and 11–13. Παιδεία entailed rigorous training that resulted in increased strength and endurance. Although the notion of punitive discipline is by no means absent from patristic and early medieval exegesis, the formative and "gymnastic" character of discipline was strongly felt.

In the twelfth century two students of the Epistle to the Hebrews deserve mention: Peter Lombard (1100–60), bishop of Paris and author of the celebrated *Sententiarum Libri IV*, and Herveus (d. *ca.* 1150), Benedictine monastic scholar in Bourg-Dieu.[24]

Both of these writers were aware of the two interpretations of ἀντὶ τῆς … χαρᾶς. This joy was either the "eternal joy, to obtain which it was necessary to undergo the passion" or the joy "set before him by the multitudes … when they wanted to make him king."[25] No preference for one interpretation over the other is expressed.

Herveus translated παιδεία as *disciplina* and saw it as the divine employment of hardship for the purpose of teaching or testing: *[disciplina] id est tribulationes per quas potes discere, quod ideo vult Deus te tribulari, ut possis velut aurum igne tribulationis probari* (Discipline, that is, afflictions through which you can learn, since God wants you to be afflicted for this reason, so that you may be tested as gold by the fire of affliction).[26] On the other hand these tribulations also have a corrective, or even cathartic function: "By adversity you are reproved and rebuked by the Lord for the wrongdoings which you have done, so that you may recognize and correct them … Through afflictions [God] makes him whom he loves pure from faults." Similarly, in his comments on verse 11 he

---

[24] *PL* 192.399–520 (Lombard), and *PL* 181.1519–1692 (Herveus).
[25] Herveus, *PL* 181.1667. See also Lombard, *PL* 192.501. In the latter phrase both authors allude to the incident in chapter 6 of John's Gospel.
[26] This and the following quote: *PL* 181.1668–9.

asserts that "discipline is affliction, which each person suffers for his own sins in order that he might be corrected." God's discipline is thus equated with the endurance of hardship, but the root cause of that hardship is wrongdoing on the part of the sufferer. For Herveus, discipline is educative in outcome, but punitive in origin.

Peter Lombard's view of παιδεία seems identical: it is educative, but also purgative and corrective. On verse 5 he writes: *Noli negligere disciplinam Domini, id est tribulationes quibus erudiris a Domino ... qui purgat peccata ... Dominus ... castigat, id est castum facit corripiendo* (Do not despise the discipline of the Lord, that is, the afflictions through which you are instructed by the Lord ... who cleanses away sins ... The Lord chastens, that is, he makes chaste by reproving).[27] Discipline is: *eruditio per molestias quando pro peccatis suis mala quis patitur, ut corrigatur* (learning through tribulations when one suffers misfortunes for one's own sins in order that one may be corrected).[28]

A third twelfth-century contribution is of uncertain authorship. The *Glossa Ordinaria*, traditionally thought to be the work of the ninth-century Benedictine abbot and theologian, Walafrid Strabo, was more likely the product of the school of Anselm of Laon.[29] The *Glossa Ordinaria* is a lengthy collection of mostly lexical notes, culled chiefly from patristic commentaries. There are several comments on Hebrews 12.1–13.[30] Two possible interpretations are given for ἀντί (vs. 2). The joy set before us (and, by implication, Jesus) may be the joy of eternity. Alternately, joy could refer to the possibility Jesus had of an earthly reign: *proposito sibi gaudio temporalis regni, quando voluerunt eum turbae rapere ut facerent regem* (the joy set before him of a temporal kingship when the multitudes wanted to seize him and make him king). Secondly, and more importantly for this study, the author argues that even Jesus, "who alone was without sin," is to be included among those who are disciplined by God. Hence we should not marvel that a saint may suffer indignities when

---

[27] *PL* 192.502. Both Lombard and Herveus (*PL* 181.1669) capitalized on the etymological connection between *castigo* and *castus*.

[28] *PL* 192.503. The striking similarity of *eruditio per molestias* to Herveus' words (*PL* 181.1671–2) is no doubt to be explained by a common source in Augustine (*PL* 37.1548).

[29] See *The Oxford Dictionary of the Christian Church* (F. L. Cross and E. A. Livingstone, eds.; 2nd edn.; Oxford: Oxford University, 1974) 572.

[30] *PL* 114.643–70.

we consider "what was endured by the most Just of the just, the most Pious of the pious."

Finally, the *Glossa* shows an awareness of the range of meanings for *disciplina* in verse 11. With obvious indebtedness to Peter Lombard and other commentators, the author cites the word and explains: "In Greek this is called παιδεία, that is, learning through tribulations when one suffers misfortunes for one's own sins in order that one may be corrected ... Discipline is also that which is called knowledge ... and in Greek is called ἐπιστήμη." Although a punitive quality (*pro peccatis*) is seen in *disciplina*, the word clearly has didactic and cognitive nuances too. Apparently *disciplina* is learning acquired through vexing experiences suffered as a result of one's sins, as well as understanding of a more intellectual nature.

Between the twelfth century and the first stirrings of the Reformation stands the great scholastic theologian of the Middle Ages, Thomas Aquinas (1225–74). Among his many works is *Super Epistolas Sancti Pauli Lectura*.[31]

Aquinas' commentary on Hebrews is exceedingly systematic and structured. From nearly every verse or paragraph of the text, two or three complementary points are derived, forming an outline for the exposition. One such point is the joy that lay before Christ in 12.2. Aquinas acknowledges two possibilities, the earthly joy of a kingly reign versus the joy of eternal life as a reward, but states no preference.[32]

According to Aquinas human beings have a proneness toward evil which the discipline of God aims at restraining. *Dominus castigat nos, ut retrahat nos a malo* (The Lord chastens us in order to keep us back from evil). The aim of this discipline is benign; the Lord chastens not for the purpose of condemnation, but for salvation.[33] Like Herveus and Lombard, Aquinas has a concept of παιδεία which combines the instructive and the punitive. His definition is similar to theirs: *[Disciplina] est eruditio per flagella et molestias* ([Discipline] is learning through scourges and tribulations).[34] The punitive nuance of παιδεία is especially evident when, in his transition to verse 12, he reflects on verses 5–11 with these words: *Supra*

---

[31] Thomas Aquinas, *Super Epistolas S. Pauli Lectura* (Raphael Cai, ed.; 8th edn.; Rome: Marietti, 1953).
[32] *Super Epistolas*, 482.
[33] *Ibid.*, 484–5.
[34] *Ibid.*, 486. On this language, see n. 28 above.

monuit Apostolus qualiter nos debemus habere ad mala poenalia sustinenda (Above, the Apostle advises how we ought to conduct ourselves so as to endure punitive misfortunes). The addition of the word *poenalia* removes any ambiguity that might remain.

In the Reformation era the Epistle to the Hebrews continued to be the object of exegetical and theological reflection.[35] The commentaries of several scholars from this period have been preserved in the magnificent *Critici Sacri*, a massive, multi-volume anthology of Biblical exposition.[36] Here one gains access to the works of over a dozen different scholars, some virtually inaccessible otherwise. Excerpts from *Critici Sacri*, along with the individual commentaries of some of the leading figures of the era, give us a sense of Reformation exegesis of our passage.

Lorenzo Valla (1407–57), an Italian humanist, literary critic, and precursor of the Reformation, called attention to the variety of meanings for παιδεία. Commenting on verses 5–9, he writes, "Because of this passage ... it is customary for some to refer to discipline as chastisement and correction, and indeed they seem to do so rightly. However, let us be aware that for discipline, chastisement, correction, and instruction there is one and the same word in Greek, παιδεία, which strictly speaking is instruction and education, as for instance, of children."[37] Here Valla not only highlights the range of possible meanings for παιδεία, but he is particularly concerned that the cognitive and developmental nuances of the word should be included.

Erasmus (1466–1536), Dutch humanist and one of the greatest classical scholars of the Renaissance, was able to blend the punitive and formative qualities of παιδεία without apparent conflict. Παιδευτάς in verse 9, he says, refers to "the process of education, as if of children, which often was a matter of floggings and reproof."[38] Censure and corporal punishment were standard fare in ancient and medieval pedagogy, and Erasmus, like many others, saw no difficulty in applying this image to God.[39]

---

[35] The sixteenth century is chronicled in Hagen, *Hebrews Commenting*.

[36] *Critici Sacri, sive, Annotata Doctissimorum Virorum in Vetus ac Novum Testamentum* (John Pearson *et al.* eds.; Amsterdam: Boom, 1698). This work was originally published in London, 1660. For full bibliographical information on the various editions see Hagen, *Hebrews Commenting*, bibliography, p. 108.

[37] *Critici Sacri*, VII, 1144.

[38] *Ibid.*

[39] On the harshness of ancient pedagogy, see Stanley R. Bonner, *Education in Ancient Rome* (Berkeley and Los Angeles: University of California, 1977) esp. 143–5.

Martin Luther (1483–1546) delivered a series of lectures on the Epistle to the Hebrews in 1517–18.[40] These lectures are troublesome for editors in that they include glosses, which were marginal comments on individual words and phrases, and scholia, or sustained expositions of the text. Gleaning from both sources, we can piece together Luther's understanding of our passage. "Joy" in verse 2 was that which lay in the future, the contemplation of which sustained Jesus in suffering. The struggle against sin (vs. 4) is broadly conceived as "fighting against the devil, the world, and one's own self." Hardship and persecution also seem to be included: "Every affliction fights in behalf of sin against us ... [Our] opponents also are the weapons of sin." The effect of this is to generalize, and ultimately to obscure, the nature of the readers' struggle. The παιδεία which God employs to sustain a person in this struggle likewise loses clarity. Generally, however, Luther understands παιδεία in terms of Jewish wisdom literature. Though he translates it as *disciplina*, he adds the gloss *flagella, castigationem*. His citations of Proverbs 22.15, "Folly is bound up in the heart of a boy, but the rod of discipline drives it far away," and 13.24, "Those who spare the rod hate their children, but those who love them are diligent to discipline them," place Hebrews 12 squarely in the wisdom tradition.[41] Nothing in Luther's exposition suggests linkage between παιδεία and the athletic imagery of the passage. There is no comment on γεγυμνασμένοις in verse 11.

John Calvin (1509–64) published a commentary on the Epistle to the Hebrews in 1549.[42] Its considerable length made possible the inclusion of many grammatical, intertextual, and theological observations. On the critical interpretation of ἀντὶ τῆς ... χαρᾶς in verse 2, Calvin recognizes two possibilities but prefers the interpretation by which Christ renounces joy.[43]

> For *for the joy* is equivalent to in place of the joy, and joy
> includes every kind of comfort. And he says, set before him,
> because it was in Christ's hand, so that if he had pleased

[40] *Luthers Vorlesung über den Hebräerbrief nach der Vatikanischen Handschrift* (E. Hirsch and H. Rückert, eds.; Berlin and Leipzig: Walter de Gruyter, 1929) 80–7, esp. 83–4. See also Kenneth Hagen, *A Theology of Testament in the Young Luther: The Lectures on Hebrews* (Leiden: Brill, 1974).

[41] Biblical quotations are from the NRSV throughout unless otherwise indicated.

[42] *Ioannis Calvini in Novi Testamenti Epistolas Commentarii* (Berlin: Eichler, 1834). ET: *Calvin's Commentary on the Epistle to the Hebrews* (London: Cornish, 1842).

[43] Translation from *Commentary* (see previous note), 170.

he had the opportunity of using it. Still if any one think the Greek preposition, rendered for, denotes the final cause, and, I do not much oppose it, the sense would then be, that Christ refused not the death of the cross, because he saw its happy end. I, however, retain the former exposition.

Calvin understands that persecution lies in the background of this text, but he seems especially concerned about sin as an "inner enemy." Hostility from external sources somehow has the effect of subduing fleshly desires. "The persecutions that we endure for the sake of the Gospel are also useful to us for another reason, since they are remedies for the destruction of sin. For in this way God keeps us under the yoke of his discipline, so that our flesh does not grow wanton." God "exercises" us in a contest, but for Calvin the contest is primarily against one's own sin: "Whether then he corrects our faults, or prevents us before we sin, he thus exercises us in this struggle against sin." Divine corrections are whips [*ferulae*] by which God "chastens our sins." The aim of God's correction is the mortification of the flesh: "The chastisements of God are designed to subdue and mortify the flesh, that we may be renewed for heavenly life ... The corrections of God are aids for our preparation because through them the Lord exercises us for the mortification of the flesh."[44] Although Calvin uses the language of *exerceo*, the context is not "gymnastic." Like Luther, he remains within the framework of the wisdom tradition and punitive discipline.

Theodore Beza (1519–1605), successor to Calvin as the leader of Reformed Protestantism, wrote a commentary on Hebrews in 1556, a fifth edition of which appeared by the end of the century. Like Calvin, Beza recognized two possible interpretations of ἀντὶ τῆς ... χαρᾶς in verse 2. On the meaning of the preposition he writes:

> Sometimes [it means] instead of and "in lieu of," other times "for the sake of." Either sense is suitable: Jesus Christ endured in lieu of and instead of the joy set before him, since it was permissible [for him] to enjoy eternal happiness ... Or by the other interpretation: the sense will be: Christ our leader endured the cross for the sake of the joy that had

---

[44] All quotes in this paragraph are from *Commentarii*, Pars Tertia, 137–40. Translations are mine.

been set before him. The same happiness has been set before us. Therefore we ought to enter into the same path.[45]

In the last two sentences, Beza shows that the second interpretation (ἀντί as "for the sake of, because of") is preferable because it makes the example of Christ more relevant to the author's paraenetic aim.

Like most Reformation exegetes, Beza interprets παιδεία primarily in the context of Israel's wisdom tradition. He is concerned, however, to distinguish between the punishment of "sinners" and the punishment of God's children: "Although the same punishments seem to envelop sinners and those who confess His name, let us remember that chastisements are called acts of paideia. Although they seem to fall by one and the same blow, nevertheless this action has two different pretexts: [God] chastises in order that he might save sons. He smites the impious in order to destroy [them]."[46] Furthermore, wrath is not necessarily the motive: "What compels [God] to chastise us? Sins. But not always. Wrath does not motivate him, otherwise he would destroy us, but rather love." As Theophylactus did centuries before, Beza emphasizes the special aim and motive of God's discipline of those regarded as God's children. It is, nevertheless, punitive discipline which Beza has in mind, for in response to the objection that God's punishments are too severe, he says: "Let us consider how great is the magnitude of our iniquities."

A few summary remarks can be made about the exegesis of Hebrews 12.1–13 in the twelfth to the sixteenth centuries. Scholars began to recognize an alternative way to interpret "joy" in verse 2. Herveus, Lombard, and Aquinas acknowledge the alternatives without further comment. Calvin describes both ways and expresses a slight preference for the earlier patristic interpretation; Luther mentions only the "prospective" view. Beza discusses both "ἀντί as *loco*" and "ἀντί as *propter*" but favors the latter.

With the possible exception of Valla (whose comment is too brief to permit certainty), twelfth- to sixteenth-century exegetes interpreted παιδεία in Hebrews 12 largely within the context of Jewish wisdom traditions. Herveus, Lombard, and Aquinas saw divine discipline as instructive but also related to the sins of the sufferer. The punitive quality was particularly strong in Calvin, who saw

---

[45] Théodore de Bèze, *Cours sur les Epîtres aux Romains et aux Hébreux (1564–66) d'après les notes de Marcus Widler* (P. Fraenkel and L. Perrotet, eds.; Geneva, 1988) 335.

[46] This quote and the next two from Bèze, *Cours*, 336–7.

discipline as a control on carnality. Beza stressed the underlying motive of divine love, but nevertheless construed παιδεία as a reproof for wrongdoings.

These two trends contrast with the earlier patristic interpretations. The second is especially important to this study. Patristic exegesis tended to see more unity in the passage, a unity based in part on athletic imagery. The idea of formative discipline as a continuous thread running through the passage, first in terms of an athletic competition, then in terms of a parent/child relationship, was incipient in patristic exegesis but virtually absent from scholarship of the subsequent era.

In the seventeenth century we find Hugo Grotius (1583–1645), Dutch jurist, scholar, and polymath. Grotius composed fairly extensive annotations on both canonical and apocryphal books. His comments on Hebrews 12 include a few remarks relevant to this study. Grotius followed Luther in preferring the "prospective" or futuristic interpretation of joy in verse 2, suggesting that ἀντί was used here instead of ἕνεκα.[47] He believed that the sin against which the readers were struggling (vs. 4) was apostasy, *defectio ab Evangelio*. His only remark relevant to παιδεία is a terse comment on verse 6: "Such chastisements are called by the Hebrews 'chastisements of love.'" The remainder of Grotius's insights pertain to minor matters.

Two massive commentaries on Hebrews appeared in the second half of the seventeenth century: those of John Owen and William Gouge.[48] Owen's exposition extends to seven volumes, Gouge's was originally three. Both works were popular with preachers owing to their immense (though often vapid and overdone) detail and ubiquitous sermon outlines. The writing is prosaic, but by much sifting one can find occasional exegetical nuggets.

Both Owen and Gouge construe ἀντί in verse 2 as "on account of." Owen observes that the common meaning for ἀντί is "in the stead of," but he insists that "there is no reason to bind up ourselves unto the ordinary use of the word, when the contexture wherein it is placed requires another sense not contrary thereunto."[49] Gouge

---

[47] This quote and the next two from *Critici Sacri*, VII, 1163.

[48] John Owen, *An Exposition of the Epistle to the Hebrews* (London, 1668–74). My edition is New York: Robert Carter, 1855. William Gouge, *Commentary on the Whole Epistle to the Hebrews* (London: Kirton, 1655). My edition is Grand Rapids: Kregel, 1980.

[49] Owen, *Exposition*, VII, 239-40.

defends the "prospective" interpretation by citing a similar use of ἀντί in 12.16 and the resulting correspondence between Christ's suffering and that of the saints. "By this joy set before Christ, we may know that we also have a joy set before us."[50]

Regarding divine παιδεία, both Owen and Gouge, sticking closely to the familial metaphor of the text, understand God as correcting errant children. "It is needful that divine institution or instruction should be accompanied with correction."[51] "[Παιδεία] is used sometimes for instruction ... sometimes for correction, as here."[52] The cathartic quality of παιδεία is especially clear in Owen: "Unto chastisement is required, that the person chastised be in a state wherein there is sin ... for the end of [chastisement] is to take away sin, to subdue it, to mortify it, to give an increase in grace and holiness."[53]

A final seventeenth-century work to consider is the commentary of Cornelius Lapide.[54] This impressive tome contains chapter-by-chapter synopses, a Latin translation of the text, and a detailed and learned verse-by-verse commentary. An especially noteworthy feature of Lapide's work is his frequent citation of and interaction with the writings of earlier scholars. Every page contains references to such writers as Chrysostom, Augustine, Athanasius, Oecumenius, Theophylactus, and Anselm. Less frequent, but almost unprecedented in scholarship, are references to early comparative literature, such as 2 Maccabees, Diogenes Laertius, and Seneca the Younger.

Lapide deals with the interpretation of ἀντὶ τῆς ... χαρᾶς at some length. He describes the first alternative, ἀντί as "instead of," "in lieu of," and notes that this is the interpretation of Chrysostom, Theodoret, Theophylactus, and Oecumenius.[55] The second interpretation construes joy as the reward of the cross. Lapide cites the use of ἀντί in 12.16 as a parallel usage, and concludes that "Christ endured the cross so that he might earn and attain to joy." The second interpretation is declared superior: "Just as this sense is simpler and more intelligible, so it is also truer and more expressive than the former."

On the central issue of divine discipline Lapide writes with insight

---

[50] Gouge, *Commentary*, 928.
[51] Owen, *Exposition*, VII, 256.
[52] Gouge, *Commentary*, 941.
[53] Owen, *Exposition*, VII, 260.
[54] C. Lapide, *Commentaria in omnes Divi Pauli Epistolas* (Antwerp: Meursium, 1665).
[55] *Ibid.*, 953–4.

and clarity. Perhaps better than any commentator prior to him Lapide recognizes both the punitive and formative dimensions of παιδεία, and rather than heedlessly conflating them as some others had done, he describes them as complementary aims. One passage is worth quoting at length.[56]

> *Omnes afflictiones, v.g. expilationes bonorum, ab Hebraeis fidei causa susceptae, omniaque tormenta Martyrum sunt* musar, *id est castigatio & disciplina Dei, non immittentis, sed permittentis ea;* partim ad hoc, *ut per ea puniantur peccata, etiamsi levia, quae fideles & Martyres quandoque admiserunt* ... Partim ad hoc, *ut per ea discant fideles patientiam, charitatem, continentiam, martyrum, aliasque virtutes. Omnem enim concupiscentiam elidit & absumit afflictio, docetque omnem virtutem.*

> All afflictions, such as the plundering of goods, sustained by the Hebrews for the sake of faith, and all tortures of the Martyrs are *musar*, that is chastisement and discipline from God, who does not inflict, but rather permits them, *in part so that* sins might be punished through them, even the trivial ones that the faithful and the Martyrs sometimes commit ... *In part so that* through them the faithful might learn the patience, charity, [and] self-control of martyrs, and other virtues. For affliction destroys and removes all wantonness, and teaches every virtue.

The main point of this excerpt is the duality of purpose in affliction; it both punishes sin and inculcates virtue. The sin that it punishes is not necessarily the cause of the affliction. The phrase *fidei causa* shows that persecution of some sort is the primary cause. (Elsewhere Lapide refers explicitly to God chastising the Hebrews *through the persecutions of the Jews.* Whether Lapide has rightly identified here the human source of the readers' afflictions is unimportant. The point is that he understands the immediate cause as social.) The sins that are punished by affliction seem to be trivial, unrelated infractions which anyone can be assumed to have committed.

One could almost infer from the former that Lapide sees the pri-

---

[56] *Ibid.*, 955, bottom right column; my emphasis.

mary function of divine discipline as formative; the punitive function is almost an afterthought. Though Lapide does not explicitly argue for the primacy of formative discipline as I shall, he is clearly conscious of the tension in Hebrews 12.4–11 that is created by the appropriation of Proverbs 3.11–12 and the distinctive exposition that follows.

The above quotation also reveals that Lapide senses a dilemma, or at least some discomfort, in attributing to God afflictions that are traceable to human agents. God does not inflict them (*non immittentis*), but rather permits them (*sed permittentis*). In the paragraph prior to the quotation he had spoken disjunctively of the discipline "that God inflicts on persons, or permits to be inflicted." Lapide apparently prefers the latter, at least in the case of martyrs and the readers of Hebrews.

The athletic imagery of the passage is fully appreciated by Lapide. Whereas many twelfth- to seventeenth-century scholars overlooked the significance of γεγυμνασμένοις in Hebrews 12.11, Lapide is careful to note the allusion, commenting briefly on wrestlers and schools of wrestling. His diligent study of medieval scholarship is evident here in his citation (by name) of Theophylactus' remark: *disciplinam vocari gymnasiam, quod Christianos quasi athletas exerceat, formet, roboret & perficiat.* (Discipline is called "gymnastic" training, because it exercises, prepares, strengthens, and perfects Christians as if they were athletes.)

Lastly, Lapide introduces Stoic ideas into the discussion via two quotations from Seneca's *De Providentia*. Gentile philosophers expressed similar thoughts, he writes, quoting: *Deus bonos ut severi patres, durius educat* (God rears good persons rigorously, as stern fathers do).[57] In addition to Seneca, a few anecdotes from other sources, sometimes unnamed, are interspersed throughout the commentary on Hebrews 12.1–13. Much more could be done in terms of collecting and categorizing such comparative texts, but Lapide must be recognized as the first, as far as I have been able to determine, to see this connection between Seneca and Hebrews.

In the mid-eighteenth century, pietist Johannes A. Bengel (1687–1752) produced his *Gnomon Novi Testamenti*, a multi-volume collection of notes which enjoyed long-lived popularity, being reprinted

[57] *Ibid.*, 956, bottom right column. The quote is from *De Prov.* 1.5.

as recently as 1982.[58] According to Bengel, Jesus was to be distinguished from the heroes enumerated in chapter 11. He is "the unique example, the unique norm and rule of faith." Bengel shows his preference for the prospective interpretation of ἀντί when he notes that the faith of Jesus was demonstrated in his willingness to endure the cross "so as to obtain joy."

Bengel understands παιδεία in Hebrews 12 to entail punishment and guilt. Commenting on verse 7 he writes: *Praesupponitur, omnes egere castigatione, ob culpam* (It is presupposed that all need chastisement because of guilt). A terse comment on γεγυμνασμένοις in verse 11 hints at, but does not develop, another view. Those who are "exercised," he says, "carry a lighter burden, and whatever burden they do carry, they bear it more easily. They are toughened by experience." Thus παιδεία imparts strength and learning.

J. J. Wettstein (1693–1754), a contemporary of Bengel, holds a secure place in the history of NT research on the basis of his text-critical work. However, the continuing importance of his *Novum Testamentum Graecum* (1751–2) and its relevance to this study derive not from the text it offers but from its extensive apparatus containing quotations from both Greco-Roman and rabbinic sources. More than 175 classical authors were scrutinized over a period of forty years in a search for texts relevant to NT interpretation. "Neither before nor after him has such a comprehensive and systematic collection of materials relevant to the NT been published."[59]

Many of these parallels are philological, pertaining to individual words, phrases or metaphors. For example, in the notes for 12.1 Wettstein adduces parallels for the figurative use of "cloud" as a multitude of persons. But by the nature of the case, some of these parallels extend to larger concepts and provide the raw data for thematic studies. The texts collected under τὸν προκείμενον ἀγῶνα (vs. 1), for example, will contribute to my investigation of athletic imagery in moral paraenesis.

The bulk of Wettstein's apparatus is the comparative material; his

---

[58] Under the title *New Testament Commentary* (2 vols.; Grand Rapids: Kregel, 1982). The following quotes are from *Gnomon Novi Testamenti* (3rd edn.; Tübingen, 1855) 916–18. Translations are mine.

[59] P. W. van der Horst, "Corpus Hellenisticum Novi Testamenti," *ABD* (New York: Doubleday, 1992) I, 1158. Wettstein's achievement deserves praise, but my own brief investigation has shown that other collections of comparative texts, e.g. Lapide and Carpzov, sometimes reveal omissions in Wettstein.

own remarks are sporadic. Nevertheless, the drift of Wettstein's viewpoint can be perceived in the texts he adduces. I find it remarkable, therefore, that with regard to παιδεία, a central concept in this passage, Wettstein adduces *not a single* Greco-Roman parallel! Granted there are philological parallels for other expressions in verses 5–11 (ὡς υἱοῖς ὑμῖν προσφέρεται, νόθοι, κατὰ τὸ δοκοῦν, πρὸς τὸ παρόν, etc.), and several rabbinical texts are cited at the end of verse 11 pertaining to (divine) chastisements, but there is no treatment of the Greek term παιδεία in its pedagogical, athletic, or religious spheres, or of similar concepts in Latin authors. Wettstein's usual thoroughness is somewhat deficient at this point. This is especially surprising since Lapide adduced comparative texts from Seneca almost a century earlier.

A third scholar from the eighteenth century made a rather substantial contribution to the scholarly investigation of Hebrews. In 1750 J. B. Carpzov's *Sacrae Exercitationes in S. Pauli Epistolam ad Hebraeos ex Philone Alexandrino* appeared. This hefty (660 pages) tome was the first thorough treatment of the points of contact between Hebrews and the writings of Philo of Alexandria. But the work is much more than a listing of Philonic parallels; it is a full commentary, and the texts drawn into the discussion include other Biblical passages, classical and Hellenistic authors, church fathers, reformers, and writers contemporary with Carpzov himself.

Carpzov notes that three different words for "discipline" or "punish" are found in Hebrews' citation of Proverbs 3.11–12: παιδεύω, ἐλέγχω, and μαστιγόω. His treatment of these words is somewhat contradictory. He states plainly that the three words have the same force: "Παιδεύειν and ἐλέγχειν have the same meaning, and they are joined in Revelation 3.19. μαστιγοῦν is the same."[60] A few lines later, however, he concedes that a contemporary scholar has some justification in distinguishing at least the first and third terms: "Gerardus Horreus contends, however, and not without a semblance of truth, that τὸ παιδεύειν differs from παίζειν, and thus from μαστιγεῖν ... [and so] the word is interpreted as 'to educate' (*erudire*), and 'to divest someone of unculturedness by stern admonitions.' "[61] Thus Carpzov acknowledges that παιδεύω carries a nuance of instruction, even enculturation, which the other words lack.

---

[60] J. B. Carpzov, *Sacrae Exercitationes in S. Pauli Epistolam ad Hebraeos ex Philone Alexandrino* (Helmstedt, 1750) 583–4.
[61] *Ibid.*, 584.

One final observation should be made regarding Carpzov's contribution. Like Lapide, he refers to the Stoics, but only by way of contrast and in very general terms. In his remarks on verse 11 he observes that the experience of discipline, first as painful, and only later as joyous, is axiomatic to human nature. But some think otherwise, says Carpzov: *aliter sentiebant illi e porticu, qui sapientem in perpetuo volebant gaudio, eumque* ἀπαθῆ *et beatum esse in tormentis* (A different view was held by those of "the Portico," who wanted the wise person to be in perpetual joy, and free from emotion and to be happy amid torment). Whereas Lapide saw a similarity between Stoic thought and that of Hebrews, Carpzov underscores a difference. It may, however, be the case that Carpzov has caricatured or at least oversimplified Stoic thought on this matter.

More could be said about the relationship between Hebrews 12.1–13 and Stoic thought. Wettstein, as we saw above, was silent on the subject; Carpzov touched on it only briefly and negatively, without citing specific texts; Lapide adduced only two texts from Seneca. A fuller treatment of this relationship is needed.

The nineteenth century witnessed an explosion in Biblical scholarship, a fact reflected in the appearance of more than twenty commentaries on the Epistle to the Hebrews. I must be selective in reviewing this literature. As representatives of this century, I will examine the commentaries of Lünemann, Delitzsch, and Westcott.[62]

By the nineteenth century the interpretation of ἀντὶ τῆς ... χαρᾶς seems to have been largely decided. Delitzsch wrote confidently that "it is now generally acknowledged that [the phrase] cannot mean, 'instead of the joy which [Jesus] already possessed as His own' ... i.e. the joy of His heavenly and divine life."[63] Lünemann enumerates three possible variants of the "ἀντί = instead of" interpretation and disallows each.[64] The verse does not assert that to endure the cross Jesus forwent (1) pre-existent, heavenly glory with God, nor (2) earthly freedom from death and suffering, nor (3) earthly joys, presumably power and popularity. The majority, says Lünemann, citing twenty-one names in a footnote, understands joy as the reward of Christ's suffering. Three arguments are offered: (1) the use

---

[62] G. Lünemann, *Commentary on the Epistle to the Hebrews* (New York: Funk & Wagnalls, 1890); F. Delitzsch, *Commentary on the Epistle to the Hebrews* (2 vols.; 3rd edn.; Edinburgh: T. & T. Clark, 1883); B. F. Westcott, *The Epistle to the Hebrews* (London: Macmillan, 1889; 3rd edn., 1920).

[63] Delitzsch, *Commentary*, II, 304.

[64] Lünemann, *Commentary*, 703.

of ἀντί in verse 16, (2) consonance with the paraenetic aim of the author, i.e. assuring the readers of their reward, and (3) the last clause of verse 2, which highlights the reward Jesus received. Westcott's remarks on this matter are brief, but in accord with the position of Lünemann and Delitzsch.

The interpretation of παιδεία is more complex. Delitzsch gives a satisfactory articulation of παιδεία as educative: "Educational discipline is the end of all suffering which God lays upon you."[65] He quotes Chrysostom approvingly when the latter says παιδεία is not κόλασις or τιμωρία, adding "I do not see what improvement could be suggested to this interpretation either in thought or expression."[66] Hence, Delitzsch seems to conceive of παιδεία in Hebrews 12 as formative and instructional. Twice he refers to God's "school of affliction," and unlike many commentators during and since the Reformation, he appreciates the significance of γεγυμνασμένοις in verse 11, suggesting that "παιδεία is a γυμνασία, an ἀγών."[67] This insight, which I deem correct, seems to have been reached intuitively. Nowhere does Delitzsch explicitly treat the diverse meanings of παιδεία; nowhere does he acknowledge any tension between παιδεία in Proverbs 3.11–12 and παιδεία in the exposition of Hebrews 12. He sees a difference between the words παιδεία, "a fatherly discipline or process of education," and ἐλέγχεσθαι, "reproof, such as makes us conscious of our faults and errors,"[68] but never demonstrates how the argument and larger context of the passage favor the former. In other words, the idea of non-punitive (educative) παιδεία, is, for the most part, not derived by a clear, forceful interpretation of the text.

Westcott entitles verses 3–6 of Hebrews 12 "Sufferings as chastisements." The language of "chastening" is used consistently for παιδεία and related terms in the translation which Westcott uses. His exposition, however, seems to favor "discipline." On one occasion he remarks that παιδεία "suggests moral training, disciplining of the powers of [the person]."[69] Overall, Westcott's treatment is no more satisfactory, and perhaps less so, than Delitzsch's. He does not wrestle with the meaning of παιδεία for the author of Hebrews. There is no elaboration of the passage's conceptual background in Jewish wisdom literature, much less pagan philosophy.

Lünemann's commentary is the least detailed of the three. His

[65] Delitzsch, *Commentary*, II, 315.   [66] *Ibid.*, 314.   [67] *Ibid.*, 324.
[68] *Ibid.*, 312.   [69] Westcott, *Epistle*, 402.

preoccupation with textual, lexical, and "small scale" literary issues sometimes leaves larger questions of meaning unaddressed. What little information can be gleaned points toward a more punitive notion of παιδεία. The word and its cognates are regularly translated with "chasten/chastisement." Nowhere does Lünemann speak explicitly of sin as the cause of the readers' suffering, but the call "to regard their sufferings as a salutary chastisement" may imply this.[70]

To conclude these remarks on Delitzsch, Westcott, and Lünemann, I should note that references to substantive parallels in extra-canonical literature are rare. Westcott occasionally cites *lexical* parallels from Philo and Josephus, less often from classical authors. Delitzsch and Lünemann also include lexical parallels of the sort collected by Wettstein a century earlier. But comparative texts containing *thematic* parallels, that is, expressions of similar topoi and ideas whether identical terms are used or not, are virtually non-existent, especially on the Greco-Roman side.

The nineteenth-century explosion of scholarship mushroomed in the twentieth. A comprehensive bibliography of twentieth-century commentaries on Hebrews would contain at least seventy titles. Again, a selective treatment is necessary. It happens that among the most recent commentaries are four which excel in detail and critical acumen, those of Attridge, Ellingworth, Lane, and Weiss.[71]

The majority view on the interpretation of ἀντὶ τῆς ... χαρᾶς continues to be "for the sake of/because of the joy." Attridge, who considers this meaning more likely, cites Moffatt, Windisch, Spicq, Michel, Teodorico, Hughes, and Braun in support of it.[72] Weiss rightly notes that the meaning of ἀντί is to be determined from the sense of the context, not vice versa.[73] The kenotic christology of Philippians 2.6–8 must not be imported as the theological backdrop for the author of Hebrews. Weiss places the phrase in the context of verses 1–3 and interprets "joy" as "the prize that is offered for the runner in the competition, and which Jesus, the 'pioneer and perfecter of faith,' has already attained on the path that is yet to be traveled by the addressees of Hebrews as well."[74]

---

[70] Lünemann, *Commentary*, 699.

[71] Harold W. Attridge, *Hebrews*; P. Ellingworth, *Commentary on Hebrews* (Grand Rapids: Eerdmans, 1993); William L. Lane, *Hebrews 1–8, Hebrews 9–13* (Dallas: Word, 1991); Hans-Friedrich Weiss, *Der Brief an die Hebräer*.

[72] Attridge, *Hebrews*, 357 and n. 63.

[73] Weiss, *Brief an die Hebräer*, 639.

[74] *Ibid.*, 640. My translation.

Nevertheless, this interpretation has not swept aside all opposition. Ellingworth has some reservations about it and, while acknowledging that most modern commentators choose it, insists that the meaning "instead of" is not impossible.[75] Lane comes down decisively on the side of ἀντί = "instead of."[76] Among the supporters of this view, he cites Nisius, Vitti, Turner, Andriessen and Lenglet, J. Schneider, Mora, Vanhoye, Riggenbach, and Gourgues.

If Delitzsch was justified in speaking of a near consensus on this question in the nineteenth century, that consensus has eroded slightly in the twentieth century. The appeal made by some twentieth-century scholars to the statistical usage of ἀντί elsewhere is questionable. The appeal to context has not yielded a consensus since interpreters seem able to find contextual evidence for both views. This miniature debate over ἀντί serves as a microcosm of Biblical research as a whole in which consensus is often elusive, and majority opinions are always subject to review.

How has the concept of παιδεία been treated by twentieth-century interpreters? Lane construes the term as "instructive discipline" or "correction." "The sufferings the community had endured were actually disciplinary in character. Properly understood, they were a means of training them for the life of committed obedience appropriate to members of God's family."[77] But the punitive element is not lacking; on the same page Lane writes, " ... παιδεία combines the nuances of training, instruction, and firm guidance with those of reproof, correction, and punishment." According to Lane, these various nuances are united in Hebrews 12.4–11 so that one can speak of God "maturing his children through responsible, corrective love."[78] Questions Lane does not raise include (1) Are some of these nuances dominant in the mind of our author? and (2) What religious and philosophical currents, other than the obvious one (Proverbs 3.11–12), could the author be in contact with?

Attridge also understands παιδεία as educative discipline. Though he is less prone than Lane to speak of "corrective" discipline, that aspect is not absent: "On the human level, [παιδεία] was regularly seen to involve chastisement and 'reproach' (ἐλεγχόμενος). The image of the stern but loving father whose affection does not 'spare the rod' was also applied to God."[79]

---

[75] Ellingworth, *Commentary*, 641.   [76] Lane, *Hebrews*, II, 399 n. l, and 413.
[77] *Ibid.*, 420.   [78] *Ibid.*, 421.   [79] Attridge, *Hebrews*, 361.

Similar exposition can be found in Ellingworth: "The meaning of παιδεία ranges between training and corporal punishment. Broadly speaking, the Greek tradition emphasized παιδεία as education, whereas the Hebrew tradition stressed the positive value of (especially God's) discipline of his people by punishment."[80] Ellingworth sees the Jewish tradition as the primary milieu of the passage, but in a suggestive remark he notes that "the physical aspect of parental discipline conveyed by μαστιγοῖ is not mentioned in the exposition."[81] This observation and similar ones have led me to re-examine the assumption that the Jewish wisdom tradition is, indeed, the primary milieu.

Weiss echoes the Greek/Jewish distinction made by Ellingworth and sees the latter milieu as the chief determinant of the meaning of παιδεία in Hebrews 12.5–11. "It is primarily this citation of scripture, then, that determines the special meaning of παιδεία, and respectively παιδεύειν, in the following verses: παιδεία, therefore, not in the sense of the classical, Greek ideal of education, but rather – entirely in line with biblical, Jewish Wisdom ... – [in the sense of] 'reprimand,' 'chastisement.' "[82] On the other hand, Weiss says that παιδεία also involves "education." Divine reproof may be "painful," but it is also "goal-directed."[83] I would not argue with this description of divine reproof, nor would I contest that Proverbs 3.11–12 (or the Jewish wisdom tradition as a whole) is *a* determinant of the meaning of παιδεία. But I would argue that what the author does *in his exposition of the citation* is of utmost importance, and that exposition inclines the meaning of παιδεία in a different direction.

As a final observation concerning these four commentaries, I would note again a general neglect of Greco-Roman comparative texts for Hebrews 12.4–11. The failure of these scholars to incorporate such texts is not a significant criticism of their work as a whole. Commentaries are concerned with many aspects of a text; a commentator cannot be expected to develop *fully* the background of a passage, discussing every comparative text and its similarities to and differences from the canonical text. Still, it is regrettable that some commentators overlook constructive parallels or cite them without allowing the exposition of the text under study to be influ-

---

[80] Ellingworth, *Commentary*, 649.   [81] *Ibid.*, 649.
[82] Weiss, *Brief an die Hebräer*, 648.   [83] *Ibid.*, 648.

enced significantly by them.[84] The commentaries of Attridge, Ellingworth, Lane, and Weiss all refer to comparative texts in their discussions of Hebrews 12.4–11, but usually in passing. As in the case of the nineteenth-century commentators, they often cite classical authors for *lexical and metaphorical* parallels, but Greco-Roman comparative texts which adduce examples of noble suffering for paraenetic purposes, or which interpret suffering as divinely imposed discipline or training are scarcely to be found. I have in mind here especially Stoic traditions, above all Seneca's *De Providentia*. Attridge, Ellingworth, and Lane, as thorough as they are, do not have a single citation from *De Providentia*. Weiss cites the work in a footnote to an excursus on the expression τὸ συμφέρον, which he notes played a role in Stoic philosophy.[85] The commentaries, thus, either omit or give scant attention to what may well be a fruitful area of study for elucidating Hebrews 12.1–13. Stoic and other Greco-Roman texts can shed light on this passage both by their affinity to and their divergence from it, for "only when we are fully aware of all the options that were available, including those Christianity did not assimilate, shall we attain a firm grasp on the place of early Christianity in its intellectual environment."[86] Seneca's *De Providentia* is particularly significant for this study since it combines two main elements of Hebrews 12.1–13, i.e. suffering as exemplary and suffering as educative.

Apart from the relentless stream of commentaries, then, what has been written on Hebrews 12.1–13 or its themes of endurance in suffering and suffering as divine discipline? The most important research consists of seven monographs which fall roughly into two chronological periods: three earlier works now a few decades old, and four recent works, including two dissertations, appearing since 1980.

---

[84] On this problem, see Abraham J. Malherbe, "Hellenistic Moralists," esp. 275–8.

[85] Weiss, *Brief an die Hebräer*, 654-5 and n. 43. Of recent commentators on Hebrews, then, only Weiss draws Stoic ideas into the discussion. This is especially surprising since commentators of the earlier part of this century did refer at least briefly to Seneca's *De Prov.* Cf. the commentaries of Moffatt (*Hebrews* [Edinburgh: T. & T. Clark, 1979]), Spicq (*L' Epître aux Hébreux. Traduction, notes critiques, commentaire* [2 vols.; Paris: Gabalda, 1977]), and Windisch (*Der Hebräerbrief* [Tübingen: Mohr, 1931]).

[86] Abraham Malherbe, "Greco-Roman Religion and Philosophy and the New Testament," in Eldon Jay Epp and George W. MacRae, eds., *The New Testament and its Modern Interpreters* (Atlanta: Scholars Press, 1989) 16.

The published dissertation of J. A. Sanders examines the notion of suffering as divine discipline in the Hebrew Bible.[87] A major part of this work is a rather tedious word study of the OT usage of *ysr*, "discipline, correct, teach." Sanders does, however, include two useful charts that summarize the nuances and distribution of this Hebrew word.[88] These are helpful in sketching the OT background of the concept, "suffering as παιδεία." Sanders' treatment of post-Biblical Judaism is less thorough. He cites texts from the Apocrypha, Pseudepigrapha, Talmud, and Midrashim, some of which are found in the commentaries on Hebrews. On the other hand, Qumran material is cited only once, perhaps because of the date of publication, and references to Philo and Josephus are entirely absent. Twice Sanders refers to verses in Hebrews 12.1–13, but, needless to say, it was not his aim to elucidate that text.

Along similar lines is the work of W. Wichmann.[89] His focus is the "theology of suffering" in late Judaism. Wichmann's study does not have the lexical orientation or the conceptual focus of Sanders. He addresses the broad question of how suffering was interpreted and is primarily concerned with post-biblical Judaism. Chapter 1 introduces "The Problem of Evil in the OT and in Late Judaism," but thereafter the OT largely drops out of view. Subsequent chapters deal with the NT, 2 Maccabees, the Syriac Apocalypse of Baruch, 4 Ezra, and rabbinic literature. The last three chapters, comprising nearly half the book, are devoted to the theology of suffering in the Tannaim and the Palestinian and Babylonian Amoraim. This concentration in Wichmann's study makes it a useful complement to Sanders. Together they cover the OT and post-biblical Judaism up to and well beyond the date of Hebrews. The texts they collect and the discussion they offer provide an adequate treatment of the Jewish background of Hebrews 12.4–13. The corresponding portion of this study need only summarize their work.

More directly related to Hebrews 12.1–13 is a small excerpt of Werner Jentsch's study on early Christian education.[90] Jentsch devotes several pages to "God as Educator: the Fatherly Education of

---

[87] Jim Alvin Sanders, *Suffering as Divine Discipline in the Old Testament and Post-Biblical Judaism* (Rochester, NY: Colgate Rochester Divinity School, 1955).

[88] *Ibid.*, 44–5, 102–4.

[89] Wolfgang Wichmann, *Die Leidenstheologie. Eine Form der Leidensdeutung im Spätjudentum* (Stuttgart: Kohlhamm, 1930).

[90] Werner Jentsch, *Urchristliches Erziehungsdenken. Die Paideia Kyriu im Rahmen der hellenistisch-Jüdischen Umwelt* (Gütersloh: Bertelsmann, 1951) 161–8.

God according to the Epistle to the Hebrews," in which he offers exegetical observations such as one finds in the commentaries, but, in contrast to most commentaries, he draws Stoicism into the discussion. Commenting on verse 11 he writes,

> [A]ll education requires time. There is a *during* and an *afterwards*. So there exists a sort of holy, pedagogical "training" and a gymnastic instruction in God's school. In this passage the milieu of the imagery, as already seen in *sympheron* [vs. 10], takes on a Stoic quality, without thereby adopting Stoic content. At the end of this education one does not find a person who is a self-sufficient measure, at peace with himself, but rather a person at peace with God.[91]

Jentsch, like Weiss, picks up on the Stoic slogan τὸ συμφέρον and implies that some similarity exists between the Stoic notion of (divine) education and that of Hebrews. But, as the above quote shows, Jentsch is more concerned to distinguish between the two. The Stoic sage is freed from all passion, which would have to include the λυπή which the author of Hebrews admits is part of the Christian's experience. Seneca may speak of the gods' fatherly disposition and love which are manifested in the testing and hardening of human beings,[92] but, says Jentsch, "the goal of all this divine education is ultimately the stoic ideal of a person, not the *soteria* of a sinful person according to the New Testament."[93] Jentsch is no doubt correct to distinguish between the goal of divine education in Stoicism and its goal in the NT, but in doing so he may have misrepresented the process of divine education in Hebrews 12.1–13. According to the text, the goal of παιδεία is τὸ μεταλαβεῖν τῆς ἁγιότητος [θεοῦ] (vs. 10) and καρπὸν εἰρηνικὸν ... δικαιοσύνης (vs. 11). The soteriological element that Jentsch introduces is not quite the point of our passage. Granted, Hebrews is concerned about salvation (1.14; 2.3, 10; 5.9; 6.9; 9.28), and σωτηρία is ultimately the result of faithful endurance, but our author does not connect παιδεία with salvation from sin.[94] Here Jentsch may be more influenced

---

[91] *Ibid.*, 166.
[92] Seneca, *De Prov.* 4.7; 2.6.
[93] Jentsch, *Urchristliches Erziehungsdenken*, 166. Earlier (162) Jentsch also wrote, "Chastisement is supposed ... to lead to repentance."
[94] The occurrence of ἁμαρτία in 12.4 does not contradict this. Here the word is virtually equivalent to ἁμαρτωλοί as the parallel in the experience of Jesus shows (vs. 3).

by the wisdom tradition that Hebrews cites than by what the author does with that tradition. Jentsch does devote more attention to Stoic analogs than any other scholar encountered in this history of research, but even his comparative work needs both elaboration and correction.

Turning to the more recent studies, I should make brief mention of Gambiza's 1981 dissertation on the concepts τελείωσις and παιδεία in Hebrews.[95] He examines these terms as they relate to the sufferings of Christ and the sufferings of Christians respectively, and attempts to show a relationship between them. This thesis has some merit, but is hindered by the fact that the author of Hebrews never explicitly connects the two terms. Moreover, there are important nuances of meaning that distinguish the application of τέλειος (and related terms) to Christ from their application to Christians. Gambiza also appears to misunderstand the significance of divine paideia in the lives of the readers.[96] Finally, the value of Gambiza's work is limited by its failure to include discussion of non-canonical literature.

More significant and of more relevance to my study is the 1986 dissertation of Stephen P. Logan.[97] The aim of Logan's monograph is "to discover the religious and cultural background against which παιδεία is best understood" (2). The author does not limit himself to the Greek word, but examines passages where the *concept* occurs. A major strength of Logan's dissertation is the breadth of sources it encompasses. After a brief introduction, chapter 2 considers the Greco-Roman background of παιδεία in ancient Sparta, the Sophists, Plato, Isocrates, and Plutarch. Chapter 3 examines the Jewish background in the OT, Apocrypha, Pseudepigrapha, rabbinic literature, Qumran, Philo, and Josephus. This section is especially strong. Nevertheless, there is a sense in which the range of texts

---

[95] Farai K. M. Gambiza, "*Teleiosis* and *Paideia* as Interpretation of Sufferings: The Perfecting of Jesus and the Disciplining of Christians in the Letter to the Hebrews," Th.D. Dissertation, Christ Seminary-Seminex, 1981.

[96] "It refers to the Christians struggling and fighting against their sinful desires" (62). This comment, apparently in reference to 12.4, although the antecedent for "it" is vague, fails to appreciate the external nature of the threat to the community. Similarly: "Christians' sufferings are like a reform school wherein they are purged of the dross of self love and love for the world (12.2–7)" (81). The reference to a "school" of sufferings has been seen before (e.g. Delitzsch), but the remainder of this quotation is foreign to the Epistle to the Hebrews, and sounds Johannine.

[97] Stephen Phillip Logan, "The Background of ΠΑΙΔΕΙΑ in Hebrews," Dissertation, Southern Baptist Theological Seminary, 1986.

considered is both too broad and too narrow. It is too broad in that the author gives considerable space to the treatment of παιδεία in its more literal sense of "pedagogy." This is particularly true in the section on the Greco-Roman background. Frankly, this adds unnecessary bulk to the dissertation. The history of pedagogy in antiquity contributes little to the understanding of Hebrews 12. Those passages which metaphorically extend the term to "divine discipline" are more relevant. Chapter 3 contributes to the interpretation of Hebrews, in part because each subdivision includes a discussion of the "Discipline of God." This dimension is absent from chapter 2.

In a different respect, the range of Logan's texts is too narrow. Although chapter 2 has a subsection on "Roman Education," it is limited to the literal notion of pedagogy and does little more than suggest that the various features of Greek education continued under Rome. The entire Stoic tradition of divine testing and strengthening of persons through adversity, which has obvious affinity with Hebrews 12, receives no attention. Logan's work on the Jewish aspect of the milieu is useful, but his dissertation still leaves a large gap in the Greco-Roman background.

A recent book by David Kraemer provides a definitive study of views of suffering in classical rabbinic literature.[98] Kraemer skillfully surveys the Mishnah, Tosefta, Midrashim, and both Palestinian and Babylonian Talmuds. Although he discovers that a fairly consistent perspective on suffering runs through much of the earlier literature, Kraemer also shows that the Babylonian Talmud, which arose in different political and geographical circumstances, gave voice to novel, even rebellious, interpretations of human suffering. Kraemer's nuanced study suggests that the picture is more complex than some have thought.

The final study which deserves mention is that of Charles Talbert.[99] Despite its small size (92 pages), it is a well-written monograph with surprising breadth and insight. As a volume in the "Zacchaeus Studies" series, it aims at concise, readable scholarship, and it succeeds. The first chapter surveys "The Educational Value of Suffering in Mediterranean Antiquity." Jewish and Greco-Roman

[98] David Kraemer, *Responses to Suffering in Classical Rabbinic Literature* (New York: Oxford University, 1995).
[99] Charles H. Talbert, *Learning Through Suffering. The Educational Value of Suffering in the New Testament and in Its Milieu* (Collegeville, MN: Liturgical Press, 1991).

backgrounds are adequately treated given the limits of a fifteen-page chapter. The Stoic tradition is represented by citations from Seneca and Epictetus. The chapter closes with the observation that Jewish traditions *generally* understand suffering as punishment for culpable acts, whereas Greco-Roman traditions tend to view suffering as training or conditioning for virtue. Talbert points out that these two streams of traditions are combined in the Hellenistic Jewish document, 4 Maccabees, and Paul's Epistle to the Romans (5.3–4). The remaining chapters treat the educational value of suffering in James, I Peter, Hebrews, and Luke–Acts. The chapter on Hebrews is organized according to two related motifs: the sufferings of Christ and the sufferings of Christians. While this division is thematically attractive, it has the unfortunate side-effect of splitting apart 12.1–13, verses 2–3 being treated under the "Sufferings of Christ," verses 5–11 under the "Sufferings of Christians." Talbert is quite aware that even the verses about the sufferings *of Christ* serve the purpose of encouraging *the readers* in their struggle (67), but the structure he chooses for the chapter does not emphasize this connection.

In his brief (slightly more than a page) discussion of 12.5–11 Talbert asks, "How should discipline (*paideia*) be understood in this context?" He rightly notes the parallel terms *elenchein* and *mastigoun* as denoting correction, even corporal punishment, and thus construes *paideia* in the sense of "parental correction of youthful misdirection."[100] But Talbert does not seem to perceive the tension between the author's use of a text from the Jewish tradition of punitive suffering and his non-punitive exposition and application of that text. The description of this tension and its implications about the author's use of παιδεία will be important features of the present work.

Talbert's survey is a useful study of the educational value of suffering in the NT and its milieu, but his treatment of Hebrews 12.5–11 could be strengthened and, I would say, corrected, by devoting more attention to (1) the description of the readers' situation and the nature of their suffering (cf. 10.32–5), (2) the literary context of 12.5–11, namely the catalog of the faithful in 11.1–12.3 and the athletic imagery throughout 12.1–13, and (3) the selective nature of the exposition and application of the text from Proverbs. The careful consideration of these "internal" factors combined with

---

[100]   *Ibid.*, 71.

a broader "external" study of comparative texts will clarify the meaning of divine παιδεία for the author of Hebrews.

1.3   Prospect: the aim and plan of this study

The prospect which arises from my own reading of Hebrews 12.1–13 and the history of research on this passage has two aspects. First, although the athletic imagery of verses 1–3 is universally recognized, the full extent of it has not been developed, nor is it often appreciated as an integrating feature of verses 1–13. Furthermore, the interpretation of ἀντί and the resulting diverse portrayals of Jesus' passion have seldom been considered in conjunction with the agon motif of the passage. Secondly, since Hebrews 12.5–6 explicitly cites the book of Proverbs, the author's understanding of suffering has primarily been interpreted via the matrix of Jewish wisdom literature. Greco-Roman interpretations of suffering, when they have entered the discussion at all, have usually been viewed in contrast to this Jewish matrix. Both halves of Talbert's antithesis need to be elaborated. The wisdom tradition's view of suffering must be located in the diverse milieu of Jewish reflections on suffering. Likewise, the full range of Greco-Roman perspectives must be sketched. Talbert's dichotomy may or may not be a helpful generalization. In either event, the place of Hebrews 12.1–13 in this framework needs to be re-examined.

I will consider three features of the passage, all of which pertain to the author's understanding of suffering. They are: (1) suffering as an agon, an athletic contest, (2) the paraenetic use of exemplars of suffering, and (3) suffering as divine discipline. The first and second of these are taken up in chapter 2; the third in chapter 3.

Chapter 2 will show that, although the language of martyrological texts is employed in Hebrews, the primary image of Jesus in 12.2–3 is as an athletic exemplar, and the call to the readers is a call to an athlete's endurance rather than a martyr's death. The use of athletic language in moral paraenesis will be traced through Greco-Roman and Jewish writers with special attention to the later Stoics. Then the agonistic features of Hebrews 12.1–13 will be displayed fully, showing both their prominence and integrative function. Lastly, the rhetorical use of exemplars, specifically athletic images as exemplars of endurance, will be highlighted. I will examine the use of Jesus as exemplar in 12.2–3 to see how it both conforms to and diverges from the rhetorical tradition.

Chapter 3 will test the thesis that the Jewish view of suffering is generally punitive and the Greco-Roman generally educative. Broad surveys of comparative texts will attempt to show the variety of perspectives in both camps. Of special importance for this study will be the later Stoic interpretations of suffering since these, in my view, reveal certain affinities with Hebrews 12.1–13 and may contribute to a better understanding of the passage. At the end of chapter 3 I will briefly consider the convergence of agonistic and educative motifs in the comparative texts, the very motifs that the author of Hebrews has combined in 12.1–13.

Chapter 4 is devoted to an interpretation of Hebrews 12.1–13 informed throughout by the findings of chapters 2 and 3 about the religious, philosophical, and rhetorical milieu of the epistle. Of chief importance to the interpretation will be an exegesis of the text in its context, the latter referring primarily to the literary context of the epistle, but also to the social situation of the readers, to the limited degree to which this can be gleaned from the epistle. A special section of chapter 4 will examine Hebrews' use of Proverbs 3.11–12 in comparison to the use of the same text in other authors, Jewish and Christian. The final chapter will gather and summarize the conclusions of the study. Several theological theses will be offered regarding the contribution of this passage to larger questions about sin, eschatology, and a theology of suffering.

2

ATHLETES AND EXEMPLARS

2.1 Introduction

The history of research in chapter 1 revealed that the preposition ἀντί in Hebrews 12.2 has been interpreted in two distinct ways, according to which two different portrayals of Jesus' suffering emerge. If by ἀντί the author means "instead of," then the readers are to understand that Jesus had possession of, or ready access to, joy, but rejected it and endured the cross instead. This was the unanimous interpretation during the patristic and early medieval periods. Although it is a minority view today, there are still several advocates for it.[1] The alternate interpretation construes ἀντί in a final sense: "for the sake of," or more precisely, "so as to obtain." According to this view, joy is in prospect, not in possession. Rather than renouncing joy at the outset, Jesus attains joy as a consequence of his suffering.

Interpreters of Hebrews 12.1–3 have detected various influences on its language and thought. The two interpretations of ἀντί lend themselves to different categories of influence. If Jesus renounces joy and chooses instead to suffer death, he makes, in effect, the choice of a martyr.[2] An influence of Jewish martyrology on this passage has been suggested, and it may be instructive briefly to examine the evidence adduced for it. The first item of evidence is found in chapter 11.

The catalogue of the faithful in 11.4–31 is punctuated by the anaphoric use of πίστει, "by faith." That pattern changes in verse

---

[1] See Lane's commentary and those cited by him, *Hebrews*, 399 n. 1 and 413–14.

[2] Lane, who opts for the "substitutionary" sense of ἀντί, sees Jesus as "confronted with a supreme moral choice. He could embrace the joy that was available to him or a humiliating death upon a Roman cross." (*ibid.*, 413). Lane then refers the reader to 4 Maccabees 15.2–3 for the use of προκείμενος in relationship to the "martyr's choice." See also *TDNT*, I, 138 and nn. 18–20.

32. A rhetorical lament of the shortness of time and a rapid volley of names signal the summation of the pericope. In the summation (33–8) we find a list of "unattributed" but dramatic acts of faith. Some of these undoubtedly allude to the persons named in verse 32, but others are rightly thought to extend the catalogue of the faithful beyond the boundaries of the Biblical canon into the period of the Maccabean martyrs.

The last two clauses of verse 34, "they were mighty in war; they routed foreign armies," are possible allusions to Maccabean resistance, although they obviously find referents in the Biblical books of Judges and Samuel too. The most likely allusions to Maccabean martyrdom are found in 35b–37. This conclusion is supported not simply by the often lethal nature of the torments described, but by specific terminology and images. Ἐτυμπανίσθησαν, "they were tortured" (35), recalls the "rack" (τύμπανον) of 2 Maccabees 6.19, 28. The refusal to accept release at the price of compromise (οὐ προσδεξάμενοι τὴν ἀπολύτρωσιν) was certainly characteristic of the martyrdoms of Eleazar (2 Macc. 6.21–3, 30) and the seven brothers (2 Macc. 7.1, 7–8, 24–30). Lastly, the hope of divine vindication by way of resurrection (ἵνα κρείττονος ἀναστάσεως τύχωσιν) was also on the lips of the Maccabean martyrs (2 Macc. 7.9, 11, 14, 23, 29). The combination of these features in Hebrews – elaborate tortures, rejection of release, and the hope of resurrection – makes an allusion to Maccabean traditions quite likely. This likelihood is strengthened by the fact that these martyrologies were highly regarded not only in Jewish but in early Christian piety.[3]

A second fact that may lend support to a martyrological air for Hebrews 12.1–3 is the expression νέφος μαρτύρων in 12.1. The meaning of μάρτυς here is debated. The context of athletic imagery has suggested to some the meaning "spectator."[4] But the proximity of the verb μαρτυρέω (11.2, 4, 5, 39) in the enumeration of the μάρτυρες would seem to favor the meaning of "witness." Since the verb was used in the passive voice in those instances, the witness is that which was borne *to* the faithful more so than the witness which they bore. The latter, i.e. the witness borne *by* Israel's faithful, is,

---

[3] See John S. Pobee, *Persecution and Martyrdom in the Theology of Paul* (Sheffield: JSOT, 1985) 14–16; and John Downing, "Jesus and Martyrdom," *JTS*, 14, 2 (1963) 279–93, esp. 281. H. Strathmann remarks that the Maccabean martyrs were so embraced by the church that they "could even be enrolled among the Christian martyrs" ("μάρτυς," TDNT, IV, 486).

[4] Lane, *Hebrews*, 408, cites Westcott, Strathmann, et al.

however, certainly implied by the lengthy description of their exploits, exploits which culminate in suffering and death. Nevertheless, the attempt to find in Hebrews 12.1 the later signification of "martyr," i.e. "one who testifies with one's own blood and life," encounters two problems. First of all, this sense by no means applies to the entire catalog in chapter 11, which is presumably the referent for μάρτυρες. Secondly, it is difficult if not impossible to demonstrate the mortal sense of μάρτυς prior to the second century. By the middle of that century, probably first in Asia Minor, the word took on "a fixed and technical martyrological use."[5] Movement toward that technical meaning is sometimes detected in the book of Revelation,[6] but there is scant evidence for it in Hebrews.

Though the mere use of the term μάρτυς does not establish a link with martyrological traditions, a third aspect of the text does. Commentators have noted that certain terminology in Hebrews 12.1–3 is characteristic of the Maccabean martyrologies.[7] The unmistakable theme of the passage is "endurance" (ὑπομονή or ὑπομένω, once in each verse, as well as 10.32, 36 and 12.7). This virtue figures prominently in 4 Maccabees 17.10, μέχρι θανάτου τὰς βασάνους ὑπομείναντες (enduring torture even to death); 17.12, ἀρετὴ δι' ὑπομονῆς δοκιμάζουσα (virtue ... tested them for their endurance); and 17.17, ἐθαύμασαν αὐτῶν τὴν ὑπομονήν (they marveled at their endurance). As the readers of Hebrews are called to "look unto Jesus," the Maccabean martyrs were described as "looking to God" (4 Macc. 17.10).[8] Lastly, both Jesus and the Maccabean martyrs are said to despise, or lightly esteem the suffering, death, and shame which they undergo: ἦσαν γὰρ περίφρονες τῶν παθῶν καὶ αὐτοκράτορες τῶν ἀλγηδόνων (For they were contemptuous of the emotions and sovereign over agonies: 4 Macc. 8.28).[9]

In summary, there is some basis for speaking of the influence of martyrological traditions on Hebrews 12.1–3. The end of chapter 11

[5] Strathmann, *TDNT*, IV, 506.
[6] See BAGD, 494 (3), and Mitchell G. Reddish, "The Theme of Martyrdom in the Book of Revelation," Dissertation, Southern Baptist Theological Seminary, 1982.
[7] See especially Attridge, *Hebrews*, 355–8; Lane, *Hebrews*, 401–10; and Otto Michel, *Der Brief an die Hebräer* (Göttingen: Vandenhoeck & Ruprecht, 1960) 287–8, n. 6.
[8] An important distinction here is that Jesus, to whom the Christians look, is not so much a vindicator of their sufferings as he is the supreme example of suffering and endurance.
[9] See other references, including Stoic and early Christian sources, in Attridge, *Hebrews*, 358, n. 72.

almost certainly alludes to the martyrs of the Maccabean era, and some of the language of 12.1–3 is shared with the accounts of that period. On the other hand, the portrayal of Jesus' suffering in 12.1–3 is shaped by the author's particular purposes and therefore lacks some of the chief features of the Maccabean martyrdoms. Jesus is not adduced as an example of courageous defiance, righteous opposition in the face of pagan oppression, nor (as I will argue) self-renunciation. He is the champion of enduring faith. His endurance of shame and hostility, not so much the agony of his physical torments and death, is the author's concern. There is none of the exquisite detail of torture and dramatic defiance of pagan authority found in the martyrologies.

In one respect it may be unfair to compare the lengthy and sometimes gruesome narratives of 2 and 4 Maccabees with the terse, rhetorical exhortation of Hebrews 12.1–3. The latter lacks many of the features of the former simply because it lacks the former's degree of development. Nevertheless, even a terse portrayal of Jesus' suffering and death such as Hebrews 12.1–3 will highlight some aspects and omit others. The goal is not to find a single category in which to "file" the pericope, but rather to allow the text to speak with its own voice. I do not deny that Hebrews 12.1–3 has a faint martyrological air, but I am convinced that another, and I would say, more influential, tradition has shaped the passage, that of the agonistic exemplar. The passage is suffused with the language and images of the ἀγών. Moreover, as I will argue in chapter 4, the prospective interpretation of ἀντί is far more likely and, if correct, lends itself much better to the portrayal of Jesus as an agonistic exemplar.

2.2 Athletic imagery in the Epistle to the Hebrews

The presence of athletic imagery in Hebrews 12.1–3 has long been recognized; my observation of it is hardly original. A few terms are unmistakably borrowed from the racecourse or arena, most notably the phrase τρέχωμεν τὸν προκείμενον ἡμῖν ἀγῶνα, "let us run the race which lies before us." Other words in the passage that have wider currency take on an athletic nuance by virtue of the context. These include: ὄγκον ἀποθέμενοι πάντα, "putting off every weight," δι᾽ ὑπομονῆς, "with endurance," ἀφορῶντες εἰς ... Ἰησοῦν, "looking unto Jesus," ἀντὶ τῆς προκειμένης αὐτῷ χαρᾶς, "for the joy which had been set before him," μὴ κάμητε ... ἐκλυόμενοι, "lest you be-

come fatigued … growing weary," and perhaps even περικείμενον
ἡμῖν νέφος μαρτύρων, "a cloud of witnesses surrounding us."

There is also language elsewhere in the epistle that offers indirect
support for the thesis that the author is portraying Jesus as an agonistic exemplar in 12.1–3. Of greatest importance is πρόδρομος in
6.20. Here the author concludes the hortatory and pastoral inter-
ruption (5.11–6.20) to his discussion of the appointment of Jesus
as high priest (4.14–7.28). He has entered inside the curtain as a
"forerunner in our behalf." The precise significance of πρόδρομος is
uncertain, but is probably to be found in the sphere of athletic or
military activity.[10] Since he learned obedience through suffering and

---

[10] Bauerfeind (*TDNT*, VIII, 235 n. 3) claims, "The athletic race hardly calls for
consideration," an odd comment since his own exposition tends in this direction.
On the same page he says, "It is quite conceivable that the word πρόδρομος corresponds to the content of 5.8f. if the word ref[ers] not just to the final end of the
course, but to the preceding course itself with all its tests and trials, so that the
frequently observed concept of the commissioned and obedient running of the
believer … may be applied to Jesus Himself." It must be admitted, though, that
the uses of the word πρόδρομος are numerous and diverse. It can refer to the first
grapes of the harvest (Num. 13.20), or similarly, the early figs (Isa. 28.4; cf.
Athenaeus, *Deipnosophistae* 3.77.c). In Wisdom 12.8 wasps (or hornets) are depicted as the forerunners or advance guard of the army of God in punishing the
Canaanites. This military usage is attested frequently in Greco-Roman authors,
especially historians. For the meaning "skirmishers," "scouts," "advance guard,"
see Appian, *Mith.* 71.2 (19); 360.3 (81); *BC* 5.3.23; Dio Cassius 41.42.2; Diodorus
Siculus, 17.17.4; Dionysius of Halicarnassus, *Thuc.* 18; Arrian, *Anab.* 1.12.7;
2.9.2; 3.7.7; Herodotus, 4.121; 7.203; 9.14; Josephus, *Ant.* 12.314; Polybius, *Hist.*
12.20; Plutarch, *Alc.* 34.5; *Crass.* 9.3; 20.1; Thucydides, 2.22.2. A significant athletic use of the word is found in Julius Pollux, a second-century CE rhetorician. In
Onomasticon 3.30.148, Pollux offers a thesaurus of words related to running
events. He lists technical terms for starting line and finishing line as well as descriptions for the runners themselves. The latter include δρομικός, σύνδρομος, ἰσό-
δρομος, θάττων, κουφότερος, ὀξύτερος, ἐλαφρότερος, σπουδαιότερος, δρομικώτερος,
ἐπίδρομος, πρόδρομος. Although a string of words does not provide much context
for meaning, the series seems to progress toward a description of the fastest runner, the one who crosses the finish line first.

Given these possibilities of military and athletic metaphors, what is the meaning
of πρόδρομος in Hebrews 6.20? The peculiar context in Hebrews 6.19–20 complicates matters. Verse 19b is an abrupt and clumsy transition back to the theme
of Jesus' Melchizedek-like priesthood (cf. 5.10). The anchor of hope in 19a is
described as ἀσφαλῆ τε καὶ βεβαίαν καὶ εἰσερχομένην εἰς τὸ ἐσώτερον τοῦ καταπε-
τάσματος. Needless to say, the first two descriptions commend themselves more
readily for an anchor than does the third. Cultic and priestly imagery have taken
over, so the attempt to link πρόδρομος with the anchor in a nautical metaphor is
misguided. The word simply means "forerunner" in the sense of "one who goes
before." As with the English word, the "runner" portion (δρομος) has lost most of
its athletic flavor.

was perfected thereby (2.10; 5.8–9), Jesus became the first to complete the course and, simultaneously, the one who enables others to complete it.

Most other passages in the epistle containing athletic language refer to the readers or other persons, not Jesus, and therefore are only indirectly relevant to the portrayal of Jesus.[11] Briefly, these include the following: the verb γυμνάζω of persons who have their moral faculties "trained" in the discernment of good and evil (5.14), and of persons "trained" through discipline (12.11); compounds of the verb ἀγωνίζω referring to Israel's heroes who "conquered" (καταγωνίζω) kingdoms (11.33), and to the readers' own "struggling against" (ἀνταγωνίζω) sin (12.4); and ἄθλησις referring to the "contest" the readers had endured (10.32). Though these verses do not contribute directly to the image of *Jesus* as agonistic exemplar, they do reinforce the concept in 12.1–13 of the *readers'* struggle as a contest and a kind of training.[12]

This combination of language in Hebrews 12.1–3 that is explicitly athletic, language in the passage that acquires an athletic hue from the context, and the occasional use of athletic language elsewhere in the epistle suggests that the chief image of Jesus in this passage is that of an agonistic exemplar: the supreme athlete who (alone) has successfully completed the course and now serves as a model to the readers.

The aim of the remainder of this chapter is therefore threefold: (1) to place the passage in the broad context of the ἀγών motif as it appears in Hellenistic moral teaching, (2) to demonstrate that the specific language of the passage, viewed alongside similar expressions in Greco-Roman comparative texts, supports a primarily athletic interpretation, and (3) to survey generally the theories found in the rhetorical handbooks about the use of exemplars, and specifically the actual employment of *agonistic* exemplars in paraenesis. Finally, Hebrews 12.1–3 (along with 11.4–40) will be situated in that broad tradition.

---

[11] Jesus is crowned (στεφανόω) in 2.7, 9. This word has a faint athletic quality in that victors in the games were crowned with a στέφανος (see *TDNT*, VII, 620 and VIII, 228), but the word's uses are too diverse to assure us of an athletic allusion. Furthermore, the immediate source of the word is Psalms 8.5–7. Neither the psalm's context nor Hebrews' exposition develops an athletic nuance.

[12] Lane, *Hebrews*, 94 note ff, suggests that τραχηλίζω in 4.13 may have the athletic nuance of "grip in a neck-hold." But the context in Hebrews provides little support for such a meaning.

2.3 Athletic imagery in moral exhortation

The origin of Greek athletics is at least as early as the Homeric age. The traditional founding of the Olympic games is dated in 776 BCE. The various events included those categorized today as "track and field," as well as boxing, wrestling, and equestrian events. The foot-race, however, remained the central event.[13] Absolute measurements of time and distance were not the chief concern; the victor was obviously the one who bested the others, who ran the fastest, jumped the furthest.

The nature of Greek athletics lent itself readily to metaphor: rigorous preparation, conditioning, and self-denial followed by extreme exertion in an individual effort to achieve a superior performance. As early as the seventh and sixth centuries BCE poets and philosophers began to appropriate the language of the games. Over the centuries, the imagery developed, reaching its acme in the Hellenistic age. The Cynic–Stoic diatribe, in particular, made extensive use of it; indeed, the moral agon "is one of the most frequently occurring images in the Cynic–Stoic diatribe, one which serves to reflect the very core and essence of its ethic."[14] The usage was thus well established long before Christian literature appeared.

The moral teaching of the early church, including that contained in the NT, was often indebted to Hellenistic moralists, especially the Stoics.[15] Pfitzner, whose work on Paul is the leading study of the agon motif in the NT, asserts that Paul "simply reflects a traditional use of the athletic image."[16] The same can be said of Hebrews. Given the long history and widespread use of the motif, there is no

---

[13] See F. A. Wright, "Olympian Games," *OCD* (New York: Oxford University, 1970) 750–1; R. L. Howland, "Athletics," *OCD*, 142–3, and the literature they cite. On the primacy of the foot-race, see Xenophanes 2.17–18 in M. L. West, ed., *Iambi et Elegi Graeci* (Oxford: Oxford University, 1972) 165; and Plutarch, *Mor.* 675c.

[14] Victor C. Pfitzner, *Paul and the Agon Motif* (Leiden: Brill, 1967) 1, n. 2.

[15] Malherbe, "Hellenistic Moralists," esp. 267–70.

[16] Pfitzner, *Paul*, 3. Pfitzner reviews the weaknesses of the previous literature (9–15), especially Lydia Schmid's 1921 dissertation, "Der Agon bei Paulus." Four years after Pfitzner the dissertation of James D. Ellsworth (University of California, Berkeley, 1971) appeared. Its title, "Agon: Studies in the Use of a Word," was initially promising, but its etymological/philological bent and chronological limits (Homer to 323 BCE) make it of little value to the present study. On combat sports in antiquity, see Michael B. Poliakoff, *Combat Sports in the Ancient World* (New Haven: Yale University, 1987); and *Studies in the Terminology of the Greek Combat Sports* (2nd edn.; Beiträge zur Klassischen Philologie 146; Frankfurt: Hain, 1986).

need to posit literary dependence on the part of Paul or any other NT writer, nor to attribute the use of the motif in Christian literature to authorial ingenuity or the specific circumstances of the readers.[17] Hence, to appreciate fully the use of the agon motif in Hebrews, it will be helpful to survey the development and character of athletic imagery in moral exhortation.[18]

It is not incidental that some of the major gymnasia, e.g. the Academy and the Lyceum, were also philosophical schools. The training of the body and the educating of the mind were natural complements and were often practiced in the same setting. But the growing importance of athletics and the praise lavished upon victors[19] gave rise to critique. Gymnastic training was faulted for an alleged lack of moral and social benefit, but often, in the devaluation of athletics, the very language of athletics was positively employed to describe the alternative, the "true" or "greatest" agon. Tyrtaeus, seventh-century poet and Spartan general, rejected the ideal of athletic excellence in favor of the brave soldier, who represented the true ἀνήρ ἀγαθός. In his "Praise of Valor" he demotes several kinds of excellence (ἀρετή) before proposing the martial ideal. Heading the list of lesser achievements is athletic prowess:

> Οὔτ' ἂν μνησαίμην οὔτ' ἐν λόγῳ ἄνδρα τιθείμην
> οὐδὲ ποδῶν ἀρετῆς οὔτε παλαιμοσύνης,
> οὐδ' εἰ Κυκλώπων μὲν ἔχοι μέγεθός τε βίην τε,
> νικῴη δὲ θέων Θρηΐκιον Βορέην ...
> οὐδ' εἰ πᾶσαν ἔχοι δόξαν πλὴν θούριδος ἀλκῆς· ...
> ἥδ' ἀρετή, τόδ' ἄεθλον ἐν ἀνθρώποισιν ἄριστον
> κάλλιστόν τε φέρειν γίγνεται ἀνδρὶ νέωι.

I would neither mention nor pose in speech a man
with prowess in running or in wrestling,
not even if he should have the stature and strength of
    Cyclops

---

[17] Nevertheless, the real-life experiences of the readers probably contributed to the effectiveness of the metaphor. Although one cannot reason with certainty from an author's use of athletic imagery to the readers' first-hand experience with formal athletics, it would be unlikely that inhabitants of a Mediterranean city in the first century would have had no experience with athletics, professional and amateur.

[18] In the following pages I am indebted to Pfitzner, especially his second chapter, "The Agon Motif in Greek and Hellenistic Philosophy" (*Paul*, 23–37).

[19] In Lucian, *Anacharsis* 10, Solon says that great throngs of people watch the games and applaud the winner, who is counted equal to the gods (ἰσόθεος).

and could outpace the Thracian North wind, . . .
not even if he should have all fame, yet lacked warlike
   strength; . . .
This is prowess, this among human beings is the noblest
and best prize for a young man to carry away.[20]

Though we do not have here the philosophical preference for moral
ἀρετή, clearly the hegemony that athletic excellence enjoyed is being
called into question. The one who prevails in battle, or dies in the
attempt, is due greater fame than the athlete.[21]

In the sixth century we find another poet "denouncing the accepted canons of ἀρετή as of less social value than his own intellectual achievement."[22] Xenophanes of Colophon exalts wisdom
over strength, speed, and athletic skill.

> ἀλλ' εἰ μὲν ταχυτῆτι ποδῶν νίκην τις ἄροιτο
>   ἢ πενταθλεύων, ἔνθα Διὸς τέμενος
> πὰρ Πίσαο ῥοῇς ἐν Ὀλυμπίῃ, εἴτε παλαίων
>   ἢ καὶ πυκτοσύνην ἀλγινόεσσαν ἔχων,
> εἴτε τὸ δεινὸν ἄεθλον ὃ παγκράτιον καλέουσιν,
>   ἀστοῖσίν κ' εἴη κυδρότερος προσορᾶν,
> καί κε προεδρίην φανερὴν ἐν ἀγῶσιν ἄροιτο,
>   καί κεν σῖτ' εἴη δημοσίων κτεάνων
> ἐκ πόλιος καὶ δῶρον ὅ οἱ κειμήλιον εἴη·
>   εἴτε καὶ ἵπποισιν, ταῦτά κε πάντα λάχοι,
> οὐκ ἐὼν ἄξιος, ὥσπερ ἐγώ· ῥώμης γὰρ ἀμείνων
>   ἀνδρῶν ἠδ' ἵππων ἡμετέρη σοφίη·
> ἀλλ' εἰκῇ μάλα ταῦτα νομίζεται· οὐδὲ δίκαιον
>   προκρίνειν ῥώμην ἠγαθέης σοφίης.

But if someone should win a victory by swiftness of foot
or by competing in the pentathlon, in the precinct of
Zeus

---

[20] Tyrtaeus 12.1–4, 9, 13–14 (see West, *Iambi et Elegi Graeci*, 157; translations of
classical sources, unless otherwise indicated, are mine). Socrates, according to
Xenophon, *Mem.* 3.12.1–4, once chided a disciple for his neglect of physical fitness. The basis of his reproach was the importance of such fitness in times of
warfare. The anecdote illustrates the preference for martial prowess over mere
athleticism.

[21] On the superiority of soldiers to athletes, see also Quintilian 10.1.33 and the references listed in W. Peterson, *M. Fabi Quintiliani Institutionis Oratoriae. Liber
Decimus* (Hildesheim: Georg Olms, 1891) 37.

[22] Allan H. Coxon, "Xenophanes," *OCD*, 1141.

by Pisa's stream at Olympia, or by wrestling
  or even by possessing the painful skill of boxing,
or the dire contest that they call the Pancratium,
  to his fellow citizens he would be more glorious to
  behold,
and he would receive a conspicuous front seat at the games,
  and there would be food from the public supplies
of the city and a gift that would be for him an heirloom;
  and also if [the victory were] by horses, he would obtain
  all this,
though not being worthy, as I am; for better than the
  strength
  of men or of horses is our wisdom;
indeed, quite ill considered is this custom; nor is it right
  to prefer strength to most holy wisdom.[23]

Xenophanes decries the prominence given to athletics and the benefits lavished on victors. Unlike Tyrtaeus, though, he does not exalt
the soldier as the ideal, but rather the sage, by whose wisdom (the
rest of the poem implies) the city is well governed. He thus "marks
the beginning of a development towards a philosophical picture of
the Agon."[24]

Before leaving the sixth century I might make brief mention of
Solon the poet and political reformer of Athens. Diodorus Siculus
(9.2.5) attributes to him the belief that the state derived no social
benefit from athletes, but only from persons who excelled in "prudence and virtue."

> Ὅτι ὁ Σόλων ἡγεῖτο τοὺς μὲν πύκτας καὶ σταδιεῖς καὶ τοὺς
> ἄλλους ἀθλητὰς μηδὲν ἀξιόλογον συμβάλλεσθαι ταῖς πόλεσι
> πρὸς σωτηρίαν, τοὺς δὲ φρονήσει καὶ ἀρετῇ διαφέροντας
> μόνους δύνασθαι τὰς πατρίδας ἐν τοῖς κινδύνοις διαφυλάτ-
> τειν.

> Solon used to think that boxers and runners and the other
> athletes contributed nothing worth mentioning to the cities
> so far as safety was concerned, but that only those who
> excelled in insight and virtue were able to preserve their
> homelands in crises.

---

[23] Xenophanes 2.1–14. See West, *Iambi et Elegi Graeci*, 165.
[24] Pfitzner, *Paul*, 24.

The superior value of moral and intellectual exercise over athletic prowess continues to be a topos in the dialogues of Plato. According to Plato (*Gorgias* 526e) Socrates invites Callicles and all persons to engage in the supreme agon of bettering their souls and to forgo the honors that most people seek. Here ἀγών embraces the whole of the philosopher's life, a contest that extends to and includes death.

καὶ σκοπῶ ὅπως ἀποφανοῦμαι τῷ κριτῇ ὡς ὑγιεστάτην
τὴν ψυχήν· χαίρειν οὖν ἐάσας τὰς τιμὰς τὰς τῶν πολλῶν
ἀνθρώπων, τὴν ἀλήθειαν σκοπῶν πειράσομαι τῷ ὄντι ὡς ἂν
δύνωμαι βέλτιστος ὢν καὶ ζῆν καὶ ἐπειδὰν ἀποθνήσκω
ἀποθνήσκειν. παρακαλῶ δὲ καὶ τοὺς ἄλλους πάντας ἀνθρώ-
πους, ... ἐπὶ τοῦτον τὸν βίον καὶ τὸν ἀγῶνα τοῦτον, ὃν ἐγὼ
φημι ἀντὶ πάντων τῶν ἐνθάδε ἀγώνων εἶναι.

And I give heed how I will show to the judge my soul as healthy as possible; so, renouncing the honors of most people, giving heed to the truth I will attempt in fact both to live, and when I die, to die, being the best person I can be. And I invite all other persons also ... to this life and this contest, which I say is worth all the contests here on earth.

Not only was the soul deemed of greater importance than the body, but the body was understood to be dependent on the soul. Indeed, this was a favorite teaching in Plato's writings. In a discussion on gymnastic training for youth (*Rep.* 403c–e), Socrates is reported to say that a sound body does not by its own virtue make the soul good, but quite the contrary. A good soul renders the body the very best. If one attends adequately to the mind, there is no need for extensive instruction on care for the body. A few lines later Socrates refers to youth who are groomed for political leadership as ἀθληταὶ ... τοῦ μεγίστου ἀγῶνος (athletes in the greatest contest). Again, we see the devaluation of athletic competition coupled with the use of athletic imagery to describe the true contest of living out the philosophic ideal.[25]

Aristotle makes frequent use of athletic similes, especially in the *Nicomachean Ethics*. The emphasis, though, is on analogy rather than critique. Runners, wrestlers, and boxers are not discredited, but

---

[25] Cf. Demosthenes 25.97 where the orator invokes the virtuous ancestors of the jurors who, by honoring the wise and punishing the unscrupulous, had become ἀθληταὶ τῶν καλῶν ἔργων (athletes of noble deeds).

are used as illustrations of the life of virtue, usually without a hint of disparagement. The following excerpts stress the importance of actualizing virtue, practicing moderation, and showing courage, respectively.[26]

ὥσπερ δ᾽ Ὀλυμπίασιν οὐχ οἱ κάλλιστοι καὶ ἰσχυρότατοι στεφανοῦνται ἀλλ᾽ οἱ ἀγωνιζόμενοι (τούτων γάρ τινες νικῶσιν), οὕτω καὶ τῶν ἐν τῷ βίῳ καλῶν κἀγαθῶν οἱ πράττοντες ὀρθῶς ἐπήβολοι γίγνονται.

And just as in the Olympic Games it is not the best and strongest who are crowned but those who compete (for of these some are victorious), so also the ones who act rightly become winners of the best things in life.

τὰ τοιαῦτα πέφυκεν ὑπὸ ἐνδείας καὶ ὑπερβολῆς φθείρεσθαι ... ὥσπερ ἐπὶ τῆς ἰσχύος καὶ τῆς ὑγιείας ὁρῶμεν· τά τε γὰρ ὑπερβάλλοντα γυμνάσια καὶ τὰ ἐλλείποντα φθείρει τὴν ἰσχύν, ὁμοίως δὲ καὶ τὰ ποτὰ καὶ τὰ σιτία πλείω καὶ ἐλάττω γινόμενα φθείρει τὴν ὑγίειαν, τὰ δὲ σύμμετρα καὶ ποιεῖ καὶ αὔξει καὶ σῴζει. οὕτως οὖν καὶ ἐπὶ σωφροσύνης καὶ ἀνδρείας ἔχει καὶ τῶν ἄλλων ἀρετῶν· ... φθείρεται δὴ ἡ σωφροσύνη καὶ ἡ ἀνδρεία ὑπὸ τῆς ὑπερβολῆς καὶ τῆς ἐλλείψεως, ὑπὸ δὲ τῆς μεσότητος σῴζεται.

Such [moral qualities] are disposed by nature to be destroyed by deficiency and excess ... just as we see is the case with strength and health. For both excessive and insufficient exercise destroy strength, so also both food and drink being too much and too little destroy health, but in proper measure they produce, enhance, and preserve it. Such is also the case with temperance and courage and the other virtues; ... So temperance and courage are destroyed by excess and deficiency, but are preserved by moderation.

οἷον κἂν τοῖς γυμνικοῖς ἀγῶσι γίνεται· τοῖς γὰρ πύκταις τὸ μὲν τέλος ἡδύ, οὗ ἕνεκα, ὁ στέφανος καὶ αἱ τιμαί, τὸ δὲ τύπτεσθαι ἀλγεινόν, εἴπερ σάρκινοι, καὶ λυπηρὸν καὶ πᾶς ὁ πόνος· διὰ δὲ τὸ πολλὰ ταῦτ᾽ εἶναι, μικρὸν ὂν τὸ οὗ ἕνεκα οὐδὲν ἡδὺ φαίνεται ἔχειν. εἰ δὴ τοιοῦτόν ἐστι καὶ τὸ περὶ τὴν ἀνδρείαν, ὁ μὲν θάνατος καὶ τὰ τραύματα λυπηρὰ τῷ

---

[26] *Eth. Nic.* 1.8.9; 2.2.6–7; and 3.9.3–4.

ἀνδρείῳ καὶ ἄκοντι ἔσται, ὑπομενεῖ δὲ αὐτὰ ὅτι καλόν, ἢ ὅτι αἰσχρὸν τὸ μή.

And such is the case in athletic contests; for with boxers, the end for which they box, the crown and the honors, is pleasant, but being pummeled is painful, since they are made of flesh and blood, and the entire task is also grievous; and because these things are many, the goal, being meager, appears to have no pleasure. If then the issue of courage is such, then death and wounds will be painful to the courageous person, who does not desire them, but endures them because it is good to do so, or because it is shameful not to.

Aristotle does not critique the games, but exploits them for the purpose of illustration. Contestants, athletes in training, courageous boxers – they all possess qualities which those pursuing moral excellence should emulate.

It was the Cynics, followed by the Stoics, who "first developed a complete and unified picture of the Agon of the sage."[27] With the Cynics, particularly Diogenes, the tone was often derisive. Devotion to athletic competition was regarded as folly, and polemic against it was a recurring theme in the diatribe. The writings of Dio Chrysostom and Diogenes Laertius provide numerous examples.

Discourse 8 of Dio Chrysostom describes the exilic wanderings of the Cynic Diogenes which eventually brought him to Corinth. Large crowds had gathered to attend the Isthmian games. According to Dio (8.11–15), a passer-by inquired whether Diogenes had come to see the contest. The Cynic replied, "No, but rather to compete!" The inquirer laughed and asked whom he had as his opponents. Diogenes answered, "The toughest and most difficult to defeat." He clarifies that he is not speaking of runners, wrestlers, jumpers, and the like, but of those opponents that teach a person prudence, namely "hardships." A noble person considers hardships the greatest opponents and never shrinks from confronting them. These hardships are then enumerated (8.16): hunger, cold, thirst, physical punishments, exile, and disrepute.[28]

---

[27] Pfitzner, *Paul*, 28.
[28] These are, of course, hardships endured by the exiled Diogenes, but there may also be an allusion to Dio's circumstances if this discourse was composed during the period of his exile by Domitian (*ca.* 82–96).

The second half of the discourse (8.20ff) describes an even more fearsome battle, a more perilous contest: ὁ [ἀγών] πρὸς τὴν ἡδονήν (the struggle against pleasure).[29] Pleasure entices persons via the senses and enslaves them through food, drink, and lusts. This ἀγών against both hardships and pleasure is the devotion of Diogenes and others who would excel, not in athletic games, but in virtue.[30]

Even more than the Cynics, it is the representatives of late Stoicism that demand attention. "The true Agon of the sage is one of the most frequently recurring pictures in the moral discourses of Epictetus, Seneca, Marcus Aurelius, and Plutarch."[31] One finds both criticism of the misplaced emphasis on physical exercise and the positive appropriation of the imagery to depict the life of the "moral athlete."

Epictetus sometimes depicts the struggles of Cynic–Stoic heroes (both legendary and historical) as quasi-athletic exercises. Heracles, for example, "did not consider himself wretched while being exercised (γυμναζόμενος) by Eurystheus" (3.22.57).[32] Socrates is praised for his "victory" over lust in resisting the youthful beauty of Alcibiades (2.18.22). "How great a victory he knew at that time, having conquered himself (νενικηκότα ἑαυτόν), like an Olympic victory!" Socrates deserved the greeting sometimes lavished on athletes, χαῖρε, παράδοξε (Hail, O Wondrous One!), for his victory surpassed that of "these rotten boxers and pancratiasts." In a similar fashion Diogenes reproaches those traveling to Olympia "to see a contest of worthless athletes" when they could behold him doing battle with a fever (3.22.58).

Stoicism tended to view life itself, that is, the philosophical endeavor to resist passion and to achieve ἀταραξία (imperturbability), as an agon, an Olympic contest. One must "enroll" in this struggle with all the earnestness and sobriety with which one enters a rigorous athletic competition. Ὀλύμπια μέλλεις ἀπογράφεσθαι, ἄνθρωπε, οὐχί τινά ποτε ἀγῶνα ψυχρὸν καὶ ταλαίπωρον (You are about to enter the Olympics, O man, not some insipid and miser-

---

[29] The juxtaposition of μάχη (battle) and ἀγών (contest, struggle) shows how easily athletic and military imagery are blended. See Pfitzner, *Paul*, 157–64.

[30] Discourse 9 contains similar anecdotes about Diogenes at the Isthmian games. Poverty, desire, and fear are added to the list of hardships. Pleasure is again cited as the chief opponent. On the contrast between exercise of the body and of the soul and Diogenes' preference for the latter, see also Diogenes Laertius 6.70.

[31] Pfitzner, *Paul*, 29.

[32] See also Epictetus 1.6.32–6 and 3.26.31.

able contest!: Epictetus 3.22.51).³³ It is God who invites one to this contest: ἐλθὲ ἤδη ἐπὶ τὸν ἀγῶνα, δεῖξον ἡμῖν, τί ἔμαθες, πῶς ἤθλησας (Come, at last, to the contest! Show us what you have learned, how you have contended!: 4.4.30). As a physical trainer, God has pitted the sage against the rugged opponent of hardship (1.24.1). Poverty, sickness, prison – they are training from Zeus (3.24.113). One must give careful consideration to the demands of the contest. It is easy to say "θέλω Ὀλύμπια νικῆσαι" (I want to be a victor in the Olympic games), but victory only comes to the one who submits to discipline, diet restrictions, training, and self-denial (3.15.1–7; cf. *Ench.* 29.2). If one can overcome every hardship, whether it be silver, a maiden, darkness, fame, abuse, praise, death, then that person is truly "the unconquered athlete" (1.18.20–3).

Though Epictetus affords the largest number of illustrative passages in a fairly compact literary corpus, other Hellenistic philosophers also make use of athletic imagery, notably the Stoics, Seneca and Marcus Aurelius, and the Platonist, Plutarch.

In Epistle 88.18–19 Seneca discusses what should be excluded from a program of liberal education. He would eliminate wrestling, the use of weaponry, and the handling of horses, for such activities do not "teach or cultivate virtue." The greatest opponents are of a different sort. *Quid prodest multos vincere luctatione vel caestu, ab iracundia vinci?* (What good is it to defeat many in wrestling or boxing, only to be defeated by anger?) Elsewhere Seneca laments the popular appeal of the games and the obsession with physical skill. The ones whose muscles and shoulders people admire are often "mental dullards." Again, exercises of a different sort are to be preferred. *Quam multi corpora exerceant, ingenia quam pauci.* (How many exercise their bodies; how few their characters!: Epist. 80.2–3). Nevertheless, moderate exercise is not to be rejected. In Epistle 15.4–5 Seneca suggests simple exercises that will not consume too much time. In any event, one should quickly return to the exercise of the mind.

But Seneca also makes positive use of athletic language. Sometimes the allusion is superficial as when he speaks of cheering on one who is running the philosopher's race (Epist. 109.6; 34.2; 17.1); sometimes it is developed at length. Athletes endure blows to the face and body for the sake of fame; the sage must also contend for a victory, not one whose prize is a garland or palm, but rather "virtue

³³ See also 3.25.1–4; 2.18.27, and *Ench.* 51.2.

and mental steadfastness and peace" (Epist. 78.16). Seneca's essay
De Providentia uses several different arguments to explain why people experience hardships. One explanation is that adversity functions like athletic training. *Omnia adversa exercitationes putat [vir
fortis]* ([The brave person] regards all hardships as exercises, 2.2).
Just as wrestlers pick the strongest opponents, or even multiple
opponents, to maximize the benefit of their training, so the moral
athlete must not shrink from adversity, for without an opponent,
virtue withers (2.3–4).

Marcus Aurelius depicts "the athlete of the greatest contest" as
the person untainted by pleasure, invulnerable to every pain, unharmed by every outrage, and undefeated by any passion (3.4.3). In
other, less well-developed metaphors he pictures the urgent contest
of life in terms of a runner or pancratiast.[34]

Plutarch also engages in the traditional critique, positive appropriation, and passing allusion to athletic competition. In *Moralia*
793–4 he contrasts athletes with elder statesmen. The former keep
themselves from necessary tasks and instead are devoted to the
useless; the latter do the opposite, devoting themselves to matters
worthy of diligence. Elsewhere Plutarch uses the agon motif to describe political leadership without any derogation of athletes. In
Lycurgus 26.1 the election of Sparta's senators is called μέγιστος ...
τῶν ἐν ἀνθρώποις ἀγώνων ... καὶ περιμαχητότατος (the greatest
and most fought over of all contests among human beings). It was a
contest in which not the swiftest or the strongest prevailed, but "the
best and wisest."[35] There are also the passing but poignant similes
such as the description of the able politician Cato who regarded his
opponents as wrestling partners: μέχρι γήρως ὥσπερ ἀθλητὴς ἀγω-
νιζόμενος ἄπτωτα διετήρησεν ἑαυτόν (Struggling like an athlete even
into old age, he kept himself from being thrown).[36]

A final observation may be made about Plutarch's use of athletic
imagery. As a neo-Platonist he held to a dualism that included the
survival of the soul beyond death. On at least two occasions Plutarch likened the afterlife and its rewards to an athlete's victory and
receipt of prizes. Just as athletes do not receive a crown while they
are contending but only afterward, so "the good" may look forward
to τὰ νικητήρια τοῦ βίου μετὰ τὸν βίον (the victory prizes of life in
the afterlife, *Mor.* 1105c). The soul engages in an agon, ἀγωνίζεται

---

[34] 4.18 and 51; 7.61; 12.9.   [35] Cf. *Mor.* 593e.
[36] *Comp. Arist. Cat. Ma.* 2. See also Plutarch, *Solon* 26.7.

γὰρ ὥσπερ ἀθλητὴς τὸν βίον, ὅταν δὲ διαγωνίσηται, τότε τυγχάνει τῶν προσηκόντων (For as an athlete it contends for the prize in life, and when it has finished the contest, then it obtains the things due it: *Mor.* 561a). But that which awaits the soul may be positive or negative; it is variously described as τιμή or τιμωρία (honor or punishment), χάρις or κόλασις (favor or chastisement). If we remember the earlier quote from Plato (*Gorgias* 526e), it becomes clear that some philosophers carried the race metaphor to its logical conclusion: the entirety of life is a race, at the end of which one receives what is due in accordance with how well one has run. This viewpoint provides an interesting comparison with the teleology and eschatology of Hebrews.

Jewish moral philosophers were likewise prone to use images from the track and arena to speak of the ethical life. In Hellenistic Judaism one finds "a wealth of evidence testifying to the continuance of the Agon tradition, above all in the writings of Philo of Alexandria, and in the Apocrypha and Pseudepigrapha of the Old Testament."[37]

Philo employs the full range of agonistic language in both the critique of athletic competition and the positive use of the image to depict the moral agon. The language is so commonly employed in Philo's many works that only a few representative texts can be examined here.[38] An extended discussion of both athletic and philosophical agons is found in *De Agricultura* 111–21. Philo urges his readers to disregard the sensational contests that cities hold, building theaters to receive huge crowds. He reproaches boxers and wrestlers for the brutality of their sport (113–14); he ridicules the achievements of runners and jumpers for being inferior in speed and distance to what animals accomplish with ease (115). He notes the contradiction between indignation at private acts of violence and the commendation of it in public (116–18). The only agon that

---

[37] Pfitzner, *Paul*, 38. Here I am indebted to Pfitzner's third chapter, "Hellenistic Judaism and the Agon Tradition" (38–72). M. B. Poliakoff, *Combat Sports in the Ancient World*, 143, remarks that "Philo is the single richest source of athletic terminology in all of Greek literature."

[38] Pfitzner, *Paul*, 38–48, gives many references. He notes (40, n. 5), however, that the image of the *runner* is less frequent in Philo. If one conceives the moral agon primarily as one *against* certain opponents – pleasure, passion, etc. – then the image of wrestling or boxing commends itself. In Hebrews, the author's chief concern is endurance, hence the foot-race is most appropriate. On Philo, see also H. A. Harris, *Greek Athletics and the Jews* (Cardiff: University of Wales, 1976) esp. 51–95.

is truly holy is ὁ [ἀγών] περὶ κτήσεως τῶν θείων καὶ ὀλυμπίων ὡς ἀληθῶς ἀρετῶν (the contest concerning the acquisition of divine and truly Olympian virtues, 119). In the latter contest, those who are stalwart in spirit, not body, compete. And though they achieve varying levels of performance, any success is commendable.

Philo's allusions to the games are usually brief and criticism is either implicit or absent. The faithful under Moses were "οἱ ... ἀθληταὶ τῷ ὄντι ἀρετῆς" (the true athletes of virtue). Moses himself practiced "the exercises of virtue," having noble reason as a trainer/ anointer. A good person who returns to the recognition of the One (God) is a victor in the "καλὸν δρόμον καὶ πάντων ἄριστον ἀγώνισμα τοῦτο" (the good race and this greatest of all contests).[39] The last sentence of *Legum Allegoriae* 2 (108) is a developed athletic image with several evocative terms. The context is a call to war against passion and pleasure, symbolized by the serpent of Genesis 3.1.

Τὴν ὀφιομάχον οὖν γνώμην ἀντίταττε καὶ κάλλιστον ἀγῶνα τοῦτον διάθλησον καὶ σπούδασον στεφανωθῆναι κατὰ τῆς τοὺς ἄλλους ἅπαντας νικώσης ἡδονῆς καλὸν καὶ εὐκλεᾶ στέφανον, ὃν οὐδεμία πανήγυρις ἀνθρώπων ἐχορήγησεν.

Therefore, array against [it] the resolve that wars against serpents, and struggle through this most noble contest, and strive to be crowned with the noble and glorious crown [in the fight] against the pleasure that conquers all other persons, [the crown] that no assembly of human beings has supplied.

Another feature of Philo's athletic imagery deserves mention: his appeals to exemplars. The narrative of Genesis 32.24–30 forms the basis for his frequent depiction of Jacob as one skilled in wrestling, not wrestling that involves the body, but that of the soul: παλαίει ψυχὴ πρὸς τοὺς ἀνταγωνιστὰς τρόπους αὐτῆς πάθεσι καὶ κακίαις μαχομένη (The soul wrestles against the tempers opposed to her, doing battle against passions and vices).[40] Other figures from Israel's past are similarly described. Abraham, Isaac, and Jacob are called "athletes who anoint themselves for the truly sacred games,

---

[39] These three quotations from *De Praemiis et Poenis* 4–5, *De Vita Mosis* 1.48, and *Leg. Alleg.* 3.48, respectively.

[40] *Ibid.*, 3.190. For other references to Jacob, see Pfitzner, *Paul*, 41 n. 4.

who, despising bodily exercise, supply vigor to the soul, striving for
victory over the antagonistic passions." (*De Abr.* 48). Elsewhere
Abraham's behavior in overcoming grief at the death of his wife
is depicted in agonistic terms: "when sorrow (λυπή) was stripping
down and sprinkling itself with dust [in preparation to wrestle]
against the soul, [Abraham] prevailed as an athlete, strengthening and greatly encouraging reason, the natural antagonist of the
passions."[41] In *De Abrahamo* 35, Philo speaks of Noah's being
crowned by God as a "victorious contestant" and given a magnificent proclamation.

Philo's appeals to the examples of Israel's forebears parallel the
evocation of Heracles in Cynic–Stoic diatribe. The question arises
whether Jacob, *et al.* function for Philo, or Heracles functions for
the Cynics and Stoics, in the same manner as Jesus does for the
author of Hebrews. This question will be postponed until the athletic
imagery of the remaining Jewish sources is investigated.

Most of the LXX contains scant evidence of athletic imagery.
Apart from Jacob's wrestling with an angel, there are some references to "running," "crowns," and "contests," but many of these
have an attenuated athletic nuance at best. "Our efforts to trace
a traditional use of the Agon metaphor or picture in hellenistic
philosophy are for the first time rewarded in the Septuagint when
we come to the Wisdom of Solomon."[42]

Two passages are of special importance here. In Wisdom of
Solomon 4.2 virtue is said to march "crowned in triumph, victor
in the contest for prizes that are undefiled." In 10.12 Wisdom is
said to have protected Jacob. "She judged a mighty contest in his
favor in order that he might know that piety is stronger than anything." The agon here is probably the wrestling contest of Genesis
32 (cf. Hosea 12.5). Pfitzner notes that both Wisdom of Solomon
and Philo portray Jacob as one of the chief contestants in an agon
of piety.[43]

Many other passages in Jewish literature could be adduced to
illustrate the agon motif, but reasons of space must limit this survey

---

[41]   *De Abr.* 256. Elsewhere Philo calls Abraham an ἀθλητὴς τέλειος (perfect athlete)
who has been deemed worthy of prizes and crowns (*Migr. Abr.* 27).

[42]   Pfitzner, *Paul*, 54.

[43]   *Ibid.*, 56–7. See also M. B. Poliakoff, "Jacob, Job, and Other Wrestlers: Reception
of Greek Athletics by Jews and Christians in Antiquity," *Journal of Sport History*,
11.2 (1984) 48–65.

to one final, highly significant text.[44] Fourth Maccabees has already been mentioned in connection with martyrdom. This first-century CE treatise, written by a Jew who was "profoundly influenced by Greek philosophical thought,"[45] contains a number of verses that depict the sufferings of the Maccabean martyrs in agonistic terms.[46] The aged Eleazar, though pummeled, nevertheless conquered his tormentors as a noble athlete (6.9–10). The seven sons respond to the tyrant that by their suffering and endurance they will obtain "the prizes of virtue" and will be with God (9.8). Other verses contain similar allusions with varying degrees of detail,[47] but one passage in particular is distinguished by its remarkable concentration of athletic terms.

In chapter 17 the author suggests a fitting epitaph for the tomb of the martyrs. Immediately following is a paragraph (17.11–16) that summarizes the events of 5.1–17.6 in thoroughly agonistic terms. The text and Anderson's translation follow.[48]

> Ἀληθῶς γὰρ ἦν ἀγὼν θεῖος ὁ δι' αὐτῶν γεγενημένος. ἠθλο-
> θέτει γὰρ τότε ἀρετὴ δι' ὑπομονῆς δοκιμάζουσα. τὸ νῖκος
> ἀφθαρσία ἐν ζωῇ πολυχρονίῳ. Ελεαζαρ δὲ προηγωνίζετο, ἡ
> δὲ μήτηρ τῶν ἑπτὰ παίδων ἐνήθλει, οἱ δὲ ἀδελφοὶ ἠγω-
> νίζοντο· ὁ τύραννος ἀντηγωνίζετο· ὁ δὲ κόσμος καὶ ὁ τῶν
> ἀνθρώπων βίος ἐθεώρει· θεοσέβεια δὲ ἐνίκα τοὺς ἑαυτῆς
> ἀθλητὰς στεφανοῦσα. τίνες οὐκ ἐθαύμασαν τοὺς τῆς θείας
> νομοθεσίας ἀθλητάς; τίνες οὐκ ἐξεπλάγησαν;

> Truly divine was the contest in which they engaged. On that day virtue was the umpire and the test to which they were put was a test of endurance. The prize for victory was incorruption in long-lasting life. The first to enter the contest was Eleazar, but the mother of the seven sons competed also, and the brothers as well took part. The tyrant was the adversary and the world and the life of men were the spec-

---

[44] I pass over pseudepigraphical sources such as the Testament of Job, the Testaments of the Twelve Patriarchs, 4 Ezra, and Syriac Baruch. See Pfitzner's discussion, *Paul*, 65–9. Josephus, despite his sizeable corpus, offers few examples of athletic imagery since he "writes as an historian and not as a moralist or interpreter of the Scriptures, as does Philo" (*ibid.*, 69). But see *War* 4.91.

[45] H. Anderson, "4 Maccabees," in J. H. Charlesworth, ed., *OTP* (Garden City, NY: Doubleday, 1985) II, 532.

[46] In addition to Pfitzner, *Paul*, 57–64, see Anderson, "4 Maccabees," 531–64.

[47] See for example, 11.20; 12.11, 14; and 16.16.

[48] Anderson, "4 Maccabees," 562–3.

tators. Piety won the victory and crowned her own contestants. Who did not marvel at the champions of the divine
Law; who were not amazed?

This dense cluster of athletic vocabulary contains several of the
motifs found in the above summary of the agon tradition. Of special
relevance to the investigation of Hebrews 12 are the following:
ἀγών, δι᾽ ὑπομονῆς, and ἀντηγωνίζετο. The three forms of ἀγωνί-
ζομαι, the simplex and the compounds with προ and ἀντι, show the
structure of the contest.[49] The athletic image, while not specific,
seems to be one of wrestling.

Before I move on to consider the specific phraseology of Hebrews
12.1–3, it might be helpful to make several general observations
about that passage in light of the agon tradition sketched above.
First of all, it is evident that the tradition was widespread and had
enjoyed a long life prior to the composition of Hebrews. Athletic
imagery in moral exhortation was commonplace, and Hebrews
12.1–3 would have been readily intelligible to its readers. To call
the language of our author "traditional" does not, however, deprive
it of all creativity. Traditional material was often adapted to an
author's particular needs.[50] Hebrews uses the language of the agon
to enjoin faith and endurance. In a single sentence (12.1–2) the
author joins Israel's past to the readers' present and adds the example of Jesus' endurance and exaltation.

On the other hand, a few features of the traditional agon motif
are lacking in Hebrews 12. There is, of course, no polemic against
athletics or bodily exercise. This is a critique with which our author
is not concerned; his appropriation of the motif is entirely positive. As for ideal figures, Hebrews exalts Israel's forebears and,
supremely, Jesus, as examples of those whose faith endures, over-
comes, and is rewarded. Our author has no interest in praising the
soldier whose military exploits save the city, nor the sage whose
counsel preserves the state, nor the philosopher whose radical engagement in the true agon constitutes a stark challenge to conven-
tional thinking.

The precise choice of a metaphor reveals the author's conception

---

[49] The martyrdom of the mother is an uncertain aspect of the tradition. There is
no mention of it in 2 Macc. and 4 Macc. refers to it "in a strangely oblique and
fleeting way" (*ibid.*, 562, n. 17a). This may account for the choice of the word
ἐνήθλει ("competed also," 17.13) to describe the mother's involvement.
[50] Malherbe, "Hellenistic Moralists," 280–1, and n. 51.

of the readers' struggle. Although the image of wrestling and boxing is quite common in the tradition, Hebrews employs running as its primary metaphor.[51] This choice coincides with the readers' need of endurance and faith, rather than aggressive action or engagement of a foe. The "enemy" is not passion or pleasure as in the case of Socrates when he resisted the youthful Alcibiades, nor the Cynic Diogenes battling his own lusts, nor the Philonic portraits of Abraham and Jacob resisting grief and passion. The struggle is against the weariness and fatigue that result from an extended contest. The agon in Hebrews 12.1–3 (cf. vss. 12–13) has more in common with Diogenes' struggle against distress, Heracles' toilsome labors, and the various hardships such as poverty, illness, exile, and imprisonment, to which the gods call the sage. Lastly, the race is oriented toward a spiritual goal; it is eschatological. Jesus' destiny was not the achievement of εὐδαιμονία (true happiness) or ἀταραξία (imperturbability) but exaltation to the right hand of God. In the case of the readers, the goal is the reception of God's promise (10.36; 11.13, 39).

2.4   Athletic language in Hebrews 12.1–13

I will now turn to the specific language of the passage in order to investigate its distinctive expression of the agon motif. The aim here is neither a detailed exegesis nor a unified interpretation of the entire passage, which are postponed until chapters 4 and 5 but rather a display of the agonistic features of the text, some quite obvious, some less so, against the broad background sketched above.

The first expression in Hebrews 12 that may have an agonistic nuance is νέφος μαρτύρων. Could the meaning here be "cloud of spectators"? Lane at first seems to allow this possibility: "In the context of the athletic metaphor, it is perhaps natural to think of an amphitheater, with its ascending rows of spectators who gather to watch the games ... The participle περικείμενον, 'surrounded by,' particularly suggests that they are witnesses to our efforts."[52] But the next sentence effectively withdraws this alternative: "In the NT,

---

[51] The image of boxing may lie behind vs. 4, but the author has chosen not to develop it as he has the foot-race image. On boxing, see the works of Poliakoff cited in n. 16 above.

[52] Lane, *Hebrews*, 408.

however, a witness is never merely a passive spectator but an active participant who confirms and attests the truth as a confessing witness." This is not convincing, however. To say that a μάρτυς is *never* "merely a passive spectator" begs the question; even if this is true elsewhere in the NT, it is not necessarily decisive for the interpretation of this passage.[53] Lane's first instinct to rely on the context is a more useful guide than his generalization about NT usage.[54] He has, however, pointed out the major obstacle to understanding μάρτυς as "spectator" in Hebrews 12.1, namely, the difficulty of adducing clear instances of this meaning.

Attridge asserts that the noun can simply mean "spectator" and cites references in Wisdom, Josephus, and Longinus.[55] These references are not as unambiguous as one might hope, but they have some force. In Wisdom 1.6 a parallelism with ἐπίσκοπος seems to support Attridge's contention. "God is a μάρτυς of the inmost thoughts, a true ἐπίσκοπος of the heart." God is by no means a "passive" spectator here. God observes with a view to judging human behavior. But why should we exclude judicial and moral interest from the idea of "spectator"? A better distinction would be whether the stress falls on "bearing testimony" or "observing." Wisdom 1.6 would incline toward the latter.

Similar qualifications could be made about the other passages cited by Attridge. Josephus' *War* 4.134 and *Antiquities* 18.299 deal with witnesses who observe valor or wrong-doing with the intent, or at least potential, of honoring or blaming. In *On the Sublime* 14.2, (Pseudo) Longinus imagines the ancient masters of style, Homer, Demosthenes, *et al.*, being present to judge his writing. This imaginary assembly is referred to as a θέατρον (theater) made up of μάρτυρες, but their judicial function is apparent in the close juxtaposition of the words δικαστήριον (court) and κριταί (judges). In each of these texts a μάρτυς is one who watches, but not with passive disengagement.

A more fruitful avenue of investigation in regard to the meaning of μάρτυς is the collocation of this word with the Greek word for "spectator," θεατής. A θεατής was one who observed plays in the

---

[53] Furthermore, the addition of the qualifier "passive" is an unwarranted restriction. A μαρτύς may be an actively engaged spectator.

[54] Context is determinative for Ellingworth, *Hebrews*, 638, and Strathmann, *TDNT*, IV, 491.

[55] Attridge, *Hebrews*, 354 n. 19.

theater, games in the arena, or war on the battlefield.[56] (In the
arena such a person is distinguished from an ἀγωνιστής, "contestant.")[57] The words μάρτυς and θεατής are often found in close
proximity with one another, sometimes even in synonymous parallels. It will be worthwhile to examine briefly some of the more
illustrative passages.

Aelius Aristides, in an oration entitled *The Embassy to Achilles*,
urges the great warrior Achilles to act promptly and use his superior strength to defend the Greeks before they are slaughtered by
Hector. Only if Achilles acts now will he be able "to display this
superiority while there are spectators and witnesses (τῶν θεατῶν καὶ
μαρτύρων) remaining for you."[58] Μάρτυς in this context is roughly
synonymous with θεατής.

Dio Chrysostom, reflecting on kingship, asserts that virtue is a
necessary possession for a monarch. The king has the greatest reason to practice virtue for he "has all people as spectators and witnesses (θεατὰς καὶ μάρτυρας) of his own soul."[59]

The Hellenistic writer who juxtaposes μάρτυς and θεατής most
often is Plutarch. In a critique of ostentatious banquets, he writes
that the wealthy consider their wealth useless "unless it has witnesses and, just as a tragedy, spectators."[60] In another context
Plutarch cautions against the public rebuke of friends, arguing that
the exposure of error should be done discreetly and in private,
without "gathering witnesses and spectators."[61] The two words are
thus virtually equated.[62]

A final reference is worthy of mention owing to its athletic context. Lucian's work *Anacharsis* is a fictive conversation on the
subject of athletics between Solon, the Athenian law-giver, and

---

[56] For spectators in the theater, see Aristophanes, *Nubes* 575 *et passim*; for the arena,
see Isocrates, *Evagoras* 79; for spectators of war, see Diodorus Siculus 13.15.5;
13.60.4; 13.72.8 and Dionysius of Halicarnassus 3.18.2.

[57] This distinction is made in Dionysius of Halicarnassus 3.19.3, and *Historia Alex-
andri Magni* 1.18, in L. Bergson, ed., *Der Griechische Alexanderroman. Rezension
β* (Stockholm: Almqvist and Wiksell, 1965).

[58] Aristides 52.435; see W. Dindorf, ed., *Aristides* (Hildesheim: Georg Olms, 1964)
II, 604. For an English translation, see Charles A. Behr, *P. Aelius Aristides, The
Complete Works* (Leiden: Brill, 1986) whose numbering differs from Dindorf. In
Behr, the above citation = 16.34. Elsewhere in Aristides μάρτυς and θεατής are
juxtaposed in 15.231 (Behr); 43.549 (Dindorf).

[59] Dio Chrysostom, 3.11.

[60] Plutarch, *Mor.* 679b. See also *Mor.* 527–8.

[61] *Ibid.*, 71a.

[62] See also *Solon* 28.3; *Mor.* 81b; 333e. For μάρτυς with ἐπόπτης, see *Agesilaus* 14.1.

Anacharsis, a Scythian sage. Anacharsis is shocked to see how Greek wrestlers and boxers abuse one another for sport. Solon explains that such events attract huge crowds, and the winners are praised as equal to the gods. Anacharsis finds it all the more unusual that athletes suffer such indignities not in the presence of a few, but "among so many spectators and witnesses (θεαταῖς καὶ μάρτυσι) of the violence."[63] The terms seem to form a simple pleonasm, but there is more taking place here. In the next sentence Anacharsis claims that such violence is intolerable in Scythia, and severe penalties are imposed when such acts are committed before even a few witnesses (ἐπ' ὀλίγων μαρτύρων). This shows that the choice of μάρτυς earlier was strategic; Lucian plays off the double meaning of "watcher" and "witness."

Although Lucian's text is not a "pure" example of μάρτυς = spectator, it may illustrate a rhetorical strategy similar to what occurs in Hebrews 12. Μάρτυς may not be the most appropriate word for "spectator at an athletic event," but it is serviceable in such a context, particularly when a second nuance is desired. Lucian desired a word with a second nuance of "legal witness." The author of Hebrews desired a word with a link to the fourfold use of μαρτυρέω in chapter 11. But this connection is more etymological than semantic. Νέφος μαρτύρων in Hebrews 12.1 may still be translated "cloud of witnesses," but the context places emphasis on the visual aspect of "watching" rather than the verbal aspect of "bearing testimony." Strathmann, therefore, is not just waxing homiletical when he says of this passage, "The readers are represented as runners who have entered the arena ... Around them on the stands are the packed ranks of spectators, the νέφος μαρτύρων, who with avid interest follow the course of the runners as eye-witnesses."[64] The μάρτυρες of Hebrews 12.1 are thus actively engaged spectators and witnesses. Such a construal of μάρτυς is semantically permissible and contextually indicated.[65]

The image of God or humanity as spectators of a moral agon

---

[63] Lucian, *Anacharsis* 11.

[64] TDNT, IV, 491.

[65] The collocation of μάρτυς and θεατής is also found in Jewish and Christian writers. See Josephus, *Ant.* 2.23; and especially Basil, *Homilia in Passionem Domini* 28.1061: θεατὰς τῆς ἀναστάσεως ... μάρτυρας τῆς ἐγέρσεως (viewers of his resurrection ... and witnesses of his awakening). Also Gregory of Nyssa, *De Virginitate* 3.1, and John Chrysostom, *In Sanctum Julianum Martyrem* 50.669, *In Joannem* 59.311 and 464.

occurs in paraenetic literature, particularly in Stoic sources. Seneca considers a brave person pitted against adverse circumstances to be a "worthy spectacle, at which God might gaze, intent upon his work" (*De Prov.* 2.9). Epictetus told the story of Diogenes who, as he lay ill with a fever, reviled passers-by saying, "You make the long trek to Olympia to see a battle of worthless athletes, but you do not wish to see a battle between a man and a fever." Diogenes considered his hardships a spectacle (θέαμα) for the moral benefit of others.[66]

The most elaborate sketch of a moral agon featuring both contestants and spectators is the scene cited above in Stoically influenced 4 Maccabees. There we saw ὁ ... κόσμος καὶ ὁ τῶν ἀνθρώπων βίος (the world and the life of men, 17.14) as the spectators of the gruesome agon of the martyrs.[67] As an example from early Christianity, Paul (1 Cor. 4.9) speaks of the apostles having become a θέατρον ... τῷ κόσμῳ καὶ ἀγγέλοις καὶ ἀνθρώποις. Lastly, in a somewhat different context, Diodorus Siculus (13.17.1) speaks of the Syracusans, engaged in a heated battle with Athens, as reproving one another for "shamefully forsaking their fatherland, which they have as a witness of their contests." So sometimes the moral agon involves an individual contestant, sometimes a group. The envisioned spectator(s) may be God, a group of persons, angelic viewers, all humanity, or even one's nation personified. The existence of this motif makes it even more likely that the author of Hebrews conceived of the cloud of Israel's faithful as an encircling throng of avid spectators.

The second expression in Hebrews 12.1 that contributes to the athletic image is ὄγκον ἀποθέμενοι πάντα, "putting off every weight." Ὄγκος derives from ἐνεγκεῖν, the (functional) aorist stem of φέρω, therefore the basic sense is "something borne" or "a burden."[68] This root idea yields such contextual meanings as "mass," "bulk," and "size." It does not appear to have any technical athletic sense, such as "weights carried by runners to increase stamina."[69]

---

[66] Epictetus, 3.22.58–9. See also 2.19.25 where Epictetus himself expresses a longing to see the θέαμα (spectacle) of a person living according to Stoic ideals.

[67] In 1 Macc. 2.37, when Antiochus' soldiers attacked non-resisting Jews on the Sabbath, the latter cried out, "Let us all die in our innocence; heaven and earth testify for us that you are killing us unjustly." The passage lacks specifically agonistic language, but the motif of cosmic witnesses to a dramatic event is evident.

[68] TDNT, V, 41 n. 1.

[69] A claim made but not substantiated by George Wesley Buchanan, *To the Hebrews* (Garden City, NY: Doubleday, 1972) 207.

But it may refer to body weight. Appian (4.7) uses the word in a description of the Gauls as intemperate in eating and drinking, having bodies given up to "bulk and heaviness" (ὄγκον καὶ βάρος), adding that they had become "wholly unfit for running or labor." In contrast Diodorus Siculus (4.20.1) describes the Ligurians as "compact in size" (τοῖς ὄγκοις ... συνεσταλμένοι) and "vigorous owing to constant exercise." Both of these passages associate fitness with a proper amount of ὄγκος in the body. Since Hebrews 12.1 refers to the removal of *all* ὄγκος, the word would have to denote "bulkiness" or "*excess* body fat." This may be the author's meaning, but a reference to clothing or a general sense of "impediment" cannot be ruled out.[70]

In τρέχωμεν the author of Hebrews reaches the linchpin of this sentence, the independent verb. Both its object, τὸν ... ἀγῶνα, and its modifier, δι' ὑπομονῆς, call for comment. The word ἀγών was seen in the above review of the motif to be a polyvalent term for almost any kind of contest or struggle.[71] In the athletic sphere, it could denote games of wrestling, boxing, jumping, throwing and running. The prominence of running events is seen in the use of ἀγών as an object of verbs of running, particularly in metaphorical contexts such as Hebrews 12.1.[72] The phrase δι' ὑπομονῆς shows the nature of the race envisioned and highlights the chief virtue enjoined by the exhortation.

Ὑπομένω did not originally denote a virtuous act. Only as a result of semantic and rhetorical development did it come to signify a central ethical quality in the writings of the Hellenistic moralists. Hauck's comment is apt.[73]

> In the first instance ὑπομένειν is ethically neutral. It simply means "to hold out." But as ὑπομονή later came to hold a

---

[70] Another reference to the athlete's avoidance of corpulence is Philo, *Special Laws* 2.91. The term ὄγκος, however, is lacking here; instead we have πολυσαρκία (fleshiness). For obesity as a hindrance to both physical fitness and military readiness, see Plutarch, *Mor.* 192d; Lucian, *Anacharsis* 25; and Dionysius of Halicarnassus 14.8.1.

[71] See LSJ, 18–19, and Ellsworth's dissertation, cited in n. 16 above.

[72] For ἀγών as the object of τρέχω/δραμοῦμαι/ἔδραμον, see Herodotus 8.102; Euripides, *Electra* 883–4, *Orestes* 878, *Iphigenia at Aulis* 1455; Eunapius, *Lives of the Philosophers* 479; Dionysius of Halicarnassus, *Roman Antiquities* 7.48.3; Libanius 40.2.44; and Philostratus, *Life of Apollonius* 8.2. The expression ἀγὼν δρόμου, meaning "foot-race," is found in Appian 2.8.55; and Pausanias 3.12.2; 3.13.7, and 5.1.4.

[73] F. Hauck, *TDNT*, IV, 581–2.

prominent place in the list of Greek virtues, so there predominates in ὑπομένειν the concept of the courageous endurance which manfully defies evil. Unlike patience, it thus has an active content. It includes active and energetic resistance to hostile power, though with no assertion of the success of this resistance ... ὑπομένειν ... means above all perseverance in face of hostile forces.

The importance of ὑπομονή was seen in both athletic and moral spheres.[74] Plutarch (*Mor.* 724–5) contrasts athletes who cannot bear up under the strain of competition with "those who endure training resolutely." Polybius (29.17.4) likens the Greek hero Perseus, who failed to endure in battle, to athletes who are in poor condition. Philo (*Prob.* 26) spans athletic and moral domains when he engages in a rather detailed comparison of the endurance of a pancratiast and that of a virtuous person. A particularly aggressive combatant whom Philo once saw was worn to exhaustion by the remarkable endurance of his adversary: εἶδον ... τὸν ... τυπτόμενον ... τὴν ... τοῦ ἀντιπάλου δύναμιν τῷ καρτερικῷ καὶ παγίῳ τῆς ὑπομονῆς καθῃρηκότα μέχρι παντελοῦς νίκης (I saw the one pummeled having worn down the strength of his opponent by the perseverance and firmness of his endurance, until [he won] a complete victory). Philo's interest is not sports commentary, however. He goes on to say that the virtuous person similarly wears down violent opposition through resolute reason.[75]

Endurance was highly esteemed among classical and Hellenistic philosophers. Ὑπομονή was closely related to ἀνδρεία, one of the four cardinal virtues of Greek philosophy.[76] Stoic philosophers likewise saw endurance as integral to moral development. Seneca (*Epist.* 67.10) asserts that when one bravely endures torture, one is employing all the virtues. Although endurance (*patientia*) is the most manifest quality in such cases, it is accompanied by fortitude,

---

[74] The value placed on endurance (in this case καρτερία) in *combat* sports is discussed by H. W. Pleket, "Games, Prizes, Athletes and Ideology," *Stadion* 1, 1 (1975) 49–89, esp. 76–7. See also Poliakoff, *Combat Sports in the Ancient World*, 9–10.

[75] On endurance in a moral agon elsewhere in Philo, see *De Congr.* 164–5.

[76] Plato articulated the four cardinal virtues: ἀνδρεία, σωφροσύνη, δικαιοσύνη, and φρόνησις (courage, self-control, justice, and prudence, *Leges* 630a–b, 964b, *Phaedo* 69b–c). Aristotle adopted this scheme (*Pol.* 1323a) and expanded it (*Rhet.* 1366a–b, *Virtues and Vices* 1249b). The ability to endure was usually seen as an integral part of ἀνδρεία. See Plato, *Phaedo* 68d, *Leges* 507b; Aristotle, *Eudemian Ethics* 1228b–1230a, *Eth. Nic.* 2.2.9, 1104b; 3.4.5, 1115a–3.9.4, 1117b.

forbearance, tolerance, prudence, and constancy. Endurance is thus integrally related to the entire complex of virtues. Epictetus elevates endurance even higher when he declares that the *lack* of endurance (*intolerantia* in the Latin source preserving this saying) is a supreme vice, one of two vices, together with the lack of self-control, that are "by far the gravest and most shameful of all." *Intolerantia* is defined as "not enduring or bearing the wrongs which we ought to bear."[77] By implication, the *practice* of endurance would be a chief virtue.

The language of ὑπομένω is fairly common in the LXX, but mostly in the positive religious sense of "waiting upon, hoping in." The meaning common in secular Greek plays a secondary role, chiefly in Job and a few apocryphal writings.[78] One book of the LXX which makes extensive use of ὑπομένω/ὑπομονή in the negative sense (enduring hardship) is 4 Maccabees. Here the verb has become a technical term for "the steadfastness of the martyr."[79] The objects of endurance are hardship (5.23; 6.9; 7.22; 16.19; 17.7, 10), pains (16.8), torments (9.6, 22; 16.1), and agonies (16.17). By endurance the martyrs overcame the tyrant (1.11; 9.30), confirmed their adherence to the Law (7.9), and hoped to receive a reward and be united with God, (9.8; 17.12–13, 17–18). This concentration of language, along with other features of 4 Maccabees, betrays its strong Stoic influence.[80] Occasionally this language is combined with agonistic rhetoric as in 17.11–16, although rarely with the image of a foot-race.[81]

In sum, then, endurance was an important virtue among Hellenistic Jews and pagans, especially the latter. Extolling this virtue did not always involve the use of athletic imagery, but as Philo shows, such imagery was readily adapted to that end.

The next phrase in Hebrews 12.2, τὸν προκείμενον ἡμῖν ἀγῶνα, makes it clear, if any doubt remained, that we are dealing with "agonistic" language. Commentators note that a strong formal

---

77 Epictetus, Loeb fragment 10 from Gellius, 17.19.
78 See Hauck, *TDNT*, IV, 583–5. For praise of Job's (athletic) endurance, see Testament of Job 27.2–7. In the latter, patience (μακροθυμία) is exalted as "better than all else" (27.7). See S. P. Brock, *Testamentum Iobi* (Leiden: Brill, 1967) 39.
79 Hauck, *TDNT*, IV, 585.
80 On the Stoic qualities of 4 Macc. see Robert Renehan, "The Greek Philosophic Background of Fourth Maccabees," *Rheinisches Museum für Philologie*, 115 (1972) 223–38.
81 In 14.5 the author portrays the martyrs as "running on a road to immortality," but the emphasis here is on the haste with which they accepted martyrdom, not the ongoing life of faith as a sustained race.

parallel exists between this phrase and τῆς προκειμένης αὐτῷ χαρᾶς in verse 3: an attributive participle of a relatively uncommon verb (five times in the NT; twice outside Hebrews) with the dative of the person involved. Because of this parallelism, which was almost certainly a conscious one on the author's part, the two phrases should be examined conjointly with regard to their athletic content.

Commentators have recognized that the description of an agon as "having been set before"[82] someone has literary precedent. Attridge calls it "a fixed classical expression."[83] It is found in a variety of authors and eras. Herodotus (9.60) describes Greece's struggle to remain free in the face of the Persian onslaught as "the greatest struggle set before us." Plato (*Phaedrus* 247b) uses the expression in speaking of the "ultimate hardship and contest set before the soul." Epictetus (3.25.2–3) uses it in an extended metaphor of the sage's struggle. "For the contest has been set before us (ὁ ἀγὼν πρόκειται), not concerning wrestling or the pancratium ... but about good fortune and blessedness itself." A character in Heliodorus' *Ethiopian Story* (7.5.5) describes the test of single combat that he faces as "the contest set before me." The examples could be multiplied.[84]

Not as widely recognized is the equally impressive precedent for the parallel phrase in Hebrews 12.2: τῆς προκειμένης αὐτῷ χαρᾶς. For in the broad tradition of games and contests (whether athletic, martial, or artistic), not only was the agon spoken of as "set before" someone, but *prizes* and *rewards* were also set forth, with a view to a winner at the outcome of the agon. Pausanias (9.2.6) mentions quadrennial games known as the Eleutheria in which "the greatest prizes are offered for running" (μέγιστα γέρα πρόκειται δρόμου).[85] A very common construction is ἆθλα (prizes) with πρόκειμαι. Such ἆθλα were offered by Hannibal to soldiers willing to engage in mortal combat for sport (Polybius 3.62). The Greek equivalent of "To the victor belong the spoils" was τὰ ... τῶν ἡττωμένων ... ἀγαθὰ τοῖς νικῶσιν ἆθλα πρόκειται (the goods of those who are defeated are set out as prizes for the conquerors).[86] Prizes were even

---

[82] The verb πρόκειμαι is used as a (perfect) passive for προτίθημι. See LSJ, 934, 1485; Herbert W. Smyth, *Greek Grammar* (Cambridge, MA: Harvard University, 1956), section 1752.

[83] Attridge, *Hebrews*, 355.

[84] Dio Chrysostom 13.118; Diodorus Siculus 8.12.9; Euripides, *Orestes* 847, *Phoenissae* 780; Herodotus 7.11; Josephus, *Ant.* 19.92; Lucian, *Anacharsis* 15; Plato, *Laches* 182a; Pseudo-Plato, *Epinomis* 975a; Plotinus 1.6.7.

[85] For γέρα with πρόκειμαι, see also Dio Cassius 56.41.6.

[86] Plutarch, *Mor.* 8d, loosely quoting Xenophon, *Cyropaedia* 2.3.2.

"set forth" for the best engineers working on the catapult in fourth-century Syracuse.[87]

The same expression is common in simile and metaphor. Dio Cassius (41.10.1) speaks of Caesar approaching Rome in 49 BCE and knowing that the city "had been set out as a prize before those who would seize it." Josephus (*Ant.* 8.208) speaks of the greatest prize of all as: προκειμένου σοι τῆς εὐσεβείας καὶ τῆς πρὸς τὸν θεὸν τιμῆς ἄθλου (the prize set before you of piety and honor toward God). Plato (*Rep.* 608c), in discussing the moral agon, refers to τά ... μέγιστα ἐπίχειρα ἀρετῆς καὶ προκείμενα ἄθλα (the greatest rewards of virtue and the prizes set forth). Philo (*De Praemiis* 13) asks in regard to the person who hopes in God, τί οὖν ἄθλον πρόκειται τῷ στεφανωθέντι τὸν ἀγῶνα τοῦτον; (What prize then is set before the one having been crowned in this contest?)

Many more examples could be given.[88] The idea of prizes set forth for winners was such a topos that the participle alone, without ἄθλα, was sufficient to convey the thought. Josephus (*Ant.* 15.269) remarks that Herod's lavish games attracted athletes "with the hope of the [prizes] set forth" (κατ᾽ ἐλπίδα τῶν προκειμένων). The strength of this topos has direct relevance to the question of the temporal or spatial proximity implied by πρόκειμαι, that is, whether πρόκειμαι means "be in one's grasp" or "lie in prospect as a goal."[89] The topos clearly points to the latter, inasmuch as the prizes serve as an incentive for the contestants and are received *after* the agon is won.[90]

Hebrews 12.1–2 should be understood in the light of these substantial precedents for the dual expressions "race lying before" and "prize(s) lying before." Attridge sees that "joy is rather like the prize or the goal that, like the contest itself, lies in front of the athlete."[91]

---

[87] Diodorus Siculus 14.42.1.

[88] Chariton 2.8.2; Dio Cassius 41.56.1; Dio Chrysostom 7.118; Diodorus Siculus 20.8.5; Herodotus 7.19; 8.26; 9.21; Lysias 1.47; Philo, *De Mutatione* 88; Plutarch, *Mor.* 156a. Related passages which lack the key word πρόκειμαι are Philo, *Migr. Abr.* 133, *Praem.* 27; and Xenophon, *Cyropaedia* 8.2.26.

[89] See BAGD, 707, and Ellingworth, *Hebrews*, 641.

[90] On this point, see especially Josephus, *Ant.* 8.302: "Those before whom a prize has been set ... do not cease striving after it." Philo (*De Vita Mosis* 1.222) similarly implies that the reward lies ahead: "The prize of the struggles and dangers that we withstood and are still now enduring is the inheritance." I might note that "inheritance" is also an important concept in Hebrews (1.14; 6.12; 9.15).

[91] Attridge, *Hebrews*, 357. The prospective use of πρόκειμαι is also seen in its collocation with σκοπός (target, goal). See Diodorus Siculus 5.18.4; 20.54.5; Josephus, *War* 4.555; Philo, *De Vita Mosis* 1.48; Plutarch, *Mor.* 1070–1. For the same idea

The author of Hebrews has adapted the traditional usage by substituting "joy" (χαρά) for "prize" (γέρας, ἆθλον, or ἔπαθλον), perhaps to avoid trivializing the heavenly session that Jesus assumed after enduring the cross. His exaltation is not explicitly styled as a prize, but the author does seem to envision a celestial reward of sorts at the end of Jesus' agon.[92]

In an effort to link the two phrases containing πρόκειμαι, I have skipped over 2a: ἀφορῶντες εἰς τὸν ... Ἰησοῦν. Although this clause contains a pregnant expression with immense christological significance, there is little of an unambiguously athletic nature in it. In some contexts ἀρχηγός may have the nuance of "champion," although in a military sense rather than athletic. It is tempting to look for foot-race imagery behind the ἀρχ/τελ antithesis, such as "first and last runner" in a race, but there is no historical or philological evidence for this.[93] Although ἀρχηγὸν καὶ τελειωτήν does not appear to involve technical, athletic terminology, the pairing of these two words makes a very significant statement about Jesus and faith. This will be explored more fully in chapter 4.[94]

In the remainder of Hebrews 12.1–13 there are scattered words that either possess an athletic nuance or are sufficiently flexible to bend in that direction. Verse 3 calls the readers to "consider the one who endured such hostility against himself at the hands of sinners." The purpose for this contemplation is ἵνα μὴ κάμητε ταῖς ψυχαῖς ὑμῶν ἐκλυόμενοι. The two terms here, κάμνω and ἐκλύω, are not borrowed from the arena or the race-track, but in the context of 12.1–3 they are adaptable to the image.

Κάμνω originally meant "work" or "toil," but also came to refer

in Christian writers, if not the exact same vocabulary, see 1 Clement 63.1 and Phil. 3.14. The motifs of agon and prizes are combined in Testament of the Forty Martyrs 1; see Herbert Musurillo, *The Acts of the Christian Martyrs* (Oxford: Clarendon, 1972) 354–5.

[92] Weiss, *Brief an die Hebräer*, 640, calls joy the "eschatological 'reward' for the patient bearing of the cross." The notion of joy as a prize is not far-fetched. Isaac receives joy as a reward for his virtue in Philo, *Praem.* 27, 31 and 50. Note that God is called a "rewarder" in Heb. 11.6 (cf. 10.35, 11.26).

[93] The meaning "trainer or chief of the games" [*entrenador o gimnasiarca*] is suggested for ἀρχηγός by G. Mora, *La Carta a los Hebreos como Escrito Pastoral* (Barcelona: Herder, 1974) 177, but I know of no precedent for this. Neither does context provide much support despite the athletic imagery of 12.1–3. An explicitly athletic meaning for ἀρχηγός makes its collocation with τελειωτής all the more inexplicable.

[94] It has long been thought that Heb. 12.2 contains the first extant use of τελειωτής and that the author may have even coined the term. In chapter 4 I discuss a previously unrecognized Greco-Roman parallel.

to the result of continued work, namely, "become fatigued, weary." This could be psychological or physical, in the latter case extending all the way to sickness and even death.[95] In Hebrews 12.1–3 the word contributes to the race imagery by stating the alternative to enduring as Jesus did, an alternative that contemplation of Jesus should preclude.[96] Ἐκλύω means "release," "loosen," or "relax" in the active voice, "to fail" or "be faint" in the passive, in which case it is nearly synonymous with κάμνω.[97] The effect is pleonastic: "so that you do not become weary, fainting in your souls."[98]

An especially interesting comparative text is found in Aristotle, *Rhetoric* 3.9.2, where both κάμνω and ἐκλύομαι occur. In a critique of the continuous style of speech that links one thought to the next by connective particles, Aristotle laments the lack of closure, the impossibility of perceiving a conclusion to the thought. A reader needs to be able to anticipate completion just as a runner does. Anticipation of the finish line sustains runners, such that at the completion of a race "they are winded and weary" (ἐκπνέουσι καὶ ἐκλύονται), but "by looking ahead to the end, they do not become fatigued (κάμνουσι) before reaching it." The similarity to Hebrews 12.1–3, 12–13 is more than lexical; the texts have in common the entire image of the renewal of one's strength through the contemplation of a goal or a person.

Some commentators detect a shift in the athletic imagery in verse 4. The language of αἷμα, ἀντικαθίστημι, and ἀνταγωνίζομαι may suggest an allusion to boxing or wrestling.[99] While it is clear that the foot-race is no longer in view, an image of boxing or wrestling is not developed significantly. Reference is sometimes made to Seneca, who likens the courageous person to a boxer who "enters a fight confidently because he has seen his own blood" (Epist. 13.2), but

---

[95] BAGD, 402, and LSJ, 872–3. For ὁ κάμνων = "one who is sick," see James 5.15.

[96] The weariness of those who must run or toil at length is referred to again in vs. 12. There the readers are enjoined to strengthen their "drooping hands" and "weak knees."

[97] BAGD, 243, and LSJ, 513. But the active means "faint" in Josephus, *War* 1.657.

[98] Whether the words ταῖς ψυχαῖς ὑμῶν go with the previous or the following verb is an open question. Both constructions are found. For ψυχή with ἐκλύω, see Diodorus Siculus 20.1.4; Polybius 20.4.7 (also with σῶμα); and 29.17.4. For ψυχή with κάμνω, see Diodorus Siculus 20.96.3; 33.26.1; Job 10.1; and Josephus, *War* 2.31.

[99] Attridge, *Hebrews*, 360; Lane, *Hebrews*, 417. Regarding blood in combat sports, see the references in C. Spicq, *Notes de Lexicographie néotestamentaire* (Göttingen: Vandenhoeck & Ruprecht, 1978) I, 102–3; also Poliakoff, *Combat Sports in the Ancient World*, 85–8.

the explicitness of this comparative text only highlights the general nature of the language in Hebrews 12.4. Ἀντικαθίστημι has the general sense of "oppose," or "resist" and is not specifically agonistic. Ἀνταγωνίζομαι means "struggle," "vie against," but covers a spectrum of athletic, martial, legal, and interpersonal contexts.[100] While an allusion to combative sports cannot be ruled out, the mention of blood has its most likely reference in Jesus' experience of violent opposition at the hands of sinners (vs. 3) and the readers' lack of such experience (10.32–4).

One final remark will conclude this survey of athletic language in Hebrews 12.1–13. In verse 11 the author commends divine παιδεία for its yield of peace and righteousness "to those who have been trained by it" (τοῖς δι' αὐτῆς γεγυμνασμένοις). The word γυμνάζω, which also occurs in 5.14, has a rather ordinary sense of "exercise" or "train," but its etymology is obvious, and this connection would have been felt even in its figurative use.[101] If the discipline (παιδεία) of enduring hardships is a means of exercising (γυμνάζω) the readers, then the two paragraphs within Hebrews 12.1–13 are not so thematically diverse after all. Divine training in faithful endurance seems to be construed first athletically and then educatively. The latter will be investigated fully in chapter 3. First, however, I must consider the use of Jesus as the prime exemplar of endurance in the light of ancient rhetoric and philosophy.

2.5 Jesus as paradigm

Hebrews 12.1–3 aims at more than a traditional, agonistic metaphor of the life of faith as a foot-race. It holds up the supreme example of faith, Jesus, who has successfully completed the course and serves as a model to those still engaged in the race. In setting forth a paradigm of the desired behavior, the author employs a rhetorical technique common to both antiquity and modernity.

The ancient rhetorical handbooks discuss the use of examples (παραδείγματα, *exempla*). The most important of these are Aristotle's *Rhetoric*, Quintilian's *Institutio Oratoria*, and two anonymous treatises, *Rhetorica ad Alexandrum* and *Rhetorica ad Herennium*. There is no need here to give a lengthy account of what each of these rhetoricians says in regard to *exempla*; this has been done

---

[100] See LSJ, 148.   [101] See TDNT, I, 775, esp. Epictetus 2.18.27 and 1 Tim. 4.7–8.

elsewhere.[102] For my purposes it will suffice to treat those points that have relevance for the argument of Hebrews 12.1–3.

An important question regarding the rhetorical use of examples was whether παραδείγματα/*exempla* had a probative function or only an illustrative one. Aristotle identified two general modes of reasoning: syllogism and induction. In rhetoric, syllogistic reasoning appears in the form of enthymemes, arguments drawn from probable premises that lead to probable conclusions.[103] Inductive reasoning employs examples. Aristotle notes that both are means of persuasion: πάντες δὲ τὰς πίστεις ποιοῦνται διὰ τοῦ δεικνύναι ἢ παραδείγματα λέγοντες ἢ ἐνθυμήματα, καὶ παρὰ ταῦτα οὐδέν πως (All [orators] produce belief through demonstration, either by examples or enthymemes and by nothing else: 1.2.8). This certainly seems to attribute a probative function to examples.[104] In actual practice, however, Aristotle implies that examples should have a subordinate role. In *Rhetorica* 2.20.9 he discusses the use of examples in combination with enthymemes. If no enthymemes are available, examples may be used as proofs (ὡς ἀποδείξεσιν); but if one has enthymemes, then examples should be used as evidence (ὡς μαρτυρίοις), as an epilogue to the enthymemes. Ideally then, syllogistic reasoning (enthymemes) should precede examples, with the latter functioning as corroboration.

The only other handbook that addresses this question in some detail is *Rhetorica ad Herennium* (*RAH*). This work tends to dismiss or at least downplay the probative function of *exempla*. In distinguishing the functions of testimony and example, the author writes,

---

[102] For concise treatments, see Michael R. Cosby, *The Rhetorical Composition and Function of Hebrews 11 in Light of Example Lists in Antiquity* (Macon, GA: Mercer University, 1988) 93–105, and B. Fiore, *The Function of Personal Example in the Socratic and Pastoral Epistles* (Rome: Biblical Institute, 1986) 26–44. Full-length treatments include Karl Alewell, "Über das rhetorische ΠΑΡΑΔΕΙΓΜΑ: Theorie, Beispielsammlungen, Verwendung in der Römischen Literatur der Kaiserzeit," Dissertation, Leipzig, 1913, and Bennett J. Price, "'Paradeigma' and 'exemplum' in Ancient Rhetorical Theory," Dissertation, Berkeley, 1975.

[103] On the definition of this term, see the glossary by J. H. Freese in Aristotle, *The Art of Rhetoric* (Cambridge, MA: Harvard University, 1926) 475–6, as well as the article to which he refers: R. C. Seaton, "The Aristotelian Enthymeme," *Classical Review* (June, 1914) 113–19.

[104] "Probative" here is not used in the sense of a strict "demonstrative proof" (ἀπόδειξις). The word which Aristotle uses, πίστις, refers to persuasive arguments that lend credence. Πίστις is not equivalent to ἀπόδειξις, and examples are better suited to the former. See *Rhet.* 1.1.11, but also 2.20.9.

"By example, the nature of what we are discussing is clarified; by testimony, it is confirmed that what we are discussing is so" (*RAH* 4.3.5). Thus, whereas Aristotle likened examples to evidence and affirmed their probative function, *Rhetorica ad Herennium* understands their function as primarily illustrative.[105] The two cannot be reconciled fully, but if we bear in mind Aristotle's counsel that *exempla* be placed *after* enthymemes if possible, there seems to be a common preference for the use of *exempla* as supportive rather than as the foundation of one's argument.

This strategy corresponds to the overall structure of the Epistle to the Hebrews. The author has reasoned in chapters 1–10 with what might be called enthymematic arguments: God has given a revelation in Christ that is superior to angels, Moses, the priesthood, the covenant, the tabernacle, the sacrifices; hence, it is all the more incumbent upon the readers that they heed this word and hold fast to their confession. This argument is elaborately developed before a single *exemplum* is given beginning in 11.4. The *exempla* of 11.4–12.3, culminating in Jesus, would not have had the same persuasive force if they had stood alone, nor if they had preceded the "enthymematic" section. Following the argument of chapters 1–10, they form an impressive rhetorical capstone.

Another aspect of the use of *exempla* merits discussion. How does the writer or speaker choose *exempla* so as to make them most effective? *Rhetorica ad Alexandrum* (1439a) advises that one should choose examples that are "suited to the matter" (οἰκεῖα τῷ πράγματι) and "nearest in time or place to the hearers" (ἐγγύτατα τοῖς ἀκούουσι χρόνῳ ἤ τόπῳ). If the latter are not available, one should use others that are the "most significant and familiar" (μέγιστα καὶ γνωριμώτατα).

All of the *exempla* adduced by the author of Hebrews in chapter 11 could be called "suited" in that they highlight people who by faith had done justice, obeyed and pleased God, and yet suffered abuse, all characteristic of the readers' experience. Furthermore, several of the descriptions in chapter 11 speak of a forward-looking

---

[105] Tension exists between *RAH* 4.3.5 and 4.49.59 and 62. In the latter, the author lists four functions of examples: to embellish, prove, clarify, or vivify. "To prove" (*causa ... probandi* in 59; *rem probabiliorem facit* in 62) would seem to be the function of testimony, not examples. The point is probably that examples strengthen an argument already established by other means.

faith that awaits the reception of God's promises.[106] According to the author, such enduring faith is a need of the congregation to which he writes (10.35–36).

As for the other criteria suggested by *Rhetorica ad Alexandrum*, proximity in time and space would obviously not apply to *exempla* drawn from the patriarchal period or the monarchy. There is, however, a certain religious proximity. If the Epistle to the Hebrews was an effective communication at all, the readers must have been steeped in the Greek scriptures of Israel. If so, the *exempla* of chapter 11 would have been γνωριμώτατα (most familiar). On the other hand, the example of Jesus in 12.2–3 fits nearly all the criteria. Jesus is certainly "suited"; he is relatively near in time to the readers; and he is surely "most significant and familiar." He is last in the author's list not simply for chronological reasons, but for teleological reasons, as 12.2 makes clear.

Finally, there is the issue of shaping the *exemplum* to meet the needs of the situation. Quintilian (5.11.6) advises that "we must consider whether the entirety of the *exemplum* is similar or only part, in order that we might know whether to employ the whole or only those parts which are useful." A historical example rarely corresponds so closely to the rhetorical exigency that it can be employed in its entirety. Thus, in Hebrews 12.1–3 the author has highlighted only those aspects of Jesus' experience that are relevant to the readers' situation.

What are those aspects? Four emerge: joy, endurance, shame, and hostility. Endurance is underscored twice (12.2, 3); its relevance to the readers is clear (12.1; 10.36). Shame was encountered but disdained by Jesus (12.2); the readers have also experienced reproaches and are called to continue to do so (10.33; 13.13; and perhaps by implication, 11.26). Great hostility was endured by Jesus (12.3); hostile treatment in various forms had been the lot of the readers too (10.32–5). Joy, which I have deliberately postponed, lay before Jesus either as a readily available, but rejected option, or as a reward beyond the cross. We have seen that the athletic metaphor favors a prospective interpretation of joy. It is clear that the rheto-

---

[106] In addition to the opening definition of faith as "the assurance of things hoped for, the evidence of things not seen," the descriptions of Noah (7), Abraham (8–10), Moses (26), and the summaries in the middle (13–16) and at the end of the chapter (35) all have this prospective notion.

rical situation favors it too. The readers have need of endurance in order to receive the promises of God (10.36; 11.39–40). Like Israel's heroes and heroines of faith, they must hold fast the confession and seek God earnestly (3.6, 14; 10.35; 11.6). There is scarcely anything in the description of the readers, explicit or implicit, that suggests they face a choice of present joy or endurance in suffering. If the example of Jesus has been shaped to meet the needs of the rhetorical situation, a shaping that is evident in other respects, then ἀντί in Hebrews 12.2 must indicate that Jesus endured the cross "to obtain the joy that lay before him."

From the above we see that the author of Hebrews (1) has employed *exempla* in the overall argument of the epistle in keeping with what the rhetoricians prescribed about their illustrative function, (2) has generally chosen them in accordance with the criteria of rhetorical effectiveness, and (3) has shaped them, especially the example of Jesus, with a view to utilizing only the appropriate parts of the *exempla*. In the final pages of this chapter, I want to move from rhetorical theory to a more philosophical and literary consideration of Jesus as exemplar.

When an author wanted to enjoin certain behaviors or attitudes, human *exempla* were deemed the most effective means. Seneca remarks that nothing is better for endowing minds with honorable thoughts or recalling the wayward to the right path than "association with good men" (Epist. 94.40). Through the use of memory and written accounts, this "association" was by no means limited to living persons. When beset by a particular problem, one may also look to the ancients. Plutarch encourages those who are the object of derision to consider Plato, who suffered abuse from Dionysius (*Mor.* 467e–f). The childless should look to the kings of Rome who did not produce heirs, and the impoverished should contemplate Epameinondas or Fabricius.[107] The sheer remembrance of a noble past life can compose and order one's life in the present, providing a guard or model for present actions.[108]

It should be apparent that the author of Hebrews stands squarely

---

[107] Seneca does express a preference for the living voice and a communal life (Epist. 6.5–6), but his writings also abound with laudatory references to the examples of Epicurus, Cato, Socrates, and others (Epist. 11.8–10; 25.5; *Brev. Vit.* 14.5–15.3; *Cons. Helv.* 13.4–8; *De Prov.* 2.9–12; 3.4–14). Indeed, in Epist. 52.7 Seneca affirms the benefits one can gain from those who have lived before: "Not only those who are, but those who were can assist us."

[108] Seneca, Epist. 11.8–10.

in the tradition of Hellenistic moralists in calling to mind the example of Jesus in order to encourage and guide his readers. In doing so, however, the author of Hebrews is not necessarily engaging in a common NT practice. It has been claimed that in early Christian literature and particularly in Paul, "Jesus is not the ideal example or paradigm to be emulated. Rather he is Lord of the believers, indeed of the world."[109] Ernst Käsemann has remarked that "the New Testament *in general* does not go to Jesus for the essence of faith. He is not a model for faith, but the Lord of the believers."[110] These statements draw the distinction too sharply; there is no reason why Jesus could not have functioned simultaneously in both capacities.[111] Nevertheless, it remains the case that Hebrews' use of the historical Jesus as the supreme model of faith was probably *not* the most common understanding of his significance. But while Jesus may have functioned in Hebrews 12.2–3 and other passages in the way that Diogenes, Heracles, Pythagoras, *et al.* functioned in Cynic and Stoic writers,[112] it is clear throughout Hebrews that Jesus was more than just the perfect example of faith to our author.

The very expression, "perfect example," calls for a few remarks. There was reluctance in antiquity, especially among the Stoics, to claim that the philosophical ideal had been achieved.[113] "Zeno did not claim to be the ideal wise man, nor did Chrysippus, who did not think that his teachers had attained to the ideal either, and while Panaetius did make use of the figure of the ideal sage in his instruction, he did so only sparingly and it remained in the background of his teaching."[114] To deal with the embarrassing realization that the virtual non-attainment of the ideal left everyone "fools," a third category was created: "those who are progressing"

---

[109] Donald A. Stoike, "De Genio Socrates," in H. D. Betz, ed., *Plutarch's Theological Writings and Early Christian Literature* (Leiden: Brill, 1975) 241.

[110] Ernst Käsemann, *Jesus Means Freedom* (Philadelphia: Fortress, 1969) 105 (my emphasis).

[111] But Stoike ("De Genio Socrates," 242) notes that Hebrews, Luke–Acts, and 1 Peter are exceptions to the "rule" that Jesus is not portrayed as the paradigm of faith. Even Paul, who views Jesus as the Lord of believers, speaks of imitating Christ (1 Cor. 11.1; 1 Thess. 1.6; cf. Phil. 2.5).

[112] See David E. Aune, "De Esu Carnium Orationes I and II," in H. D. Betz, ed., *Plutarch's Theological Writings and Early Christian Literature* (Leiden: Brill, 1975) 305.

[113] See Abraham J. Malherbe, "Hellenistic Moralists," 285, n. 80, and, by the same author, "Pseudo-Heraclitus, Epistle 4: The Divinization of the Wise Man," *Jahrbuch für Antike und Christentum*, 21 (1976) 42–64, esp. 54–6.

[114] *Ibid.*, 54.

(οἱ προκόπτοντες or *proficientes*). Under the pressure of both external critique and the compulsion of their own logic, Stoics under the
Empire "affirmed, with some hesitation, that [the ideal] could be
realized, but that the number of those who had [realized the ideal]
was exceedingly small."[115] Seneca, who viewed himself as a *profi-
ciens*, suggested that such a person might appear, like the Phoenix,
every 500 years (Epist. 42.1).[116] Epictetus did not consider himself
to have attained the ideal (4.1.151; 4.8.43) and claims never to have
seen the perfect Stoic (2.19.24–6).[117] Given this reluctance to claim
attainment of the ideal, combined with Hebrews' strong affinities to
Cynic–Stoic agon traditions and, we will see in the next chapter,
with Stoic notions of divine discipline, it is noteworthy that Hebrews
12.2 unqualifiedly styles Jesus as "the pioneer and perfecter of faith."
For this early Christian writer there definitely was one person who
had reached perfection and was the ideal *exemplum* of faith for all
others; indeed he enabled others to have faith.

In summary, then, Hebrews 12.1–3 presents Jesus not so much as
a martyr or a model of self-renunciation, but as the paradigm of
faithful endurance who has completed the course in advance of
all others. In creating this image, the author has employed a long-
established tradition of an athletic agon which enables him to under-
score endurance in suffering as a quality needed by the readers. The
author has located his *exempla* toward the end of his argument, and
chosen and shaped them in accord with rhetorical theory. In holding
up Jesus as a model to be emulated, he has done something *relatively* uncommon in the NT. In portraying him as having attained
the ideal of faith, he has done something quite uncommon in his
philosophical milieu.

In the next chapter I will investigate the background of the second
construal of suffering in Hebrews 12.1–13: suffering as divine discipline. To answer the question of how παιδεία should be understood
in the context of Hebrews 12.1–13, I will cast my net broadly to see
how suffering was variously understood in a large number of texts,
both Jewish and Greco-Roman.

---

[115] *Ibid.*, 55.
[116] See also *De Ira* 2.10.6, and *De Const.* 7.1. In the latter, Marcus Cato is given as
an example of the realized *bonus* (good person).
[117] Epictetus, on the other hand, speaks at length about "making progress" (προ-
κόπτων, προκοπή). See *Discourses* 1.4; *Ench.* 48 and 51. The Cynics, however,
remained more optimistic; for them the ideal had been achieved by such figures as
Socrates and Diogenes.

3

PUNITIVE AND NON-PUNITIVE SUFFERING

3.1 Introduction

The history of research in chapter 1 revealed that παιδεία and related terms in Hebrews 12.5–11 have been variously understood by different interpreters. Παιδεία can refer to corrective punishment, rigorous training, or the end result of training, i.e., education or culture.[1] The nuances of the English word "discipline" approximate this range of meanings. I suggested that a useful way to frame the investigation of the background of Hebrews 12.5–11 was the antithesis of punitive versus non-punitive discipline. The former presupposes wrongdoing on the part of the sufferers and construes their suffering as divine punishment for those misdeeds. The latter makes no such assumption; it disavows a *necessary* connection between suffering and sin. In addition, non-punitive interpretations often attribute a positive benefit to suffering, a kind of formative experience whereby the sufferers advance in virtue, righteousness, etc. Punitive discipline may, of course, also result in learning or personal formation. Punitive discipline and formative discipline are not mutually exclusive categories. But by framing the investigation in terms of punitive and non-punitive discipline, we obviously do have mutually exclusive categories. The distinguishing factor then is not whether learning results, but whether wrongdoing is presupposed. When learning does result, its precise nature may also help distinguish between punitive and non-punitive discipline. The former produces a chastened spirit, an eagerness to avoid further error; the latter produces a mature, hardy spirit, a toughness and endurance.

It was seen that earlier exegetes and homileticians were especially sensitive to the formative nuance of παιδεία. Chrysostom saw

---

[1] The loftier sense of παιδεία is seen in Werner Jaeger's choice of this word as a title for his *magnum opus* on Greek culture. See Werner Jaeger, *Paideia: The Ideals of Greek Culture* (3 vols.; Oxford: Oxford University, 1946).

παιδεία as a kind of γυμνασία or athletic training, an insight that not only does justice to Hebrews 12.5–11, but grasps the literary unity of 12.1–13. Other patristic interpreters, such as Saint John of Damascus, Oecumenius and Theophylactus, echoed this insight.

Beginning with the twelfth century, the punitive nuance of παιδεία began to be felt more strongly. Herveus, Peter Lombard, and Thomas Aquinas understood suffering as instructive but also related to the sins of the sufferers. The Reformers, Erasmus, Luther, Calvin, and Theodore Beza, to varying degrees all saw a punitive aspect to divine παιδεία. For them the most obvious context for Hebrews 12.5–11 was the Jewish wisdom tradition in which suffering represents divine punishment for the purpose of correction. Modern reflection on Hebrews 12.5–11 reveals an awareness of the various possible construals of παιδεία. Recent commentators, including Attridge, Ellingworth, Lane, and Weiss, generally conclude that the author of Hebrews combines the nuances of correction and education. But this observation seems to derive more from the semantic range of the word than from the argument of Hebrews 12.1–13, its literary context, and its place in the larger milieu of ancient reflections on human suffering. Hebrews' concept of suffering as παιδεία was rarely compared with similar concepts in Greco-Roman authors. Commentators usually neglected, or at most made passing reference to, the Stoic notion of hardship as education or training. The presence of a citation in Hebrews 12.5–6 from Jewish wisdom literature, namely Proverbs 3.11–12, seems to have skewed the discussion toward Jewish concepts of suffering.

Other writers have supplemented this deficiency in the commentaries by surveying both Jewish and Greco-Roman views on educative suffering. The monographs of Logan and Talbert broaden the discussion and, despite the criticisms made in chapter 1, serve well as a springboard for the topic of the present chapter.

Talbert in particular offers a useful thesis that corresponds closely to my own distinction of punitive versus non-punitive discipline. Under the heading "Suffering as Divine Discipline in Ancient Israel," Talbert discusses the view of suffering as "correction of one's misdirection."[2] The father/son relationship becomes a metaphor for God's dealings with Israel. Motivated by love, God punishes Israel (or certain individuals) with a view to their growth and improvement. "Presupposed in this particular Jewish view *usually* is the as-

---

[2] Talbert, *Learning Through Suffering*, 11.

sumption that the sufferer has strayed from the right path either consciously or unconsciously, knowingly or unwittingly."[3] Under the heading "Suffering as Divine Education in Greco-Roman Antiquity,"[4] Talbert examines several passages from classical and Hellenistic authors, concluding that suffering in the Greco-Roman world is "not so much correction of one's misdirection, as in the mainstream of Jewish thought, but rather conditioning that builds one up for greater virtue."[5]

The plan of this chapter is to investigate the two halves of Talbert's thesis. I will examine primary Jewish texts that pertain to "Divine Discipline in Ancient Israel," proceeding through them in this order: prophets, wisdom literature, psalms, Maccabean literature, Josephus, Philo, Qumran, and rabbinical literature. The available treatises on the topic of suffering and divine discipline will also be consulted. Primary texts pertaining to the second half of Talbert's thesis, "Suffering as Divine Education in Greco-Roman Antiquity," will be examined in a similar fashion, with the later Stoics, Seneca, Epictetus, and Musonius Rufus being given special attention. The goal will be both to judge the validity of Talbert's thesis and, if possible, to refine it by considering an additional dimension: the nature and source of the suffering in each case.

The methods of text selection vary. Lexical searches are helpful to a degree. Key terms, e.g. *musar* and παιδεία, led to a number of useful texts. But as is often the case with lexical searches, this procedure also generated many useless texts. This was particularly so in the Greco-Roman portion of this chapter since παιδεία in those sources most often refers to the human educational process and has nothing to do with divinely purposeful suffering. Moreover, theology does not inhere in individual words, but in thoughts. Lexical searches will always omit some relevant texts simply because the key terms may be lacking even when the theme is present.[6]

In addition to lexical searches, I made extensive use of secondary sources, gleaning many references from charts, indexes, and footnotes. This process is admittedly a dependent and somewhat hap-

---

[3] *Ibid.*, 16 (Talbert's emphasis).

[4] The shift from "Discipline" to "Education" is, of course, crucial.

[5] Talbert, *Learning Through Suffering*, 20.

[6] This point was persuasively made by James Barr in his landmark work *Semantics of Biblical Language* (Oxford: Oxford University, 1961) esp. 238–62. See also Schuyler Brown, "Philology," in Epp and MacRae, eds., *The New Testament and its Modern Interpreters*, 129.

hazard one, but it is sufficient for my purposes. I do *not* intend to do a comprehensive study of Jewish and Greco-Roman views of suffering. This would be an enormous task, far beyond my capabilities and beyond the needs of this investigation. A glance at the secondary literature on this topic will show that whole volumes have been written on the meaning of suffering in single groupings of the Jewish literature alone, such as the Psalms or rabbinical literature. My aim is not to be comprehensive, but to present an adequate collection of texts to give the reader a sense of the diversity of views.

Before investigating the merits of Talbert's thesis, I should briefly consider more elaborate schemata that have been proposed for understanding suffering. Talbert's two-fold scheme may be over-simplified not only in its dichotomy along Jewish and Greco-Roman lines, but the two-fold scheme in itself may be unfairly simplified. No less than in modern times, ancient solutions to the problem of human suffering were numerous and complex. Earlier in this century H. Wheeler Robinson outlined six "great principles for the interpretation of human suffering" found in the OT.[7] They are (1) Retributive: suffering is punishment for sin; (2) Educational: suffering chastens and disciplines the soul; (3) Probationary: the "furnace" of suffering tests faith; (4) Revelational: through suffering a person gains a deeper knowledge of God; (5) Sacrificial: sufferings are a vicarious offering to God (e.g. Isaiah 53); (6) Eschatological: suffering is a sign of the impending end through which deliverance comes. Robinson's first category corresponds to my "punitive." Most of the remaining categories can be seen as species of my "non-punitive" category. This is fairly clear in the case of educational, probationary, and revelational. Sacrificial or vicarious suffering, I will argue, belongs under the punitive heading although it represents a variation in this tradition. Robinson's sixth category, "eschatological," is perhaps the most difficult to correlate with my two-fold scheme. It is presumably non-punitive, but it differs from the other non-punitive principles in that it seems to offer little personal benefit to the sufferer. At most eschatological suffering reveals the nearness of the end.

Some years after Robinson, J. A. Sanders offered an eight-fold list of "solutions found in the Old Testament to the problem of suffer-

---

[7] H. Wheeler Robinson, *Suffering Human and Divine* (New York: Macmillan, 1939) 31–48.

ing."[8] His discussion is extremely terse, and OT illustrations are not provided for all eight solutions, making it difficult to be sure of his meaning in every case. Sanders lists the following: retributive, disciplinary, revelational, probational, illusory (or transitory), mysterious, eschatological, and meaningless. Sanders' list is reducible. The first two, retributive and disciplinary, are roughly equivalent to my "punitive" category. Sanders' revelational solution is harder to categorize. What is being revealed? If sin and the will of God are revealed, this solution may be a subtype of the disciplinary.[9] The probational solution, using an image of metallurgy, views suffering as a process of testing and refining the nation or an individual as gold and silver are tested in a fire. The significance of this image varies. In some cases it implies a refining that purges a person of sin and, therefore, would be punitive and corrective. Elsewhere, the presupposition of "sinful impurities" is not evident, and we may have a subtype of non-punitive suffering.[10]

Sanders' other solutions are encountered less often in the OT. Habakkuk 2.4 and the Psalms are cited as representing the "transitory" solution, wisdom literature as one source of the "mysterious" solution, post-exilic works for the "eschatological" solution, and Ecclesiastes and Job for the "meaningless" solution.[11] These differ from the first group in their failure to identify a religious function of suffering. The "illusory–transitory" solution denies the significance of suffering, obviating the need for an explanation; the "mysterious" solution admits ignorance; the "eschatological" solution defers an

---

[8] Jim Alvin Sanders, *Suffering as Divine Discipline in the Old Testament and Post-Biblical Judaism*, 1. Sanders refers to Robinson but makes no attempt to correlate their two lists.

[9] This must be Sanders' meaning for he says the disciplinary and revelational views "are closely related and stem from the basic beliefs which underlie faith in an ethical deity." (p. 1). But he cites no Biblical passages to illustrate the revelational view.

[10] For refinement as purgative, see Jer. 6.27–30, 9.6–9, and Isa. 1.25. Purging of sin is less explicit in Prov. 17.3, Isa. 48.10, Zech. 13.8–9, and Mal. 3.2–4. In a few cases the refining image occurs with no hint of wrongdoing (Ps. 17.3, 26.1–3, 66.8–12) and sometimes with a strong disavowal (Job. 23.10–12). Some of these examples approach the formative interpretation of suffering. See also below on Sirach and Wisdom of Solomon.

[11] I will argue below that Job makes a more significant contribution to the problem of suffering than simply declaring it "meaningless." Ecclesiastes' interpretation of suffering might better be designated "mysterious" than "meaningless." Other examples that might fall into the "meaningless" (or "mysterious") category are Psalms 44 and 88. The suffering depicted in these psalms is attributed to God but is not explicitly punitive nor educative.

explanation; and the "meaningless" solution denies the possibility of one. These four "solutions" may provide ways of dealing existentially with suffering, but they fail to explain it theologically.[12] For the purposes of this study, I am primarily interested in solutions that interpret human suffering as divinely purposeful. Given this limitation, the most critical factor in distinguishing the various solutions is the presence or absence of the punitive element with its presupposition of wrongdoing.

Fredrik Lindström has recently highlighted the important difference between the punitive and non-punitive solutions. (Lindström uses "pedagogical" for my "non-punitive.")[13]

> [T]he starting-points of the pedagogical model, on the one hand, and the retributional/punitive, on the other, are basically opposite. While the idea of individual retribution assumes that suffering is a sure sign that the person has been rejected or punished by God, the starting-point for the pedagogical model is instead that suffering is a sign, a confirmation that he is accepted by God, that is, it is the pious one whom God corrects, like a father disciplines his beloved son ... the pedagogical model, by a diametrically opposite point of departure, is a completely different alternative interpretation of suffering.

When the issue is framed in this way, it becomes necessary for my non-punitive category to be inclusive of various subtypes and images: fatherly correction, parental instruction, refiner's fire, athletic training, etc. Lindström suggests a three-fold division of "Human suffering with pedagogical overtones," namely educative, probative, and redemptive.[14] By the latter Lindström refers to those instances of purificatory suffering involving the image of refining. This category is arguably divisible into probative and punitive depending on whether sin is being purged, but the point is that the rubric "non-punitive" gathers several different nuances together.

The schemata of Robinson, Sanders, and Lindström are obviously more elaborate than Talbert's and mine. But the aim of this

---

[12] The "eschatological" solution is a partial exception to this in that it sees the increase in suffering as the culmination of a divine plan for the cosmos.

[13] Fredrik Lindström, *Suffering and Sin. Interpretations of Illness in the Individual Complaint Psalms* (Stockholm: Almqvist and Wiksell, 1994) 139.

[14] *Ibid.*, 140.

study is not to categorize every possible nuance of the meaning of suffering, but to frame theological construals of suffering in a manner that will serve the examination of Hebrews 12.1–13. On the one hand, my two-fold scheme is admittedly heuristic in that it serves the special purpose of this study. On the other hand, it accommodates nearly all the views mentioned above, highlights the critical issue of culpability, and has the virtue of simplicity.

One final qualification is needed with regard to the categories used in this study. I exclude altogether "eschatological suffering" which, in effect, is futuristic judgment rather than this-worldly suffering. Again, the categories are chosen with a view to Hebrews 12.1–13. I am concerned with the theological interpretation of actual experiences of suffering as divinely purposive. One might regard the threat of hell for the impious as an instance of "punitive suffering." But this would be to confuse temporal suffering with eschatological judgment. The result would be a broadening of the scope of this chapter beyond its already unwieldy size. My concern is with communities or individuals who have undergone or are undergoing suffering *in this life*, and with the theological interpretation of these experiences. Because of this I will not treat those texts, such as apocalypses and oracles, that connect sin with eschatological suffering alone.

3.2   Jewish perspectives on suffering

3.2.1   The "Orthodoxy" of the prophets

The problem of suffering in the Jewish Scriptures has attracted the sustained attention of many writers.[15] The aim here is not necessarily

---

[15] In this century alone, see Arthur S. Peake, *The Problem of Suffering in the Old Testament* (London: Robert Bryant, 1904); J. Y. Batley, *The Problem of Suffering in the Old Testament* (Cambridge: Cambridge University, 1916); Kaufmann Kohler, *Jewish Theology* (New York: Macmillan, 1918); H. W. Robinson, *The Religious Ideas of the Old Testament* (New York: Scribner, 1919); E. Balla, "Das Problem des Leides in dem israelitisch-jüdischen Religion," in Hans Schmidt, ed., *EYXAPIΣTHPION: Studien zur Religion und Literatur des Alten und Neuen Testaments* (Göttingen: Vandenhoeck & Ruprecht, 1923); Norbert Peters, *Die Leidensfrage im alten Testament* (Biblische Zeitfragen 11/3–5; Münster, 1923); H. Schmidt, *Gott und das Leid im alten Testament*, 1926; L. B. Paton, "The Problem of Suffering in the Pre-Exilic Prophets," *JBL*, 46 (1927) 111–31; Wichmann, *Leidenstheologie*; Wheeler Robinson, *Suffering, Human and Divine*, 31–48; Johann Jakob Stamm, *Das Leiden des Unschuldigen in Babylon und Israel* (Zürich: Zwingli, 1946); Edmund R. Sutcliffe, *Providence and Suffering in the Old and New Testa-*

to controvert those studies nor to rehearse them in detail, but to survey the most important passages that interpret suffering as divinely purposeful. The key terms for this portion of the study are *ysr* and the related noun *musar* in the Hebrew Bible and παιδεία/ παιδεύω in the LXX. Both word groups have the semantic range necessary to include both punitive and formative categories ("punish," "correct," "discipline," "educate").[16] The use of παιδεία/ παιδεύω in particular provides access to important comparative texts for the interpretation of Hebrews 12.5–11, where those words figure prominently.[17]

The idea of divine discipline appears in a number of prophetic passages in the Hebrew Bible. Zephaniah 3.1–8 contains an oracle against Jerusalem in which the city is condemned for its corrupt officials, judges, prophets, and priests. The city is twice reproached for not accepting the Lord's discipline (vss. 2, 7). This refusal "refers to the leaders' unwillingness to learn from the disasters that had overtaken them in history, disasters that the prophets interpreted as God's punishment of his people, intended to bring them back to obedience."[18] The calamities described in verse 6 may refer to the devastation wrought by Assyrian king Sennacherib's campaign several decades earlier in which many Judean cities were destroyed. The suffering of that period, according to the prophet, should have served as *musar* (LXX παιδεία) for Jerusalem.

The book of Jeremiah also contains several oracles against Israel. The flagrant apostasy of the nation is set forth in 2.1–37. Idolatry (vss. 4, 8, 11, 27–8), Baal worship (vss. 8, 23), and violence toward the poor (vs. 34) had defiled Israel. God's discipline is a direct result of these sins, so much so that Israel's sin is personified as the punisher: "Your wickedness will punish (*ysr*; LXX παιδεύω) you, and

---

ments (London: Thomas Nelson, 1953); Sanders, *Suffering as Divine Discipline*; Josef Scharbert, *Der Schmerz im Alten Testament* (Bonn: Hanstein, 1955); Sam K. Williams, *Jesus' Death as Saving Event: The Background and Origin of a Concept* (Missoula, MT: Scholars Press, 1975); Erhard S. Gerstenberger and Wolfgang Schrage, *Suffering* (Nashville: Abingdon, 1980).

[16] In addition to the standard lexica, see Gerhard von Rad, *Old Testament Theology* (New York: Harper, 1962) I, 431 n. 32.

[17] In some cases I will treat passages in which the key terms do not appear. This is, after all, a thematic study, not merely a lexical one. However, most of the Hebrew and Greek texts discussed in this chapter have been selected on the basis of terminology.

[18] J. J. M. Roberts, *Nahum, Habakkuk, and Zephaniah. A Commentary* (Louisville: Westminster/John Knox, 1991) 212.

your apostasies will convict you."[19] In the prophet's mind, God's *musar* apparently included even the death of certain members of the community (vs. 30). Here we may have an allusion to the violence and persecution of Manasseh (2 Kings 21.16) or Jehoiakim (Jer. 26.20–3).[20] The prophet's theological viewpoint finds the purposeful action of God even in these events.

Other relevant passages in Jeremiah include the following. In 7.28 we again hear the complaint that Israel has not heeded God's voice and has not "accepted discipline." The latter is a common phrase in Jeremiah (5.3, 17.23, 32.33, 35.13), and, as in 7.28, it is often parallel with a failure to hear the voice or words of Yahweh (cf. Zeph. 3.2). In 30.14 the Lord's *musar* is described by the prophet as cruel or harsh[21] and is substantiated by the greatness of Israel's evil and the multitude of her sins (cf. 30.15b). Jeremiah 31.18–20, part of what is known as the Book of Consolation, imagines a penitent Israel in the guise of Ephraim pleading, "You disciplined me, and I took the discipline; I was like a calf untrained." The following verses clarify that the meaning of *ysr* here is corrective punishment; Ephraim has repented in shame and returned to the Lord whose mercy is assured (vs. 20). Rather consistently, then, in the book of Jeremiah, divine *musar* presupposes disobedience to Yahweh.

Ezekiel contains *ysr/musar* only in 5.15 and 23.48. In the former, the prophet inveighs against rebellious Jerusalem, describing her coming devastation. Because of the city's failure to obey God's statutes (5.6) and their desecration of the sanctuary (vs. 11), they face a three-fold catastrophe: pestilence, violent death, and exile (vs. 12). As a result they will become "a mockery and a taunt, a warning (*musar*) and a horror" to the nations around them. In 23.48 Samaria and Jerusalem are allegorized in the adulterous sisters, Oholah and Oholibah. The sins of Samaria and Jerusalem, child sacrifice, idolatry, and profanation of the Sabbath, will be punished with violent judgment, plunder and fire (23.46–7). This destruction, says the prophet, will be a warning. All women "will take warning" (nitpael

---

[19] Only here in the OT does *ysr* have a subject other than God or a human authority figure; see William L. Holladay, *Jeremiah 1* (Philadelphia: Fortress, 1986) 96.

[20] John Bright, *Jeremiah* (Garden City, NY: Doubleday, 1965) 16. The textual, literary, and historical problems of vs. 30 are rather complex. Among other things, the referents for "children" and "prophets" are unclear. See the discussion in Holladay, *Jeremiah 1*, 106–7.

[21] Or, "the punishment of a merciless one," if the noun is revocalized as the construct.

of *ysr*) and not commit the lewdness of Oholah and Oholibah. Although the verb is used here not of those punished, but of those
"warned" through the punishment of others, the passage is clearly
still a punitive interpretation of suffering. The infidelity of Samaria
and Jerusalem is the basis of the coming dire circumstances.

Of the many other prophetic passages in which *ysr*/*musar* occur,[22]
one is especially important because it involves a variation of the
traditional punitive interpretation of suffering. Isaiah 52.13–53.12 is
perhaps the best known of the so-called Servant Songs (also 42.1–4;
49.1–6; 50.4–11). Whether the Servant represents the nation or an
individual is not important here; the crucial point is the explanation
of the Servant's suffering. In 53.5–6 a six-fold expression forcefully
maintains that the source of the affliction is the wrongdoing *of
others*: "Surely he has borne our infirmities and carried our diseases
... he was wounded for our transgressions, crushed for our iniquities; upon him was the punishment (*musar*) that made us whole,
and by his bruises we are healed." The innocence of the Servant is
affirmed or implied at several points: "By a perversion of Justice he
was taken away" (8a); "He had done no violence, and there was
no deceit in his mouth" (9cd); "My righteous one, my servant, shall
make many righteous" (11c).

This text is a celebrated example of vicarious suffering, suffering
that somehow confers a benefit upon others. Specifically, the suffering of the Lord's Servant is the means by which persons are restored
and healed.[23] I suggest that Isaiah 53 still belongs to the category of
punitive suffering. The critical characteristic is present: sin is presupposed. Furthermore, God is the source of the suffering: "struck
down by God, and afflicted" (4d). But it differs from the texts examined above in that the sufferer and the sinner(s) are not one and
the same. In this way it diverges from the usual prophetic understanding of suffering as punishment for one's *own* sins.

Isaiah 53 broadens the category of punitive suffering, but should
not necessarily be viewed as a protest against it. One commentator
on this text remarks, "The sufferer is innocent; and this by itself ...
is a declaration that the simplistic explanation of suffering proposed

---

[22] See the list in Sanders, *Suffering as Divine Discipline*, 7.

[23] Precisely *who* is restored and healed is, like the identity of the Servant, a conundrum. See the discussion in John L. McKenzie, *Second Isaiah* (Garden City, NY:
Doubleday, 1968) 132–6. For a history of the interpretation of this difficult passage, see Christopher R. North, *The Suffering Servant in Deutero-Isaiah* (London:
Oxford University, 1956).

by traditional wisdom is false."[24] The innocence of the Suffering Servant *is* apparent, as I noted above. But it is scarcely the chief point of Isaiah 53 to defend the Servant against the traditional charge that his suffering implies wrongdoing. The innocence of the Servant is a secondary motif. The writer is far more concerned with the connection of the Servant's suffering to the sin *of others*. Since sin is involved and divine punishment of sin is inflicted, although "redirected" against a third party, Isaiah 53 should be viewed as a subtype of the punitive view rather than as a protest against it. In any case, apart from the Servant Song of Isaiah 53 one would be hard pressed to find an OT text that construes the punishment of a nation or an individual as vicariously suffered for the sins of others. This was not a common Jewish mode of thinking.[25] We will see, however, that this idea finds an echo in one strand of the Maccabean literature and, of course, its influence on the NT and Christian theology as an interpretation of the suffering of Jesus is well known.[26]

The prophetic texts presupposing a causal relationship between sin and human suffering could be multiplied almost endlessly, especially if the list is not limited to passages containing certain key words. Robinson claims that "the idea of suffering as the just recompense and reward of sin" is "fundamental to the prophetic religion." "Almost any chapter of the prophetic writings illustrates the application of this principle."[27] Isaiah (1.5–9) interprets the devastation

---

[24] McKenzie, *Second Isaiah*, 133.

[25] Isaiah 53 is arguably the only text in the Hebrew Bible that teaches "vicarious suffering," and even the view that *it* does has been called into question; e.g. Sam K. Williams, *Jesus' Death as Saving Event*, 107–11. For other points of view, see Claus Westermann, *Isaiah 40–66* (Philadelphia: Westminster, 1969); and John D. W. Watts, *Isaiah 34–66* (Waco, TX: Word, 1982). Another permutation of suffering (though not vicariously) for the sins of others is the notion of "inherited guilt," that is, suffering for the sins of one's ancestors. The punishment of sins "to the third and the fourth generation" is mentioned in Exod. 20.5–6 and 34.7, but is vigorously denied in Deut. 24.16, Jer. 31.29–30, and Ezek. 18.20. In the NT "inherited guilt" is proposed but rejected as an explanation for congenital blindness in John 9.2.

[26] Most notably, Acts 8.26–35. See the references in F. F. Bruce, *The Acts of the Apostles, The Greek Text with Introduction and Commentary* (Grand Rapids, MI: Eerdmans, 1990) 228–9.

[27] Robinson, *Religious Ideas*, 161. Paton (see n. 15 above) argues that numerous difficulties arose in the way of the "penal theory of suffering," such as the suffering of the innocent, a new socio-economic order that favored the unjust, political upheavals in which entire nations suffered, and the suffering of the prophets themselves. It was, of course, true that many human experiences contradicted a

of foreign armies as divine punishment; Amos (4.6–12) sees the discipline of God in famine, drought, and pestilence; for Joel (1.2–2.27), judgment comes in the form of a locust plague. From these and the previous examples we see that the prophetic understanding of divine discipline is usually national in scope. The events interpreted as divine discipline are *usually* recent history, in which case the interpretation is *ex post facto*, but they may also be proleptic in that the prophet warns of dire circumstances that will result from the nation's infidelity. Divine discipline is construed differently, however, in the next group of writings to be considered.

3.2.2   Diversity in wisdom literature – Proverbs, Sirach, and Wisdom of Solomon

A large number of wisdom texts express the idea of divine discipline or instruction. The setting, however, is almost always the household, and the image is that of a parent in relationship to children.[28] Because of the aphoristic nature of most wisdom literature, there is usually no narrative context that might describe the circumstances in which one is being disciplined. Unlike prophetic literature, wisdom writings seldom appeal to Israel's history or to specific persons suffering afflictions causally related to acts of disobedience. Wisdom authors simply praise the benefits of discipline and enjoin others to heed it. Nevertheless, the punitive or formative nature of discipline is usually evident from the accompanying language, especially parallel terms. Owing to the nature of the material, an investigation of divine discipline in wisdom texts will more closely resemble a "word study" than the historical/theological observations of prophetic literature above. A suitable place to begin is with the very passage that Hebrews 12 appropriates: Proverbs 3.11–12.

These two verses are addressed to "my son." Verse 11 consists of parallel prohibitions in chiastic arrangement with their objects: "The discipline of the Lord (*musar*; LXX παιδεία) do not despise; and do not loathe his reproof." Verse 12 substantiates the prohibitions with an assurance of divine love: "For the Lord loves the one whom he

---

punitive interpretation of suffering, but there are scarcely any alternative interpretations of suffering in the prophets or any theological protest of the type that appears in Job. The prophets sometimes lament their own, presumably undeserved, suffering (especially Jeremiah), but they hope for divine vindication rather than positively interpret their suffering or fault divine justice.

[28] Georg Bertram, "παιδεύω," *TDNT*, V, 606 and 608.

reproves"; and a simile of parental discipline: "As a father [loves] the son in whom he is well-pleased." Divine discipline is rooted in God's love for the individual. God relates to the one disciplined as a parent to a child.

The significance of *musar*/παιδεία in this verse is clearly punitive. The parallel noun in verse 11 of the MT is "reproach, reprimand," a word which implies a correction of wrongdoing. The punitive aspect is intensified by the LXX, which in verse 12 has apparently read the first Hebrew word of 12b, "and as a father," as a hiphil form of a Hebrew verb meaning "cause pain," and has translated with μαστιγοῖ, "whip, flog, chastise."[29]

Three observations, then, can be made about Proverbs 3.11–12. First, the nuance of παιδεία is punitive or corrective. Second, the image by which divine παιδεία is conceived is the father/son relationship. Third, the divine motive behind discipline is love.[30] The punitive aspect is stronger in the LXX; the fatherly aspect in the MT. These three characteristics are found frequently, but by no means invariably, in the many wisdom passages dealing with παιδεία.[31]

The nuance of παιδεία in Proverbs is sometimes punitive, as an examination of the surrounding language reveals. As noted above, in Proverbs 3.11–12 the parallel terms are clearly punitive. The Greek verb ἐλέγχω and the related noun ἔλεγχος are common parallels for παιδεύω/παιδεία in Proverbs. In addition to 3.11–12 they are paralleled in 5.12; 9.7; 12.1; 13.18; 15.10 and 15.32. In 6.23 the two nouns are simply conjoined. In a few other contexts the punitive quality of παιδεία is made clear by its collocation with "the rod." According to 22.15 the "rod of discipline" will drive folly from a child.[32] In 13.24 and 23.13–14 the proper employment of παιδεία with children is said to involve "the rod."

On the other hand παιδεία sometimes had an educational nuance. In Proverbs 1.2, 7 and 15.33 the word is linked with σοφία (wisdom).

---

[29] Talbert, *Learning Through Suffering*, 71, notes the terms in the synonymous parallelisms and concludes that παιδεία in Heb. 12.5–6 has a punitive nuance; likewise Bertram, *TDNT*, V, 609. As I will argue in chapter 4, this reasoning is more persuasive in regard to Prov. 3.11–12 than Heb. 12.5–6.

[30] These three features are found in 2 Sam. 7.14–15. The Lord promises to be a father to David's offspring, to punish him with a rod and blows, but not to remove from him divine love.

[31] From here on I will primarily refer to the LXX since the author of Hebrews used either that version or a similar Greek translation of the Jewish scriptures.

[32] The LXX uses parataxis here, ῥάβδος ... καὶ παιδεία (rod ... and discipline), whereas the MT uses the construct.

In 1.29 σοφία is even a variant reading for παιδεία. Other parallel terms reveal a similar aspect. In 4.1 παιδεία is parallel to ἔννοια (insight); in 8.10 to γνῶσις (knowledge); in 15.5 to ἐντολαί (commandments). In 24.30–2 the observation of a field owned by a lazy person serves as an "object lesson" in negligence and sloth. The writer says of the field, ἐπέβλεψα τοῦ ἐκλέξασθαι παιδείαν, "I considered [it] so that I might draw from it learning." A remarkable use of the word occurs in 25.1 where a collection of Solomonic sayings is called αἱ παιδεῖαι Σαλωμῶντος. Here the word must mean "instructive saying" or "teaching." (Παροιμίαι is a variant reading.) It is clear even from this brief survey that παιδεία in Proverbs contains elements of correction and punishment, but also of instruction, wisdom, and insight. In any given passage the meaning might be shaded in one direction or the other.

The agent of discipline in Proverbs is almost always human. The setting may be a household with the mention of parents, children, or slaves: 1.8; 4.1; 13.24; 15.5; 19.18; 22.15; 23.13; 28.17a; 29.17, 19. Less often the agent of παιδεία is a person outside the family unit, a teacher (5.13) or an indefinite person (9.7). But most often addressees are simply enjoined to "accept," "love," or "heed" παιδεία, not to "despise" or "ignore" it, and the agent of παιδεία is left unspecified. Virtually the only text in Proverbs that explicitly speaks of *the Lord's* discipline is 3.11–12, the text that Hebrews appropriates.

In the category of wisdom literature the book of Job presents a strikingly different perspective on suffering and human existence. I will postpone consideration of Job briefly since two other books, Sirach and Wisdom of Solomon, should be examined in conjunction with Proverbs.

The author of Sirach is in many ways a traditionalist whose themes echo the book of Proverbs. Discipline figures prominently in its verses. The noun παιδεία and the verb παιδεύω appear about fifty times in all. Quite often παιδεία has the positive nuance of "instruction." The prologue praises Israel for παιδείας καὶ σοφίας (line 3; cf. line 12). These two terms are conjoined or paralleled elsewhere in the book: 1.27; 4.24; 6.18; 21.18–19; and 24.25–7. Similarly, note the close relationship with ἐπιστήμη (knowledge), in 16.25, κρίματα (judgments), in 18.14, and διδασκαλία (teaching) in 24.31–2. In 50.27 the author describes the entire contents of the book as παιδεία συνέσεως καὶ ἐπιστήμης (instruction in understanding and knowledge). Clearly the term possesses an educative or formative sense in these contexts.

Alternately, παιδεία is sometimes punitive. This is occasionally the sense when the author speaks of disciplining children.[33] Parents are to discipline their children and "bend their necks from their youth" (7.23; cf. also 42.5). According to 30.1 "He who loves his son will whip him often" (ἐνδελεχήσει μάστιγας αὐτῷ). Synonymous parallels in the next two verses speak of the one "who disciplines his son" (παιδεύων) and "who teaches his son" (διδάσκων).[34] The punitive aspect is also found in reference to the discipline of slaves. In 33.25 the author likens the function of παιδεία with household servants to the function of a rod with a donkey (cf. 42.5).

As in Proverbs, the agent of παιδεία in Sirach is usually human. The discourse and maxims of the wise are a source of discipline (8.8). As noted above, the author says of the contents of his book, "Instruction (παιδείαν) in understanding and knowledge I have written in this book" (50.27). Most often, then, παιδεία is a quality of humans, and παιδεύω an activity of humans: parents and householders, teachers (51.23), rulers (10.1), etc. There are, nevertheless, a few exceptions. Wisdom personified is a source of discipline in 4.17. The Lord rebukes, trains, and teaches in 18.13–14. Likewise, in 22.27–23.3 the Lord is implicitly the one who will guard a person from sins by, among other things, placing the discipline of wisdom (παιδείαν σοφίας) over one's mind.

Discipline is a less prominent theme in the Wisdom of Solomon. The noun and verb occur about ten times in all. The nuance of the words is most often formative and educative (1.5; 3.11; 6.11, 17, 25; 7.14). Sometimes the agent of discipline is God (3.5; 11.9; 12.22), sometimes a person (6.11, 25). When the agent is God, the object is the people of God. These passages and similar ones in Sirach call for special comment.

Wisdom 3.1–12 deals with the death of "the souls of the just." The author asserts that the fate of just souls departed is falsely perceived as calamitous by foolish human beings. Though "their end was reckoned as distress and their journey from us as ruin," in fact they enjoy the peace and blessing of God (3.2–3). From a human perspective they seemed to be punished; in reality, they have entered

---

[33] But the child is also addressed in non-punitive contexts: 6.18, 32; 16.24–5.

[34] In this triad of verbal expressions, "whip ... discipline ... teach," παιδεύω both in order and in meaning stands in the middle, between two terms whose meanings παιδεύω can approximate in certain contexts. A similar triad occurs in 18.13: ἐλέγχων καὶ παιδεύων καὶ διδάσκων (reproving and disciplining and teaching). On the collocation of μάστιγες (whips) and παιδεία, see also 22.6.

into an immortal hope. In a nicely balanced line with contrasting adverbial accusatives the writer says, ὀλίγα παιδευθέντες μεγάλα εὐεργετηθήσονται (Though disciplined slightly, they will be benefited greatly: vs. 5). In the following lines (5b–6) the image of refining shows that God's purpose in the affliction of the just was probative: ὁ θεὸς ἐπείρασεν αὐτοὺς καὶ εὗρεν αὐτοὺς ἀξίους ἑαυτοῦ· ὡς χρυσὸν ἐν χωνευτηρίῳ ἐδοκίμασεν αὐτοὺς (God tested them and found them worthy of himself; as gold in a smelting-furnace he proved them). In this case the refining does not seem to be purgative in function; there is no indication of sinful impurities to be removed. After all, these are "the just" who were found worthy of God! It is the impious who will receive punishment (ἐπιτιμία, vs. 10). This is a type of formative suffering. The just are "proved" and "approved" by their affliction; they are found to be trustworthy.

Two other passages in the Wisdom of Solomon support this interpretation. In 11.1–14 an elaborate comparison illustrates how God benefited Israel through the same means by which Egypt was tormented. Israel thirsted in the desert and received water from the rock; Egypt's plentiful source of water became polluted with blood. By thirsting, Israel learned how God had punished her enemies. "The author here enunciates a principle ... to the effect that it was *pedagogically* necessary that the Israelites should have a taste of their enemies' punishments."[35] Egypt was punished because of impiety; Israel suffered milder afflictions in order that she might understand divine punishment. The language of 11.9–10 distinguishes between Israel's experience and Egypt's. It is worth quoting at length.

> ὅτε γὰρ ἐπειράσθησαν, καίπερ ἐν ἐλέει παιδευόμενοι,
> ἔγνωσαν πῶς μετ᾽ ὀργῆς κρινόμενοι ἀσεβεῖς ἐβασανίζοντο·
> τούτους μὲν γὰρ ὡς πατὴρ νουθετῶν ἐδοκίμασας,
> ἐκείνους δὲ ὡς ἀπότομος βασιλεὺς καταδικάζων ἐξήτασας.

> For when they were tried, though they were being disciplined in mercy, they learned how the ungodly were tormented when judged in wrath. For you tested them as a parent does in warning, but you examined the ungodly as a stern king does in condemnation.

---

[35] David Winston, *The Wisdom of Solomon* (Garden City, NY: Doubleday, 1979) 228 (my emphasis). See especially 11.5 for the statement of this principle.

The contrast is reinforced by several parallel expressions. Israel was tested (ἐπειράσθησαν) and disciplined with mercy (ἐν ἐλέει παιδευόμενοι); Egypt was tormented (ἐβασανίζοντο) and judged in wrath (μετ' ὀργῆς κρινόμενοι). God tested (ἐδοκίμασας) Israel, admonishing her as a parent (ὡς πατὴρ νουθετῶν); God examined (ἐξήτασας) Egypt, passing judgment like a severe king (ὡς ἀπότομος βασιλεὺς καταδικάζων). What was punitive for Egypt was probative or formative for Israel.

The second passage is Wisdom 12.19–22. Here the author observes that God grants opportunity for repentance to all, even to Israel's enemies. But God's treatment of Israel differs: ἡμᾶς οὖν παιδεύων τοὺς ἐχθροὺς ἡμῶν ἐν μυριότητι μαστιγοῖς (So, though you disciplined us, our enemies you scourge ten thousandfold: vs. 22). The stated purpose of this divine discipline is that Israel might consider God's goodness when judging, and hope for mercy when being judged (22bc).[36] Though there is no language of "testing" or "proving" in this passage, the divine purpose of Israel's experience still seems to be educative rather than punitive.

Sirach also contains two passages that seem to articulate a formative or probative view of suffering. Quite compelling in this regard is 2.1–6 in which "Ben Sira warns his disciples about the adversity that the Lord allows as a test of whether or not fear of the Lord is genuine."[37] Those who come to serve the Lord are advised to prepare their souls for testing (εἰς πειρασμόν). They are told to persevere and not to act impetuously in a time of affliction. A string of commands and prohibitions in verses 1–4 enjoining patience, fidelity, and acceptance of one's lot are then grounded in the concept of probative suffering: ὅτι ἐν πυρὶ δοκιμάζεται χρυσὸς καὶ ἄνθρωποι δεκτοὶ ἐν καμίνῳ ταπεινώσεως (For gold is tested in the fire, and those found acceptable, in the furnace of humiliation). Whatever the precise nature of the affliction is, there is no suggestion that its function is punitive; rather it is probative.

The image is somewhat less developed and more obscure in the second passage, Sirach 4.17. Wisdom personified is said to

---

[36] Winston (*ibid.*, 244), notes that a strong case has been made for reading μετριότητι (with moderation) instead of μυριότητι (with a myriad, ten thousandfold) in 22a. This unquestionably suits the context better. Though this emendation lessens the severity of the contrast between God's treatment of Israel and Egypt, the choice of verbs and the purpose clause in 22bc still favor a formative or educative understanding of God's discipline of Israel.

[37] Patrick W. Skehan, *The Wisdom of Ben Sira* (New York: Doubleday, 1987) 150.

walk with her children, putting them to the test (βασανίσει) with her
παιδεία until the point that she trusts their heart.[38] She will test
(πειράσει) them with her ordinances. There is no hint of divine
punishment here; rather the point seems to be a test of one's fidelity
to Wisdom.

I should mention here two Pentateuchal texts which, while obviously not belonging to the same genre as Sirach and Wisdom of
Solomon, nonetheless share some features with the passages just
discussed. Deuteronomy 8.2–5 interprets Israel's wilderness experience as a lesson in humility and faithfulness. Moses addresses the
people:

> Remember the long way that the Lord your God has led
> you these forty years in the wilderness, in order to humble
> you, testing you to know what was in your heart, whether
> or not you would keep his commandments. He humbled
> you by letting you hunger, then by feeding you with manna,
> with which neither you nor your ancestors were acquainted,
> in order to make you understand that one does not live by
> bread alone, but by every word that comes from the mouth
> of the Lord ... Know then in your heart that as a parent
> disciplines a child so the Lord your God disciplines you.

The function of Israel's adversity is probative. By subjecting the
Israelites to the hardships of hunger and thirst, God will see if
they are dependent on divine mercy and provision. They are tested
(ἐκπειράζω) to see if they will keep his commandments. The image
of parental discipline is present in verse 5 (*ysr*, παιδεύω). In this
context "discipline" should be understood as formative testing, not
punishment. The wilderness provision is described in similar terms
in Exodus 16.4. The Lord devises the daily provision in order to test
(πειράζω) the people to see if they will obey the Lord's instruction
(*tôrah*, νόμος).

---

[38] The adverb διεστραμμένως with "she will walk" is difficult. The verb διαστρέφω
means "to turn different ways, twist, distort, or pervert." LSJ, 426, suggests
"perversely" for the adverb in Sir. 4.17. The NRSV translates "on tortuous
paths." Skehan, *Wisdom of Ben Sira*, 172, suggests "in disguise." The word is only
one of several difficulties in the verse. "She will put them to the test" is preferable
to NRSV's "torment." The latter is a common derived meaning of βασανίζω, but
the basic sense of the word is "to rub upon the touchstone" (βάσανος), i.e. "put to
the test." See LSJ, 308–9. The subject of the verb ἐμπιστεύσῃ (17d) might be
construed as the child of Wisdom rather than Wisdom herself. The use of the word
in 16a may support this.

These passages from the Wisdom of Solomon (3.1–12; 11.1–14; 12.19–22), Sirach (2.1–6; 4.17), and Deuteronomy (8.2–5) are evidence that a formative view of suffering is occasionally to be found among Jewish writers. Sometimes this view is expressed by the figure of the refiner's fire, sometimes by parental discipline.[39] It is of interest that this viewpoint is found especially in wisdom literature, for this same genre also offers numerous examples of the alternate view: punitive discipline.

3.2.3   Protest in wisdom literature – Ecclesiastes and Job

Before leaving the category of wisdom, I must call attention to two important "non-orthodox" views about the nature of suffering. The first is represented by the book of Ecclesiastes, or Qoheleth, according to its Hebrew title. Ecclesiastes is a blunt, even cynical, response to the religious crisis created by the recognition of life's vanity and inequity. Qoheleth rejects the dogma that the righteous will be rewarded and the wicked punished. "The wise have eyes in their head, but fools walk in darkness. Yet I perceived that the same fate befalls all of them. Then I said to myself, 'What happens to the fool will happen to me also; why then have I been so very wise?'" (2.14–15). "In my vain life I have seen everything; there are righteous people who perish in their righteousness, and there are wicked people who prolong their life in their evil-doing" (7.15). "The same fate comes to all, to the righteous and the wicked, to the good and the evil, to the clean and the unclean, to those who sacrifice and those who do not sacrifice" (9.2). These passages address the vanity of seeking wisdom rather than the problem of suffering, but one can at least make some inferences from them about the author's view of suffering. Clearly Qoheleth sees little correspondence between a person's righteousness or lack thereof and the prosperity or evil befalling that person. Implicitly, then, a punitive view of suffering is rejected. Since, for Qoheleth, the sum of life's experiences is vanity

---

[39] A further instance of the refining image is found in Jdt. 8.25–7 where the testing of Abraham, Isaac, and Jacob is recalled. The language employed includes πειράζω (test) and πυρόω (prove by fire). The purpose of the testing is two-fold: "to search the heart" and "to counsel or admonish." The *New Oxford Annotated Bible* (NRSV) notes, "Their present sufferings are not punitive, but educative." Cf. Carey A. Moore, *Judith* (Garden City, NY: Doubleday, 1985) 183, who speaks of "the benevolent intent and the salutary effects of God's discipline."

(1.2; 12.8), no positive interpretation of suffering is offered in its place.

The main representative of the "protest" view is the book of Job. Less cynical than Ecclesiastes, Job constitutes a vigorous and elaborate repudiation of the doctrine of retribution, namely, that the wicked suffer for their misdeeds and, conversely, that those who suffer are necessarily guilty of some wrongdoing. Job himself serves as a vivid case study that refutes any rigid application of this doctrine. From the outset the reader is informed that Job is "blameless and upright, one who feared God and turned away from evil" (1.1). Even after the complete loss of his livestock, servants, children, home, and health, Job remained righteous (1.22; 2.10). Job's friends, Eliphaz, Bildad, and Zophar, articulate the traditional doctrine in a series of speeches interrupted by Job's defense of himself (4.1–27.23).[40] A final speaker, Elihu, is particularly arrogant and accusatory, insisting that Job's professed innocence cannot possibly be true (33.9–12). Finally God responds in a lengthy series of reproaches couched in rhetorical questions such as, "Where were you when I laid the foundation of the earth?" (38.4). The sum of them is, "Shall a faultfinder contend with the Almighty?" (40.2). After a second speech by God, Job finally replies. He acknowledges the power and purpose of God and his own ignorance (42.1–6). The Lord commends Job and rebukes his three friends. Never does Job admit any wrongdoing, nor does the Lord ever contradict Job's claim of innocence. The book is thus a powerful refutation of the traditional view.

The question remains: What is the *positive* contribution of the book of Job to the understanding of suffering? The sheer existence of the book confirms that, at least at the time of its composition, the punitive view held sway. Perhaps Job should be viewed as one of the first hammer swings at the monolith of punitive suffering. If so, this in itself is a significant achievement. Job certainly proves that the traditional view needs modification. Moreover, Job may be seen to hint at the necessary direction of that modification. Although Job says little about the divine purpose of suffering, there is an indication of probative or formative suffering in Job 23.10: "When [God] has tested me, I shall come out like gold." One commentator re-

---

[40] The first speech of Eliphaz contains a likely allusion to Prov. 3.11–12. Job 5.17 shares three key words with that text: "reprove," "discipline," and "despise." Here divine discipline is understood punitively.

marks, "Here Job's assurance that God is concerned with his well-being rises to its highest point ... Job longs for a golden character."[41] Although this small affirmation of hope is nearly lost in a book filled with accusations and denials, it should perhaps be seen as the probative/formative interpretation in embryo. Job does not solve the problem of evil, but neither does it deserve to be called "a conspicuous failure."[42] Job advances the discussion by identifying a dead end and hinting at a new direction.

3.2.4   Interpreting disease and devastation – Psalms

Hymnic literature, both canonical and pseudepigraphical, also furnishes some important texts on the subject of suffering and its interpretation. Prayers for healing sometimes imply that bodily afflictions are divine punishments for sin.[43] Psalm 6 is a prayer for deliverance from distress caused by enemies or perhaps disease. The first verse suggests that the psalmist's plight is related to the Lord's wrath: Κύριε, μὴ τῷ θυμῷ σου ἐλέγξῃς με, μηδὲ τῇ ὀργῇ σου παιδεύσῃς με. (O Lord, do not rebuke me in your anger, or discipline me in your wrath.) Note here the parallelism of ἐλέγχω and παιδεύω, a common one in wisdom literature. The precise relationship between the writer's malady and the Lord's disciplinary action is

---

[41] John E. Hartley, *The Book of Job* (Grand Rapids: Eerdmans, 1988) 340. The refining image in Job 23.10 suggests that the probative category is the best classification for this verse. The testing of Job seems to pertain more to the *demonstration* of his good character than to the formation of it.

[42] M. H. Pope, "Book of Job," *Interpreter's Dictionary of the Bible* (Nashville: Abingdon, 1962) II, 922: "If the purpose of the book is to 'solve' [the problem of evil], it must be admitted to be a conspicuous failure."

[43] F. Lindström has written a lengthy monograph (see n. 13 above) whose thesis runs counter to my observations here. He questions "the supposed self-evident connection between sickness and sin in the individual complaint psalms" (429). While Lindström has shown that the individual complaint psalms, as a genre, do not display the features of human sin, divine wrath, and resultant illness as consistently as several scholars have claimed (see his survey of the literature, 3–6), he has not convinced me that a causal connection between sickness and sin is to be found "in none of these psalms" (445). Lindström minimizes the evidence that does exist, noting that a sin motif occurs in *only* eight of the complaint psalms; divine wrath in *only* ten (10). The most serious problem is Lindström's tendential use of redaction criticism. In psalm after psalm, lines that clearly refer to sin and associate it with the writer's suffering are classed as redactional (70–3, 130–1, 242–4, 281–3, 299–300, 329–32). Even where such textual reconstruction might have merit, it only shifts the problem of a punitive view of illness from the psalmist to the redactor. These psalms clearly contain the punitive view in their final form, and many of them probably did in their original form.

unclear, but the detrimental nature of the latter is obvious. The psalmist prays for grace and healing (vs. 2), not παιδεία. The first verse of Psalm 38 (LXX 37.2) expresses the same thought.[44] Here the affliction is explicitly associated with the Lord (vs. 2) and with the psalmist's sin: "There is no soundness in my flesh because of your indignation; there is no health in my bones because of my sin" (vs. 3). Psalm 39, also a prayer for healing, identifies sin as the cause of the author's distress (vss. 8–11):

> Deliver me from all my transgressions. Do not make me the scorn of the fool. I am silent; I do not open my mouth, for it is you who have done it. Remove your stroke from me; I am worn down by the blows of your hand. You chastise mortals in punishment for sin, consuming like a moth what is dear to them; surely everyone is a mere breath.

Alternately, there are passages in the Psalms in which suffering is understood as formative. Psalm 66.8–12 (LXX 65) is a noteworthy example. Here again is the image of refining precious metals: ἐδοκίμασας ἡμᾶς, ὁ θεός, ἐπύρωσας ἡμᾶς, ὡς πυροῦται τὸ ἀργύριον· (You, O God, have tested us; you have tried us as silver is tried). This psalm praises and thanks God for blessings and deliverance from peril. Not a hint of confession or guilt is to be found in it. Psalm 105.16–19 (LXX 104) is similar. Here the psalmist praises God for the providential care wrought through Joseph. The latter was sold as a slave, his feet fettered and neck bound with iron. These hardships are viewed as a sort of probation: τὸ λόγιον κυρίου ἐπύρωσεν αὐτόν (The word of the Lord tested him). The painful and humbling experiences of Joseph are regarded as a refining fire, apparently in preparation for his pivotal role as master of the king's possessions and, ultimately, for the deliverance of Israel.

The pseudepigraphical Psalms of Solomon, probably written in Jerusalem in the first century BCE, deal extensively with the theological problem of suffering and God's justice. The author's faith is sorely challenged by the recent desecration of Jerusalem, a likely allusion to Pompey's invasion in 63 BCE.[45] If God is just, how can

---

[44] The Greek in both verses (6.2 and 37.2) is identical; the Hebrew (6.1 and 38.1) varies only in the first noun for "anger."

[45] On dating and other matters, see R. B. Wright, "Psalms of Solomon," *OTP*, II, 639–70. On the meaning of chastisements in the Psalms of Solomon, see E. P. Sanders, *Paul and Palestinian Judaism: A Comparison of Patterns of Religion* (Philadelphia: Fortress, 1977) 397–8. For a punitive interpretation of the de-

the innocent suffer, especially at the hands of profane gentiles? The author of these Psalms is compelled to conclude: the victims are *not* innocent. They are suffering for sins that are sometimes known and sometimes involuntary and hidden.

The priests of Jerusalem seem to be targeted by the indictments in 2.3–7:

> Because the sons of Jerusalem defiled the sanctuary of the Lord, they were profaning the offerings of God with lawless acts; ...
> ... The sons and the daughters [were] in harsh captivity, their neck in a seal, a spectacle among the gentiles.
> He did [this] to them according to their sins, so that he abandoned them to the hands of those who prevailed.[46]

Even those deemed righteous are not entirely without sin and, there-fore, are subject to the Lord's discipline. In a faint echo of Proverbs 3.11 the author writes, οὐκ ὀλιγωρήσει δίκαιος παιδευόμενος ὑπὸ κυρίου (A righteous person will not lightly esteem being disciplined by the Lord: 3.4a). The following context (3.4–8) reveals that the discipline of the Lord here purges the sins of the righteous, remov-ing all possible sins: repeated, accidental and unknown.[47] There-fore, the author argues, God's judgment and discipline of Israel are just (8.26–9).

The Lord's discipline can be painful. Just as Proverbs 3.11–12 conjoins παιδεία and the word μαστιγόω (whip, flog) so does the author of the Psalms of Solomon.[48] "We are under your yoke for-ever, and [under] the whip of your discipline" (7.9). Another passage speaks of "the rod of discipline" (18.7). The punitive nature of God's παιδεία is nowhere more evident than in 10.1–3.

> Happy is the man whom the Lord remembers with rebuk-ing, and protects from the evil way with a whip [that he may] be cleansed from sin that it may not increase.
> The one who prepares [his] back for the whip shall be puri-fied, for the Lord is good to those who endure discipline.

---

struction of Jerusalem in 587 BCE, see 2 (Syriac Apocalypse of) Baruch 13.1–10; 79.1–4 *et passim*. A more general statement of condign punishment via foreign nations is found in the Testament of Moses 12.10–13.

[46] This and other citations are from Wright, "Psalms of Solomon."

[47] *Ibid.*, 654–5, note m.

[48] For the use of μαστιγόω for divine affliction, see also Tob. 13.2, 5, 10 (LXX).

> For he will straighten the ways of the righteous, and will
> not bend [them] by discipline; and the mercy of the Lord
> is upon those who truly love him.

Lastly, the discipline of God is sometimes framed in terms of a
parental relationship. God "will admonish the righteous as a be-
loved son, and his discipline is as for a first born" (13.9). "Your
discipline for us [is] as [for] a firstborn son, an only child, to divert
the perceptive person from unintentional sins" (18.4). There is, then,
a whole complex of language in these Psalms held in common with
wisdom literature: παιδεία, μάστιξ, ὀλιγορέω, ἁμαρτία, υἱός, and
ὑπομένω (on the latter see 10.2, 14.1, 16.11–15).

The Psalms of Solomon are thoroughgoing in their punitive interpretation of suffering. Even given a historical incident (Pompey's
invasion) that would seem to furnish clear instances of undeserved
suffering, the author is persistent in justifying this presumably divine
action against Israel.

> The righteous must be guilty of some sins, even if unwit-
> tingly, and God alerts the righteous person to these sins
> through affliction so that he may improve himself and thus
> escape a worse punishment ... The psalmist believes that
> suffering is purgative and salutary ... and will say that the
> righteous are singled out for especially exacting discipline,
> but he never moves toward assigning a positive meaning to
> suffering or [toward] making it the sign of election. For the
> psalmist, suffering remains suffering for sin.[49]

3.2.5 "For the sake of our sins"/"For the sake of virtue" –
Maccabean literature

This is an appropriate place to examine the Maccabean literature,
for portions of it have much affinity with the perspective of the
Psalms of Solomon treated above. Second Maccabees relates the
persecution of the Jews under the Seleucid kings from about 180 to
161 BCE.[50] Just as the author of the Psalms of Solomon decried the

---

[49] Wright, "Psalms of Solomon," 644. (V. Schwartz co-authored this portion of
Wright's essay.)

[50] Works on 2 Macc. include: P. F.-M. Abel, *Les Livres des Maccabées* (Paris:
Gabalda, 1949); J. R. Bartlett, *The First and Second Books of the Maccabees*
(Cambridge: Cambridge University, 1973); Robert Doran, *Temple Propaganda:*

Romans' devastation of Jerusalem under Pompey, so 2 Maccabees laments the profaning of the city by Antiochus IV (6.3–6).

> Harsh and utterly grievous was the onslaught of evil. For the temple was filled with debauchery and reveling by the Gentiles, who dallied with prostitutes and had intercourse with women within the sacred precincts, and besides brought in things for sacrifice that were unfit. The altar was covered with abominable offerings that were forbidden by the laws. People could neither keep the sabbath, nor observe the festivals of their ancestors, nor so much as confess themselves to be Jews.

How could God allow such outrages? According to the author of 2 Maccabees, the sins of the people were the explanation. When he entered the temple "Antiochus was elated in spirit, and did not perceive that the Lord was angered for a little while because of the sins of those who lived in the city, and that this was the reason he was disregarding the holy place" (5.17). The outrages included forced participation in pagan rituals and the execution of those who persisted in Jewish practices such as circumcision and Sabbath keeping (6.7–11). After describing such heinous acts of the Seleucids against the Jews, the author digresses briefly to explain the "purpose" of these atrocities (6.12–16).[51]

> Now I urge those who read this book not to be depressed by such calamities, but to recognize that these punishments were designed not to destroy but to discipline (πρὸς παιδείαν) our people. In fact, it is a sign of great kindness not to let the impious alone for long, but to punish them immediately. For in the case of the other nations the Lord waits patiently to punish them until they have reached the full measure of their sins; but he does not deal in this way with us, in order that he may not take vengeance on us afterward when our sins have reached their height. Therefore he never withdraws his mercy from us. Although he disciplines us

---

The Purpose and Character of 2 Maccabees (CBQMS 12; Washington, DC: Catholic Biblical Association of America, 1980); and Solomon Zeitlin, *The Second Book of Maccabees* (New York: Harper, 1954).

[51] On these two digressions (5.17–20 and 6.12–17), see Doran, *Temple Propaganda*, 53–4.

with calamities (παιδεύων ... μετὰ συμφορᾶς), he does not forsake his own people.

The very next section in the narrative is the celebrated account of the martyrdoms of Eleazar, the seven brothers and their mother (6.18–7.42). When Antiochus had the last of the seven brothers brought forward to be tested, the youth refused to obey and, moreover, reviled the king. "You who have contrived all sorts of evil against the Hebrews, will certainly not escape the hands of God. For we are suffering because of our own sins.[52] And if our living Lord is angry for a little while, to rebuke and discipline us (χάριν ἐπιπλήξεως καὶ παιδείας), he will again be reconciled with his own servants" (7.31–3). The final words of the seventh brother reinforce this view by describing "the wrath of the Almighty" as having "justly fallen on our whole nation" (7.38).[53]

In chapters 8 and 9, the Maccabeans under Judas turn the tide of battle and gain several victories. Antiochus falls ill, smitten by God with a devastating disease, and dies. Judas and his followers recover the temple and purify the sanctuary. There they offer sacrifices and incense, light lamps, and pray to God "that they might never again fall into such misfortunes, but that, if they should ever sin, they might be disciplined (παιδεύεσθαι) by [God] with forbearance and not be handed over to blasphemous and barbarous nations" (10.4).

There is, then, a pattern in the narrative. Descriptions of the outrages of the gentiles alternate with brief justifications of God's disciplinary action. This occurs at particularly traumatic junctures in the narrative. Note the sequence: (1) Antiochus profanes the temple (5.15–16); the people's sins are given as the cause, and the hope of a restored temple is expressed (5.17–20). (2) Jews are coerced and the first martyrdoms occur (6.7–11); there is reassurance that God's discipline will be followed by mercy (6.12–16). (3) The particularly gruesome martyrdoms of Eleazar, the seven and their mother are

---

[52] Abel (*Livres des Maccabées*, 375) sees expiatory suffering here and at 7.18: "God ... sends persecution to the Jews for the expiation of their sins." But the texts do not bear this out, suggesting only that sin is the cause of their suffering, not that guilt is removed thereby.

[53] Contrast the justice of God's wrath in 2 Macc. 7.38 with the explicit injustice of the deaths of Jewish resisters in 1 Macc. 2.37. Facing their Seleucid foes they refused to fight on the Sabbath, but exhorted one another saying, Ἀποθάνωμεν πάντες ἐν τῇ ἁπλότητι ἡμῶν· μαρτυρεῖ ἐφ᾽ ἡμᾶς ὁ οὐρανὸς καὶ ἡ γῆ ὅτι ἀκρίτως ἀπόλλυτε ἡμᾶς. (Let us all die in our innocence; heaven and earth testify for us that you are killing us unjustly.)

narrated (6.18–7.42); the youngest son testifies that the Hebrews' suffering is just, but minor compared to Antiochus' coming torment (7.30–8). (4) At the conclusion of the Antiochus episode, the temple is restored (10.1–3); the Maccabeans pray that future sins will be disciplined more mercifully (10.4).

In each case the ways of God are justified by imputing guilt to the Jews in the present and depicting a more just and favorable outcome in the future. The former is of special importance for this study. The theological position of the author of 2 Maccabees is much like that found in the Psalms of Solomon. Every disaster in Israel's experience must be explained within the context of divine sovereignty and justice; nothing occurs outside God's will. Therefore, suffering, no matter how manifestly human in its origin, must also be expressive of God's justice; in other words, it is deserved. Even those who suffer courageously, defying tyrants and standing firm in their piety, somehow merit the punishment they receive. The narrative portrays the immediate, human agents of suffering, namely, the Seleucids, but the author's theology demands that divine causation be involved as well.

The author of 3 Maccabees shares this perspective.[54] At two major points in the narrative, a gentile oppressor, Ptolemy IV Philopator, is on the verge of committing a heinous act against the Jews and is only averted by the pious prayer of a Jewish representative followed by divine intervention. The most remarkable feature of these episodes for our purposes is the way in which the prayers interpret the impending horrors in the framework of divine justice.

The first instance occurs when Ptolemy, following his victory at the Battle of Raphia, visits Jerusalem and wishes to enter the most holy place of the temple. The Jews are naturally aghast, and when Ptolemy persists in his request, the priests and the citizenry flock to the temple and prostrate themselves in prayer (1.9–21). Simon, the high priest, prays that God would deliver them from the wicked and insolent men who would defile the sacred place. But Simon does not protest that such sacrilege would be unfair to the Jews, rather that it would dishonor God and lend credence to their enemies' boasts. The potential violation of the temple is construed as punishment for the people's sins: διὰ τὰς πολλὰς καὶ μεγάλας ἡμῶν ἁμαρτίας καταπονούμεθα καὶ ὑπετάγημεν τοῖς ἐχθροῖς ἡμῶν καὶ παρείμεθα ἐν

---

[54] On 3 Macc., see H. Anderson, "3 Maccabees," *OTP*, II, 509–29; and M. Hadas, *The Third and Fourth Books of Maccabees* (New York: Harper, 1953).

ἀδυναμίαις. (Because of our many and great sins we are crushed with suffering, subjected to our enemies, and overtaken by helplessness: 2.13.) An even more specific connection is made a few verses later: "Do not punish us for the defilement committed by these men, or call us to account for this profanation" (2.17). Verse 19 asks that God "wipe away our sins and disperse our errors." Simon's prayer does not object to the fact of the people receiving punishment; it assumes that punishment must be deserved. It is the pagan agent that is unacceptable.

Similarly in chapter 6, Ptolemy, now back in Egypt, has imprisoned in the hippodrome all Jews who resisted his program of religious syncretism and threatens to have them crushed by rampaging elephants. This time Eleazar, a respected priest, prays for deliverance. But again, the imminent disaster is thought possibly to be merited by the people's sins. Eleazar prays, "If our life is subject to penalty because of impious deeds in the course of our sojourn abroad, rescue us from the hand of our enemies, Lord, and destroy us by a fate of your own choosing" (6.10).[55]

The author of 3 Maccabees works within a rigid framework of sin and punishment. He is "an ardent champion of the old Deuteronomic orthodoxy ... the conviction that God rewards the righteous and punishes the wicked."[56] Moreover, for this author as for the author of 2 Maccabees, it seems that the connection works both ways. Not only is it assumed that the wicked are punished, but conversely, those who suffer (i.e. are punished) must have committed some wickedness. According to the author of 3 Maccabees, the persecution of the Jews by Ptolemy IV can be traced back to the Jews' "many and great sins."

This perspective is lacking in 4 Maccabees; in fact, it seems to have been deliberately edited out.[57] Fourth Maccabees has been well characterized as "a philosophical exercise on the subject of devout reason's mastery over the passions."[58] The supreme martyrs of the Maccabean period, Eleazar and the seven brothers and their

---

[55] Translation from Anderson, "3 Maccabees," 526.

[56] *Ibid.*, 514.

[57] It is quite likely that the author of 4 Macc. "had at his disposal 2 Maccabees and rearranged and reshaped it freely to suit his own taste and purpose." (H. Anderson, "4 Maccabees," 541.) On the sources of 4 Macc., see also Hadas, *Third and Fourth Books of Maccabees*, 92–5.

[58] Anderson, "4 Maccabees," 532. See also Renehan, "The Greek Philosophic Background of Fourth Maccabees."

mother, are portrayed as champions of virtue, noble examples who through λόγισμος (reason), εὐσεβεία (piety), and ἀρετή (virtue) overcame the evil tyrant Antiochus. Nowhere, however, does the author suggest that they suffered even in part for their own sins as part of God's punishment. It was for the sake of virtue and piety that they endured and ultimately died.[59] Their deaths were in every way noble, a fulfillment of piety (11.6, 12; 12.14; 16.16).

This emphasis is seen in the use of the word παιδεία in 4 Maccabees and the starkly contrasting use in 2 Maccabees.[60] In 2 Maccabees we saw that παιδεία was linked to the calamities (συμφοραί) brought on by Antiochus, which were understood as divine punishments (τιμωρίαι) (6.12–16). Παιδεία is also coupled with ἐπιπλήξις (reproof) and viewed as the purpose of the Lord's anger toward sin (7.32–3). The use of παιδεία in 4 Maccabees is strikingly different. In 1.17 the παιδεία τοῦ νόμου is equated with wisdom. Through this παιδεία we learn both human and divine matters. When the third brother is at the point of death, he says, διὰ παιδείαν καὶ ἀρετὴν θεοῦ ταῦτα πάσχομεν (We suffer these things for the sake of instruction and the virtue of God: 10.10). This probably involves a hendiadys for "training in divine virtue." In any case, the nuance of παιδεία is formative and educative. Similarly, in 13.22 the close fraternity of the seven brothers is expressed by a complex of four terms: shared nuture (συντροφία), daily companionship (ἡ καθ' ἡμέραν συνηθεία), general instruction (ἡ ἄλλη παιδεία), and training in the law of God (ἡ ... ἐν νόμῳ θεοῦ ἀσκήσεως). Again, παιδεία is viewed as formative and educative.[61]

There is perhaps one sense in which the martyrs' suffering in 4 Maccabees involves sin. When Eleazar is at the point of death, he prays to God: "Be merciful to your people and let our punishment be a satisfaction on their behalf. Make my blood their purification and take my life as a ransom for theirs" (6.28–9). After the opening words we have a three-fold expression of vicarious atonement.

---

[59] This is stated repeatedly in 4 Macc. The expression "for the sake of virtue," or something similar, occurs in 1.8; 7.22; 9.18; 10.10; 11.2; "for the sake of piety" and similar expressions are found in 6.22; 9.6, 7, 24, 29, 30; 11.20; 12.14; 13.7–12; 14.3; 15.12, 14; 16.13, 17, 23; 17.7; 18.3. One might also note "for the sake of the Law" (6.28) and "for the sake of God" (16.19, 21; 17.20).

[60] The word group does not occur in 3 Macc.

[61] The verb παιδεύω occurs in 4 Macc. 5.24 parallel to non-punitive terms, ἐκδιδάσκω and ἐξασκέω. Related, but not involving the word παιδεία, is the sixth son's description of the trial (ἀγών) to which they are being subjected as "an exercise in suffering" (γυμνασία πόνων: 11.20).

In some way "the suffering and death of the martyred righteous had redemptive efficacy for all Israel and secured God's grace and pardon for his people."[62] The thought occurs again in 17.21–2: the martyrs became, as it were, a ransom (ἀντίψυχον) for the sin of the nation through whose blood and the propitiation (ἱλαστήριον) of whose death God had rescued Israel.

As I observed earlier in this chapter in the discussion of Isaiah 53, the notion of vicarious suffering is related to punitive suffering in that sin is presupposed, but it diverges from the traditional punitive understanding in that the sufferer and the sinner are not one and the same. No one suffers in 4 Maccabees for his or her own sins, as the object of God's wrath. The purpose of suffering in 4 Maccabees should not be construed punitively in the sense articulated in 2 Maccabees. Rather, suffering is seen primarily as formative, "for the sake of piety," but also vicarious, "for the sake of the nation."

Three groupings of material remain in this survey of Jewish views of suffering and divine discipline: the first-century writers Josephus and Philo, the documents from Qumran, and the vast collection of material known by the rubric of rabbinic literature. I will proceed in that order.

3.2.6   Views of a historian and a philosopher – Josephus and Philo

Josephus supplies a wealth of lexical examples of παιδεύω/παιδεία,[63] but none of these refers to divine action toward persons, either punitively or educatively. On the purely lexical level, however, it should be pointed out that Josephus uses these words exclusively in an educative sense. The noun denotes "training" or "instruction." It often extends to the resultative sense of "learning," "culture," or "erudition." Josephus claims to have made significant gains in παιδεία early in life (*Vita* 8). Indeed, as an adult he boasted that he far exceeded the people of his own nation in the παιδεία of the Jews (*Ant.* 20.263). In this way, the word is sometimes coupled with the name of a people or nation to denote, for example, the "culture" of the Greeks (*Ant.* 19.213; *Vita* 40, 359; *Apion* 1.73) or of the Hebrews/Chaldeans (*Ant.* 10.187, 194). The possession of παιδεία

---

[62] Anderson, "4 Maccabees," 539.

[63] The noun occurs thirty times; the verb about twenty times. See Karl H. Rengstorf, *A Complete Concordance to Flavius Josephus* (Leiden: Brill, 1973–83) 265–6.

was a highly regarded quality and was sometimes linked with goodness and virtue (*Ant.* 12.53; 19.164). Similarly, the verb means "teach," or "instruct," less often "rear." Nowhere in Josephus is the word used in the punitive sense of "chastise" or "correct."[64]

There is, however, one passage in the *Antiquities* (3.13–16) that depicts hardship as divine testing. The Israelites were greatly disgruntled because of the hardships they experienced as Moses led them in the wilderness. Preoccupied with their misfortunes, they began to protest and even to threaten Moses' life (3.11–12). Moses exhorted them not to forget the benefits they had already received at God's hand, but to hope for deliverance from their present difficulties. For God was probably "exercising" (γυμνάζειν) them by these present hardships, testing their virtue and endurance (καρτερία, ὑπομονή), a test in which the Israelites were being proven (ἐλέγχεσθαι) not to be noble. Although the terms παιδεύω and παιδεία are absent, some of the language of this passage (γυμνάζειν, ὑπομονή, ἐλέγχεσθαι) is found in Hebrews 12.4–11, making the concept of probative and formative suffering in *Antiquities* 3.13–16 similar to that of Hebrews. Moreover, the use of the word γυμνάζειν gives the passage a faint athletic cast, another point in common with Hebrews 12.

A punitive interpretation of suffering is found, as one would expect, in the discussion of the plagues inflicted on the Egyptians (*Ant.* 2.293–314). Among the reasons Josephus gives for reciting the plagues is the potential educative function of such a recital: συμφέρει τοῖς ἀνθρώποις μαθοῦσι φυλάττεσθαι ταῦτα ποιεῖν, ἐφ᾽ οἷς μὴ δυσαρεστήσει τὸ θεῖον μηδ᾽ εἰς ὀργὴν τραπὲν ἀμυνεῖται τῆς ἀδικίας αὐτούς. (It behooves people that they learn to guard themselves so as to act in a way that the Deity will not be displeased, nor, provoked to wrath, will repay them for their wrongdoing: 2.293.) Thus, while the plagues were punitive for the Egyptians, Josephus hoped that others would gain a moral lesson from the Egyptian experience.

Pharaoh's guilt runs throughout the narrative. At first his error is to scorn the words of Moses, God's representative (293). Later, his false promises of release are condemned as "deceit" (ἀπάτη, 300) and "wickedness" (πονηρία, 304). The latter word is picked up

---

[64] Since Josephus wrote with the assistance of Greek translators, his use of παιδεύω and παιδεία is evidence that the educative meaning was dominant among late-first-century Hellenistic readers. Cf. Bertram, *TDNT*, V, 617. Bertram (*ibid.*, 614, n. 103) notes that Josephus substitutes μάστιξιν νουθετεῖν (to admonish with floggings) in *Ant.* 8.217 for the LXX's punitive use of παιδεύειν in 1 Kings 12.11.

again in an explicit statement that Pharaoh's problem is not "ignorance apart from wickedness" (τὸν δίχα πονηρίας ἀνόητον). If that had been the case, Pharaoh would have quickly learned the right course of action. On the contrary, the flaw of the Egyptian king was less folly than vice (307). Pharaoh is being punished.

Another passage bears terse witness to the idea of punitive suffering. The gruesomeness of the terminal disease of Herod the Great, described in the *War* (1.656), led some diviners to declare that this malady was a penalty for Herod's murder of certain rabbis who had instigated a seditious act (1.648–50). This is a clear instance of suffering interpreted in a punitive fashion, but the statement consists of a single subordinate clause in a lengthy period that highlights the disease more than its interpretation, an interpretation to which Josephus adds no comment.[65]

The punitive sufferings of the Egyptians, Pharaoh, and Herod the Great are past examples of relatively minor significance. Of greater importance for Josephus' theological interpretation of suffering and hardship is the single most catastrophic event of his own lifetime, the Jewish War. The consistent perspective of Josephus' *War* is that the Jews were dreadfully wrong to resist the Romans, particularly because God had joined the Romans' side in response to the transgressions of the Jews.

This is especially evident in the speeches of Josephus himself and Eleazar in the later stages of the war. In *War* 5.378 Josephus attempts to persuade his comrades to surrender, warning them that they are "waging war not only against the Romans, but against God." In 5.401–3 Josephus inveighs against alleged sins of the Jews: thefts, treacheries, adulteries, plundering, and murder. How could the Jews expect that God would be their ally after this? (Cf. 5.411–14.) Perhaps the most forceful of all Josephus' statements is found in 6.110: "God, therefore, God Himself, is bringing a purifying fire along with the Romans and is plundering the city filled with such pollutions."

The speech of Eleazar, the leader of the Sicarii at Masada, also refers to God's disfavor with the Jews. "We should have recognized," Eleazar acknowledges, "that [God] had condemned the nation of the Jews once dear to Him" (7.328). "We have been de-

---

[65] As a final example of God punishing wicked individuals, one might consider *Ant.* 10.262 in which God uses deadly lions to destroy the impious enemies of Daniel.

prived, clearly by God Himself, of the hope of deliverance" (7.331). The Romans' successes in war and the Jews' setbacks are indications of "[God's] anger for many wrongdoings which in our folly we inflicted on our fellow Jews" (7.333). "It is by God's will and of necessity that we are going to die ... For it is not by the might of [the Romans] that these things have happened, but a greater cause having intervened has given to them the apparent victory" (7.359–60).

Throughout such speeches the presupposition of Jewish unfaithfulness is manifest. God has abandoned them and is, in fact, now in concert with the Romans. Although Josephus does not specifically use the language of παιδεία for God's action through the Romans, it is clear that he understands the destruction of Jerusalem as a divine response to the sin of its inhabitants. Their suffering at the hands of the Romans is punitive.

Philo uses the language of παιδεία/παιδεύω even more than Josephus. His writings are permeated by the concept.[66] The educative nuance of the words is pervasive; they rarely refer explicitly to chastisement.[67] Ideas typically associated with the words include "admonishment" (νουθεσία, νουθετέω),[68] "wisdom" (σοφία),[69] and "teaching" (διδασκαλία, διδάσκω).[70] As the etymology would suggest, the word is often associated with childhood. The phrase "from the earliest age" (ἐκ πρώτης ἡλικίας) is sometimes found with the verb.[71] The verb is sometimes part of a triad: "beget" (γεννάω), "raise" (τρέφω), and "educate" (παιδεύω).[72] Παιδεία is by no means limited to childhood, however; it encompasses "the general culture which transcends and gathers up specialized training and which consists in the moral establishment of character and the fulfillment of [human] nature as *humanitas.*"[73]

---

[66] Bertram, *TDNT*, V, 612.

[67] A punitive nuance is acquired from the context in *Migr.* 116 and *Post.* 97.

[68] *Post.* 68; *Immut.* 54; *Congr.* 172; *Spec.* 2.239; *Spec.* 4.96.

[69] *Fug.* 52, 137; *Som.* 2.71; *Spec.* 2.29; *Prob.* 107.

[70] *Spec.* 4.107; *Praem.* 162.

[71] *Praem.* 162; *Legat.* 210; *Spec.* 1.314.

[72] *Leg. Alleg.* 1.99; *Flac.* 158.

[73] Bertram, *TDNT*, V, 613. Philo calls ὀρθὸς λόγος (correct reason) and παιδεία (instruction) the father and mother, respectively, of virtuous persons; the father establishes laws and the mother institutes customs by which the virtuous live (*Ebr.* 80–1). Among the positive effects of παιδεία on a person's character are the promotion of virtue and the avoidance of passion and pleasure (*Leg. Alleg.* 2.90).

On the question of human suffering as divine discipline, Philo presents a mixed picture. Perhaps his most comprehensive discussion of punitive suffering is found, not surprisingly, in the work, *De Praemiis et Poenis* (*Rewards and Punishments*). In this writing Philo considers narrative portions of "the sacred oracles delivered by the prophet Moses" with special regard to the rewards proposed for virtuous persons and the punishments for the wicked (*Praem.* 3). The latter section seems to be incomplete, but an additional work appended to *De Praemiis*, known as *De Exsecrationibus*, provides much material similar in nature to the "punishments" section of the former.[74]

Cain serves as the first example of a wicked person. As the first fratricide, he was deserving of a severe and novel punishment. God laid a curse on Cain, condemning him to "an unending death," to "griefs, and pains, and incessant calamities" (*Praem.* 68–73). Cain's sufferings are thus divinely inflicted and directly related to his sins. *De Praemiis* proceeds to discuss Korah's rebellion (Num. 16.1–11), but an apparent lacuna breaks the text at section 78. I skip ahead to the relevant material in *De Exsecrationibus*.[75]

In sections 126–62 Philo offers an extensive list of disasters, hardships, and bodily ailments, all of which befall the wicked as a result of their impiety. The list includes: poverty (127); locust, worms, and blight (128–9); barren fields and drought (130–2); war and its concomitant, starvation (132–6); slavery and oppression (137–42); diseases of every imaginable sort (143–7); fear and paranoia (148); and attacks by wild beasts (149). The punitive nature and divine origin of these disasters is never in question. The list is introduced as "the curses appointed against the lawless and transgressors" (126). Destitution gives rise to many other evils, when it is a visitation of "heaven-sent vengeance" (θεήλατος ... δίκη, 136). Everything that the impious do will be vain and useless "in consequence of their evil pursuits and actions" (142). The purpose of all these calamities is to "chasten" the wicked (148); they are not aimed at their destruction, but rather at their "admonition," and "if they are shamed throughout their whole heart, and change their ways ... they will then find favor from their merciful saviour, God" (163). Here we see that

---

[74] On the structure and integrity of these essays, see Emil Schürer, *The History of the Jewish People in the Age of Jesus Christ* (rev. and ed. by G. Vermes, F. Millar and M. Goodman; Edinburgh: T. & T. Clark, 1987) III.2, 853–4.

[75] I follow the Loeb edition which numbers *De Exsecrationibus* continuously with *Praem.*

suffering that is unmistakably punitive in nature can be still educative in intent.

Punitive suffering is also evident in certain stories of divine judgment related in *Vita Mosis*. The impious who died in the Noachian flood (*Vita Mosis* 2.53–4) and in the destruction of Sodom and Gomorrah (2.55–6) "were chastised with ... punishments" (57). The interpretation is punitive, but given the shape of the original stories, it could hardly be otherwise. The same is true of God's treatment of the Egyptians just prior to the Exodus. The miraculous signs performed by Moses and Aaron did not persuade the Egyptians (*Vita Mosis* 1.90–5). They required a more severe threat, so the Lord sent "a flurry of plagues by which the foolish were admonished, whom reason had not chastened." The sins of the Egyptians were complete; hence, God inflicted the perfect number of plagues (ten) on them in punishment (1.96). In Philo's lengthy description of the plagues (1.96–146) two points are made repeatedly: their punitive nature and their corrective function.[76]

But non-punitive construals of suffering are also found in Philo. In *De Praemiis* 119, perhaps referring to Exodus 15.26, Philo understands Moses to promise that "complete freedom from disease will be given to those persons who cultivate virtue and who set up the sacred laws as guides of all their words and actions in life both private and public." Then, as if realizing the inadequacy of such a statement, he adds, "and if some infirmity should arise, it will not be for the sake of injuring them, but in order to remind mortals that they are mortal, so as to destroy overbearing pride and improve their disposition." Philo acknowledges that virtuous followers of the law may still suffer illnesses. Such persons are taught humility by their suffering. But guilt cannot be inferred here in view of the description of these persons in the context.[77]

Philo handles the wilderness episode and the strife that arose between Moses and the people somewhat differently from Josephus. As hunger, thirst, and uncertainty about the future oppressed the Hebrews (*Vita Mosis* 1.191–2), they began wistfully to remember the abundance of Egypt and they became indignant at Moses (1.193–7). God had pity and relieved their distress through a daily

---

[76] The plagues are referred to as κόλασις (1.102) and τιμωρία (1.106, 113, 130, 133, 143). The corrective function is expressed in 1.110, 134, 143.

[77] The educative effect of the suffering of the pious is not equivalent to that of the impious discussed in *Praem.* 163. The latter presupposes contrition and confession of sin.

provision of heavenly manna. The purpose of this divine benevolence is explicitly stated: ὅπως ... παιδευθῶσιν ἤδη μὴ δυσανασχετεῖν ... τλητικῶς δ᾽ ὑπομένειν (so that [the people] would be taught not to bear up grudgingly, but to endure steadfastly: 1.199). This educative image differs from the one seen in Josephus' reflection on the same story (*Ant.* 3.13–16) in two ways. First, linguistically the picture is of God "teaching" rather than "training" and "testing." More importantly, Philo seems to view *the provision of manna* as that which teaches, rather than the hunger and privation! In other words, Josephus viewed the people's *suffering* as potentially, though unsuccessfully, educative, whereas Philo viewed the *cessation* of their suffering as educative. But in both cases the divine aim was to instill "patience."

Patience in suffering plays a prominent role in another important text in Philo. A verse from the Pentateuch (Exod. 15.9) forms the basis of a rather detailed reflection on the nature of suffering in *De Cherubim* 77–82. It is the special attribute of God, says Philo, to act (τὸ ποιεῖν), whereas the special attribute of created beings is to be acted upon or to suffer (τὸ πάσχειν).[78] Whoever accepts this will bear even the most grievous calamities easily (78). Philo is not advocating passive submission to life's hardships, however. In the same paragraph he declares that one must be brave and fortify one's resolve "by means of one's patience and endurance (καρτερίᾳ καὶ ὑπομονῇ), the mightiest virtues." This statement is followed by two bipartite illustrations, the acts of being sheared and being beaten (τὸ κείρεσθαι ... τὸ τύπτεσθαι). A sheep, when sheared, is utterly passive.[79] But when a person's hair is cut, he or she cooperates with the barber, positioning the head and accommodating the "doer." In a similar fashion, when wrongdoers, slave or free, are beaten for their crimes, they suffer in subjection. But athletes, such as boxers and pancratists, block and dodge the blows of their opponents. In spite of the tension between the two analogies (one recommending cooperation with the "doer," the other, active opposition), the point is made clear in the final paragraph. Suffering is inevitable, but we must not acquiesce in it. Rather we should aim for "the contrary type of suffering" (τὸ ... ἀντιπεπονθός) exemplified by the boxer. Being strengthened by the forces of the mind, we must be strong

---

[78] Πάσχω here serves as the passive of ποιέω, "to be acted upon." See LSJ, 1347.
[79] A commonplace made famous by Isa. 53.7. Cf. Acts 8.32.

"so as to lighten the load of the misfortunes that threaten us" (82). Suffering is never explicitly attributed to divine agency in this text, but the opening antithesis of God as "actor" and human beings as "the ones acted upon" may imply this. Two additional brief observations: (1) Suffering is an opportunity for demonstrating (developing?) patience and endurance, and (2) an athletic metaphor lends itself quite naturally to Philo's argument.

Another important text is *De Congressu* 157–80. The theme of this lengthy section, which runs to the end of the work, is "affliction." Philo's thesis is that affliction is used by God for admonishment and discipline. Indeed, according to Philo, "affliction" is another name for admonishment (νουθεσία, 157). Thus when Genesis 16.6 says "[Sarah] afflicted her," Philo would have us understand, "[Sarah] admonished and chastened her" (158). The essay rambles on, picking up words and phrases from various Pentateuchal texts. A phrase from Exodus 15.25, "and there [God] tested him," prompts this remark: ἡ γὰρ ἄδηλος ἀπόπειρα καὶ δοκιμασία τῆς ψυχῆς ἐστιν ἐν τῷ πονεῖν καὶ πικραίνεσθαι (For the uncertain trial and testing of the soul lies in toil and bitter experiences: 164). The language of testing and proving then combines with athletic imagery. Those who fail the test are like weary athletes who consider toil a formidable wrestling partner and lose heart. But others face adversities bravely and "struggle on through the contest of life" (τὸν ἀγῶνα τοῦ βίου διήθλησαν, 165). Affliction, therefore, should be viewed as beneficial, not harmful. Τρέφεται γὰρ τοῖς παιδείας δόγμασιν ἡ νουθετουμένη ψυχή (For the soul that is admonished is nurtured by the lessons of discipline: 167).

Philo seems to assume throughout that God is the source of testing and discipline. When he comes to Deuteronomy 8.2, however, he is clearly uncomfortable with the attribution of famine to God. τίς οὖν οὕτως ἀνόσιός ἐστιν, ὡς ὑπολαβεῖν κακωτὴν τὸν θεὸν καὶ λιμὸν, οἴκτιστον ὄλεθρον, ἐπάγοντα ...; (Who is so impious as to suppose that God is an oppressor and one who inflicts famine, a most wretched destruction ...?: 171.) A quick resort to allegorical interpretation rescues the biblical text. When it says God "oppressed," we are to understand that God "disciplined, admonished, and chastened" (ἐπαίδευσε καὶ ἐνουθέτησε καὶ ἐσωφρόνισε, 172). Moreover, "famine" here does not refer to food, but to a dearth of the works of vices and passions. In view of Philo's punitive construal of the plagues, it is clear that he does not shrink from attributing certain calamities to God. But famine, which Philo deemed particularly severe, was apparently unworthy of God.[80]

As Philo approaches the end of *De Congressu*, he reaffirms his thesis that affliction is profitable (175). Like the author of Hebrews, he cites Proverbs 3.11–12. This passage highlights[81] the word παιδεία, which Philo has used twice already in the preceding pages. For Philo, the special significance of Proverbs 3.11–12 is the link between admonition and kinship with God.

The final proof of the benefit of affliction is found in Exodus 22.22. Philo's failure to understand the Hebrew idiom of the infinitive absolute in the expression, "if afflicting you afflict" (LXX ἐὰν δὲ κακίᾳ κακώσητε), prompts him to inquire, With what is one afflicted if *not* with evil?[82] He responds that the text surely means one may be "rebuked by virtue and disciplined by wisdom" (ὑπὸ ἀρετῆς ἐλεγχόμενον καὶ ὑπὸ φρονήσεως παιδευόμενον, 179). Therefore, he says, "I do not regard all affliction as blameworthy." In this terse, but crucial statement Philo implicitly acknowledges that *some* afflictions are blameworthy, but not all can be so construed. There is an "affliction of righteousness" that does not reprove error so much as test the mettle of one's soul. This kind of affliction is probative and formative, not punitive.

One Philonic text remains: *De Providentia*. The title of this work might suggest that it would be the most crucial witness for Philo's understanding of human suffering. But the usefulness of *De Providentia* is hampered by two factors. First, its manuscript tradition is scant, and, perhaps related to this, its accessibility for English readers is limited.[83] Second, more of the text is devoted to disputing

---

[80] *Vita Mosis* 1.110 states that God *would* have inflicted famine and pestilence on the Egyptians if God had wanted to destroy them. Since this is a contrary-to-fact condition, it does not necessarily contradict *De Congr.* 171. But *Ebr.* 79 refers to "famine or pestilence or any other evil *inflicted by God*." The key word is θεήλατος, "god-driven." It is hard not to see a contradiction between *Ebr.* 79 and *De Congr.* 171. See also *De Prov.* 41 and 53 where the same contradiction in a single writing of Philo's is irresolvable.

[81] The word order of Philo's citation thrusts παιδεία to first position from fourth where it occurs in the LXX. Philo's text does not, however, repeat the word in vs. 12 as most MSS do.

[82] On this common use of the infinitive absolute to strengthen the verbal idea, see *Gesenius' Hebrew Grammar* (E. Kautzsch and A. E. Cowley, eds.; Oxford: Clarendon, 1910) 342.

[83] The full text of *De Prov.* is extant only in Armenian. A Latin translation was made by J. B. Aucher, *Philonis Judaei Sermones tres hactenus inediti*, 1822. Two Greek fragments are preserved by Eusebius in *Praep. Evang.* 7.21 and 8.14. No

the alleged happiness of the wicked than to explaining the suffering of the righteous. There are, nevertheless, a few noteworthy passages, the discussion of which will complete this survey of Philo.

A punitive interpretation of suffering is given for certain instances involving egregious crimes such as temple robbery. Philo tells of three such robbers who perished in precisely the ways prescribed by law for their crimes. This, he says, was hardly coincidental. Rather, they "succumbed to the judgment of God" (34). What about the wicked who go unpunished? Philo acknowledges these, but insists that God's judgment in these matters is just and not to be questioned.

Divine discipline may be mediated or direct. Tyrants are sometimes used to purge wickedness. God, as the governor of the entire world, sets up tyrants as executioners to stem injustice and impiety (39). On other occasions God does not use such "underlings" to sweep away wickedness, but acts directly (41). Specifically, God may use famine, pestilence, or earthquakes, in which large numbers of people die, all "for the sake of the provision of virtue."

The latter is a remarkable statement. We have already seen that Philo equivocates about the ultimate source of famine and other calamities.[84] In this passage he unmistakably attributes them to the direct agency of God. But in *De Providentia* 53 Philo denies this: σεισμοὶ τε καὶ λοιμοί, καὶ κεραυνῶν βολαὶ, καὶ ὅσα τοιαῦτα, λέγεται μὲν εἶναι θεήλατα, πρὸς δ' ἀλήθειαν οὐκ ἔστι, Θεὸς γὰρ οὐδενὸς αἴτιος κακοῦ τὸ παράπαν. (Earthquakes and plagues, and thunderbolts, and other such things are said to be divinely sent, but, in truth, this is not the case; for God is the cause of no evil whatsoever.) In addition to the problem of the coherence of Philo's thought, there is the glaring ethical and theological question of how natural disasters, which destroy so indiscriminately, could be considered instances of divine activity, i.e. "acts of God." Philo, who wants to have it both ways, seems not to have resolved the problem. In any event, whether disasters are divinely caused or not, Philo says that the death of the innocent thereby can serve to chasten others from afar (55).

To conclude this survey of Josephus and Philo: Certain instances of suffering recounted in the OT suggest, if not demand, either a

English translation of the Armenian or the Latin is available. I use the Loeb edition of the Greek fragments and English translation (Philo, vol. IX). For fuller bibliography and a brief description of the work, see Schürer, *History of the Jewish People*, III.2, 864–5.

[84] See n. 80 above.

formative/probative or a punitive interpretation. It is not surprising, then, that both Josephus and Philo construe the hardships suffered by Israel in the wilderness formatively and the plagues inflicted on Egypt punitively. In addition, Josephus saw the Jewish war as an outstanding instance of divine chastisement of the folly of his own people. Josephus' personal involvement in this conflict undoubtedly colored his perspective, but there are numerous precedents of similar interpretations of foreign invasions in the prophets and Maccabean literature. Philo, on the other hand, reflected philosophically about the purpose of human suffering. His "view," unsystematic as it is, can only be called a hybrid, having elements of both punitive and non-punitive interpretations of suffering. On the one hand, tyranny, natural disasters, and seemingly chance accidents may represent divine judgment; on the other hand, hardships, calamities, and toil can serve as testing, instruction, and admonition, all of which promote virtue and endurance.

3.2.7   The crucible of affliction – the literature of Qumran

The scrolls from the Qumran settlement make up a substantial body of literature, diverse in genre, sometimes technical and esoteric in nature, and partially fragmentary in form. These obstacles have not restrained, and in some ways may have contributed to, the continuing flood of research on Qumran.[85] A survey of Jewish perspectives on human suffering and divine discipline would be incomplete without at least some reference to this unique corpus.[86] Though I have no expertise in this area and must, therefore, rely on the specialists, there are a few useful studies that will serve as guides to the material.[87]

A study by Jean Carmignac, "La Théologie de la souffrance dans

---

[85] Jerome Murphy-O'Connor, writing in the mid-80s, estimates the number of contributions at seven thousand. See "The Judean Desert," in *EJMI*, 119–56.

[86] J. A. Sanders' study (*Suffering as Divine Discipline*) can be excused for omitting the Dead Sea Scrolls because of its date (1955). He refers to the Manual of Discipline as a "newly found document" (75).

[87] The two most valuable studies are: Jean Carmignac, "La Théologie de la souffrance dans les Hymnes de Qumran," *Revue de Qumran*, 3 (1961–2) 365–86; and Barbara Thiering, "Suffering and Asceticism at Qumran as Illustrated in the Hodayot," *Revue de Qumran*, 31 (March 1974) 393–405. See also A. R. C. Leaney, "The Eschatological Significance of Human Suffering in the Old Testament and the Dead Sea Scrolls," *Scottish Journal of Theology*, 16 (1963) 286–96; E. P. Sanders, *Paul and Palestinian Judaism*, 286–7; and Logan, "Background," 106–9.

les Hymnes de Qumran," lays out the relevant material under two headings, "Suffering of the Impious" and "Suffering of the Just," and then discusses the causes and aims of each category of suffering respectively.[88] The collected material is impressive (twenty citations in the first category, twenty-two in the second), but on closer examination some of these texts fail to contribute to a theology of suffering in the way one would hope.

The majority of the texts cited under the heading "Suffering of the Impious" refer to eschatological suffering, namely the final destruction of the wicked by God. The following are typical.[89]

> But Thou, O God, Thou wilt answer them to execute judgment upon them through Thy might, [according] to their (abominable) idols and according to their manifold transgression ... (4.18–19).

> For then the sword of God shall hasten the period of judgment, and all His t[r]ue children shall be roused to destroy the sons of wickedness; and all the sons of guilt shall no longer be (6.29–30).

> And all iniquity [and wi]ckedness Thou shalt exterminate forever (14.16).

> And Thou didst create the wicked into [the periods of] Thy [wra]th and from (the) womb Thou didst set them apart for the day of slaughter. ... [Through the mystery of] Thy [understanding] Thou didst establish them, to wreak great judgments upon them ... (15.17, 19).

This is suffering of the terminal variety; hence, it does not compare with the instances examined throughout this chapter. There is no thought of correction, education, or reproof; the "function" is extermination. Granted, one might still categorize the theology of such texts as "punitive suffering,"[90] but the special nature of this

---

[88] See previous note.

[89] Translations of the Hymns are from Menahem Mansoor, *The Thanksgiving Hymns, Translated and Annotated with an Introduction* (Grand Rapids: Eerdmans, 1961). Mansoor uses square brackets for suggested restorations of letters or words; parentheses are used for words added to the English translation for stylistic purposes only (95–6).

[90] So Carmignac ("Théologie," 368–9) writes, "the *Hymns* see in the suffering of the impious the consequence and the punishment of their crimes."

suffering makes it properly a matter of eschatology rather than divine providence.

Of the texts which Carmignac adduces under "Suffering of the Impious," only two may pertain to this-worldly suffering, and even their force is uncertain.

> In Thy wrath are all judgments of affliction, but in Thy goodness there is abundance of forgiveness, and Thy mercies are on all Thy favored sons (11.8–9).

> And [Thou who art] great [in merc]y, who pardonest them that repent (their) transgression; and who visitest the iniquity of the wicked ... (14.23–5).

Both of these texts contrast divine goodness and mercy with divine judgment of the wicked. There are no contextual clues in either case that require an eschatological interpretation. The question remains whether those who are recipients of "judgments of affliction" or divine visitations have the opportunity to repent and receive any benefit from their chastisement. The juxtaposition of judgment and pardon may imply this, but it is equally possible that the texts express a rigid dualism of the wicked versus God's favored ones, a dualism that admits little or no redemption.[91]

The texts Carmignac adduces under "Suffering of the Just" provide more fertile ground for generating something like a theology of suffering in the Hymns, though here too the ambiguities abound. The following are the most pertinent texts.

> (1) For Thou, in Thy mercies and Thy great lovingkindness didst strengthen the spirit of man in the face of affliction[s] ... [And Thou didst] clean[se him] from the multitude of his iniquity so that he may recount Thy wonders in the presence of all Thy handiworks ... the judgments of my afflictions ... (1.31–3).

> (2) But I, trembling and shivering have seized me and all my bones are broken and my heart hath melted as wax before the fire. And my knees drip as waters that are poured down a slope, for I have remembered my guilts together with the treachery of my fathers, when wicked men rose

---

[91] On the lack of any hope of conversion of the impious in the Hymns, see *ibid.*, 373–4: "For the 'impious' ... no hope of conversion, of pardon, of salvation is ever envisioned, neither in the present nor in the future."

against Thy covenant and tyrants (rose) against Thy [w]ord. Then I said in my transgression: I have been abandoned by Thy covenant. But whenever I remember the might of Thy hand with the overflowing of Thy compassion, I am fortified; yea, I rise, and my spirit hath held firmly (its) position in the face of a blow, for [I] lean on Thy lovingkindness and the overflowing of Thy compassion. For Thou atonest a sin, and cl[eansest ma]n from guilt through righteousness (4.33–7).

(3) Thou hast wrought marvels with a poor (soul) and Thou hast put him into a crucible [for refining as go]ld by the work of fire and as silver refined in the furnace of the smelters to cleanse (him) sevenfold (5.15–16).

(4) And I, (though I go) from ruin to desolation, from pain to blows; yea, from pangs to throes, yet, my soul speaketh of Thy wondrous works. And Thou hast not rejected me, through Thy lovingkindness. ... Thy judgment I shall vindicate, for I know of Thy truth and (therefore) I shall choose (Thy) judgment upon me. And my afflictions I willingly accept, for I have waited for Thy lovingkindness and Thou hast set a supplication in the mouth of Thy servant and hast not rebuked my life nor hast Thou spurned my well-being (9.6–7, 9–11).

(5) And Thou, my God, ... Thou pleadest my cause for Thou reproveth me through the mystery of Thy wisdom. And Thou hast concealed the truth until [its appointed time] ... [unto] its appointed season and Thy rebuke of me hath turned into gladness and joy. And my wounds (were turned) unto per[petual] healing [and unto] eternal [times] and the crown of mine adversaries [was turned] unto a crown of glory and my failure unto an everlasting might (9.24–6).

(6) I have come to understand that whomsoever Thou choosest ... [Thou prolon]gest [Thy lovingkindness] to him so that he sinneth not to Thee and to [recompen]se him for his affliction through Thy chastisements ... (17.21–2).

The first text affirms God's fortifying of the sufferer amid afflictions and juxtaposes this thought with God's cleansing of the person from manifold sins. Does the conjunction of these two ideas suggest a causal relationship between affliction and purification from sin? It is difficult to say, especially since lacunae occur at two key points in the text. What is certain is that the writer associates affliction and sin; and it is implied that cleansing from sin brings deliverance, or at least relief, from affliction. The final phrase, "the judgments of my afflictions," strongly suggests that the suffering of the writer results from divine displeasure.[92]

The second text begins with a vivid description of physical affliction resulting from the remembrance of sin. But the knowledge of God's compassion and lovingkindness reassures and strengthens the sufferer, leading to a renewal. Atonement and purification from sin are involved in this renewal. Here the logical relationships are more explicit: consciousness of sin leads to affliction; pardon leads to renewal. There is no explicit statement, however, that God is the source of the affliction.

The third citation contains the smelting image found in several texts of the Hebrew Bible and Apocrypha. The use of this imagery in the Hymns should occasion no surprise since they consciously imitate the canonical Psalms, and the smelting image occurs there (Ps. 17.3; 26.1–3; 66.8–12; 105.19). "Crucible" occurs only once in the Hebrew Bible (Prov. 17.3), but is frequent in the scrolls as "a symbol for the testing of the Sons of Light in the 'epoch of Belial.' "[93] The result of this refining is cleansing.

The fourth text depicts the author in deep affliction yet still conscious of God's wonders and compassion. Rather enigmatic is the statement, "I shall choose Thy judgment upon me. And my afflictions I willingly accept." Again, the author associates the judgment of God with affliction, and it is moreover implied that God's judgment is just.

In the fifth citation the author has been reproved by the wisdom of God. But in a four-fold affirmation of reversal, the author proclaims that this rebuke has had a quite positive outcome: "glad-

---

[92] Geza Vermes (*The Dead Sea Scrolls in English* [3rd edn.; London: Penguin, 1987], 168) translates, "the judgments by which I was scourged." Mansoor, *Thanksgiving Hymns*, 103 n. 10, observes that "judgments of afflictions" is a common expression in the Hymns and cites 11.8 and fragment 3.16.

[93] Yigael Yadin, *The Scroll of the War of the Sons of Light against the Sons of Darkness* (London: Oxford University, 1962) 339. See the references Yadin gives on p. 221 n. 4.

ness," "joy," "healing," "a crown of glory," "everlasting might." These words describe the salutary and unexpected result of God's rebuke (discipline?).

The last passage may also allude to a sort of reversal, for it speaks of the recompense of God's elect person. Divine lovingkindness is designed to recompense the elect for "affliction through Thy chastisements." Here is perhaps the clearest connection yet between affliction and divine discipline. The precise nature and purpose of the affliction is not specified, but its means is chastisement by God. Does the moral improvement implied in the clause "that he sinneth not to Thee" result from the chastisement, the lovingkindness that follows it, or both? As is often the case, the terseness and obscurity of the text do not permit a certain answer.

These are the most relevant texts in the Hymns for this study.[94] A few passages in other Qumran documents deserve brief mention. In the Manual of Discipline (8.2–4) the following instructions are given to the Council of the Community: "They shall preserve the faith in the Land with steadfastness and meekness and shall atone for sin by the practice of justice *and by suffering the sorrows of affliction.*"[95] Perfect obedience to the law, combined with suffering, was thought to procure pardon for Israel (or the community). In this text, then, suffering has an expiatory function.[96]

One final text is found in The Words of the Heavenly Lights (4Q 504) 3. Its explicit references to suffering and divine chastisement make it worth quoting at length.[97]

> Behold, all the nations are as nothing beside Thee, they are counted as void and nought before Thee. We have called on

---

[94] I have not discussed the elaborate image of the woman in childbirth (3.7–12) although this text surely symbolizes a person (or community) in travail. The nature of any real suffering behind the text is shrouded by the imagery. There is also disagreement about the meaning of the woman's male child. See Mansoor, *Thanksgiving Hymns*, 112 n. 6, 113–14, and Thiering, "Suffering and Asceticism," 402–4.

[95] Translation is that of Vermes, *Dead Sea Scrolls*, 72 (emphasis mine).

[96] On this text, see A. R. C. Leaney, *The Rule of Qumran and its Meaning* (London: SCM Press, 1966) 213–14. On the expiatory function of suffering, Thiering, "Suffering and Asceticism," 404, also cites 4Q 183 fragment 1, col. II, line 7: "They expiated their iniquity by their afflictions." For a different evaluation of the evidence, see Carmignac, "Théologie," 382–5, who downplays the significance of Manual of Discipline 8.2–4.

[97] Vermes, *Dead Sea Scrolls*, 217–18.

Thy Name alone. Thou hast created us for Thy glory and
made us Thy children in the sight of all the nations. For
Thou hast named Israel "My son, my first born," and hast
chastised us as a man chastises his son. Thou hast brought
us up throughout the years of our generations [by means
of] evil diseases, famine, thirst, pestilence, and the sword
... of Thy Covenant. Because Thou hast chosen us [from
all] the earth [to be Thy people,] therefore hast Thou
poured out Thine anger [and jealousy] upon us in all the
fury of Thy wrath. Thou hast caused [the scourge] of Thy
[plagues] to cleave to us of which Moses wrote, and Thy
servants the Prophets, that Thou wouldst send evil against
us in the last days.

Several features of this text are noteworthy. The unifying theme is
not so much the suffering of the community as its election by God.
Election is expressed in terms of a parent/child relationship, and the
evidence for that parental relationship is the community's suffering
perceived as God's chastisement: "Thou ... hast chastised us as a
man chastises his son."[98] The specific means of God's chastisement
are enumerated: evil diseases, famine, thirst, pestilence, and the
sword. The writer sees these adversities not only as having a divine
origin, but as directly related to the community's election: "Thou
hast chosen us ... *therefore* hast Thou poured out Thine anger."[99]
In relation to Hebrews 12.4–11 and other texts we have examined,
we might note that whereas the image of fatherly discipline is common, it is more often combined with an emphasis on divine benevolence than on wrath. For the author of Hebrews and Proverbs
3.11–12, God disciplines out of love; for this Qumranian author,
God disciplines out of anger.

How, then, should we assess the contribution of Qumran to the
range of Jewish views of human suffering? Any conclusions must
be prefaced with a frank admission of the difficulties of the material.
The writings of Qumran pose greater interpretive problems than
perhaps any other group of texts included in this study. The state of
the manuscripts is the first difficulty, a particularly acute one in the

---

[98] The text, borrowing loosely from Deut. 8.5, twice employs the root *ysr*. See
Maurice Baillet, *Discoveries in the Judaean Desert* (Oxford: Clarendon, 1982) VII,
141–3.

[99] My emphasis. For the Hebrew text, see *ibid.*, 141.

case of the Hymns.[100] A closely related problem is the difficulty of interpretation. In addition to a poorly preserved text, the interpreter must reckon with "the cliché-ridden language, the tortuous and barely grammatical sentences, [and] the incessant filching of Scriptural 'tags.'"[101] Lastly, there are the historical difficulties of determining the subject(s) and nature of the suffering. Do the Hymns describe the afflictions of the author or the community? Can any specific historical references be gleaned from the Hymns?[102]

Having made these disclaimers, I think it is still possible to make some general observations about a Qumranian theology of suffering, at least as it is represented in the Hymns. Like many Jewish writings, the Qumran hymns often associate affliction and sin. In a small number of texts this relationship was explicitly causal. Affliction was sometimes symbolized by a "crucible" and the image of smelting. God was portrayed as chastising persons, but the outcome of divine chastisement was joy and healing. In one text a parent/ child image was employed and various natural and human calamities were seen as the means of divine chastisement. A lesser theme, not evident in the Hymns but found elsewhere, was the expiatory function of suffering to atone for sins.

In general, then, the Qumran scrolls offer several instances of the punitive view of suffering seen in most other strands of Jewish literature. Whether the scrolls give evidence of non-punitive interpretations of suffering is more difficult to determine. The above excerpt from The Words of the Heavenly Lights grounds the discipline of the community in divine election. It is not clear that this discipline, as severe as its forms are (diseases, famine, thirst, pestilence, violence), necessarily entails punishment for sin. This text may possibly belong in the non-punitive category. In any event, one can hardly draw conclusions about the full range of views from so small a sample of texts drawn mostly from the Hymns. Suffice to say that the "orthodox" view seems well represented at Qumran. To what extent it was also the dominant view, I leave to future studies by specialists in that field.

---

[100] Vermes, *Dead Sea Scrolls*, 165, speaks of "a good deal of deterioration," a problem that complicates even the division of the Hymns from one another.

[101] T. H. Gaster, *The Dead Sea Scriptures* (New York, 1956) 8, cited in Mansoor, *Thanksgiving Hymns 94*, n. 6.

[102] On such questions, see Thiering, "Suffering and Asceticism," 393–4.

3.2.8   "Suffering without sin?" – rabbinic literature

The last body of writings to be considered is rabbinic literature. This corpus is daunting because of its sheer magnitude. The following treatment makes no pretense of being comprehensive. I will simply highlight several of the more noteworthy texts to which other researchers have drawn attention.[103]

An ever-present concern for students of rabbinical literature is the possibility of anachronism. As one expert observes, "Evidence for rabbinic Judaism is derived from collections that date from 200 CE and later. Stories, anecdotes, halakic and historical statements may also be suspected of anachronism or distortion by later experience and have become increasingly uncertain as sources for the reconstruction of *early* rabbinic Judaism."[104] The relevance of these documents to NT interpretation is likewise uncertain. Nevertheless, since the present study is not concerned with literary dependence, and, as a comparative, theological project, need not draw rigid chronological boundaries, a brief examination of some rabbinic texts is in order.

The earliest rabbinical document, i.e. the Mishnah, "overwhelmingly neglects the imperfections of history, preferring to picture a world controlled and stabilized by Torah."[105] Therefore, suffering is regarded not as a problem to be explained, but as evidence of divine justice meted out to deserving sinners. Although the world-to-come will assure that *perfect* justice is achieved, much of God's punishment is imparted in the present age. All manner of evil,

---

[103] The most thorough study is David Kraemer, *Responses to Suffering*. See also Solomon Schechter, "The Doctrine of Divine Retribution in Rabbinical Literature," *Studies in Judaism* (1st Series; Philadelphia: Jewish Publication Society of America, 1896) 213–55; George F. Moore, *Judaism in the First Centuries of the Christian Era* (Cambridge, MA: Harvard University, 1927) II, 248–56; Wichmann, *Leidenstheologie*; A. Büchler, *Studies in Sin and Atonement in the Rabbinic Literature of the First Century* (New York: Ktav, 1939) 119–211, 327–74; and Yaakov Elman, "The Suffering of the Righteous in Palestinian and Babylonian Sources," *Jewish Quarterly Review*, 80, no. 3–4 (January–April 1990) 315–39.

[104] Anthony J. Saldarini, "Reconstructions of Rabbinic Judaism," in *EJMI*, 438; Saldarini's emphasis. Cf. the statement by Herbert Danby, *The Mishnah* (New York: Oxford University, 1933) XIV, "It is a matter of extreme difficulty to decide what historical value we should attach to any tradition recorded in the Mishnah."

[105] Kraemer, *Responses to Suffering*, 211.

from natural calamities to social turmoil, was attributed to human transgressions, sometimes with very specific linkage. One Mishnaic passage is worth quoting at length.[106]

> Seven kinds of retribution come upon the world for seven classes of transgression. If some give tithe and some do not give tithe, there comes famine from drought: some suffer hunger while some have enough. If [all] resolved that they would not give tithe there comes famine from tumult and drought. And if they will not set apart Dough-offering there comes an all-consuming famine. Pestilence comes upon the world because of crimes deserving of the death penalties enjoined in the Law that are not brought before the court; and because of [the transgressions of the laws of] the Seventh Year produce. The sword comes upon the world because of the delaying of justice and the perverting of justice; and because of them that teach the Law not according to the *Halakah*. Noisome beasts come upon the world because of false swearing and the profaning of the Name. Exile comes upon the world because of idolatry and incest and the shedding of blood; and because of [neglect of the year of] the Release of the land.

Elsewhere in the Mishnah the death of women in childbirth was attributed to three causes: heedlessness of menstrual laws, neglect of the Dough-offering, and violations pertaining to the lighting of the Sabbath lamp.[107]

The Jerusalem Talmud continues the Mishnaic tradition of construing suffering as punishment for sin. "[I]t adds almost nothing of substance to earlier approaches to this subject. The most notable development in its relevant traditions is its condemnation of those who respond to suffering with contempt."[108] This commitment to tradition is especially evident in the Yerushalmi's reflections on the destruction of the Jerusalem temples, both by Babylon and Rome.

---

[106] *m.* 'Abot 5.8–9; translation from Danby, *The Mishnah*, 456–7. Strictly speaking, Tractate 'Abot is post-Mishnaic. See Kraemer's remarks on this passage and others (*Responses to Suffering*, 53–65).

[107] *m.* Šabb. 2.6; Danby, *The Mishnah*, 102.

[108] Kraemer, *Responses to Suffering*, 104.

The following excerpt shows differing opinions about specifics, but agreement on the punitive interpretation.

> [T]he first Temple was destroyed only [on account of the fact] that they worshiped idols and engaged in prohibited sexual relations and shed blood. And the same is true with the second [Temple]. R. Yohanan b. Torta said: ... We find that the first Temple was destroyed only because they worshiped idols and engaged in prohibited sexual relations and shed blood. But in the second, we know that they toiled in Torah and were careful in [performing] the commandments and in tithing, and they had every good manner, [so, if they were so good, why was their Temple destroyed?] but they loved money and hated one another for no good reason ...[109]

The same interpretation obtained in instances of individual suffering. The result was an "almost exclusive insistence that suffering is punishment for sin."[110]

In the Babylonian Talmud, the attribution of specific calamities to specific sins was continued with a lively mix of opinions among the rabbis. Certain authorities saw the death of a wife or child as punishment for unfulfilled vows; others blamed it on the neglect of Torah study. Drought and economic hardship were blamed on failure to pay tithes; locusts and famine resulted from robbery.[111] Specific historical events may lie behind such statements as "Through the crime of bloodshed the Temple was destroyed and the Shechinah departed from Israel," and "As a punishment for incest, idolatry and non-observance of the years of release and jubilee exile comes to the world, they [the Jews] are exiled, and others come and dwell in their place."[112] The sum of the matter is tersely expressed in a

---

[109] *y.* Yoma 38c (translation from *ibid.*, 105–6).

[110] *Ibid.*, 113. Kraemer discusses "The Hint of Alternatives" in which a few texts imply that the suffering of the righteous is protective or expiatory for other persons (108–9).

[111] *b.* Šabb. 32b; I. Epstein, ed., *Hebrew–English Edition of the Babylonian Talmud* (London: Soncino, 1960–   ).

[112] *b.* Šabb. 33a (*ibid.*). On an anecdotal level, when 400 jars of Rabbi Huna's wine turned sour, the cause was found in the Rabbi's unlawful management of his vineyard (*b.* Ber. 5b).

statement attributed to Rabbi Ammi: "There is no death without sin, and there is no suffering without iniquity."[113]

But the distribution of suffering in the world remained problematic. If suffering is tied to sin, why do the righteous appear to suffer more than the wicked? Rabbi Akiba answered this dilemma by an appeal to eschatology: "[God] deals strictly with the righteous, calling them to account for the few wrongs which they commit in this world, in order to lavish bliss upon and give them a goodly reward in the world to come; [God] grants ease to the wicked and rewards them for the few good deeds which they have performed in this world in order to punish them in the future world."[114] Thus when Rabbi Eliezer fell sick, one of his students, Rabbi Akiba, was able to rejoice, knowing that a great reward lay in store for him in the next world.[115]

Suffering was not solely punitive, with no thought of positive benefit to the sufferer. Adversity led one to repentance, and in this way was also expiatory. When he suffered a foreign invasion and exile, Manasseh, the son of king Hezekiah, was humbled and brought to repentance.[116] Since suffering serves this purpose, a person should welcome it: "A man should even rejoice when in adversity more than when in prosperity. For even if a man lives in prosperity all his life, it does not mean that his sins have been forgiven him. But what is it that does bring a man forgiveness? You must say, suffering."[117] Suffering, interpreted as divine chastisement, was able to atone for sins just as sacrifice was, and even more: "For just as sacrifices are the means of atonement, so also are chastisements. ... And not only this, but chastisements atone even more than sacrifices. For sacrifices affect only one's money, while chastisements affect the body."[118]

Because of the positive benefits of divine discipline, the refrain was

---

[113] b. Šabb. 55a (*ibid.*). The necessity of a connection between sin and suffering is seen in the suggestion that the executions of Rabbi Simon and Rabbi Ishmael were due to the slightest negligence in their religious service. See Jacob Z. Lauterbach, ed., *Mekilta De-Rabbi Ishmael* (Philadelphia: Jewish Publication Society of America, 1933) Nezikin 18; III, 141.

[114] Genesis Rabbah 33.1; H. Freedman and Maurice Simon, eds., *Midrash Rabbah* (London: Soncino, 1939) I, 257.

[115] *b.* Sanh. 101a. See E. P. Sanders, "Rabbi Akiba's View of Suffering," *Jewish Quarterly Review*, 63 (1972–3) 332–51.

[116] Lauterbach, ed., *Mekilta De-Rabbi Ishmael*, Bahodesh 10; II, 281–2. See also *b.* Sanh. 101a.

[117] Lauterbach, ed., *Mekilta De-Rabbi Ishmael*, Bahodesh 10; II, 278.

[118] *Ibid.*, 280.

often heard among the rabbis: "Precious are chastisements." They are precious because the name of the Omnipresent One rests upon the one who suffers them. They are precious because through them God gave Israel the gifts of the Torah, the Land, and the world-to-come. They are precious because they effect atonement. They are precious because they avail, as in Manasseh's case, where instruction and toil do not.[119]

The punitive interpretation of suffering was clearly the "orthodox" view among the rabbis, but there is evidence of counter-opinions.[120] Human experience forced some persons to doubt so rigid a connection between suffering and sin. The saying of Rabbi Ammi cited above, "There is no death without sin, and there is no suffering without iniquity," was included in the Babylonian Talmud but so was its refutation. The deaths of Moses, Aaron and a few other persons were thought to be unrelated to transgressions. The Bavli thus reasons that "there is death without sin and there is suffering without iniquity. Thus the refutation of R. Ammi is [indeed] a refutation."[121]

A new category, "chastisements of love," was devised to account for those rare occurrences of suffering in which self-examination discovered no underlying sin or negligence. The following saying, attributed by some to Rabbi Hisda, explains this idea.

> If a man sees that painful sufferings visit him, let him examine his conduct. For it is said: *Let us search and try our ways, and return unto the Lord*. If he examines and finds nothing [objectionable], let him attribute it to the neglect of the study of the Torah. For it is said: *Happy is the man whom Thou chastenest, O Lord, and teachest out of Thy law*. If he did attribute it [thus], and still did not find [this to be the cause], let him be sure that these are chastenings of love. For it is said: *For whom the Lord loveth He correcteth*.[122]

---

[119] Reuven Hammer, *Sifre: A Tannaitic Commentary on the Book of Deuteronomy* (New Haven and London: Yale University, 1986) 60–2 (Piska 32). See also Lauterbach, ed., *Mekilta De-Rabbi Ishmael*, Bahodesh 10; II, 279–82. On the atoning power of suffering, see E. P. Sanders, *Paul and Palestinian Judaism*, 168–72.

[120] Kraemer devotes a chapter to "the rebellious side of the Bavli" (*Responses to Suffering*, 184–210). He highlights the three texts from the Babylonian Talmud that I consider here: Shabbat 55a–b, Berakhot 5a–b, and Hagiga 4b–5a. These texts articulate innovative interpretations of suffering.

[121] *b.* Šabb. 55b.

[122] *b.* Ber. 5a.

A "chastisement of love," then, is an infliction of divine punishment that is not merited by sin, but simply is evidence of "God's peculiar love."[123]

A third text from the Babylonian Talmud deals with the specific problem of premature death. In a curious anecdote, a conversation between the Angel of Death and his messenger is witnessed by Rabbi Bibi ben Abbaye.[124] The messenger is instructed to bring Miriam the Hairdresser. He errs and returns with Miriam the children's nurse. The Angel of Death asks, "How were you able to get her [since it was not yet her time to die]?" The messenger explains that Miriam the children's nurse had accidentally burned herself, and this misfortune provided an opening for her to be brought to the realm of the dead. Rabbi Bibi asks, "Have ye permission to act thus?" The Angel of Death, alluding to Proverbs 13.23, argues that there are those who are swept away without justice. He goes on to explain that the years that were rightly due to Miriam or anyone else who dies prematurely will be added to the life of some deserving rabbi.

Beneath the droll details of this fanciful conversation is the remarkable and radical viewpoint that a person does not always reach his or her appointed end in life. "There can be premature death. God's justice is not necessarily done."[125] Given the uniformly punitive interpretations of suffering in the Mishnah and Jerusalem Talmud, such texts as the tale of two Miriams, Rabbi Hisda's notion of "chastisements of love," and the refutation of Rabbi Ammi's maxim, constitute daring innovations. In this way the canon of rabbinic Judaism, especially the Bavli, legitimizes novel responses to suffering and acknowledges that not all suffering can be traced to transgressions.[126]

3.2.9 Summary of Jewish perspectives

Before I proceed to Greco-Roman texts, a summary of the Jewish literature is in order. A chart found at the end of this chapter

---

[123] George F. Moore, *Judaism in the First Centuries of the Christian Era* (Cambridge, MA: Harvard University, 1927) II, 256.

[124] *b*. Hagiga 4b–5a.

[125] Kraemer, *Responses to Suffering*, 203.

[126] *Ibid.*, final chapter, especially pp. 213–14. Yet it remains the case that "in all forms *of Palestinian Judaism* ... suffering was almost always connected with the conception of God's justice: suffering is punishment for sin": E. P. Sanders, "Rabbi Akiba's View of Suffering," 333 (my emphasis).

(section 3.5) categorizes most of the texts cited here. I have entitled
the two broad categories "punitive" and "non-punitive." I use the
latter instead of "formative" or "educative" since it is inclusive of all
those views that deny, or at least do not seem to presuppose, a
causal connection between sin and suffering. Texts that view suffering as instruction in virtue, rigorous training, or fiery testing, as well
as those that simply protest the assumed connection of suffering and
sin, are all included in the non-punitive category. In a few cases the
assignment of a passage might be debated, but most categorizations
are self-evident. Passages within each category are gathered together
according to their genre or corpus. At the bottom of the chart a few
sub-categories are shown.

The chart reveals a number of things. Most importantly for this
study, it shows that non-punitive interpretations of suffering, though
not as common as the "orthodox" view, were by no means rare.
They are found in a variety of genres and authors: wisdom literature, the Psalms, the Pentateuch, 4 Maccabees, Josephus, Philo, and
the Babylonian Talmud. The hardships that were interpreted in this
way included the physical sufferings of the Israelites in the wilderness (Josephus, Philo), historical events such as the atrocities and
persecution of the Maccabean era (4 Macc.), fictive accounts of a
righteous person's afflictions (Job), the premature death of a person
(Babylonian Talmud), or, as a general principle, the afflictions that
serve to test the pious (Wisdom of Solomon, Sirach). A variety of
images is employed: a refining fire, a father's care, instruction in
virtue, athletic exercise, chastisements of love, or sheer protest
against the prevailing punitive view. Of special importance for this
study were the clearly educative interpretations of suffering such as
that found in 4 Maccabees. Thus, it is apparent that in Jewish literature, non-punitive construals of suffering were widely employed
and diverse.

Suffering as punishment for wrongdoing was the "orthodox" position. Prophetic literature seems to have operated exclusively in the
punitive mode. The assumption of the prophets was expressed by
Amos: "Does disaster befall a city, unless the Lord has done it?"[127]
The rigorous monotheism of the prophets traced all human fortunes

---

[127] Amos 3.6b. It has been argued, however, that neither this passage nor similar
ones prove that the notion of divine "pancausality" of misfortune was a widely
held dogma. In other words, Amos may be arguing the case to an audience un-
convinced of the connection rather than presupposing that they shared his view.

to one divine source. Thus, "every experience of suffering was ascribed to the direct will of Yahweh, and interpreted by the simple and obvious principle of moral retribution."[128] Wisdom literature and psalms, especially the Psalms of Solomon, also contained punitive construals of suffering, although both of these genres also offered examples of the non-punitive view. The Maccabean literature (apart from 4 Macc.) provides perhaps the most striking instances of suffering interpreted as punishment. What makes 2 and 3 Maccabees so remarkable (and portions of Josephus and Psalms of Solomon might be included here) is that military catastrophes that clearly have human origins and are acts of aggression by foreign powers, nevertheless, are explained, at least in part, as due to sin on the part of Israel. This dogged persistence in viewing all human events as expressive of divine retribution was found frequently, though not uniformly, in the foregoing survey. Finally, the punitive view was well represented in the writings of Qumran and the Rabbis, although the latter showed traces of independence in its later stages.

The variety of Jewish explanations of suffering (punitive, formative, probative, expiatory, vicarious, etc.) is in part due to the complexity of ancient Judaism. Some communities were committed to a rigorous view of divine sovereignty and justice according to which all events were understood as (at least indirectly) the will of God. (The Book of Job qualifies this notion slightly by the introduction of Satan in its opening narrative. Although Satan can act only with God's permission, the effect of his presence in the narrative is to distance God from the direct, intentional causation of Job's calamities.) Other writings in the above survey were influenced by forces outside traditional Judaism (e.g. Stoic influence in 4 Macc.) as well as by the common observation that suffering is not proportional to transgressions. Of even greater importance, however, is the complexity of suffering itself, which does not lend itself to any single explanation. Philo and Josephus are examples of individual authors who moved freely back and forth between punitive and non-punitive interpretations as their religious convictions or the historical circumstances of the incidents dictated. Instances of suffering that did not seem capable of divine causation (e.g. famine or the suffering of the

---

Even if this is true, it remains the case that punitive suffering is the *prophet's* perspective. See Fredrik Lindström, *God and the Origin of Evil. A Contextual Analysis of Alleged Monistic Evidence in the Old Testament* (Lund: Gleerup, 1983) 199–214.

[128] Robinson, *Religious Ideas*, 170.

pious) were usually otherwise explained by Philo and Josephus. On the other hand, they could quickly resort to a punitive interpretation when the circumstances (such as the apparent guilt of the afflicted) made this view plausible.

I now return to the first half of Talbert's thesis, namely, that the Jewish view of suffering *usually* assumes that the sufferer has strayed from the right path.[129] The survey done in this chapter indicates that, for this thesis to be upheld, a liberal qualification must be seen in the word *"usually."* The thesis can be affirmed of prophetic literature, and with minor qualifications, of rabbinic literature. But texts from several bodies of Jewish literature reveal ways of understanding suffering that make no such assumption. When Talbert expands the description of suffering's purpose to include correction, refinement, purification, and growth, he encompasses nearly all the texts considered in this chapter.[130] But this obscures the distinction between punitive and non-punitive. Generalizations, by nature, admit exceptions, but a more nuanced version of Talbert's thesis would indicate that while the punitive view of suffering was dominant, it nonetheless shared the field with several, sometimes significant, counter-currents.[131]

A final observation may offer a partial explanation for the various non-punitive, that is, "unorthodox," interpretations of suffering. It seems to be the case that among Jewish authors the strongest representatives of the non-punitive view of suffering have this in common: evidence of non-Jewish influences and, in some cases, non-Palestinian origin. Jewish wisdom literature, which contained several non-punitive texts (Wisdom, Sirach) as well as protests of the "orthodox" view (Job, Ecclesiastes), is generally characterized by a less parochial and more universal outlook on life. It shares many themes, viewpoints, and expressions with similar literature from non-Jewish cultures. Fourth Maccabees, which departed dramatically from the punitive interpretations of 2 and 3 Maccabees, was clearly influenced by Hellenistic philosophy, particularly Stoic ideas. Philo's writings, several of which favored a non-punitive understanding of suffering, have long been recognized as containing elements of Stoic, Pythagorean, and Neo-platonic philosophy. Lastly,

---

[129] I remind the reader that Talbert emphasized *"usually"*. See above, pp. 78–9.
[130] Talbert, *Learning Through Suffering*, 12.
[131] The brief scope of Talbert's book limited the degree of elaboration.

it is surely no accident that within rabbinic literature it is the *Babylonian* Talmud, a late non-Palestinian corpus, that begins to evidence novel interpretations of suffering. The Babylonian Talmud betrays other non-Jewish influences (magic, sorcery, and astrology) much more prominently than its Palestinian counterpart.[132]

Conversely, writings that stem from or seem closely linked to Palestine (Hebrew prophets, Psalms of Solomon, Qumran, Jerusalem Talmud) more often expound the punitive view. Chronology does not seem to play a role since punitive interpretations are found in writings from the earliest period (Amos, Isaiah) and the later period (Mishnah, Jerusalem Talmud). The distinction of non-Palestinian versus Palestinian origin cannot be pressed too far, however. Punitive interpretations of suffering did arise in the diaspora as well. (3 Macc. for example, is widely thought to be of Alexandrian origin. Moreover, the provenance of a writing is often difficult to determine.) But the *tendency* remains: Jewish writers in Palestine who betray few contacts with non-Jewish modes of thought are more likely to view suffering as divine punishment. This observation suggests that, with this modification, Talbert's thesis may have more validity than was granted above. Jewish writers *usually do* understand suffering as punishment for sin, except for Jewish writers who venture out intellectually and/or geographically, in which case *non*-punitive interpretations appear more often.

3.3   Greek and Roman perspectives on suffering

The second half of Talbert's thesis suggests that in the Greco-Roman world suffering was generally regarded as "a discipline intended by Providence to educate and improve the sufferer." "Suffering in this view is not so much correction of one's misdirection, as in the mainstream of Jewish thought, but rather conditioning that builds one up for greater virtue."[133] Most of the remainder of this chapter will be devoted to surveying Greco-Roman texts, from the archaic period to the later Stoics, in order to portray the variegated background of non-Jewish perspectives on suffering, and thereby further to test and elaborate Talbert's thesis.

Greek literature provides a multitude of passages illustrating a

---

[132] Gary G. Porton, "Talmud," *ABD*, VI, 312.
[133] Talbert, *Learning Through Suffering*, 17 and 20.

keen awareness of the severity and prevalence of life's hardships.[134] "A profound strain of melancholy makes itself heard in nearly all the reflective passages of Greek writers."[135] Homer envisions Zeus having two urns[136] on his doorstep from which he distributes sorrows and blessings. For some persons Zeus mingles the contents of the urns and bestows shifting fortunes. To others he gives undiluted sorrows, making them utterly wretched (*Iliad* 24.527–33). Thus it is the lot of mortals, at best, to suffer vicissitudes, at worst, to endure unmitigated hardship, and Zeus is the source of both.[137] Solon is equally pessimistic: οὐδὲ μάκαρ οὐδεὶς πέλεται βροτός, ἀλλὰ πονηροὶ πάντες, ὅσους θνητοὺς ἠέλιος καθορᾷ. (Not one mortal is blessed, but all on whom the sun looks down are wretched.)[138]

This view is generally more pessimistic than that of the Hebrew scriptures (with the exception of Ecclesiastes), but the idea that all things, good and evil, are traceable to deity is something Homer and Solon share with certain biblical authors.[139] Still the question remains, If God/Zeus is the source of woe, what is the divine purpose in afflicting humankind?

[134] For some of these references I am indebted to James Adam, "Ancient Greek Views of Suffering and Evil," in A. M. Adams (ed.), *The Vitality of Platonism* (Cambridge: Cambridge University, 1911) 190–212.

[135] *Ibid.*, 192. See also S. H. Butcher, "The Melancholy of the Greeks," in *Some Aspects of the Greek Genius* (Port Washington, NY: Kennikat, 1969) 130–65.

[136] The grammar of this *locus classicus* is ambiguous and has led both ancient and modern readers to construe the text as speaking either of two urns (good and evil) or three urns (one good and two evil). The question is not without significance since the "three urns" interpretation is more pessimistic, implying that all persons experience a preponderance of evil. For the "two urns" interpretation, see Plato, *Rep.* 379d (loosely adapting Homer); Plutarch, *Mor.* 24b, 600d (following Plato); W. Leaf, *The Iliad* (Amsterdam: Adolf M. Hakkert, 1960) II, 574; and C. W. Macleod, *Iliad, Book XXIV* (Cambridge: Cambridge University, 1982) 133. For the "three urns" interpretation, see Pindar, *Pyth.* 3.81–2 (a probable allusion); Plutarch, *Mor.* 105c (quoting Homer); and David C. Young, *Three Odes of Pindar* (Leiden: Brill, 1968) 50–2. An interesting facet of the Pindaric passage is the antithesis between the νήπιοι and the ἀγαθοί based on their endurance of suffering. Cf. Heb. 5.13–14.

[137] A saying quoted (disapprovingly) by Plato (*Rep.* 379e) calls Zeus "the dispenser of both good and evil things." On Zeus/God as the source of good and evil, see also *Iliad* 16.249–52, *h. Cer.* 147–8, 216–17, and Pseudo-Orpheus 14. The latter text is extant in several recensions; this line was altered in later recensions to remove the offense of attributing evil to God. See the discussion by Carl R. Holladay, *Fragments from Jewish Hellenistic Authors.* Vol. IV: *Pseudo Orpheus* (SBL Texts and Translations; Pseudepigrapha; Atlanta: Scholars Press, 1996).

[138] Frag. 14; West, ed., *Iambi et Elegi Graeci*, II, 150. As the antithesis to μάκαρ, πονηρός has its original meaning here, "oppressed," "worn down by toil." (Cf. πονέω.) An almost identical saying is found in Theognis, *Elegies* 167–8.

[139] Deut. 32.39; Amos 3.6; Isa. 45.7; Job 2.10; 5.18.

3.3.1   Human sin and folly as a source of suffering

One answer to this question echoes the "orthodox" Jewish view: human folly or sin is responsible for suffering. In a meeting of the gods, Zeus complains that mortals find fault with the gods: ἐξ ἡμέων γάρ φασι κάκ' ἔμμεναι, οἱ δὲ καὶ αὐτοὶ σφῆσιν ἀτασθαλίῃσιν ὑπὲρ μόρον ἄλγε' ἔχουσιν. (For they say that evils are from us! But they themselves have sorrows in excess of fate by their very own reckless folly: *Odyssey* 1.32–4.) In Aeschylus' *Persians*, Darius foresees great suffering for his men due to their impiety in plundering sacred sites in Greece. A sort of reciprocity is at work: "Having perpetrated evil, no less evil do they suffer; and other evils they are going to suffer: the spring of sorrows has not yet been quenched, but it still gushes forth" (813–15).

Such reflections were not intended as comprehensive explanations of human suffering. Indeed, the phrase, "in excess of fate," in the Homeric passage just cited implies that a certain measure of misery is destined to all, but one may worsen matters by evil behavior.[140] These texts simply reflect the awareness that some suffering has its origin in human wrongdoing. This seems to operate "naturally," that is, there is no explicit mention of this suffering being sent by the gods.

Popular religion, however, often did operate on the assumption that evil befell people because the gods were offended and needed to be propitiated. This was especially true of more mysterious calamities whose causes were dimly understood.

> All the great crises that leave men helpless even when united may be interpreted as caused by the wrath of the Stronger Ones, gods and heroes: bad harvests and infertility of the soil, diseases of men and cattle, barrenness of women and abnormal offspring, civil wars and defeat by a foreign army. Conversely, if these powers are appeased, all kinds of blessings must return, rich harvest, healthy children, and civic order.[141]

The traditional means of averting calamity and restoring blessing were sacrifice and prayer. Appeal was made to the various deities in

---

[140] See LSJ, 1147.
[141] Walter Burkert, *Greek Religion* (Cambridge, MA: Harvard University, 1985) 264.

accord with their respective areas of authority: Apollo for illness, Demeter for agriculture, Poseidon for seafaring and earthquakes, etc.[142]

The association of Poseidon with earthquakes furnishes examples of the way in which natural calamities might be attributed to moral evil. In 464 BCE an earthquake that struck Sparta was thought to be the result of a curse stemming from an earlier outrage. Some time before, helot suppliants had taken asylum at the altar of Poseidon on the Spartan promontory, Taenarus. The Spartans had removed and killed the suppliants in violation of the site's sacred status. Some saw a causal connection between the sacrilege and the quake.[143] Similarly, in 373 an earthquake that demolished the Peloponnesian towns of Helice and Bura was attributed to the sacrilege that the towns' inhabitants committed against certain Ionians who were sacrificing at the altar of Poseidon in Helice. The disaster is recounted in some detail by Diodorus Siculus (15.48–9), who also explains the popular reasoning behind the attribution: (1) Poseidon is the deity who holds the power of earthquakes and floods; (2) Poseidon has a special connection to the Peloponnese; (3) The Peloponnese is laced with underground rivers and caves; and most remarkably, (4) it was claimed that, apart from the impious, not one other person perished in the disaster! The latter shows how far popular piety would go for the sake of consistency. If the destruction of Helice and Bura was divine retribution for the sacrilege of certain inhabitants, the justice of Poseidon would certainly insure the safety of those who had not participated.[144]

Elsewhere Diodorus Siculus reports another incidence of sacrilege in which the perpetrators met with divine retribution. In about 345 BCE a group of Phocian soldiers led by Philon perpetrated a temple robbery at Delphi (16.56.3–8). The members of this group, and Philon in particular, received the condign punishment of the gods: death by fire, war, or disease (16.56.4, 8; 58.5–6; 61–4).

---

[142] *Ibid.*, 264–8; and, more broadly, W. K. C. Guthrie, *The Greeks and their Gods* (London: Methuen, 1950) 27–112.

[143] Thucydides, 1.128.1; Burkert, *Greek Religion*, 137–8.

[144] The pious interpretation was challenged even in Diodorus' day. He notes (15.48.4) that there had been much discussion about the disasters, and he contrasts the interpretation of the natural scientists (φυσικοί) to that of the pious. The former attribute earthquakes and floods to natural, mechanical forces. Even this brief mention of a rationalist explanation shows the diversity of opinion among the ancients. See also Pausanias (7.24.5–25.4), who mentions the disasters at both Helice and Taenarum and gives a thoroughly religious explanation.

The above three incidents involve human wrongdoing of a particular sort: the violation of a sacred site either by violence against suppliants or robbery of temple goods. It is not surprising that such deeds, consisting of brazen effrontery against particular gods, were thought to evoke divine wrath. The punishments, especially earthquakes and disease, were especially amenable to supernatural explanation. The point here is not that all people of antiquity were "primitive" or "superstitious," but that supernatural and natural explanations existed side by side (a situation that still obtains today), and that certain crimes followed by certain calamities lent themselves well to a religious interpretation.

Plutarch wrote an entire essay on the sort of piety that attributes every adversity to the work of the gods (*On Superstition, Mor.* 165e–171). In his view this naive perspective was even more harmful than atheism. The atheist disbelieves in the gods and is indifferent to them. The superstitious person believes in the gods but regards them as the source of grief and injury (165b). Illness, loss of property, death of children, etc. are all classed as "afflictions of God" (168c). The essay shows that superstition and atheism (not to mention a more rational form of piety that the treatise presupposes) existed side by side in the first century and offered their respective explanations of suffering.

A variation of punitive suffering was the idea of "inherited guilt," that is, the punishment of persons for the sins of their ancestors. This was perhaps an attempt to explain the conspicuous fact that some of the wicked enjoyed prosperity. The penalty for their wickedness, so the argument went, fell upon their descendants. Thus Solon muses: ἀλλ᾽ ὁ μὲν αὐτίκ᾽ ἔτεισεν, ὁ δ᾽ ὕστερον· οἳ δὲ φύγωσιν αὐτοί, μηδὲ θεῶν μοῖρ᾽ ἐπιοῦσα κίχηι, ἤλυθε πάντως αὖτις· ἀναίτιοι ἔργα τίνουσιν ἢ παῖδες τούτων ἢ γένος ἐξοπίσω. (One pays the penalty immediately, another at a later time; and those who escape, whom the pursuing Fate of the gods does not overtake, assuredly [Fate] comes [to them] in turn. Innocent people pay for their deeds, either their children or descendants coming thereafter.)[145] The justification for this was a belief in family solidarity: "[T]he family was a moral unit, the son's life was a prolongation of his father's, and he

---

[145] Solon, 13.29–31; West, ed., *Iambi et Elegi Graeci*, II, 128. Similarly, Theognis (731–52) laments that the children of the wicked seem to bear the penalty of their parents' misdeeds. Theognis' protest indirectly witnesses to the persistence of this way of interpreting unrequited evil and undeserved suffering.

inherited his father's moral debts exactly as he inherited his commercial ones. Sooner or later, the debt exacted its own payment."[146]

3.3.2   Protests against the punitive view

There were, of course, protests against the punitive interpretation
of suffering. The Greeks had an occasional Job and Qoheleth. One
variety of protest is implicit in the simple observation of life's in-
equities. Solon rightly perceived that "Many wicked persons are
rich, and many virtuous persons poor."[147] The latter might be explained by an appeal to "inherited guilt," but the former could
not. Among the ancient poets, Theognis was especially troubled by
the disparities he observed. He laments that the wicked and the just
either share the same fate or receive a portion opposite what they
are due.

> πῶς δή σευ, Κρονίδη, τολμᾶι νόος ἄνδρας ἀλιτροῦ ἐν
> ταὐτῆι μοίρηι τόν τε δίκαιον ἔχειν;

> How, O son of Kronos, does your mind bear for criminals
> to have the same fate as the just person?

> ἔπης δ' ὄλβον ἔχουσιν ἀπήμονα· τοὶ ἀπὸ δειλῶν ἔργων
> ἴσχοντες θυμὸν ὅμως πενίην μητέρ' ἀμηχανίης ἔλαβον τὰ
> δίκαια φιλεῦντες ...

> Yet [the wicked] have carefree wealth, and those who
> keep their heart from base deeds nevertheless receive
> poverty, the mother of helplessness, despite their love
> of justice ...[148]

Implicit in these remarks is a protest, or at least a questioning, of a
thoroughgoing view of retribution. If such were the case, one would
expect only the wicked would suffer poverty and other ills; the just
would be free from undue hardships.

A second kind of protest against the punitive view of suffering
criticized the idea that the gods could be the cause of evil at all,

---

[146] E. R. Dodds, *The Greeks and the Irrational* (Berkeley: University of California,
1966) 34. See the entire chapter "From Shame-Culture to Guilt-Culture," pp.
28–63, esp. notes 25 and 26. For "inherited guilt" in the Bible, see n. 25 above.
[147] Solon, frag. 15; West, ed., *Iambi et Elegi Graeci*, II, 150.
[148] Theognis, *Eleg.* 377–8, 383–5; text from Douglas Young, *Theognis* (Leipzig:
Teubner, 1961) 25. See also lines 743–52.

especially gratuitous evil. The earlier protest, represented above by Theognis, was empirical: it was an observable fact that people do not suffer in proportion to the moral quality of their lives. This second sort of protest is theological: God, by nature, is good, and therefore nothing (gratuitously) evil can have its origin in God. Plato articulates this viewpoint clearly.[149] God cannot be the cause of all things, but only of what is good. The poets ought not to say, as they are prone to do, that Zeus metes out both good and evil; we must not regard woe as the work of God.

Plato permits an exception, however, if one rightly understands God's punishment and its effect on the sufferers. If punishment is attributed to God, it must meet these two requirements: ὁ μὲν θεὸς δίκαιά τε καὶ ἀγαθὰ εἰργάζετο, οἱ δὲ ὠνίναντο κολαζόμενοι. (On the one hand, God acted justly and nobly; on the other hand, those who were punished profited from it.)[150] Plato thus severely restricts the punitive view of suffering. Suffering can only be construed as divinely sent chastisement if it has some beneficial effect on those punished.[151]

3.3.3   Educative suffering: the archaic and classical eras

The view that suffering was salutary or educational was widespread among Greek writers from the mid-fifth century on. It was frequently summed up in Greek by the juxtaposition of two similar sounding words: ἔπαθον ... ἔμαθον (I suffered ... I learned). A survey of passages containing this wordplay and similar phrases is in order.[152]

---

[149] See especially *Rep.* 379a–380d, in which the Homeric passage cited above (*Iliad* 24.527–33) is flatly rejected: οὐκ ... ἀποδεκτέον οὔτε ʿΟμήρου οὔτ' ἄλλου ποιητοῦ ταύτην τὴν ἁμαρτίαν περὶ τοὺς θεοὺς ἀνοήτως ἁμαρτάνοντος ... (It is not to be accepted when Homer or any other poet foolishly makes this error concerning the gods ...)

[150] *Rep.* 380a–b.

[151] Plato's doctrine of punishment, whether human or divine, generally requires that it be remedial, for those whose crimes are curable, or that it serve as a deterrent to others in the case of incurable crimes. See *Gorgias* 525b–c and, in general, Mary Margaret Mackenzie, *Plato on Punishment* (Berkeley: University of California, 1981).

[152] Here I draw upon two excellent articles: J. Costé, "Notion grecque et notion biblique de la 'souffrance éducatrice,'" *Recherches de Science Religieuse*, 43 (1955) 481–523; and Heinrich Dörrie, "Leid und Erfahrung. Die Wort- und Sinn-Verbindung παθεῖν – μαθεῖν im griechischen Denken," *Akademie der Wissenschaften und der Literatur*, 5 (1956) 303–44 (alternative numbering, 1–42). Pithy, rhyming expressions of the educational value of suffering also occur in English.

The earliest poetic expressions of the educative value of suffering were usually stated negatively. That is, the accent was not on the positive benefit that accrued to a noble person who suffered incidentally, but on the inevitable awakening of the foolish person who suffered as a result of folly. In the *Iliad* (17.1–32) Menelaus guards the fallen body of Patrocles and warns the advancing Trojan, Euphorbus, to back away or risk bodily harm, for "even a fool understands after a thing has been accomplished" (32). This is not a question of lofty religious insight gained from adversity, but the brutish lesson of a sound thrashing. Even at this level the expression achieves the status of a proverb.[153] It recurs verbatim in the *Iliad* at 20.198 and in slightly altered form in Hesiod. In the latter (*Works and Days* 218), Perses, the poet's brother, is urged to pursue the path of justice rather than hubris. In so doing he will act wisely and avoid evil, whereas "a fool learns [only] after having suffered" (παθὼν δέ τε νήπιος ἔγνω). There is no theological dimension here; the means of instruction are not divine, but the very natural process of trial and error.

One of the chief mythological examples of the failure to foresee perilous consequences was Epimetheus, who, lacking the insight of his brother Prometheus, opened Pandora's box and released manifold harm on humankind. Hesiod notes that "after he took possession of the evil, he understood" (*Works and Days* 89). Again, the lesson is a harsh, after-the-fact recognition of folly, yielding insight mingled with regret.[154]

The first instance of the pairing πάθημα ... μάθημα is found in the fifth-century historian, Herodotus (1.207).[155] Croesus of Lydia advises the Persian king Cyrus to take an aggressive stance in the war against Tomyris, queen of the Massagetae. This advice stems from Croesus' personal experience. For, he says, τὰ δέ μοι παθήματα ἐόντα ἀχάριτα μαθήματα γέγονε. (My experiences, being unfavorable, have become lessons for me.) Croesus had known defeat in

Athletes are familiar with "No pain, no gain." I once heard a preacher speak of "the University of Adversity."

[153] The proverbial status is clear in Plato (*Symp.* 222b) when Alcibiades warns Agathon to beware lest he be like the fool "in the adage" who learned after having suffered.

[154] Pindar (*Isthmian* 1.40) observes: ὁ πονήσαις δὲ νόῳ καὶ προμάθειαν φέρει. (The one who suffers at heart also gains foresight.) On the translation, see G. Kirkwood, *Selections from Pindar, Edited with an Introduction and Commentary* (Chico, CA: Scholars Press, 1982) 283.

[155] See Dörrie, "Leid und Erfahrung," 310 (8).

battle, imprisonment, and the threat of death. These past events supposedly enabled him to see the proper course of action in the present.[156]

This passage from Herodotus is echoed in two later historians.[157] In Dionysius of Halicarnassus (8.33.3), the legendary hero Coriolanus waxes arrogant in a speech to his Volscian army. He attributes his success to his own piety and the resultant favor of the gods. But if he should change this course and dishonor the gods, he suspects that his fortunes would likewise change: ἐκ μεγάλου ταπεινὸς γενήσομαι, καὶ τἀμὰ παθήματα παιδεύματα γενήσεται τοῖς ἄλλοις; (From my great estate shall I [not] be made low, and my sufferings become lessons to others?) The variations on Herodotus' expression consist of vocabulary (παιδεύματα versus μαθήματα) and reference (lessons for *others* versus oneself).[158] Later, Appian of Alexandria, writing in the second century CE, mentions the raising of a new army by Tigranes and Mithridates (12.13.87). These troops were placed under the command of Mithridates since Tigranes judged that "[Mithridates'] misfortunes (παθήματα) had become lessons (διδάγματα) for him." Again, the vocabulary is altered, but the three passages make nearly the same point: misfortunes suffered in war make one (or others) wiser.

Tragedy is the genre where the pairing of suffering and learning comes to full flower. By its very nature, tragedy gives a central role to human suffering. "The problem of suffering is grasped more profoundly in tragedy than in the philosophical ethics of antiquity, since tragedy shows, 'not in theoretical generality but in actual disaster, that through suffering we learn who we are and what befalls us.'"[159] Moses Hadas identifies four essential qualities of Greek tragedy: (1) the person affected must possess stature, (2) the suffering must be the consequence of morally defensible choices, not a natural disaster, (3) the issue must have a certain magnitude, and, most importantly for our purposes, (4) the tragedy "must serve to educate, first the personage involved, whom suffering ripens to wis-

---

[156] The fact that Croesus' advice was disastrous for Cyrus gives the adage an ironic twist.

[157] Dörrie, "Leid und Erfahrung," 322 (20), overstates the connection: "These passages in Herodotus are twice quite obviously imitated and thereby in a certain sense interpreted."

[158] Of course, from the viewpoint of Coriolanus, his hypothetical sufferings would be punitive since they would result from his dishonoring the gods.

[159] W. Michaelis, "πάσχω, etc.," *TDNT*, V, 906 n. 11, quoting G. Nebel, *Weltangst und Götterzorn*, 1951, 115–16.

dom, and through that personage the community to whom the play is addressed."[160] The essence of tragedy is thus the recognition of the great disparity between the divine world of bliss and the human world of hardship and the consequent human capacity to achieve excellence by the endurance of hardship.[161]

In the dreadful scene of Iphigenia's sacrifice, Aeschylus (*Agam.* 250–1) alludes to the calamity coming upon the house of Agamemnon and issues a cryptic warning: Δίκα δὲ τοῖς μὲν παθοῦσιν μαθεῖν ἐπιρρέπει. (Justice allots learning to those who suffer.) Earlier in the same play, Zeus is lauded as "the one who sets mortals in the right path of understanding, who has established as a fixed rule that learning (μάθος) comes by suffering (πάθος)" (177–8). We have clearly progressed beyond the adages of Herodotus and the epic poets, not only by the affirmation of divine agency, but by the scope of the insight gained through suffering. "Plainly this learning through suffering is not just a later understanding of the salutary purpose of individual sufferings or a growing wise through painful experiences as in Hes[iod]. It is a deeper view of human existence in its totality."[162]

Sophocles offers various formulations of the same idea. The elderly king Oedipus speaks of three teachers he has had: στέργειν γὰρ αἱ πάθαι με χὠ χρόνος ξυνὼν μακρὸς διδάσκει καὶ τὸ γενναῖον τρίτον (For misfortunes, and time, long my companion, and, thirdly, nobility teach me to be content: *OC* 7–8). Similarly, in the final lines of *Antigone* (1350–3), the chorus identifies wisdom as the chief part of happiness, and piety toward the gods as a strict obligation. Then the play concludes: μεγάλοι δὲ λόγοι μεγάλας πληγὰς τῶν ὑπεραύχων ἀποτίσαντες γήρᾳ τὸ φρονεῖν ἐδίδαξαν. (Great words of the over-proud, having paid the price of great calamities, have taught wisdom in old age.)[163] In *Philoctetes* (534–8), the title char-

---

[160] Moses Hadas, *Humanism. The Greek Ideal and its Survival* (Gloucester, MA: Peter Smith, 1972) 55–7.

[161] *Ibid.*, 58.

[162] Michaelis, "πάσχω, etc.," 906. Cf. E. Fraenkel, *Aeschylus' Agamemnon* (Oxford: Clarendon, 1950) II, 106: "With φρονεῖν as the goal of man's journey we are on a much higher plane of ideas than is reached by the traditional verdict παθὼν δέ τε νήπιος ἔγνω or in proverbial expressions such as παθήματα μαθήματα and the like." See also *Eumenides* (520–1): "It is expedient to gain wisdom by hardship."

[163] On the peculiar word order of these lines, see J. C. Kamerbeek, *The Plays of Sophocles, Part III Antigone* (Leiden: Brill, 1978) 212. For other Sophoclean expressions relating suffering and learning, see *Electra* 1462–3, and *Trachiniae* 143.

acter bemoans the life that he has been forced to live in exile. The mere sight of his home in exile would have been intolerable for a lesser person. "But I, by necessity, have learned to bear misfortunes."

These passages associate suffering with learning, but none explicitly connects suffering with the gods (though this may be implied in *Antigone*). A Sophoclean fragment, however, does make this connection: αἴσχη μέν, ὦ γυναῖκες, οὐδ' ἂν εἷς φύγοι βροτῶν ποθ', ᾧ καὶ Ζεύς ἐφορμήσῃ κακά· νόσους δ' ἀνάγκη τὰς θεηλάτους φέρειν. (Disgraces, O women, not even one mortal would ever escape, against whom even Zeus would stir up evils. So, it is necessary to bear the plagues sent by the gods.)[164] It may be that Sophocles conceives the sufferings of Oedipus, Creon (in *Antigone*), and Philoctetes as divine in origin, but this is not certain. Sophocles associates suffering with learning, and, in a few scattered references, associates suffering with the gods. But he does not explicitly state that the gods inflict suffering on human beings in order to instruct them. What is explicitly stated by Aeschylus is at best hazily suggested by Sophocles.

Among the major genres of Greek literature, then, tragedy possesses the greatest development of the idea of educative suffering.[165] Comedy was not too concerned with human suffering, at least in its religious and pathetic dimensions.[166] Philosophers occasionally spoke of the pain and toil connected with suffering, but generally they did not reach the level of theological or existential reflection

---

[164] Fragment 680; A. C. Pearson, ed., *The Fragments of Sophocles* (Amsterdam: Adolf M. Hakkert, 1963) I, 298. See also fragment 961 (*ibid.*, III, 121): θεοῦ δὲ πληγὴν οὐκ ὑπερπηδᾷ βροτός (But a blow from God a mortal does not escape). Similarly, *Ajax* 278–9 speaks of "a plague from God."

[165] Thus Dörrie, "Leid und Erfahrung," 338 (36): "Only tragedy, strictly speaking only Aeschylus, has ... grasped the idea that a higher power wants to teach human beings something through suffering." See also Michaelis, "πάσχω, etc.," 906: "[The educational value of suffering] is most impressively stated by Greek tragedy, esp. Aesch[ylus]." Costé, "Notion grecque," 492, agrees: "The Agamemnon of Aeschylus offers us ... the most vigorously striking expression of our theme and one of its richest uses."

[166] When Aristophanes refers to "passions" he intends sexual innuendo. See *Thesmophoriazusai* 195–9, and Dörrie, "Leid und Erfahrung," 323–4 (21–2). A maxim attributed to Menander, a writer of New Comedy, associates pain with learning: ὁ μὴ δαρεὶς ἄνθρωπος οὐ παιδεύεται (The person who is not beaten is not instructed); Siegfried Jaekel, ed., *Menandri Sententiae* (Leipzig: Teubner, 1964) 66.

found in Aeschylus.[167] We saw above that Plato ascribed to God only those sufferings that had a beneficial effect.[168] There were, moreover, currents in some schools of philosophy that hindered serious discussion of the beneficial effects of suffering. If a philosophy regarded virtue as the only good, then suffering was incidental, an indifferent matter. Philosophy enables the sage to rise above ill health, calamity, and loss, for these things "cannot alter the internal attitude of the sage."[169] This attitude was characteristic of Socrates and a few Stoic philosophers.[170]

3.3.4   Educative suffering: the Hellenistic era

The fourth century BCE saw a decline in the use of the precise word-play, πάθος ... μάθος due to the increasing tendency to use πάθος to denote an irrational impulse of the soul rather than an external misfortune, calamity, or punishment.[171] But in other Greek formulations and their Latin equivalents, the motif stayed very much alive. The element of divine intentionality in human suffering was rarely present, however.

Sometimes the later sayings reflect the archaic notion of learning by trial and error. In a letter of Pseudo-Aeschines, the writer admires a friend whose wisdom surpasses his own: ἃ γὰρ ἐγὼ παθὼν ἐδιδάχθην, ταῦτα πρὶν παθεῖν φυλάττεται, σοφίᾳ καὶ οὐχ ὥσπερ οἱ

---

[167] The presocratic philosopher, Democritus, is credited with the following saying: τὰ μὲν καλὰ χρήματα τοῖς πόνοις ἡ μάθησις ἐξεργάζεται, τὰ δ᾽ αἰσχρὰ ἄνευ πόνων αὐτόματα καρποῦται (Learning, through sufferings, produces noble results; but shameful results are borne as fruit automatically without sufferings); fragment 182, Hermann Diels, *Die Fragmente der Vorsokratiker* (Berlin: Weidmansche, 1952) II, 182. Aristotle also associated learning with pain: μετὰ λύπης γὰρ ἡ μάθησις (For learning comes with grief: *Pol.* 7.4.4); also: τῆς παιδείας ἔφη τὰς μὲν ῥίζας εἶναι πικράς, τὸν δὲ καρπὸν γλυκύν ([Aristotle] said that the roots of discipline were bitter, but the fruit was sweet: Diogenes Laertius, *Aristotle* 5.1.18).

[168] *Rep.* 380 a–c.

[169] Costé, "Notion grecque," 491; see the entire section on "The silence of the philosophers," 490–2.

[170] See Plato, *Meno* 87e–88a, *Euthyd.* 280e, and *Gorg.* 467e; cited in A. A. Long and D. N. Sedley, *The Hellenistic Philosophers* (Cambridge: Cambridge University, 1987) II, 350. The position of utter neutrality toward "indifferent matters" (things that were neither virtue nor vice) was not held by all Stoics; indeed, it was the "non-orthodox" view of a few (e.g. Aristo and Herillus). Most Stoics, beginning with their founder, Zeno, believed that some indifferent things were intrinsically preferable, and others were generally to be avoided. "Orthodox" Stoics might very well have sought to avoid suffering or to seek positive benefit in it. See *ibid.*, I, 354–9; II, 355.

[171] Dörrie, "Leid und Erfahrung," 330–1.

ἄφρονες πείρᾳ διδασκόμενος. (For the things that I learned after having suffered, these things he bears in mind before suffering, being taught by wisdom, and not by trial as fools are.)[172]

Unsuccessful martial exploits continued to instruct and chasten military leaders. Caesar sent a communiqué to Pompey in the course of their hostilities, suggesting that each put an end to his resistance and lay down his arms. Rather serious losses had been suffered by each side, losses that "they could regard as instruction and injunctions in order that they might be wary of further casualties" (*Bellum Civile* 3.10).

The wide currency of the notion of suffering's educative value is also apparent in Aesop's fables. A few of these fables, which often relate insight gained through mishaps, conclude with the saying, ὁ λόγος δηλοῖ, ὅτι πολλάκις τὰ παθήματα τοῖς ἀνθρώποις μαθήματα γίνονται. (The story shows that sufferings often become lessons for people.)[173] Other references could be given to demonstrate the motif's continued existence in the imperial period, but these need not detain us here.[174] The final stage of this survey will consider the theme (not the wordplay *per se*) of educative suffering in a few authors of an era closer to that of the Epistle to the Hebrews, the later Stoics.

We are fortunate that a large number of the writings of Lucius Annaeus Seneca, a Stoic philosopher contemporary with the apostle Paul, has been preserved. His several extant prose works, including a collection of 124 letters, are valuable sources for late Stoicism. Several of these letters reveal Seneca's thoughts on suffering.[175]

First, it is clear that Seneca viewed suffering as an "indifferent"

---

[172] Epistle 5.4; F. Blass, ed., *Aeschines Orationes* (Stuttgart: Teubner, 1978) 296.

[173] August Hausrath, ed. *Corpus Fabularum Aesopicarum* (Leipzig: Teubner, 1959). See fables 134 (Vol. I, Pt. 1, 159–60) and 223 (Vol. I, Pt. 2, 45–6). The form of the saying varies; sometimes μῦθος appears for λόγος, sometimes φρονίμοις for ἀνθρώποις.

[174] See the list of classical sources in Dörrie "Leid und Erfahrung," 344 (42), and both classical and biblical references in Costé, "Notion grecque," *passim*. To Dörrie's list one might add the late (fourth century CE) examples found in Libanius, *Progymnasmata* X.α.13: παρ' αὐτῶν ὧν ἔπαθον μεμαθηκότες (having learned from what they suffered), and XI.δ.1: παθὼν μεμάθηκε (having suffered, he learned). See R. Foerster, ed., *Libanii Opera* (Stuttgart: Teubner, 1915) VIII, 337, 381.

[175] A helpful, topical arrangement of Seneca's philosophy is available in Anna Lydia Motto's *Seneca Sourcebook: Guide to the Thought of Lucius Annaeus Seneca* (Amsterdam: Adolf M. Hakkert, 1970). I am especially indebted to her entry on "Adversity."

matter, neither essential to the sage's practice of virtue, nor necessarily detrimental to it. Nevertheless, because of its intrinsic nature, suffering was normally to be avoided. *Plurimum interesse inter gaudium et dolorem; si quaeratur electio, alterum petam, alterum vitabo* (There is a great difference between joy and pain; if a choice is to be made, I will seek the former and avoid the latter: Epist. 66.19). But suffering was not to be avoided at all cost; when virtue demanded it, the sage would undergo hardship and torture (Epist. 66.21). Suffering itself is "against nature," but to maintain a resolute spirit in suffering is "according to nature" (Epist. 66.38). This view accords with Stoic "orthodoxy."[176]

Secondly, Seneca often speaks of benefits that one may derive from suffering. *Unum habet assidua infelicitas bonum, quod quos semper vexat, novissime indurat* (Unrelenting misfortune has one advantage: those whom it continually distresses, it eventually toughens: *Ad Helviam* 2.3). Wisdom is another likely by-product of suffering. *Nam quasi ista inter se contraria sint, bona fortuna et mens bona, ita melius in malis sapimus; secunda rectum auferunt* (For it is as if these things were contrary to one another: good fortune and a good mind; thus we are more prudent in adversity. Favorable circumstances take away our virtue: Epist. 94.74). Seneca also makes the common observation that misfortune often contains a disguised blessing. *Quotiens enim felicitatis et causa et initium fuit, quod calamitas vocabatur?* (For how often has the source and beginning of happiness been something that was called a calamity?: Epist. 110.3). Finally, suffering has a probative function in that it presents an opportunity for one's mettle to be demonstrated. A ship's pilot is not tested by calm waters and a favorable wind; rather "it is necessary that some hardship encounter [the pilot] that will try the soul" (*Ad Marciam* 5.5).

The proper response to hardships is, of course, patient endurance: *Posse laeto animo adversa tolerare* (To be able to endure adversity with a cheerful spirit: *Quaest. Nat.* 3, Pref. 12). Penitence or self-examination is not called for since Seneca is generally concerned with adversities that befall *just* persons.[177] But how do the gods

---

[176] See n. 170 above. Seneca regarded utter indifference to suffering as inhuman. See *Ad Polyb.* 17.2: *Nam et non sentire mala sua non est hominis, et non ferre non est viri.* (For indeed, not to feel one's afflictions is not human, and not to bear them is not manly.)

[177] Epist. 74.10: *Multa incommoda iustis viris accident* (Many misfortunes befall just men).

fit into this schema? What is their connection, if any, to human suffering?

Seneca affirms that "all things happen by the decree of god" (*Quaest. Nat.* 3, Pref. 12). Therefore, hardship, suffering, and pain are part of a divine plan. I indicated above that Seneca thought various benefits could be derived from suffering. Nowhere are the benefits of suffering and the divine intentions behind suffering so explicitly treated as in the work *De Providentia*. I conclude this survey of Seneca with a discussion of this important work.

De Providentia is a dialogue or philosophical essay, prompted by an inquiry of Seneca's friend Lucilius and punctuated occasionally by further questions and remonstrations.[178] Apart from the initial inquiry, which may very well reflect an actual communication from Lucilius, the later "quotations" are probably Seneca's rhetorical devices to move the essay along.

The opening sentence poses the essay's theme: *Quid ita, si providentia mundus regeretur, multa bonis viris mala acciderent* (Why, if the world is governed by Providence, do many evils befall good persons?: 1.1).[179] Seneca's answer may seem to ramble at times, but three points that emerge repeatedly constitute the core of his response.[180]

First, Seneca argues that, in fact, "no evil can befall a good person" (2.1). This statement, seemingly refuted by human experience, must be seen in the context of Stoic philosophy, particularly its understanding of "good' and "evil." The former was restricted to moral goodness, virtue, wisdom, etc.; the latter to their opposites. Other things, such as health, wealth, and social standing, were morally indifferent. They could be desirable, just as their opposites,

---

[178] See 1.1; 2.1; 3.2; 5.3, 9; 6.1, 6. *De Prov.* is not a dramatic dialogue of the Platonic type, but rather of a later kind in which the chief speaker (here also the author) expounds a view in a lengthy speech with few interruptions from an imaginary opponent. In *De Prov.* the role of Lucilius almost disappears.

[179] The amount of secondary literature specifically on *De Prov.* is modest. A helpful commentary has been provided by Earl George Delarue, "Lucii Annaei Senecae *De Providentia*: A Commentary," Dissertation, Cornell University, 1974. See his bibliography, 106–11.

[180] Some scholars see a basic, if somewhat obscure structure in *De Prov.* See Delarue, "Senecae *De Providentia*," xxv–xxvii; L. Theron, "Progression of Thought in Seneca's 'De Providentia,'" *Acta Classica*, 13 (1971) 61–72; and J. R. G. Wright, "Form and Content in the 'Moral Essays,'" in *Seneca* (C. D. N. Costa, ed.; London: Routledge and Kegan Paul, 1974) 39–69, esp. 48–54. The essay may not ramble as much as a cursory reading suggests. In any case, my concern has much more to do with the content of the essay than with its structure.

illness, poverty, and social obscurity, were undesirable, but they were not constitutive of virtue or goodness. This philosophy is carefully reinforced by Stoic vocabulary.

> The most distinctive characteristic of Stoic ethics is its re-striction of the ordinary Greek terms for "good" and "bad" to what we would call the moral sense of these words. In the case of "good" this is expressed most generally by claiming that the only good thing is "rectitude" or "the honorable."

> The conception of good and bad as moral benefit and moral harm respectively gave rise to some of the most famous Stoic paradoxes: no harm can affect the good man, since he cannot be injured by vice, and nothing except vice is harmful in the strict sense.[181]

Thus, a good person by definition is unharmed by evil since (Stoic) evil entails a moral choice that a good person would never make.[182] Furthermore, God protects good persons from true evils: *Omnia mala ab illis removit, scelera et flagitia et cogitationes im-probas et avida consilia et libidinem caecam et alieno imminentem avaritiam* ([God] removes all evils from them – sins and crimes and base thoughts and greedy schemes and secret lust and avarice that longs for another's goods: 6.1). This list reveals Seneca's exclusively moral conception of *mala*. The hardships that the ordinary person shuns are not *mala*.[183] These are more typically called *adversa or incommoda*.

A second emphasis in Seneca's *De Providentia* is God's parental care for the good person. A friendship exists between God and the sage. Indeed, beyond friendship, there exists a relatedness and re-semblance (*necessitudo et similitudo*, 1.5). The sage is thus described: *discipulus eius aemulatorque et vera progenies, quam parens ille mag-*

---

[181] Long and Sedley, *Hellenistic Philosophers*, I, 374 and 377. These statements about Greek sources for Stoic philosophy also hold true for Seneca's Latin. The good person in Seneca's vocabulary is the *bonus*; the evil by which the good person is untouched is *malum*. See Epist. 76.19; 82.14; 94.8; *De Vita Beata* 4.3; 16.1; *De Beneficiis* 7.2.2.

[182] The denial that evil can befall the sage is found elsewhere in Seneca. See *De Constantia Sapientis* 2.1 and *De Beneficiis* 2.35.2. In the latter, Seneca acknowl-edges that Stoics sometimes avoid the ordinary meaning of words.

[183] *De Prov.* 5.1: *Haec quae vulgus appetit, quae reformidat, nec bona esse nec mala.* (These things which the crowd seeks, which it shuns, are neither good nor evil.)

nificus, virtutum non lenis exactor, sicut severi patres, durius educat
([God's] pupil, imitator and true progeny, whom that magnificent
parent, no mild enforcer of virtues, educates quite sternly, just as
strict fathers do: 1.6).

Although Seneca uses the gender-neutral term *parens* to refer
to God in 1.6, he primarily has in mind a father image. In 2.5–6
he distinguishes between maternal and paternal love. The former he
characterizes as gentle and protective; the latter as stern, demanding, almost cruel. Divine love, according to Seneca, is akin to the
latter: *Patrium deus habet adversus bonos viros animum et illos for-
titer amat* (God has a paternal disposition toward good men and
loves them firmly: 2.6). It is entirely within God's character and
purpose, says Seneca, to expose persons to toil, pain, and loss.
Those whom God loves are disciplined. This strict, fatherly love of
God is even likened to the Spartans' practice of publicly lashing
their children (4.11–12). The image is brutal to the modern con-
science, but it would have been less offensive to the Roman mind.
Neither is it far removed from some statements in the Jewish wisdom tradition.[184]

Third, Seneca viewed the hardships (*adversa, incommoda*) endured by the wise as instructive and salutary. This is the most important point of the essay; it occurs repeatedly in a number of images. I have already noted the parental image above. God "rears"
(*educat*) the wise person like a son (2.5). The sage is not kept as a
favored pet; rather God "tests, hardens, [and] prepares" the sage for
Himself (*experitur, indurat … parat*: 1.6). After citing the extreme
practices of Spartan fathers, Seneca asks, *Quid mirum, si dure gen-
erosos spiritus deus temptat?* (Why is it strange if God puts noble
spirits to a severe test?: 4.12.)

Athletic imagery, as a way of depicting the meaning of suffering,
is used quite extensively in *De Providentia*. Brave persons regard
adversity as "training" (*exercitationes*, 2.2) and eagerly pit themselves against it as against a formidable opponent. The gods enjoy
such a spectacle: *vir fortis cum fortuna mala compositus* (a brave
man pitted against misfortune, 2.9). Various aspects of the athletic
image are developed at length in 2.2–4, 7–9, and 4.1–3.

A further metaphor of one who benefits from hardship is the

---

[184] See above, pp. 89–91. On the extent of parental authority over children in
Seneca's day, see Bonner, *Education in Ancient Rome*, 5–6 and 18–19. On the
Spartan practices, see Cicero, *Tusc.* 2.46, and Plutarch, *Mor.* 239d.

soldier. Suffering is an accepted part of the soldier's glory. "Those who return from the battle intact may have performed the same, but the one who returns wounded is more highly esteemed" (4.4). The veteran of war is not shaken by the sight of blood, knowing that "often one prevails [only] after the shedding of blood" (4.7).

Other images play minor roles in the essay. The refining image, which was seen in some Jewish traditions, occurs once: *Ignis aurum probat, miseria fortes viros* (Fire tests gold, misfortune brave men: 5.10). In another figure, the painful, but beneficial, nature of suffering is likened to medical procedures.[185] Surgery, cautery, and amputation, which were excruciatingly painful in times prior to anesthesia, were nevertheless credited with healing some people. In a similar way, Seneca argues, "some misfortunes are for the benefit of those whom they befall" (3.2). Even animal imagery is present in references to calamities as "goads" of the soul (*stimulos*, 4.6) or as a "yoke" (*iugum*, 4.7). Sailors and farmers (4.13), trees (4.16), and Vestal Virgins (5.3) are also among those whose hardships and strains ultimately work to their benefit.

These diverse figures converge and contribute to the central argument: *Hos ... deus quos probat, quos amat, indurat, recognoscit, exercet* (Those whom God approves and loves, [God] toughens, examines, and exercises: 4.7). Suffering in all its forms benefits the sufferer. In Stoic thought it could not be otherwise since the gods decree everything, and their actions must be for the good of mortals. Seneca's explanation of the suffering of the sage is clearly to be classed as formative and almost invariably non-punitive.[186]

Epictetus, as we saw in chapter 2, was especially fond of athletic metaphors. The hardships of life were interpreted as divine training, sometimes quite explicitly. Cynics, says Epictetus, are persuaded that whatever they suffer, Zeus is training them (γυμνάζει). By his many labors, Heracles, an important exemplar to Stoics, "was

---

[185] Cf. Philo, *Praem.* 33.
[186] I have emphasized the personal benefit of suffering in this summary of *De Prov.*, but at least twice Seneca also mentions the function of suffering as a lesson *for others*. See 3.1 and 6.3. Seneca has little to say about suffering that people bring on themselves through folly. Once he calls the indulgence of pleasure "the source of all evils" (Epist. 110.10). Apparently then, the suffering of the vulgar crowd (the non-*boni*) might be due to their foolish indulgence of pleasure. They might also suffer from *adversa*. The *sapiens* would experience only the latter.

being trained and exercised by Zeus" (ὑπὸ τοῦ Διὸς ἀθλούμενος καὶ γυμναζόμενος, 3.22.57; see also 1.6.32–6). The sage is God's exhibit to the world. In poverty, without political status, in sickness, in exile, or in prison, Zeus is "training (γυμνάζων) and using [the sage] as a witness to others" (3.24.113).[187]

Hardships (περιστάσεις), a favorite word of Epictetus', are the things that reveal a person's character (1.24.1). When one is called to face a hardship, the time has arrived to show "if we have been educated" (εἰ πεπαιδεύμεθα, 1.29.33). The source of one's education here is the study of philosophy. Epictetus' point is not that hardships make a person a philosopher, but that the study of philosophy prepares a person for hardships. The effect of enduring hardships is certainly educative, but Epictetus much prefers to describe that process with athletic language.[188]

Two minor addenda conclude this brief examination of Epictetus. First, Epictetus like Seneca, does not see Zeus' training by means of hardships as hateful or destructive in intent. Zeus does not hate, nor even neglect his creatures; on the contrary he has equipped them with all the resources they need to endure, "as was characteristic of a good king and, in truth, a father" (1.6.40).[189] Though Epictetus employs a father image for Zeus, there is generally a less severe characterization of Zeus as father than was found in Seneca's *De Providentia*. Both the use of this metaphor and the kindly portrayal of God as father may remind us of Hebrews 12.4–11. Secondly, in connection with Heracles, there is a statement strongly reminiscent of Hebrews 5.8. Epictetus notes that God did not give Heracles abundance so as to live luxuriously: οὐδὲ γὰρ τῷ Ἡρακλεῖ παρεῖχεν, τῷ υἱεῖ τῷ ἑαυτοῦ ... ὁ δ' ἐπετάσσετο καὶ ἐπόνει καὶ ἐγυμνάζετο (For God did not even give much to Heracles, [although] he was God's own son ... but [Heracles] accepted orders, toiled, and exercised: 3.26.31). The irony between Heracles' divine sonship and his lot in life serves Epictetus' aim of calling people to a life of dignified austerity, much as Hebrews 5.8 uses Jesus' obedience as a model for those who find salvation in him.

Musonius Rufus, the teacher of Epictetus, was a Stoic philosopher

---

[187] Cf. 3.26.28 which speaks of God using good persons as "examples to the uninstructed" (παραδείγμασιν πρὸς τοὺς ἀπαιδεύτους).

[188] See, for example, 3.10.6–9.

[189] See also 3.24.113, and generally, 3.24.15–16 and 1.13.3–4.

of some influence and reputation. A number of his essays and sayings have been preserved in the anthologies of Stobaeus and the writings of Epictetus and others. Two texts in particular deserve comment for our purposes.[190]

The sixth essay of Musonius is entitled "On Training" (Περὶ ἀσκήσεως). The thrust of this essay is the necessity of complementing theoretical knowledge with practical application, but included is a discussion of the training that involves both soul and body. Examples of the latter include accustoming oneself to "cold, heat, thirst, hunger, meager rations, hard beds, avoidance of pleasures, and patience under suffering."[191] Such training has certain benefits: "For by these things and others like them the body is strengthened and becomes capable of enduring hardship, sturdy and ready for any task; the soul too is strengthened since it is trained for courage by patience under hardship and for self-control by abstinence from pleasures."[192] Twice in the space of a few lines the phrase "patience under suffering/hardships" (ὑπομονὴ τῶν ἐπιπόνων) is used. Endurance pays the dividends of a stalwart body and brave soul. Yet the passive verbs leave the subject of the strengthening unnamed. Do the gods play a role?

The seventh essay of Musonius is entitled "That One Should Disdain Hardships" (ὅτι πόνου καταφρονήτεον). Although his chief concern is hardship suffered in behalf of virtue and goodness, he begins by recognizing that people often suffer in pursuit of unworthy goals: illicit love, financial profit, fame, retaliation. Since everyone suffers hardship for some reason, those who pursue noble goals should be especially willing to suffer. He cites as examples acrobats who risk injury for the sake of a small payment and fighting cocks who, though they lack an understanding of virtue, nevertheless fight bravely to the death. How much more then, should we endure suffering "when we know that we are suffering for some good purpose, either to help our friends or to benefit our city, or to defend our wives and children, or, best and most imperative, to become good

---

[190] The critical edition is O. Hense, *C. Musonii Rufi Reliquiae* (Leipzig: Teubner, 1905). The Greek text along with a translation and helpful introduction are found in Cora E. Lutz, "Musonius Rufus, The Roman Socrates," *Yale Classical Studies*, 10 (1947) 3–147.

[191] Translation from *ibid.*, 55, lines 12–14 (Hense, *C. Musoni Rufi Reliquiae* 25, lines 7–9).

[192] Lutz, "Musonius Rufus," 55, lines 14–18 (Hense, *C. Musoni Rufi Reliquiae*, 25, lines 9–14).

and just and self-controlled, a state which no man achieves without hardships."[193]

A few observations can be made regarding this essay in comparison with other Stoic philosophers. First, Musonius, more explicitly than Seneca and Epictetus, acknowledges and discusses suffering due to one's folly or ignoble aims. Seneca was more often concerned with the suffering of virtuous persons, and therefore it was rarely punitive. In Musonius, some persons suffer because they are not pursuing the goal of virtue, and therefore, at least implicitly, they deserve their lot. Secondly, just as in the sixth essay, the religious dimension is lacking. Musonius does not describe the suffering of the just as a God-sent lesson in virtue, but apparently as the natural means by which one acquires virtue. Neither is the suffering of the ignoble explicitly called punishment from God. God is absent from his reflection on hardships.[194] Lastly, I might note that the sage is called not only to endure hardship (ὑπομένειν, ἀνέχεσθαι, καρτερεῖν), but also to disdain it (πόνου καταφρονητέον). This thought occurs in the title of the seventh essay and also in its final words.

Hierocles, a lesser known Stoic, was roughly contemporary with Epictetus. Little of his writing is extant and, by most estimates, little of it is original. Furthermore, what little has survived is not easily accessible. Fragments of Hierocles' "On Duties" (Περὶ καθηκόντων) have been preserved in the anthology of Stobaeus but are not fully translated into English.[195] Two passages in "On Duties" pertain to human suffering and the gods; they are worth citing at length.

> We should certainly not neglect noting that, even though the gods are not the causes of evil, they attach some evils to certain people and surround those who deserve corporal punishment and loss of their property. They do this not because of malice, thinking that man of necessity must live in distress, but for the sake of punishment. For just as pesti-

---

[193] Lutz, "Musonius Rufus," 59, lines 21–6 (Hense, *C. Musoni Rufi Reliquiae*, 31, lines 3–9).

[194] Musonius is by no means an atheist, of course. For him, as for all Stoics, Zeus is the father of humankind and to be imitated by us. See, for example, essay 17.

[195] C. Wachsmuth and O. Hense, eds., *Ioannis Stobaei Anthologium*, 5 vols. (Berlin: Weidmann, 1974). See also Hans Friedrich August von Arnim, *Hierokles Ethische Elementarlehre* (Berlin, 1906). The lack of an English translation has been partially remedied by extensive selections in Abraham J. Malherbe, *Moral Exhortation: A Greco-Roman Sourcebook* (Philadelphia: Westminster, 1986) 85–104.

lence and drought, and also deluges of rain, earthquakes, and everything of this kind are for the most part produced by certain other physical causes, but at times are caused by the gods when it is critical that the sins of the masses be punished publicly and generally, so also in the same way the gods sometimes afflict an individual's body or cause him to lose his property in order to punish him and to turn others and make them choose what is better ...

I think that comprehending that the divine is never the cause of any evil contributes greatly to proper conduct toward the gods. Evils issue from vice alone, but the gods are of themselves the causes of good and of what is useful, yet we do not admit their beneficence but surround ourselves with voluntary evils ... God is good, and has been naturally filled from the beginning with all virtues, so he could not do evil or cause anyone to do evil. On the contrary, he furnishes every good to all people who are willing to receive it, and, in addition to the good, he freely bestows on us, of those things which are intermediate [between virtue and vice], that which is according to nature as well as that which produces what is according to nature. The one sole cause of evil is vice.[196]

Hierocles' chief concern in these two passages seems to be the benevolence of the gods. They are not the cause of evil, either on the large scale of natural disasters, or on the individual scale of illness and loss. Nevertheless, the gods are apparently able to direct or inflict evils that were not of their creation so that they affect appropriate persons. As in Seneca and Epictetus, Hierocles stresses that there is no malice on the part of deity. On the other hand, the punitive function of these calamities is more explicit in Hierocles than in other Stoic writers.

There is tension in Hierocles' thought and perhaps outright contradiction in his language. It is explicitly denied that the gods cause evil, but in the latter half of the first quotation he acknowledges that natural disasters "at times are caused by the gods." One might remove the tension by appealing to the distinctiveness of Stoic vocabulary in which "evil" would refer exclusively to "moral evil,"

---

[196] Wachsmuth and Hense, eds., *Anthologium*, 1.3.54 and 2.9.7; translation from Malherbe, *Moral Exhortation*, 87–8.

leaving adversity and hardships in the realm of divine provenance.
But it is not clear, at least from the above selections, that Hierocles
is using this distinction. In any case, Hierocles clearly believed that
some suffering was punitive (and monitory) in function. Whether he
held along with other Stoics that non-punitive suffering could be
educative cannot be determined from the limited sources we have.

The last figure to be considered is Marcus Aurelius, the Roman
Emperor from 161–80 CE. His *Meditations* contain a few reflections
on the nature of suffering. Marcus Aurelius embraced the Stoic
orthodoxy of the existence, providence, and benevolence of the
gods: ἀλλὰ καὶ εἰσί, καὶ μέλει αὐτοῖς τῶν ἀνθρωπείων· καὶ τοῖς μὲν
κατ᾽ ἀλήθειαν κακοῖς ἵνα μὴ περιπίπτῃ ὁ ἄνθρωπος, ἐπ᾽ αὐτῷ τὸ
πᾶν ἔθεντο (In fact, the [gods] do exist and are concerned with
human affairs; and so that humankind might not fall into anything truly evil, they have bestowed on them every [needed] thing:
2.11).[197] The qualification "truly evil" presupposes the Stoic conception of evil as vice or moral error. It goes without saying that the
gods have not safeguarded humankind against "evils" in the popular sense. The latter, things such as dishonor, pain, and poverty,
befall evil and good persons indiscriminately. Aurelius' view of
these conditions is in accord with Stoic "orthodoxy": οὔτε καλὰ
ὄντα οὔτε αἰσχρά. οὔτ᾽ ἄρ᾽ ἀγαθὰ οὔτε κακά ἐστιν ([They are]
neither honorable nor shameful. Therefore, they are neither good
nor evil: 2.11).

Aurelius' emphasis on the moral irrelevance of intermediate
matters is strong. Perhaps as a result, and certainly in contrast to
other Stoics, Aurelius shows little concern for any positive construal
of suffering or adversity. Since all things stem from one universal
source,[198] "every injurious thing" is simply "a subsequent manifestation of the grand and beautiful" (6.36). Therefore, one should not
regard harmful things as alien to the divine purpose; rather one
must simply "ponder the source of all things" (6.36). However satis-
fying this reflection might have been to Aurelius and his ancient
readers, it leaves unanswered the question – What positive benefit is
there in suffering adversity? On the specific issue of physical pain,
Aurelius can only parrot the *dictum* of Epicurus: οὔτε ἀφόρητον

---

[197] The divinely granted sufficiency of the individual was "a central tenet of Stoicism." See the citations in A. S. L. Farquharson, *The Meditations of the Emperor
Marcus Antoninus* (2 vols.; Oxford: Clarendon, 1944) II, 520.

[198] See *Meditations* 6.36; 8.23; 9.39.

οὔτε αἰώνιον (It is neither unbearable nor interminable: 7.33).[199] For Aurelius, hardship and suffering are not explicitly punitive, educative, probative, or monitory. The most he says is that they are inconsequential.

3.3.5   Summary of Greek and Roman perspectives

This completes the survey of Greek and Roman texts pertaining to punitive and non-punitive construals of suffering. The most important texts cited above are collected in a chart found at the end of this chapter (section 3.6). A few summarizing remarks can be made here. In several instances a punitive interpretation of suffering is, in fact, affirmed. Homer's Zeus attributed the sorrows of mortals at least in part to their own "reckless folly." Specific historical events were sometimes viewed in this framework. Popular piety saw a causal relationship between sacrilege and suffering when such crimes were followed, even after a significant lapse in time, by calamitous events destroying either the perpetrators or the region involved. This mode of thought sometimes seemed to be embraced by the writer, but other times was only reported as a popular view. A variation of the punitive idea was found in the notion of "inherited guilt," the belief that, when persons escaped punishment for evil acts, their descendants inherited their moral debts and paid the penalty. This belief enabled one to explain ostensibly undeserved suffering.

Apart from these reactions of popular piety, though, Greek and Roman writers generally seemed less prone to attribute punitive motives to deity than did Jewish writers. The only place (within the limit of the texts examined in this study) in which a comprehensive, thoroughly retributive view of human suffering is in evidence among Greeks and Romans was Plutarch's essay *On Superstition*, which, of course, was not that author's personal belief but a critique of popular naivety. In contrast, several Jewish sources (certain prophetic texts, 2 and 3 Maccabees, Psalms of Solomon, and several voices within rabbinic literature) do promote such a rigorously consistent view.

A few Greek and Roman philosophers (Plato, Musonius, Hierocles) engaged in broader reflection on the possibility of human beings suffering for wrongful acts. There was, however, usually some qualification. Plato restricted divine causality to suffering that

---

[199] See Diogenes Laertius 10.140, and Farquharson, *Meditations*, 737–8, 748.

was just and beneficial since God could not be the cause of gratui-tous evil. Musonius Rufus readily admitted that people sometimes suffer as a result of wrongful acts: illicit love, greed, pride, etc. But Musonius did not explicitly speak of the deity as inflicting suffering. Hierocles equivocated, wanting to blame human vices for suffering and to exculpate the gods from responsibility for natural cata-strophes, but admitting that at least some of these events were divinely caused (or perhaps divinely appropriated) and punitive in function.

In general, then, it seems to be true that Greeks and Romans more often questioned the punitive interpretation of suffering than affirmed it. Early poets knew well that the punitive theory did not account for many circumstances. Several writers either rejected or de-emphasized the punitive interpretation and instead highlighted the moral and practical benefits of suffering, ranging from simple insights gained by trial and error to the lofty achievement of a good and just character. Tragedy (notably Aeschylus) viewed suffering and the understanding that ensues as essential features of human existence. Whatever its origin, suffering was a "given" in human affairs, and its potential for benefitting the sufferer was axiomatic for several Greco-Roman authors. Stoics of a later period (most notably Seneca) saw in suffering the means by which the gods exer-cised, tested, and trained persons.

This jumble of ideas forms the milieu in which Hebrews 12.1–13 raises its voice. We have seen that both halves of Talbert's thesis are, as Talbert himself no doubt knew, simplified expressions. Jewish writers often challenged the "orthodox" association of sin and suffering, sometimes simply protesting, sometimes articulating specific alternatives. The views of Greco-Roman authors likewise were not monolithic, but varied and even contradictory. This should occasion no surprise. A complex, existential problem like suffering does not permit easy solutions. Given such a variety of possible interpretations, one's exegesis of Hebrews 12.1–13 must not be done within a rigid framework. True, the author of Hebrews appropriates Proverbs 3.11–12 as a text for exposition, but the intellectual milieu of the author, who gives evidence of being in tune with the rhetor-ical and philosophical currents of his day, was rich with alternatives, any of which could exert an influence without intruding in the form of a citation.

The next chapter gives detailed attention to Hebrews 12.1–13. One matter remains, however, before I turn to the biblical text.

Inasmuch as the key text juxtaposes motifs examined in chapters 2 and 3 namely athletic imagery and formative suffering, it might be instructive briefly to consider other contexts where these motifs converge.

3.4 The convergence of γυμνασία and παιδεία

In depicting the moral life of the sage or saint, ancient writers used a variety of images such as those of an athlete, child, student, or soldier. Sometimes an author employed two or more of these images in order to provide a fuller picture of the struggle to acquire or maintain virtue, goodness, wisdom, or faith, while avoiding evil, passion, sin, and lethargy. In his study of the "agon" motif Pfitzner observed, for example, that "the military image ... often accompanies and complements the athletic image."[200]

In Hebrews 12.1–13 a mingling of athletic and educative language occurs. Such a combination had both logic and precedent. The logic of the combination stems from the fact that the concepts of γυμνασία and παιδεία are overlapping. Both denote a process of "training," the former obviously veering toward physical training, the latter toward social and intellectual training.[201] But both could be employed in a pleonastic expression, as when Polybius (1.1.2) says that the study of history is the truest παιδεία καὶ γυμνασία.[202] The terms were also associated in the Greek system of education. Here παιδεία was usually the comprehensive category of which γυμνασία was a division.[203]

The precedents for combining athletic and educative images are found especially in Stoic authors. Most of these texts have been touched on above. Seneca envisions God as "a glorious parent" who "rears [children] quite strictly" (*De Prov.* 1.5). Several lines later the image shifts to an athletic one. Adversities are no longer parental discipline, but physical exercises, opponents against which one tests one's prowess (2.2–4). Epictetus says that a hardship is an occasion

---

[200] Pfitzner, *Paul*, 157. See the entire chapter on "The Agon Motif and the Military Image in Paul," 157–64.

[201] See Plutarch, *Mor.* 764c, which speaks of a σῶμα ἀγύμναστος (untrained body) and a ψυχὴ ἀπαίδευτος (undisciplined mind).

[202] For the close juxtaposition of cognates of παιδεία and γυμνασία, see Philostratus, *Lives of the Sophists*, 2.619; Lucian, *Timon* 36; and Herodian 5.7.5.

[203] See Isocrates, *Antidosis* 181–2; Plato, *Rep.* 376e, 430a, 521e, 548b–c; *Leges* 743d–e; Aristotle, *Pol.* 8.2.3; Plutarch, *Mor.* 7d.

to show "if we are educated" (εἰ πεπαιδεύμεθα). The challenge of a hardship is likened to a student demanding to be given complex syllogisms to analyze. The next sentence likens the same challenge to an athlete's desire for a formidable wrestling opponent (1.29.33–5). A similar blend of athletic and educative language occurs in 4.4.30–2. Epictetus refers to one who declines to enter the contest and engage another athlete as "uninstructed" (ἀπαίδευτος). Elsewhere he insists that "your teacher and educator" (διδάσκαλον ὑμῶν καὶ παιδευτήν) ought "to engage in the contest" (ἀγῶνα ἀγωνίζεσθαι) of living an austere life (1.9.12). Further examples of this convergence of terminology can be found in Musonius Rufus, Philo, and Diodorus Siculus.[204]

Thus, the convergence of athletic and educative language in Hebrews 12.1–13 is neither surprising nor unique. However, the particular emphases of the author of Hebrews must not be obscured by the raft of comparative texts surveyed in chapters 2 and 3. In examining the biblical text, I will look for those emphases in order to discern the distinctive statement of Hebrews about endurance in suffering.

---

[204] Musonius' sixth essay ("On Training") combines many instances of μανθάνω and its cognates with γυμνάζω and its cognates, although the latter has little of its original athletic sense. Philo combines the images in *De Congr.* 164–7 and 180. Diodorus Siculus speaks of a person who "became an athlete (ἀθλητής) of all virtue. For as a child he availed himself of the best teachers (παιδευταί)" (9.2.1).

3.5   Jewish perspectives on suffering

Punitive suffering	Non-punitive suffering
Zephaniah 3.1–8	
Jeremiah 2.1–37; 7.28; 30.14; 31.18–20	
Ezekiel 5.15; 23.18	
Isaiah 1.5–9	
Amos 4.6–12	
Joel 1.2–2.27	
Proverbs 3.11–12	Wisdom 3.1–12; 11.1–14; 12.19–22
Sirach 22.27–23.3	Sirach 2.1–6; 4.17
	Deuteronomy 8.2–5
	Exodus 16.4
Psalm 6.1; 38.1–3; 39.8–11	
Psalms of Solomon 2.3–7; 10.1–3, *passim*	
2 Macc. 5.17; 6.12–16; 7.18, 31–3, 38; 10.4	4 Macc. 10.10; 11.20
3 Macc. 2.13–20; 6.10	
Tobit 13.2, 5, 10	
2 Baruch 13.1–10; 79.1–4 *et passim*	
Testament of Moses 12.10–13	
Josephus, *Ant.* 2.293–314 *War* 1.656; 5.378, 401–3; 6.110; 7.328–33, 359–60	Josephus, *Ant.* 3.13–16
Philo, *Vit. Mos.* 1.90–5; 2.53–7 *De Prov.* 34 *De Praem.* 126–62	Philo, *Vit. Mos.* 1.191–9 *De Prov.* 55 *De Congr.* 157–80 *De Cher.* 77–82
Thanksgiving Hymns (1QH): various	Words of Heavenly Lights (4Q 504, 3)
m. 'Abot 5.8–9	*b.* Ber. 5a
m. Šabb. 2.6	*b.* Hagiga 4b–5a
y. Yoma 38a	*b.* Šabb. 55b
b. Šabb. 32b, 33a, 55a	
Probative (punitive)	**Probative (non-punitive)**
Jeremiah 6.27–30; 9.6–9	Psalm 17.3; 26.1–3; 66.8–12; 105.16–19
Isaiah 1.25	Judith 8.25–7
	Wisdom 3.6

Expiatory for oneself
Mekilta De-Rabbi Ishmael,
   Bahodesh 10
Manual of Discipline (1QS) 8.2–4

Anti-orthodox protest
Job, *passim*
Ecclesiastes, *passim*

Expiatory for others (vicarious)
Isaiah 52.13–53.12
4 Macc. 1.11; 6.28–9; 17.21–2

3.6   Greek and Roman perspectives on suffering

Punitive suffering	Non-punitive suffering
Homer, *Odyssey* 1.32–4	Solon, Frag. 15
	Theognis 377–8, 383–5
	Herodotus 1.207
Aeschylus, *Persians* 813–15	Aeschylus,
	Agam. 177–8, 250–1
	Eumenides 520–1
	Sophocles,
	Oedipus Coloneus 7–8
	Antigone 1350–3
	Philoctetes 534–8
Thucydides, 1.128.1	
	Democritus, Frag. 182
Plato, *Republic* 380a–b	Plato, *Republic* 379a–380d
Diodorus Siculus 15.48–9; 16.56–64	Diodorus Siculus 15.48.4
Pausanias 7.24.5–25.4	
Plutarch, *Moralia* 165b, 168c	
Dionysius of Halicarnassus 8.33.3	Dionysius of Halicarnassus 8.33.3
	Appian of Alexander 12.13.87
	Pseudo-Aeschines, Epist. 5.4
	Aesop, Fables 134, 223
	Seneca,
	Ad Helviam 2.3
	Epist. 94.74; 110.3
	Ad Marciam 5.5
	De Providentia, passim
	Epictetus 3.22.57; 24.113
Musonius Rufus, Essay 7	Musonius Rufus, Essays 6 and 7
Hierocles (Stobaeus), 1.3.54; 2.9.7	
	Marcus Aurelius 2.11; 6.36

4

ENDURANCE IN SUFFERING
INTERPRETING HEBREWS 12.1–13

4.1 The social context of the readers

The historical circumstances of the Epistle to the Hebrews are
notoriously difficult to determine. The identity of the author was
debated as early as the third century.[1] The date of composition can
be determined no more precisely than the second half of the first
century, with the last quarter perhaps more likely. The geographical
location of the readers is a major conundrum. Suggested locales
have spanned the Mediterranean: Alexandria, Judea, Asia Minor,
Rome, and Spain. But while a location in time and space cannot be
determined, a few facts about the social and religious circumstances
of the readers can be gleaned from the epistle. Though meager, they
aid the interpretation of our passage, for any insight into the readers'
struggles may shed light on the nature of the ἀγών to which they are
called in 12.1–3 and the παιδεία for the purpose of which they are
called to endure in 12.4–11.

The most fruitful passage in sketching the socio-religious circumstances of the community that received the Epistle to the
Hebrews is 10.32–6. These verses constitute a "comfort" passage
following the stern warning of 10.26–31, which concluded with,
"It is a fearful thing to fall into the hands of the Living God."[2]
The author appeals to the readers' past endurance as a basis for
continued endurance (vs. 32 ὑπεμείνατε; vs. 36 ὑπομονῆς ... ἔχετε
χρείαν). By persevering through an earlier crisis, they had shown
courage and confidence that should not be abandoned in their
present circumstances. The brief description of that former ordeal

---

[1] See the well-known comment of Origen (first half of the third century) preserved
in Eusebius, *Hist. Eccl.* 6.25.11: τίς δὲ ὁ γράψας τὴν ἐπιστολήν, τὸ μὲν ἀληθὲς θεὸς
οἶδεν. (But who wrote the epistle, in truth, God knows.)
[2] This pattern of exhortation, stern warning, reassurance is used elsewhere by the
author. See especially 6.1–12; less fully in 2.1–4, 4.11–16, and 12.25–9.

gives us some indication of the nature of their relationship with the larger society.

They are called to remember "the former days in which they were enlightened" (τὰς πρότερον ἡμέρας, ἐν αἷς φωτισθέντες, 32). "Former days" could by itself refer to any previous period in the community's existence, but combined with φωτισθέντες it denotes the time immediately following their reception of the gospel message (cf. 6.4). Presumably the affliction described in the following verses was precipitated by that conversion. In those early days of their Christian existence they endured "a great contest of sufferings" (πολλὴν ἄθλησιν ... παθημάτων). Three things are worth noting in this clause: (1) the theme of endurance, which is central to our passage (cf. 12.1, 2, 3, 7); (2) the sportive imagery of ἄθλησις, which refers especially to a contest of athletes[3] and therefore prepares for 12.1–3; and (3) the notion of suffering, which elsewhere is associated with the testing and perfection of Jesus (2.18; 5.8), as well as with his atoning death (2.9–10; 13.12). Although the language of suffering is not found in 12.1–13, the community's experience of it is assumed and interpreted there.

The "great contest of sufferings" is elaborated in 10.33–4. Two different aspects of this contest are distinguished. Some suffered reproach and abuse; some became the partners of those who suffered. The first aspect refers to exposure to public scorn that involved both verbal and physical ill-treatment. Members of the community were in some way "put on display" (θεατριζόμενοι). The rarity of this word thwarts a more precise definition.[4] The second aspect involves persons not directly affected by this public shaming. They shared vicariously in the ordeal. How they did so is then explained (γάρ). They sympathized, or more precisely, suffered along with fellow members who had been imprisoned.[5] In addition, they suffered the confiscation of their property and did so with joy, confident of a superior, lasting possession.

Although the community's first experience of abuse, imprisonment,

---

[3] The athletic sense of ἄθλησις is evident in Athenaeus, *Deipnosophistae* 10.414c; Philo, *De Congr.* 46.4, *Mut.* 84, *De Spec.* 2.98; Plutarch, *Phil.* 3.2; Polybius, *Hist.* 7.10.2–4; 27.9.7–11; and Strabo 6.1.12. A military nuance is found in Diodorus Siculus 15.16.2 and 16.17.3.

[4] It is tempting to think of Nero's outrages recorded in Tacitus, *Annales* 15.44, but Heb. 12.4 seems to exclude the experience of martyrdom.

[5] The alternate reading, δεσμοῖς (chains), is divided against itself (αὐτῶν, μου) and is easily explained by a transcriptional error. The reading of δεσμίοις is confirmed by 13.3.

and despoliation had occurred in the past and was prompted by
their initial acceptance of the gospel, another passage suggests that
such affliction was an ongoing reality for them. In 13.4 the readers
are enjoined to "remember the prisoners as if bound with them,
[and] those who are mistreated as if you yourselves were in their
body." The community's ongoing struggle with a hostile environment was no doubt the source of their fatigue and disillusionment, a
malaise which the epistle hopes to remedy.

This, then, is a sketch of the situation of the readers. The specifi-
city of the information given in 10.32–4 and its partial echo in 13.4
argue in favor of these being genuine historical circumstances. Lane
notes that some scholars have read these verses as generic exhortations: "By a one-sided emphasis upon the homiletical aspects of the
description, it has sometimes been argued that these verses have no
specific reference; they are concerned solely with theoretical, typical
circumstances characteristic of younger churches."[6] This charge can
be leveled at general paraenesis such as we have in 13.1–2: "Let
mutual love continue. Do not neglect to show hospitality." It is
unwarranted to see descriptive statements about the historical community behind every imperative and prohibition. But 10.32–4 does
not consist of such non-specific, independent exhortations that could
be addressed to any church.[7] Although this passage is introduced by
an imperative, it contains three aorist indicatives that refer to actual
experiences of the community: ὑπεμείνατε ... συνεπαθήσατε ...
προσεδέξασθε. We may conclude, then, that the recipients of the
Epistle to the Hebrews had undergone and were undergoing a period
of great affliction from a hostile, external source. This hostility was
(at least in part) religiously motivated. The source of this hostility
cannot be determined with precision, but the occurrence of impri-
sonments over a period of time suggests persons with some degree of
official sanction.

4.2 The function, boundaries, and unity of the passage

Hebrews 12 is nestled between two clearly identifiable blocks of
material. The first is chapter 11, the recital of the faithful from

---

[6] Lane, *Hebrews*, 301, cites Wrede and Dibelius.

[7] On the nature of epistolary paraenesis, see Abraham J. Malherbe, "Hellenistic
Moralists," 267–333, esp. 280–1. For an example of reading too much history
into general paraenesis, see Barnabas Lindars, *The Theology of the Letter to the
Hebrews* (Cambridge: Cambridge University, 1971) 7–8, 114.

Israelite tradition. This chapter constitutes a shift in the author's earlier argument from "scriptural proofs" in chapters 1–10 to an argument based on *exempla*. We saw in chapter 2 that this strategy was recommended by rhetorical theorists, notably Aristotle.[8] Chapter 11 does contain numerous echoes from the Hebrew Bible, but it functions by amassing paradigms rather than by arguing from textual premises. The second block of material is chapter 13, a volley of commands, instructions, and greetings which conclude the letter. The primary themes of the epistle, the primacy of Christ and the call to faithful endurance and hope, are briefly reprised in chapter 13 (cf. vss. 10–14), but they are not significantly elaborated. Most of the final chapter consists of general moral paraenesis (1–2, 4–6, 9, 15–16), instructions about community leaders (7–8, 17), a benediction (20–1), and epistolary greetings (18–19, 22–5). Thus, chapter 12 may be seen as the apex of this "word of exhortation" (13.22).[9] Here the author makes his final, urgent appeal that the readers not succumb to fatigue, but press on with endurance and hope as did the pioneer and perfecter of faith, Jesus.

Certain grammatical features also mark the transition. Chapter 11 employed the indicative almost exclusively, primarily the secondary tenses, to narrate Israel's past. Chapter 12 reintroduces paraenesis with a hortatory subjunctive (τρέχωμεν, vs. 1) and an imperative (ἀναλογίσασθε, vs. 3). The 3rd-person verbs of chapter 11 shift to 1st and 2nd person in keeping with the personal application of the author's appeal.[10] The words χωρὶς ἡμῶν (vs. 40) insinuate the author and readers into the litany of the faithful; the strong conjunction of 12.1 thrusts them into full view.

There is no consensus on the end of the section which begins with 12.1. McCown divides the chapter into these parts: 1–11, 12–17, and 18–29. George Guthrie's recent text-linguistic analysis uses the following divisions: 1–2, 3–17, 18–24, 25–9.[11] Vanhoye identifies the first section as 1–13 on the basis of an *inclusio* between τρέχωμεν in verse 1 and τροχιά in verse 13. Lane argues that "A single verb

---

[8] Aristotle, *Rhet.* 2.20.9; see also *RAH* 4.3.5.
[9] Ellingworth, *Hebrews*, 637, calls 12.18–24 the rhetorical climax of the epistle. Is there any reason the entire chapter cannot be seen in this light?
[10] Lane, *Hebrews*, 403. Spicq, *Commentaire*, II, 382, calls 12.1–4 a commentary on 10.36.
[11] W. G. McCown, "Ο ΛΟΓΟΣ ΤΗΣ ΠΑΡΑΚΛΗΣΕΟΣ: The Nature and Function of the Hortatory Sections in the Epistle to the Hebrews," Dissertation, Union Theological Seminary, Richmond, VA 1970, 98–110. George H. Guthrie, *The Structure of Hebrews, A Text-Linguistic Analysis* (Leiden: Brill, 1994) 72–3, 132–3.

and its euphonic echo are an insufficient basis for determining the limits of a section ... the limits of this unit must be determined thematically." On the basis of thematic features, however, Lane reaches the same conclusion as Vanhoye.[12]

The theme of Hebrews 12.1–13 can be summed up by the words "endurance in suffering." Nevertheless, neither the conclusion nor the unity of the passage is entirely unambiguous. A paragraph break is variously located after verse 11, after verse 13, or after both 11 and 13, making the last two verses a paragraph in themselves.[13] The last of these options is the best. On the one hand, the *inclusio* produced by the imagery of verses 1–2 and 12–13 argues in favor of a paragraph break after verse 13; verses 14–17 leave the athletic imagery behind. This *inclusio* is admittedly imprecise; the imagery of verses 1–2 is athletic whereas the imagery of verses 12–13 is somatic or medical. But since the somatic terms of verses 12–13 call for the restoration of one's capacity for movement and exertion, they complement the exhortation to run with endurance (vs.1). These verses thus show a stronger connection with what precedes them than with what follows. On the other hand, the *inclusio* of verses 1–2 and 12–13 leaps over verses 5–11, a passage that contains little explicitly athletic language.[14] Hence, 12–13 are best set off as a separate paragraph, though one that brings closure to the entire pericope.

The unity of the passage also requires comment. An initial examination seems to reveal two distinct sections: verses 1–3 and 4–11 (for the moment taking vss. 12–13 as a conclusion to the whole).[15] The first exhorts the readers to "run with endurance" while surrounded by a great cloud of witnesses and while looking to the example of Jesus. The second section contains a similar exhortation to endure, this time substantiated by an understanding of suffering as divine παιδεία, derived from Proverbs 3.11–12. There is a clear shift

[12] Lane, *Hebrews*, 404–5; A. Vanhoye, *Structure and Message of the Epistle to the Hebrews*, (Rome: Pontifical Biblical Institute, 1989) 30, 104–5. The *inclusio* was noticed as early as Theophylactus (*PG* 125.376b).

[13] Nestle[26] divides the text after vs. 11; UBS[3] makes paragraph breaks after 11 and 13, with a new section title for vss. 14–29. Both the NIV and the NRSV set off 12–13 as a separate paragraph.

[14] An important exception to this is γεγυμνασμένοις in vs. 11.

[15] Guthrie, *Structure of Hebrews*, 72–3 puts the break between vs. 2 and vs. 3 on the basis of "cohesion shifts" in topic, temporal indicator, and (verbal) subject. But the topic shift does not occur until vs. 4, or arguably even vs. 5; the temporal focus (present/future) has not changed from vs. 1; and, since the first person subject of τρέχωμεν (vs. 1) is inclusive of the readers, no significant shift occurs in ἀναλογίσασθε.

in focus between the two sections.[16] The contemplation of Jesus which dominates verses 1–3 (ἀφορῶντες, ἀναλογίσασθε) is absent from verses 4–11. The notion of suffering as divine discipline, central to verses 4–11 (note the cluster of παιδεία/παιδεύω words), is absent from verses 1–3. Despite this tactical shift from a paradigm to a scriptural/theological rationale, the aim remains unchanged: the encouragement of the beleaguered readers in their faith struggle. This unity is seen most clearly in the occurrence of ὑπομένω in both sections (vss. 2, 3, 7). Other links between the sections include the danger of fatigue (ἐκλύω, vss. 3, 5), the struggle against sin/sinners (vss. 3, 4), the agonistic language (ἀγών, ἀνταγωνίζομαι, vss. 1, 4), and joy as the outcome of suffering (vss. 2, 11).

4.3 Interpreting Hebrews 12.1–13
part 1 – the example of Jesus

The entirety of chapter 11 constitutes the prior context of Hebrews 12.1–13 and prepares for the latter's paraenetic thrust. The author begins chapter 11 with a functional definition of faith and a brief comment on the relation of faith and creation. He then launches into a review of Hebrew luminaries including prehistoric figures (vss. 4–7), patriarchs (vss. 8–22), and notables from the period of the exodus and the conquest (vss. 23–31). The encomium is punctuated some eighteen times by the Greek πίστει.[17] The penultimate section of the chapter (vss. 32–8) complains of the shortness of time fully to relate the names of those who have performed faithfully. The chapter concludes strategically with the reminder that, despite their faith, these persons did not "obtain the promise"; they did not obtain the ultimate object of faith.[18] God foresaw "something better," the perfection of all God's people under the new covenant.

The surprising note of non-fulfillment with which chapter 11 ends is clearly not the goal toward which the catalog was moving. The

---

[16] Weiss, *Brief an die Hebräer*, 633, notes that the theme of endurance in suffering is discussed first from a christological aspect (12.2–3) and then from the aspect of wisdom theology (12.4–11).

[17] For a discussion of this use of anaphora, as well as other rhetorical devices in chapter 11, see Cosby, *Hebrews* 11.

[18] Elsewhere in the epistle "obtaining" or "inheriting" the promise is an expression for achieving the goal of faith (4.1; 6.12; 9.15; 10.36). Although certain individuals are said "to have obtained promises" with reference to specific, intermediate objectives (6.15; 7.6; 11.17, 33), their ultimate attainment of faith's end is clearly denied (11.13, 39).

denial of fulfillment in verse 39 and the glimmer of hope in verse 40 prepare for Jesus, the supreme example of faith, in 12.1–3, the one through whom the promises are obtained (9.15) and through whom perfection is achieved (10.14). Hebrews 12.1–3 represents the rhetorical culmination of the author's argument in chapter 11 just as the example of Jesus represents the soteriological culmination of the author's theology.[19]

The text begins with a strong inferential conjunction, τοιγαροῦν, a compound of three particles, each of which probably had inferential force.[20] The word indicates an emphatic relationship of premise/inference between 11.39–40 and 12.1–3. The premise of 12.1–3 is the vivid witness of so many faithful predecessors who nevertheless fell short of perfection. The inference is that, like those predecessors, the readers too must show endurance in their struggle. The link between the readers and the OT exemplars is strengthened grammatically by an adverbial καί and the emphatic pronoun ἡμεῖς. "We too," he writes, must demonstrate faith and endurance in suffering. The way in which this must be manifested becomes clear in the metaphor that unfolds.

Elsewhere in the epistle, the author has based hortatory sections on some "possession" of the community. In 4.14–16 the possession of a great high priest undergirds a call to "hold fast the confession" and "approach the throne of grace with confidence." In 10.19–25 the possession of "confidence to enter the sanctuary" and "a great priest over the house of God" supports a three-fold exhortation to "approach ... hold fast ... and consider." Here in chapter 12 the argument is similar. The possession of "so great a surrounding cloud of witnesses" is part of the basis for the following paraenesis.

The metaphor of a cloud to describe a great throng of people is found in both classical and Hellenistic writers.[21] A construction

---

[19] A.T. Robertson, *A Grammar of the Greek New Testament in the Light of Historical Research* (Nashville: Broadman, 1934) 432, calls these verses a "splendid peroration" to chapter 11.

[20] *Ibid.*, 1154, cites three possible etymologies for the particle τοί but is unable to designate any one as certain. Smyth, *Greek Grammar*, 669, however, connects τοί with the locative case of the old demonstrative τό, which had an inferential meaning. The compound is, therefore, more emphatic. See BAGD, 821. In its only other NT occurrence (1 Thess. 4.8) the conjunction has a similarly emphatic force.

[21] In addition to Herodotus 8.109, Attridge, *Hebrews*, 354 n. 18, cites Homer, *Iliad* 4.274, Vergil, *Aeneid* 7.793, and Philo, *Legatio* 226.

similar to the one used by the author of Hebrews appears in Herodotus 8.109 where Themistocles, the Athenian general, speaks of a Greek victory over the Persians as having routed "so great a cloud of men" (νέφος τοσοῦτο ἀνθρώπων). The demonstrative in 12.1, τοσοῦτον, probably calls attention to both the number and the magnificence of that assembly.[22] The position of the demonstrative, separated from the word it modifies, adds additional emphasis.[23] This assembly of exemplars surrounds the readers to encourage them in their "agon."

The word μάρτυς normally has three possible nuances.[24] The basic meaning of the word is "one who bears witness." In its strictest sense, this would involve a judicial setting. This is its meaning in Hebrews 10.28 where the context concerns judicial decisions under the Mosaic law. More broadly, μάρτυς refers to anyone who observes some activity or event and is able, or obligated, to testify to it. A second possible nuance, "martyr," became a common one in the early church as more of those who bore witness to Christ suffered violent death as a result of their testimony. The NT shows signs of "the beginning of the semantic change by which the ordinary Greek word for 'witness' acquired its distinctive Christian sense of 'martyr.' "[25] The third possibility, "spectator," was examined above in chapter 2.[26] There it was found that, although μάρτυς seldom refers to a completely "*passive* spectator," there are cases in which the element of vision is more prominent than the element of "testifying."[27] It was seen in chapter 2 that although μάρτυς was not wholly synonymous with θεατής, the Greek word for spectator, it was often collocated with it. The semantic fields of these words overlap. Μάρτυς is serviceable for the meaning "spectator," especially if other factors call for its use. The explanation for its presence in Hebrews 12.1, then, is that it contains a trace of athletic meaning

---

[22] BAGD, 823, suggests a qualitative rather than quantitative force for the adjective.

[23] BDF, section 473 (2). The device is known as hyperbaton. See Smyth, *Greek Grammar*, 679. Cf. τοιαύτην and ἀντιλογίαν in vs. 3.

[24] BAGD, 494.

[25] F. F. Bruce, *The Epistle to the Hebrews* (Grand Rapids: Eerdmans, 1964) 347.

[26] See section 2.4.

[27] Westcott, *Epistle to the Hebrews*, 393, asserts that "there is no apparent evidence that μάρτυς is ever used *simply* in the sense of 'spectator'" (emphasis added). This may be the case in Biblical Greek, but even there one should not exclude the possibility of an equivocal usage that *combines* the nuances of "spectator" and "witness."

and yet still evokes the recurring motif of bearing and receiving good testimony in chapter 11. Westcott's conclusion strikes a good balance:

> The passage would not lose in vividness though it would lose in power if θεατῶν were substituted for μαρτύρων. These champions of old time occupy the place of spectators, but they are far more than spectators. They are spectators who interpret to us the meaning of our struggle, and who bear testimony to the certainty of our success if we strive lawfully.[28]

In addition to the lexical possibility of μάρτυς portraying a stadium filled with spectators, there is the precedent of the literary motif of a vast, or even "cosmic," group of spectators for an agon. In chapter 2 (section 2.4) we saw that Seneca, 4 Maccabees, Paul, and Diodorus Siculus used such an image. The author of Hebrews, thus, has good precedent for envisioning Israel's faithful assembled to watch his readers' agon of faith.

How, then, do the witnesses function in the exhortation? The author no doubt hopes to inspire the faith of the readers by reminding them of their "possession" of a magnificent assembly of faithful predecessors. The litany of names includes persons who endured testing (Abraham) and abuse (Moses) and every sort of indignity (11.35–8), but did so with faith, trusting that God would reward them (11.6, 26). The correlation with the readers' lives is apparent. Moreover, the addressees will be roused to greater endurance particularly because their own era has the hope of the full realization of God's promise (11.39–40). The relationship between the ancients and the readers is, therefore, not just one of continuity, but of culmination.[29]

The athletic imagery of the passage becomes unmistakable in the second and third clauses of the verse. Like runners preparing for a race, the readers are enjoined to "lay aside every weight." The term

---

[28] *Ibid.*, 393.

[29] Weiss, *Brief an die Hebräer*, 631, notes the syntactical structure of vs. 1 is like 4.14–16 and 10.19–24: "Therefore, as those who have ..., let us ... " An indicative reference back to what "we have" is joined directly to an imperative. The difference, Weiss notes, is that 4.14–16 and 10.19–24 refer to a christological "possession." The exhortation to endurance in 12.1–3 is not motivated solely by Jesus, but also by Israel's heroes of faith, especially those mentioned in 11.36–8.

ὄγκος, slightly emphatic by its position, means "weight," or "impediment."[30] It refers to any encumbrance which hampers movement. Attempts by some scholars to render it "pride" or "arrogant disposition" ignore the metaphor.[31] Such meanings are within the semantic range of the word but are inappropriate here.[32] The verb for "putting off," ἀποθέμενοι, is used literally of clothing and figuratively of all sorts of habits and hindrances.[33] What is the weight to be put off? Conjectures have included clothing,[34] weights carried by runners to increase stamina,[35] excess body fat,[36] or some combination thereof. In chapter 2 I cited texts that associated (excessive) ὄγκος with the inability to run swiftly, or conversely, being compact in ὄγκος with the practice of frequent exercise.[37] These comparative texts, along with the athletic metaphor of Hebrews 12.1–3, make the meaning of "(excessive) body fat" possible for our passage. Seesemann, however, cautions against over-confidence in the matter: "It is hardly possible to define more closely what kind of a burden the author has in mind. By using the adjective πάντα, he himself abandons any such attempt."[38]

The nature of the impediment is uncertain, but a clue to its spiritual effect is provided by the next phrase: καὶ τὴν εὐπερίστατον ἁμαρτίαν. If καί is epexegetical,[39] the meaning would then be "putting off every impediment, *namely*, sin which so easily besets." In this case, sin *is* the impediment. But attempts to designate a precise referent for either ὄγκον or ἁμαρτίαν ultimately fail owing

---

[30] BDF, section 473 (2); BAGD, 553.

[31] Heinrich Seesemann, "ὄγκος," *TDNT*, V, 41.

[32] See Josephus, *War* 4.319, and the citations in LSJ, 1197.

[33] BAGD, 101. The force of the middle voice here is "laying off from oneself." See Robertson, *Grammar*, 810. The participle is circumstantial but derives imperative force from the main verb.

[34] Theodore H. Robinson, *The Epistle to the Hebrews* (New York: Harper, 1933) 175. Also Westcott, *Epistle to the Hebrews*, 394–5. Spicq, *Commentaire*, II, 385, even refers to the custom of Greeks performing naked.

[35] Buchanan, *To the Hebrews*, 207; Bruce, *Epistle to the Hebrews*, 335. Although such a technical meaning would strongly support the athletic imagery, I know of no clear instance of ὄγκος being used in this way.

[36] *Ibid.*, 349; A. Tholuck, *A Commentary on the Epistle to the Hebrews* (Edinburgh: Clark, 1842) 116.

[37] Respectively, Appian 4.7 and Diodorus Siculus 4.20.1. See above, section 2.4 and n. 70, for the discussion and other pertinent references.

[38] Seeseman, *TDNT*, V, 41. Delitzsch's suggestion (*Epistle to the Hebrews*, 299) that ὄγκος refers to "the encumbering weight of Judaic notions, rites, and observances" can be dismissed as tendentious.

[39] Tholuck, *Commentary*, 116. See also Grotius (*Critici Sacri*, vii, 1162).

to the general nature of the author's language. *Anything* which impedes free movement is to be thrust aside.

In the adjective εὐπερίστατον, we have both a textual and a semantical problem. This reading is supported by a wealth of Greek manuscripts, lectionaries, and translations. The only variant, εὐπερίσπαστον, meaning "easily distracting," has very slender support in an early papyrus, p^{46}, and a tenth-century minuscule, 1739. Metzger notes that this variant could have entered the textual tradition either by a palaeographical error or a deliberate modification of the more obscure εὐπερίστατον.[40] In any case, the reading εὐπερίσπαστον, is to be rejected.[41]

There are several possibilities for the meaning of εὐπερίστατον. The prefix εὐ- means "readily," "well," or "easily." The remainder of the word is a verbal adjective of περιΐστημι which has either an active or passive force. Based purely on the form, Moulton and Howard suggest four possible meanings: (1) easily avoided, (2) admired (literally "well surrounded"), (3) easily surrounding, besetting, or (4) dangerous.[42] The first two meanings are wholly inappropriate in the context. Whatever this "sin" is, it impedes one's progress in the race and is, therefore, detrimental. The third meaning is preferable to the fourth since it specifies the way in which sin impedes. Thus the translation "easily besetting" or "ensnaring" conveys the best sense.[43]

"The sin which easily besets" has sometimes been thought to be apostasy.[44] This dire possibility is certainly warned against in the epistle (2.1–3; 12.25–9; and especially 6.4–8; 10.26–31), but a reference to apostasy in 12.1 is unlikely. First of all, although the author warns of apostasy, he ultimately does not think the community is likely go down this path (6.9–12; 10.35–9). More importantly, the

[40] Bruce M. Metzger, *A Textual Commentary on the Greek New Testament* (New York: UBS, 1975) 675. Note that the committee's decision favoring εὐπερίστατον has been up-graded from {B} in UBS³ to {A} in UBS⁴.

[41] The only argument favoring εὐπερίσπαστον is the rarity of the alternative. Lane *Hebrews*, 398–9, nevertheless, prefers it and cites several other scholars sharing this view. On the other hand, the verb ἀποθέμενοι favors the reading εὐπερίστατον since one puts off that which easily ensnares or besets.

[42] J. H. Moulton and W. F. Howard, *A Grammar of New Testament Greek* (Edinburgh: T. & T. Clark, 1919) II, 282.

[43] As most modern commentators have chosen. See the list in Attridge, *Hebrews*, 355, and BDF, section 117.

[44] Tholuck, *Commentary*, 116; E. Käsemann, *The Wandering People of God: An Investigation of the Letter to the Hebrews* (Minneapolis: Augsburg, 1984) 45–8; Spicq, *Commentaire*, II, 385.

sin of apostasy scarcely would fit the image of a runner stripping (or slimming) down for a race. Apostasy would disqualify one altogether, not simply hinder one's progress.[45] More appropriate language for the sin of apostasy would involve avoidance or turning back from it, rather than removing it. The article with ἁμαρτία is probably generic; hence, a general meaning is best.[46]

The syntactical linchpin of the exhortation in verses 1–2 is the verb τρέχωμεν. The hortatory first person, as opposed to an imperative, has a pastoral tone. The author implies a solidarity between himself and the readers.[47] The protracted nature of the race is indicated by the present tense and the modifying expression δι' ὑπομονῆς. The need is not for a sprint, but rather "the grim and resolute determination of the long-distance runner."[48] The object of the verb, ἀγών, is a general term for a contest or struggle. In classical usage, this included athletic, musical, legal, and psychological struggles.[49] Its collocation with τρέχω in Hebrews 12.1 demands the meaning "race." This collocation also occurs in classical writers, usually in a figurative sense as here.[50] I noted in chapter 2 that the use of ἀγών with πρόκειμαι is a common construction.[51] Herodotus, Plato, Lucian and others spoke of contests as "having been set" before a person or group.

The use of athletic imagery in Greco-Roman literature was traced in chapter 2. Here I would only note that the NT supplies many examples in addition to the few found in the Epistle to the Hebrews. Paul's correspondence is a rich source. In 1 Corinthians 9.24–7, the apostle employs the imagery of a race. As athletes compete with seriousness and purpose, so must followers of Christ show earnestness in their endeavors. Paul also speaks of his apostolic ministry in terms of running (Gal. 2.2, Phil. 2.16).[52]

The specific choice of images in Hebrews 12.1–2 is instructive. Whereas the Pauline tradition employed running and boxing meta-

---

[45] H. Montefiore, *A Commentary on the Epistle to the Hebrews* (New York: Harper, 1964) 214.

[46] On the article, see Attridge, *Hebrews*, 355, n. 27. For the image of removing sin like a garment, see Rom. 13.12, Eph. 4.22, Col. 3.8, 1 Pet. 2.1, and Jas. 1.21.

[47] Attridge, *Hebrews*, 64, n. 14, notes other examples of this *captatio benevolentiae*.

[48] Robinson, *Epistle to the Hebrews*, 179.

[49] See the examples cited in LSJ, 18–19.

[50] Bauernfeind, *TDNT*, VIII, 227. For references, see above, section 2.4, n. 72.

[51] See above, section 2.4, and LSJ, 1485 (3); Attridge, *Hebrews*, 355, n. 37.

[52] 1 Cor. 9.24–7 arguably pertains more to Paul's apostolic ministry than to the Christian life in general. See Pfitzner, *Paul*, 82–98.

phors in paired expressions (1 Cor. 9.26; 2 Tim. 4.7), the author of Hebrews has used only the former. As I observed in chapter 2, the paraenetic needs of the readers determine the choice. Their primary need is endurance, not strength or swiftness. As Ellingworth points out, neither is the readers' struggle conceived primarily in terms of competition, but rather of success or failure. There is no hint of overtaking or defeating others in the race, only of successful completion.[53]

Endurance, we saw in chapter 2, was a highly esteemed virtue. It was associated with ἀνδρεία, one of the four cardinal virtues of Greek philosophy. It was seen as closely related to several other virtues: fortitude, prudence, and constancy. The lack of endurance was a supreme vice. Endurance was especially praised by Stoic and stoically influenced writers: Seneca, Epictetus, and the author of 4 Maccabees. Although the ancient moralists did not always couch their exhortations to endure hardships and suffering in athletic images, they frequently and quite naturally did. Our author, then, employs a well-established tradition in calling his readers to "run with endurance."

In 12.2 a participial clause and a relative clause conclude the sentence. The readers are to look away to Jesus as they run this race. The prefix ἀπό adds to the sense. The verb means "to look *away from* all others toward one."[54] It occurs in the description of the Maccabean martyrs, who "avenged their nation, looking unto God (εἰς θεὸν ἀφορῶντες), and enduring torments to the point of death" (4 Macc. 17.10). Josephus describes the associates of Judas Maccabeus as "having no one to look to" (πρὸς μηδένα ... ἀφορᾶν ἔχοντες) after his death (*Ant.* 12.431). In these contexts and in Hebrews 12.2, the word clearly implies more than "to direct one's eyes toward." As with the English expression "to look to," there is a sense of relying upon, looking to with the expectation of support or inspiration.[55]

---

[53] Ellingworth, *Hebrews*, 639. Chrysostom noted that the metaphor chosen by the author was *not* boxing, wrestling, or combat (*PG* 63.193). Cf. Theophylactus (*PG* 125.368C).

[54] LSJ, 292. The re-direction of one's gaze is made more explicit by the preposition εἰς, as in Heb. 12.2, but it was not a necessary part of the construction.

[55] This sense occurs in Epictetus 3.24.16, where it is said of Odysseus that πρὸς ἐκεῖνον [sc. Zeus] ἀφορῶν ἔπραττεν ἃ ἔπραττεν (looking to him, he did the things that he did). See also Epictetus 2.16.42; 2.18.29; 2.19.29, and Plutarch *Consol. ad Apoll.* 119d. In Plutarch, *Mor.* 467e the verb ἀποθεωρεῖν is used similarly. Windisch, *Hebräerbrief*, 109, calls this "the strengthening gaze." See also Weiss, *Brief an die Hebräer*, 634–5, 636 n. 21.

For the author (and presumably his readers), that source of help and inspiration is Jesus.[56] The use of this name emphasizes the humanity of Christ; the postponement of the name adds emphasis.[57] This technique is a favorite one of our author who likes to pile up modifiers and appositional nouns, and place the name at the end of the clause.[58]

The phrase in apposition to the name Jesus is τὸν τῆς πίστεως ἀρχηγὸν καὶ τελειωτήν. Here we see the author's penchant for antithesis.[59] The first half, ἀρχηγός, occurred in 2.10 where Jesus was called τὸν ἀρχηγὸν τῆς σωτηρίας. The meaning in both passages is "originator" or "founder."[60] The second half of the antithesis uses an exceedingly rare word, τελειωτής. The standard lexicons and theological dictionaries offer no instances of the word prior to Hebrews, and some plainly assert that our passage is the first occurrence.[61] But a parallel has been overlooked.[62] Dionysius of Halicarnassus, rhetor and historian of the late first century BCE, uses the word in an essay on Dinarchus, the last of the so-called Attic orators.[63] At the beginning of the essay, Dionysius justifies

---

[56] Lane, *Hebrews*, 406–7: "The writer recognizes ... that an earnest appeal for Christian endurance cannot finally be based upon the antecedent exposition of faithfulness to God under the old Covenant. There can be an appropriate response to the appeal only in the light of the struggle and triumph of Christ.... [Jesus is] the supreme example of persevering faith." The supremacy or primacy of Jesus' example has often been noted. Lapide (*Commentaria*, 953) calls Jesus "the most complete exemplar." Grässer (*Aufbruch und Verheissung*, 109) calls Jesus' example "archetypical." Cf. 1.2 where Jesus is distinguished from the prophets. It is also clear from 11.13, 39 that the OT heroes are not a sufficient motivation.

[57] Note its position in 2.9 and 3.1 also. "Jesus" last appeared in 10.19. See the statistics in Grässer, *Aufbruch und Verheissung*, 109, n. 40.

[58] See 3.1, 6.20, 7.22, and especially 13.20.

[59] Attridge, *Hebrews*, 190, n. 57, notes similar antitheses in 2.10 and 3.14. The juxtaposition of the roots αρχη- and τελ- is found in 3.14b and 7.3.

[60] BAGD, 112. The word also occurs in Acts 3.15 and 5.31, and about thirty times in the LXX. Its many classical meanings include "founder," "creator," and "military leader." The tempting interpretation of G. Mora that ἀρχηγός means "trainer or chief of the games" (see section 2.4, n. 93) lacks philological support. Moreover, in the light of the parallel in Dionysius of Halicarnassus (see n. 62 below), the collocation of ἀρχηγός and τελειωτής almost certainly has a non-technical, non-athletic signification.

[61] BAGD, 810; TDNT, VIII, 86; LSJ, 1770; H. Balz and G. Schneider, eds., *Exegetical Dictionary of the New Testament* (Grand Rapids: Eerdmans, 1993) III, 346; Joseph H. Thayer, ed., *A Greek–English Lexicon of the New Testament* (New York, 1889) 619.

[62] N. Clayton Croy, "A Note on Hebrews 12:2," *JBL*, 114 (1995) 117–19.

[63] The essay "On Dinarchus" appears in the second Loeb volume of "The Critical Essays," trans. Stephen Usher (Cambridge, MA: Harvard University, 1985) and

the omission of Dinarchus from his earlier works on oratory since Dinarchus was neither the "inventor" (εὑρετής) of a style of rhetoric, nor the "perfecter" (τελειωτής) of styles invented by others. This antithesis is quite similar to that of Hebrews 12.2. Dionysius uses εὑρετής instead of ἀρχηγός in the first half of the antithesis, but the two words are nearly synonymous. The parallel illustrates the fairly commonplace experience that in human affairs one person or group often originates something, and then others refine and perfect it. The distinction of Hebrews 12.2 seems to be that *both* terms, in an overarching expression, are applied to a single person, Jesus. He is, according to the author, both the originator *and* the consummator of faith. The faith of Jesus is the "prototype," but not one to be transcended by later improvements, for he is also faith's paragon. Lane renders the phrase "the champion in the exercise of faith and the one who brought faith to complete expression."[64]

In what sense does Jesus originate faith? Jesus was not temporally the first to possess faith. The list of exemplars in chapter 11 establishes the possibility of faith in the pre-Christian era. Michel rightly dismisses the temporal sense (*zeitlich*) in favor of the material sense (*sachlich*).[65] Jesus *originates* faith in the sense that "he is the first person to have obtained faith's ultimate goal, the inheritance of the divine promise."[66] The faith of the ancients as sketched in chapter 11 was forward-looking; the fulfillment to which it looked was Jesus. Yet the same person, according to our author, *perfects* faith. Jesus brought faith to its goal by his perfect obedience and endurance, and finally by his exaltation to God's right hand. In perfecting faith, Jesus has inaugurated "a new and living way" by which to approach God (10.20).[67]

the fifth volume of the Teubner edition, ed. H. Usener and L. Radermacher (Stuttgart: Teubner, 1899).

64 Lane, *Hebrews*, 411. In chapter 2 (see section 2.5) we saw that moralists, particularly the Stoics, were reluctant to claim that the ethical ideal was ever achieved. The author of Hebrews has no such scruples in regard to Jesus.

65 Michel, *Brief an die Hebräer*, 292. The decision here has nothing to do with Christ's "pre-existence," although the author of Hebrews clearly affirms that belief (1.2). See Fred B. Craddock, *The Pre-Existence of Christ in the New Testament* (Nashville: Abingdon, 1968) 128–37.

66 Attridge, *Hebrews*, 356.

67 Weiss, *Brief an die Hebräer*, 635–6, suggests that "faith" here refers to Jesus' own faith, demonstrated in his endurance and suffering. But since, in the context of the whole epistle, the "pioneer of faith" is also the "pioneer of salvation" (2.10), one can say that Jesus is both the archetype and the basis of faith. Hebrews 12.2 thus makes a contribution to the "faith of Christ" debate, even though it does not use

Elsewhere in Hebrews the language of "perfection" (τέλειος/ τελειόω) occurs frequently. Christ himself was perfected through suffering (2.10, 5.9, 7.28) and he brings others to perfection (10.14). The law and the cultic system were incapable of perfecting anyone (7.19, 9.9, 10.1). But here in 12.2, faith itself is perfected, not faith in the sense of "the content of Christian belief, but the fidelity and trust that [Jesus] himself exhibited in a fully adequate way and that his followers are called upon to share."[68]

The relative clause which concludes verse 2 contains one of the major interpretive problems of the passage. Jesus is said to have endured the cross ἀντὶ τῆς προκειμένης αὐτῷ χαρᾶς. The ambiguity lies in the preposition ἀντί. The history of research in chapter 1 revealed that this word has been the crux of a debate for centuries. In the first millennium there was a consensus that Jesus endured the cross "instead of the joy that was set before him," i.e. construing ἀντί as substitutionary. Two closely related factors contributed to this view. First, there was a desire to preserve the autonomy of Jesus. If the Son of God died an ignominious death, surely he had chosen to do so. Interpreting ἀντί as "instead of" shows that Jesus had an alternative to the cross. Secondly, this interpretation harmonized the verse with gospel passages such as John 10.18, which stressed the voluntary nature of Jesus' death, and John 6.15, in which Jesus rejects an earthly kingship, the "joy" of Hebrews 12.2 by this interpretation.

In the centuries from the turn of the first millennium up to the reformation, it began to be widely recognized that there were two possible interpretations of ἀντί. Some scholars, such as Herveus, Peter Lombard, and Aquinas, acknowledged the alternatives without stating a preference. Luther argued that a prospective "joy" sustained Jesus in suffering; Calvin favored the earlier substitutionary

exactly the same language as the contested phrases in Paul (see especially Rom. 3.22). In Hebrews, Jesus is the supreme model of faith; nowhere does the epistle explicitly speak of Christ as the *object* of faith, although he enables the faith of others. See also Attridge, *Hebrews*, 357. Generally, then, Hebrews aligns with the "faithfulness of Christ" side of the debate in Paul. For a discussion of the profoundly christological nature of faith in Hebrews, see Dennis Hamm, "Faith in the Epistle to the Hebrews: The Jesus Factor," *CBQ* 52 (1990) 270–91. On the "faith of Christ" debate in Paul, see the literature cited in James D. G. Dunn, *Romans 1–8* (Dallas: Word, 1988) 166–7.

[68] Attridge, *Hebrews*, 356. Generally, see David Peterson, *Hebrews and Perfection. An Examination of the Concept of Perfection in the Epistle to the Hebrews* (Cambridge: Cambridge University, 1982).

view. Theodore Beza saw that the prospective interpretation made the verse more effective as paraenesis.

Seventeenth-century interpreters began to call attention to the use of ἀντί in Hebrews 12.16 as favoring the prospective construal. By the late nineteenth century a consensus was forming that Jesus had endured the cross "for the sake of the joy set before him," nearly a complete reversal from the consensus of the patristic period. This remains the majority view in the late twentieth century, but the older substitutionary interpretation still has prominent advocates, most recently William Lane.

The interpretation of ἀντί is bound up with the meaning of the participle προκειμένης.[69] It may mean "to lie before" in the sense of "be at hand," "be present," or it may mean "to lie before" as a goal, in the distance. The first meaning of πρόκειμαι combines with the first meaning of ἀντί to yield the sense "instead of the joy which was at his disposal." The second meaning of πρόκειμαι unites with the second meaning of ἀντί, to convey the sense "in order to obtain the joy which was in prospect for him."

The meaning of a word is derived from three factors: etymology, usage, and context, in ascending order of importance. Etymology reveals the origin of a word, but origins can be (and often are) far removed from current usage. Usage refers to the full range of a word's possible meanings as established by a study of the word in various contexts. With regard to ancient languages, our knowledge of usage is sometimes limited by poor representation in extant texts. A word may have had several meanings and been by no means rare, but if the vagaries of literary and scribal activity (not to mention war, climate, fire, etc.) have only preserved intact two or three occurrences of the word, our understanding of its usage is obviously hampered. Lastly, context determines meaning and is, in fact, the decisive criterion. If context requires a meaning that usage has shown to be rare, context must prevail. How do these considerations apply to Hebrews 12.2?

The preposition ἀντί originally had the sense of "over against," "opposite" or "facing." It is cognate with Latin *ante* and German *ant-* as in "Antwort."[70] Its usage in the NT, the LXX and extra-biblical sources amply attests to the meaning "instead of," "in the place of," "in return for." Matthew 2.22 speaks of Archelaus ruling

---

[69] For ἀντί, see BAGD, 73–4 (1) and (3); for πρόκειμαι, see BAGD 707 (2) and (3).
[70] LSJ, 153; Smyth, *Greek Grammar*, 373.

Judea ἀντὶ τοῦ πατρός after the death of Herod. 1 Peter 3.9 urges its readers not to pay back κακὸν ἀντὶ κακοῦ (cf. Rom. 12.17). The alternate meaning is also illustrated by several passages. Matthew 17.24–7 records the story of Jesus' payment of the temple tax with a coin found in the mouth of a fish. Jesus instructs Peter to take the coin and give it to the authorities ἀντὶ ἐμοῦ καὶ σοῦ. Another example would be the celebrated logion, Mark 10.45 (cf. Matt. 20.28), that the Son of Man came to give his life as a ransom ἀντὶ πολλῶν.

In both of these examples ἀντί means "in behalf of X" where X is a person. When X is a thing, "personal" interest is no longer involved, and "in behalf of" shades over into "so as to obtain." Two Hellenistic texts in particular illustrate this meaning. The first is found in Appian's *Roman History* (11.60.314). Seleucus, the king of Asia, has a son, Antiochus, who is gravely ill, pining away with a secret love for his stepmother. Unaware of the identity of his son's love, Seleucus thinks that perhaps the woman is merely reluctant and could be persuaded to marry his son by gifts and enticements. Seleucus remarks that his entire kingdom will some day pass on to his son, and would be given to him even now ἀντὶ τῆς σωτηρίας if the unknown woman desired it. The meaning is clearly "for the sake of" or "so as to obtain [Antiochus'] deliverance [from his illness]." The second example comes from Aristotle's *Nicomachean Ethics* (3.1.7). In a discussion of the moral value of voluntary versus involuntary actions, Aristotle concedes that some actions are a composite of the two types. As an example, he notes that people will jettison a ship's cargo, an action no one would voluntarily perform, if a storm made such a measure necessary in order to save lives. Sometimes these "composite" acts are even praiseworthy, such as "when people endure something disgraceful or painful in order to obtain greater and more noble goals" (ὅταν αἰσχρόν τι ἢ λυπηρὸν ὑπομένωσιν ἀντὶ μεγάλων καὶ καλῶν). The pertinence of this statement to Hebrews 12.2 is apparent, and the verbal similarities are striking.[71]

It is clear that both meanings of ἀντί were in use in the first century CE.[72] One might ask – Was one more common than the other?

---

[71] In addition to ὑπομένω and ἀντί, which occur in Heb. 12.2, note Aristotle's αἰσχρόν and λυπηρόν, which have cognates in Hebrews' αἰσχύνη (12.2) and λυπή (12.11).

[72] For another example of the "prospective" use of ἀντί, see Libanius, Oration 16.3.

Dana and Mantey confidently state "there is conclusive proof that the dominant meaning for ἀντί in the first century was 'instead of.' " This assertion is based on Moulton and Milligan's celebrated research into the papyri.[73] Though the assertion may be statistically correct, two cautions need to be expressed. First, as Dana and Mantey themselves admit, this statement refers to papyri usage. These are *non*-literary documents, often of a commercial nature, and, therefore, the range of the word's usage may not reflect the same distribution found in literary documents. Secondly, and more importantly, a word's "dominant" meaning has little to do with its meaning in a given passage. Context, not statistics, determines meaning.

Before turning to the immediate context of Hebrews 12.2, we should consider 12.16, the only other occurrence of ἀντί in the epistle. That occurrence is instructive. The author warns "Let no one be immoral or irreligious as Esau was, who for (ἀντί) a single meal gave up his birthright." The meaning is "for the sake of" or "in order to obtain." The meaning "instead of" would make no sense in this context.

Part of the immediate context of ἀντί in Hebrews 12.2 is the word προκειμένης. I noted above that the meaning of the preposition is linked to the meaning of this participle. The latter, to reiterate, means "to lie before" either in the sense of "being immediately present" or "being in view as a goal." In choosing between these two options, one cannot help but notice the strikingly similar expression at the end of verse 1: τὸν προκείμενον ἡμῖν ἀγῶνα. Notice the pattern: article, participle, pronoun, noun. The phrase in verse 1 speaks of the race which lies before Christians. The meaning of προκείμαι here, so deeply embedded in the athletic imagery, is clearly "to lie before," but in which sense, "lie at hand" or "lie ahead"? The author might have avoided this ambiguity by using a different expression such as "run toward the goal" or "the prize." To be sure, the ἀγών is one in which the readers are already engaged (10.32–6), but it also extends into the future. This element of extension or "goal-orientedness" is required by the imagery. A race and an exhortation to run "with endurance" necessarily entail duration in time and (figurative) space.

---

[73] H. E. Dana and J. R. Mantey, *A Manual Grammar of the Greek New Testament* (Toronto: Macmillan, 1957) 100. J. H. Moulton and George Milligan, *The Vocabulary of the Greek Testament* (Grand Rapids: Eerdmans, 1980) 46–7.

There is, then, a *syntactical* parallel which can hardly be accidental. This parallel favors the interpretation of ἀντί in 12.2 as "for
the sake of" or "in order to obtain." It is the word ἀγών which
slightly impairs what would otherwise be a flawless *paraenetic* parallel between 1c and 2b. (The first clause might have been better
expressed by something like τρέχωμεν εἰς τὸ βραβεῖον [prize]. Cf.
Phil. 3.14 and 1 Cor. 9.24–5.) Despite this slight imperfection, the
author clearly wants to draw an analogy between Jesus' experience
and that of the readers. Jesus was also in an ἀγών. Just as he endured and obtained joy, so must the readers. The notion of a futuristic joy "beyond the cross" is also supported by verse 2c, which
highlights Jesus' exaltation. His enthronement at God's right hand
is precisely that joy for the sake of which he endured the cross. Joy
also plays a part in the experience of the readers, for 12.11 speaks of
joy as an eventual result of their παιδεία.

In chapter 2 I showed that the popular literary motif of the agon
used the word πρόκειμαι to express *both* "the contest that lies before" *and* "the goal, prize, or reward that lies before" a person.[74]
The latter expression was common in descriptions of athletic contests as well as in metaphorical usages. The prevalence of this language suggests that it forms the conceptual background for the
phrase "the joy that lay before him" in Hebrews 12.2b. Our author
conceived of Jesus as enduring the agon of the cross with a view to
obtaining the joy that lay ahead just as an athlete longs for the prize
of victory. This joy was then realized in his heavenly session at the
right hand of God (2c).

Finally, the larger paraenetic context of 10.32–12.13 strongly
supports the above interpretation. Throughout chapter 11 faith is
that which sustains a person through hardship when reward and
fulfillment are unseen. "Faith is the substance of things hoped for,
the evidence of things not seen" (11.1). Those who come to God
must have faith that God "is a rewarder for those who earnestly
seek him" (11.6). "By faith Noah was warned about things not yet
seen" (11.7). "By faith Abraham went forth not knowing where he
was going" (11.8). "[Abraham] looked forward to the city that has
foundations, whose architect and builder is God" (11.10). "All
these died not having obtained the promises, but having seen them
from afar" (11.13). Moses endured "the shame of Christ, for he was

---

[74] For references to πρόκειμαι with ἀγών, see above, section 2.4 and n. 84; for πρόκειμαι with prizes and rewards, see section 2.4 and n. 88.

looking ahead to his reward" (11.26). Overwhelmingly, the experience of the faithful in chapter 11 is adversity combined with a longing for vindication and fulfillment. By faithful endurance they obtain a more permanent possession in the future.[75]

This interpretation (ἀντί = for the sake of) has been favored by the majority of translators[76] and commentators.[77] It is without a doubt lexically possible; it is in accord with the author's usage (albeit limited) of ἀντί; and it is most consonant with both the immediate and broader context. The paraenetic aim of the author, i.e. to encourage the readers to endure until they obtain their reward (10.35), lends support to the prospective interpretation of ἀντί.[78] Finally, the prevalence of promissory, forward-looking language and the relative lack of martyrological language *in the paraenesis* argue for joy as a prospect that sustained Jesus in his agon.

There are few arguments to commend the "substitutionary" interpretation of ἀντί. Sometimes reference is made to 11.24–26a in which Moses is said to "refuse to be called a son of Pharaoh's daughter, choosing to suffer abuse with the people of God rather than to enjoy the fleeting pleasure of sin, considering the reproach of Christ a greater wealth than the treasures of Egypt." Moses renounces pleasure in favor of suffering, and to that extent Hebrews 11.24–26a might be seen to support a martyrological reading of 12.2. But this appeal to 11.24–26a is superficial and selective. It parallels "the fleeting pleasure of sin" with "joy" in 12.2. But joy is clearly a positive virtue in Hebrews, something for which the readers are commended (10.34), something they are to encourage in their community (13.7). The example of Moses, in fact, serves the prospective interpretation. Hebrews 11.26b reads: "For he was looking away toward his reward (μισθαποδοσίαν)." Even the description of Egypt's

---

[75] See also 10.35–6 and 13.14. Luke T. Johnson notes that the faith heroes "all acted in view of what had not yet appeared" (*The Writings of the New Testament, An Interpretation* [Philadelphia: Fortress, 1986] 424). The paradox of "seeing" what is yet "unseen" is at the heart of faith.

[76] See the Jerusalem Bible, KJV, Moffatt's translation, NEB, NIV, Phillips' translation, TEV, RSV, and NRSV (though the latter offers the alternative rendering in a footnote.)

[77] See those listed in Attridge, *Hebrews*, 357, n. 63. Add to them Bruce, *Epistle to the Hebrews*, 353, n. 45, Moffatt, *Hebrews*, 196, and Robertson, *Grammar*, 574. Ellingworth, *Hebrews*, 641, observes that a weakness of the "in lieu of joy" interpretation is that "joy" would then seem to refer to Jesus' escape from death, a strange use for such a strong word.

[78] On the shaping of the example of Jesus according to the author's aim, see section 2.5.

pleasure as "fleeting" suggests a greater reward lay elsewhere. Again, in verse 27, Moses is said to have set out from Egypt not fearing the wrath of the king "for he persevered as though seeing the One who is unseen." So Moses exemplifies prospective, forward-looking faith as much as self-denying faith.

Not only is there little to commend the substitutionary sense of ἀντί, there are also difficulties with this view. It produces an awkward syntactical construction. Rendering ἀντί as "instead of" would imply that χαρά was also an object of the verb ὑπέμεινεν. In other words, the expression "Instead of X, he did Y" normally means "Instead of *doing* X, he did Y." The same verb would apply to both nouns. But this would produce gibberish in Hebrews 12.2 and would only be possible by means of a harsh zeugma or the ellipsis of some verb with χαρά.[79]

Another difficulty is the question – What would Jesus' renunciation of joy mean? Joy in his pre-incarnational union with God? Joy in the continuation of earthly life? Joy in avoiding the cross? None of these ideas receives significant support in the epistle. Although the author of Hebrews accepts the early Christian belief in the pre-existence of Christ (cf. 1.2), nowhere in Hebrews is there any exposition of the incarnational event that explicitly treats the relinquishment of divine privileges (such as the renunciation of joy.) The closest thing to this is 2.7–9 which speaks of Jesus' "being made a little lower than the angels." But this is not the self-denying kenosis of Philippians 2, a passage that sometimes becomes the lens through which Hebrews 12.2 is read.[80]

The precise definition of the "joy" renounced by Jesus has been a problem for those interpreters who opt for the substitutionary sense. Patristic exegetes, who adopted the substitutionary interpretation almost without exception, split on the exact meaning of the joy which Jesus supposedly renounced. Some took it to mean pre-existent bliss with God; others envisioned an earthly joy free from the suffering of the cross.[81] Modern scholars are similarly

---

[79] Eduard Riggenbach, *Der Brief an die Hebräer* (Wuppertal: Brockhaus, 1987) 390. Windisch, *Hebräerbrief*, 108, believes that the interpretation of ἀντί as "instead of" makes the entire expression "somewhat careless."

[80] Lane, *Hebrews*, 413. See also P.-E. Bonnard, "La Traduction de Hébreux 12:2: 'C'est en vue de la joie que Jésus endura la croix,'" *Nouvelle Revue Théologique*, 97 (1975) 415–23, esp. 416–17.

[81] See the lists in Attridge, *Hebrews*, 357 n. 59 and n. 60, and H. Braun, *An die Hebräer* (Tubingen: Mohr-Siebeck, 1984) 390, n. 29.

divided.[82] If ἀντί is construed as "for, in order to obtain," then the "joy" very naturally becomes the prospective joy of Jesus' exaltation, an idea that is a recurrent theme in the epistle (1.3, 13; 2.7–9; 8.1; 10.12; 12.2).[83] The juxtaposition of Jesus' suffering and his entry into heavenly glory occurs elsewhere in the NT. First Peter 1.8 speaks of "the sufferings of Christ and the subsequent glory." In Luke 24.26 the risen Christ asks the Emmaus travelers, "Was it not necessary that the Christ should suffer these things and enter into his glory?"

William Lane, the most recent major commentator to construe the text in the sense of "renunciation of heavenly joy," does not offer a detailed defense, but rather refers the reader to other studies, most notably those of Nisius and Andriessen.[84] Nisius' arguments are weakened by specious philological reasoning (ἀντί should only be translated as "for" in commercial contexts), tendentious translations (the prospective interpretation would be redundant: "In order to attain his glory, Christ endured the cross and attained his glory"), and the assumption of Pauline authorship (ἀντί as "for" yields a non-Pauline thought).

Andriessen spends an inordinate amount of space discussing how Hebrews 12.2 was interpreted by patristic exegetes and translated in the ancient versions.[85] This provides an interesting history of research, but it does not constitute an exegetical argument. Andriessen also tends to restrict unjustly the meaning of ἀντί. He claims that the final sense of this preposition is found nowhere in the NT. He even denies this sense to Hebrews 12.16.[86] A causative sense occurs a few times, but only, says Andriessen, in stereotyped phrases such

---

[82] See the lists of those opting for pre-existent joy versus deliverance from the cross, Lane, *Hebrews*, 413 and 414, respectively, and Lünemann's lists of ancient and modern opinions (*Commentary*, 703, nn. 2–4).

[83] Outside Hebrews, see Rom. 8.34, Eph. 1.20, and Col. 3.1.

[84] J. B. Nisius, "Zur Erklärung von Hebr. 12,2," *Biblische Zeitschrift*, 14 (1917) 44–61; P. Andriessen, "Renonçant à la joie qui lui revenait," *Nouvelle Revue Théologique*, 97 (1975) 424–38. See also P. Andriessen and A. Lenglet, "Quelques passages difficiles de l'Epître aux Hébreux (5,7.11; 10,20; 12,2)," *Biblica*, 51 (1970) 207–20, esp. 215–20.

[85] Andriessen, "Renonçant," 425–9.

[86] Andriessen's argument in favor of a substitutionary sense for ἀντί in Heb. 12.16 is unpersuasive and somewhat circular. His interpretation of ἀντί in 12.2, which is the crux of the article, is used to support his interpretation of ἀντί in 12.16, which is itself part of the argument for his interpretation of ἀντί in 12.2. See Andriessen and Lenglet, "Quelques passages difficiles," 219–20.

as ἀνθ' ὧν and ἀντὶ τοῦτο.[87] But, as I argued above, context, not the statistics, determines meaning. Finally, Andriessen asks, "Can it be that Jesus endured the cross only, or primarily, for the purpose of finding joy?"[88] Such an idea, he says, would contradict the affirmations of the epistle that the sacrifice of Jesus had as its purpose the atonement of sin and the perfection of God's people (9.14; 10.14). Needless to say, Andriessen's query is a distortion of Hebrews 12.2, and his strict dichotomy of seeking joy or atoning for sin is a false one.[89]

Andriessen's uneasiness with the implications of the prospective interpretation of ἀντί points to a problem for some modern readers. No one takes issue with Jesus' exaltation following his suffering. The discomforting feature is the portrayal of Jesus having subsequent joy *as a conscious motive*, or perhaps even compensation, for enduring the cross. To some minds this mitigates the suffering of the cross.

Modern notions of altruism and selflessness may make us demur at the thought of Jesus' having joy in view while suffering the cross, but two basic hermeneutical points must be borne in mind. First, if our aim is to interpret the text in accordance with the author's intent, i.e. historically, modern sensitivities have little bearing on the process. The relevant question is whether *the author of Hebrews* demurs at a certain portrayal of Jesus. Secondly, we must remember that we are, in fact, dealing with a *portrayal* of Jesus. The psychological state of the historical Jesus as he contemplated and endured the cross was no more recoverable for the author of Hebrews than it is for us. The issue is the *paraenetic use* of the Jesus tradition. It apparently did not trouble our author to portray Jesus as suffering on the cross, sustained by the thought of joy lying ahead, and to use this portrayal as an encouragement to readers.[90] We should conclude that the author meant "*for the sake of* the joy which lay before him," and that the joy of Jesus' exaltation served as the "prize" or "reward" of his race.

Let us proceed with the remainder of verse 2. Only here in the NT

---

[87] Andriessen, "Renonçant," 429–31.
[88] Andriessen and Lenglet, "Quelques passages difficiles," 215.
[89] For a full response to Andriessen and Lenglet, see Bonnard, "Traduction de Hébreux 12:2."
[90] The author was clearly *not* reluctant to understand faithful endurance as rewarded by God (10.35; 11.6, 26).

is Jesus said to have "endured" (ὑπέμεινεν) the cross.[91] The choice of this word is quite deliberate inasmuch as it serves the hortatory purpose of the author. The verb and its related noun occur four times in the passage (vss. 1, 2, 3, 7). It unifies the thought by connecting the endurance enjoined on the Christian community to the endurance exemplified by Jesus. If the author had emphasized the *death* of Jesus or used the language of violent suffering so common in martyrologies, the paraenetic thrust would have been lost since the readers' experience had not reached that extreme (vs. 4). We saw in chapter 2 that the example of Jesus was carefully shaped to meet the needs of the rhetorical situation (section 2.5). Only those aspects of Jesus' experience that are relevant to the readers – endurance, shame, hostility, joy – have been appropriated.

The ignominy of crucifixion in antiquity is well known.[92] Cicero calls it "*crudelissimum taeterrimumque supplicium*" (the most cruel and hideous punishment, *In Verrem* 2.5.62, 165). Elsewhere he pleads that the very mention of a cross "be far not only from the body of Roman citizens but also from their thought, their eyes, their ears" (*Pro Rabirio* 5.16). The significance of this mode of execution did not escape the NT writers. Paul's celebrated "kenosis" passage in Philippians 2.6–11 reaches its nadir at the end of verse 8 with the words ὑπήκοος μέχρι θανάτου, θανάτου δὲ σταυροῦ.[93] In Hebrews 12.2, "cross"[94] sums up the suffering of Jesus, his endurance of which serves as an example to the community.

In enduring crucifixion Christ disregarded the ignominy of the cross. The author's juxtaposition of the words "cross" and "shame" may even be deliberate.[95] The aspect of crucifixion that our author wants to highlight is not its lethal nature or the physical torments

---

[91] Braun, *An die Hebräer*, 406, notes other biblical expressions involving the cross as a direct object. Spicq, *Commentaire*, II, 388, notes that the verb is unusual with "cross" as the object. In this passage of Hebrews the cross is viewed "not so much as a redemptive event (as in 1.3) but as an ordeal inflicted through the active opposition of sinners" (Lane, *Hebrews*, 414).

[92] J. Schneider, "σταυρός," *TDNT*, VII, 573–4; Martin Hengel, *Crucifixion in the Ancient World and the Folly of the Message of the Cross* (Philadelphia: Fortress, 1977).

[93] This is a powerful combination of anastrophe, brevity and final word order.

[94] The anarthrous noun is qualitative. It thus emphasizes the nature of Christ's death rather than the fact. A good English rendering might be: "He endured crucifixion."

[95] The chiastic word order brings together two related concepts. It must be acknowledged, however, that the object of καταφρονέω often precedes the verb in the NT.

that it inflicted, but its shame.[96] Here again the paraenetic use of the tradition is evident. The readers' ordeal had not involved crucifixion (12.4); it had involved public displays, reproaches, and afflictions (10.32). The same language (ὀνειδισμός) was used anachronistically to describe the sufferings of Moses (11.26), and will be used later in a final appeal to the readers to imitate Jesus' sufferings (13.13).

The verb καταφρονέω can mean "despise" or "scorn," but the sense here is "lightly esteem, disregard, count insignificant."[97] The motif of persons disregarding suffering and death is found frequently in Hellenistic literature.[98] This is an instance where a clear lexical similarity exists between the language of our passage and that of martyrologies. Fourth Maccabees provides a number of examples: Eleazar, the elderly priest (6.9), the seven brothers (13.1, 9; 14.1), and their mother (14.11; 16.2). The terms for "despising" vary (καταφρονέω, περιφρονέω, and ὑπερφρονέω), but a more important observation for our purposes is the object of those verbs. The Maccabean martyrs typically "despise" coercive means (ἀν-αγκή, 6.9), suffering (πόνος, 13.1), agony (ἀλγηδών, 14.1, 11), and torture (βάσανος, 16.2). Such experiences were obviously part and parcel of the dreadful persecutions related in the Maccabean literature. The point is that the crucifixion of Jesus could have been portrayed with similar gruesome detail in Hebrews 12.2–3, but was not.[99] The needs of the rhetorical situation have shaped the portrayal.

The final clause of verse 2 repeats the familiar refrain of Psalm 110.1. This passage is appropriated five times by the author to

---

[96] On the categories of shame and honor in Hebrews, see David A. DeSilva, "Despising Shame: A Cultural–Anthropological Investigation of the Epistle to the Hebrews," *JBL*, 113 (1994) 439–61; and, by the same author, *Despising Shame. Honor Discourse and Community Maintenance in the Epistle to the Hebrews* (SBLDS 152; Atlanta: Scholars Press, 1995).

[97] BAGD, 420. Cf. Aristotle, *Rhet.* 2.2.3.

[98] Appian, *BC* 5.4.36; Dio Cassius 43.38.1; 46.26.2; 46.28.4; Diodorus Siculus 5.29.2; 17.43.6; 17.107.5; Diogenes Laertius 1.6; Epictetus 4.1.70–1; Herodian 3.3.5; Josephus, *War* 2.377; 3.475; 5.458; 6.42; 7.406; Lucian, *Peregr.* 13; Marcus Aurelius 4.50; 12.34; Philo, *Abrahamo* 183; Plutarch, *Brut.* 12.1; *Mor.* 210–11; 216c. Musonius Rufus devoted an entire essay to "Despising Hardship" (Essay 7). On the association of "despising death or terror" and "endurance," see Aristotle, *Eth. Nic.* 1104b (Loeb 2.2.9) and Lucian, *Peregr.* 23.

[99] The most important passage in Hebrews dealing with the agony of Jesus' death (or, more precisely, its anticipation) is 5.7–8. This text contains none of the vocabulary of torture found in the Maccabean literature and, indeed, portrays Jesus as obedient, rather than resolute and impassive.

depict the exaltation of Christ. The opening scripture catena concludes with a quotation from the LXX (1.13). The other occurrences in the epistle (1.3, 8.1, 10.12, 12.2) shift the construction from an imperative to a third-person indicative so that the action is explicitly predicated of Christ. The other slight variations (throne versus God versus majesty) are examples of metonymy and are not theologically significant. The use of the perfect tense (κεκάθικεν) in 12.2 is noteworthy, however.[100] It indicates not simply the past action of taking one's seat, but the continued session of Christ. As Bruce laconically puts it, "He is still there."[101] As I have argued above, Christ's assumption of a position at God's right hand represents the joy for the sake of which he endured the cross, the prize that awaited him at the end of his agon. In view of this, it is fitting that the final allusion to Psalm 110 employs the perfect tense. Jesus assumed a place of honor at the end of his agon. When the faithful, who are still in the thick of the agon, fix their gaze on him (2a), it is as the one who is the *perfecter* of faith (2a), who *has* taken a seat at God's right hand (2c), and *has* endured such great hostility at the hands of sinners (3a).

In the third verse the focus on Jesus as the paradigm of endurance continues. He endured faithfully; therefore,[102] his followers are urged to consider him carefully. The contemplation[103] of Jesus has been elevated from a circumstantial action related to the exhortation (2a) to the central imperative (3a). "*Consider* the one who has endured[104] such great[105] hostility at the hands of sinners!" The

---

[100] Of the five references to Ps. 110.1 this is the only one that uses the perfect.

[101] Bruce, *Epistle to the Hebrews*, 353 n. 44. On the tense, see also Ellingworth, *Hebrews*, 642, and Montefiore, *Commentary*, 215.

[102] The conjunction γάρ is inferential; BAGD, 152.

[103] The comparative nuance of ἀναλογίζεσθαι may be present. The readers may be asked to consider how Jesus' ordeal compares to their own (Westcott, *Epistle to the Hebrews*, 399). H. Niederstrasser, *Kerygma und Paideia: Zum Problem der erziehenden Gnade* (Stuttgart: Evangelisches Verlagswerk, 1967) 402, notes that the reference to the historical Jesus is "in no way meant only 'historically,' but is simultaneously a call to discipleship." If this comparative nuance is present, then the link to vs. 4, which probably alludes to Jesus' experience of violence, is made even stronger. On the latter, see Moffatt, *Hebrews*, 198.

[104] The perfect again stresses the continuing validity of Christ's example. See Lane, *Hebrews*, 400, and BDF, section 342 (5). Ellingworth, *Hebrews*, 643, comments that the perfect participle "properly indicates resistance over a period of time." But this is not necessarily the emphasis of the perfect tense, which more likely stresses the successful completion of Jesus' endurance. He now serves as an example of one who has suffered the supreme hardship and emerged victorious. For the perfect tense elsewhere in Hebrews, see 1.4; 2.9, 18; 4.14, 15; 7.26, 28; 9.26; 12.2.

[105] Note the emphasis on τοιαύτην through hyperbaton.

choice of the word ἀντιλογία, just like the choice of ὑπομένω and αἰσχύνη, facilitates the analogy with the readers' experience. "Endurance of hostility at the hands of sinners" is precisely their need (10.32–6). This hostility is not necessarily limited to verbal contradiction.[106] Chrysostom and others saw here an allusion to the full range of abuses that befell Jesus in his passion.[107] Still, the *primary* connotation of the word is verbal, not physical opposition. Again we see the shaping of the Jesus tradition for paraenetic purposes.

The words εἰς ἑαυτόν constitute the second major textual problem of the passage. If we omit the variation between the simple pronoun and the reflexive, the choice is basically between the singular, which would refer to Christ, and the plural, which would probably refer to "sinners."[108] The manuscript evidence weighs heavily in favor of the plural, but the extreme difficulty of construing it has made editors reluctant to place it in the text.[109] Textual critics normally prefer the more difficult reading, but as "difficult" approaches "impossible" it becomes more likely that the reading is corrupt.[110]

Most attempts to construe the plural depend on the idea of sinners' self-destructiveness.[111] Thus, ironically, Jesus endured hostility at the hands of sinners "against themselves." Parallels are adduced from the OT,[112] classical,[113] and Hellenistic[114] literature. These are

---

[106] *Pace* Lünemann, *Commentary*, 703.

[107] *PG* 63.195–6. Cf. Oecumenius (*PG* 119.425) and Theophylactus (*PG* 125.369).

[108] The attempt to connect ἑαυτούς with the main verb ἀναλογίσασθε ("consider in yourselves") breaks down in view of the word order (Braun, *An die Hebräer*, 407).

[109] The singular is printed by the UBS[3], UBS[4], Nestle[26] and Constantinus de Tischendorf's *Novum Testamentum Graece* (Leipzig: B. Tauchnitz, 1904). B. F. Westcott and F. J. A. Hort (*The New Testament in the Original Greek* [New York: Harper, 1895]) opt for the plural.

[110] Windisch, *Hebräerbrief*, 110, calls the plural "impossible."

[111] Lane offers a sometimes convoluted defense of the plural reading largely based on Heb. 6.6 as an alleged parallel expression; likewise Montefiore, *Commentary*, 216.

[112] Korah's rebellion in Num. 17.3 (LXX); Prov. 8.36. Ellingworth (*Hebrews*, 643–4, and "New Testament Text and Old Testament Context in Heb. 12:3," in E. A. Livingstone, ed., *Studia Biblica 1978* = *JSNT*, Suppl. 3 [1980] 89–96) argues that "sense can be made of the plural if, and only if, it is seen as a verbal allusion to the LXX of Num. 17.3" (p. 90). Moreover, he suggests that the author may also have in mind the hostility of OT sinners against the pre-incarnate Christ. But Bruce, *Epistle to the Hebrews*, 332, questions this idea on the basis of the weakness of the verbal parallel and the word order of Heb. 12.3.

[113] Xenophon, *Hellenica* 1.7.19: εὑρήσετε σφᾶς αὐτοὺς ἡμαρτηκότας τὰ μέγιστα εἰς θεούς τε καὶ ὑμᾶς αὐτούς. (You will find yourselves having committed the greatest sins against both the gods and yourselves.)

[114] Philo, *Quod Deterius Potiori Insidiari Soleat* 52: ὁ βλάπτων τὸν ἀστεῖον ἐπιδέδεικται ζημιῶν ἑαυτόν. (The one who hurts a good person is shown to be harming himself.) See also Jude 11.

self-defeating, though, because the clarity of their expression of self-destructiveness only casts more doubt on its obscurity in Hebrews 12.3. Zuntz concludes: "The singular is the only imaginable reading that fits the context ... The attempts at making sense of [the plural] only prove its absurdity. It would, then, have to be put down as one more instance of the 'primitive corruption' which Westcott and Hort recognized in this epistle."[115]

The last clause of the pericope states the intended result of considering Jesus and, in doing so, returns to the athletic metaphor. The author hopes that the contemplation of Jesus will prevent his congregation from growing weary and fatigued as they run their race. Both words (κάμνω and ἐκλύομαι) can refer to physical or spiritual fatigue.[116] The first originally meant simply "to work" or "toil"; then it came to denote the effect of continual work, namely, "to be weary."[117] The latter verb, in the active voice, means "set free" or "release"; only the passive occurs in Christian literature, however. The passive sense of "relaxed" or "slack" developed into "become faint, give out." The word appears again in 12.5 in the quotation from Proverbs 3.11–12 and thus constitutes one of the lexical links between verses 1–3 and 4–11.[118]

These two verbs (κάμνω and ἐκλύομαι) occur together in Aristotle (*Rhet.* 3.9.2–3), a passage with a very different larger context, but one nevertheless having certain affinities with our author's metaphor.

> διόπερ ἐπὶ τοῖς καμπτῆρσιν ἐκπνέουσι καὶ ἐκλύονται προορῶντες γὰρ τὸ πέρας οὐ κάμνουσι πρότερον

> So at the finishing line [runners] are out of breath and become faint; for by looking ahead to the end, they do not give out beforehand.

This is how our author understands the example of Jesus. By looking ahead to "joy," he endured the ἀγών of the cross. This is also the author's aim with regard to the readers: to inspire them to

---

[115] G. Zuntz, *The Text of the Epistles* (London: Oxford University, 1953) 120. Advocates of the plural include Montefiore (*Commentary*, 216), Buchanan (*To the Hebrews*, 210), A. Wikgren (in Metzger, *Textual Commentary*, 675), and Lane (*Hebrews*, 400). See also Moffatt, *Hebrews*, 198.

[116] See the references in Attridge, *Hebrews*, 358, n. 79, n. 80.

[117] LSJ, 872.

[118] In addition to ἐκλύομαι, note the following links: ἀγῶνα (1), ἀνταγωνιζόμενοι (4); ἁμαρτωλῶν (1), ἁμαρτίαν (4); ὑπομονῆς (1), ὑπομένετε (7); χαρᾶς (2), χαρᾶς (11).

run with endurance so they do not give out before reaching the goal.

Two remaining issues are the structure and the function of these few verses in the Epistle to the Hebrews. Estella Horning has addressed these matters in a brief article.[119] Regarding structure, she sees an elaborate, four-step chiasmus in verses 1 and 2. Four sets of matching elements center around the participial clause beginning verse 2. Below is her translation arranged to show the chiastic pairs.

> Therefore we,
>> A   having *seated around about* us such a cloud of witnesses,
>>> B   *setting aside* every weight and every clinging sin
>>> . . .
>> C   with *patient endurance* . . .
>> D   let us run the *race that is set before us* . . .
> Keeping our eyes on Jesus the pioneer and perfecter of the faith,
>> D'   Who for the *joy that was set before him* . . .
>> C'   *patiently endured* a cross . . .
>>> B'   *despising shame* . . .
>>>> A'   and *is seated* at the right hand of the throne of God.

Horning's structural analysis is ingenious but, like so many chiastic arrangements, over-refined. The parallel between D and D' is unmistakable. It expresses in athletic terms the analogy between the experience of the readers and that of Jesus. Likewise C and C' share a common theme, but whether they are part of a chiasmus is debatable. The two (Greek) words that Horning has isolated as part C really belong to D, and can scarcely have been intended as a separate element in a chiasmus. Thereafter, the analysis is weak. Part B has little to do with B', and part A only aligns with A' because of Horning's translation. The observation of parallels in C/C' and D/D' is valid, but I would regard them simply as a comparison rather than a chiasmus. "We face a 'contest' as *Christ* faced a cross. *We* must have endurance just as *He* had endurance. *We* must not give out until we reach the end just as *Christ* reached His goal at the right hand of God." This analysis is less elaborate than Horning's

---

[119] Estella B. Horning, "Chiasmus, Creedal Structure, and Christology in Hebrews 12.1–2," *Biblical Research*, 32 (1978) 37–48.

schema, but there is a higher degree of certainty that this much was in the author's mind. I should point out again that the most certain pair in this chiasm, parts D and D', lends support not only to a rhetorical comparison between Jesus' agon and that of the readers, but also to the prospective interpretation of ἀντί. If the "joy set before Jesus" is parallel to "the race set before us," then both are to be pursued. If the readers are to *engage* in their race, but Jesus *renounced* joy, then the parallel is destroyed.

Horning has rightly pointed out that these verses gather up several of the principal christological themes of the book: perfection, testing, endurance, suffering, faithfulness and exaltation. Psalm 110, a scriptural linchpin for the author, is also alluded to here. There is, then, a synoptic quality to the passage.

Hebrews 12.1–3 does not argue, as most of the material in the first ten chapters did, that one ought to be faithful because the revelation (priesthood, covenant, sacrifice) given in Christ is superior to what existed before. It argues from examples, not exposition, from paradigms, not precepts. This recalls Aristotle's advice about rhetorical strategy: exemplars should follow enthymemes.[120] As the agonistic exemplar who culminates (and makes possible) all previous exemplars, Jesus serves as the supreme model of endurance, scorning a shameful cross and finally assuming the victor's position at the right hand of God. The paradigm displayed to the readers of the epistle is, then, not one who has forgone joy and suffered a martyr's death, but a contestant who has faithfully endured an agon similar to that of the readers and has completed the race.

4.4   Interpreting Hebrews 12.1–13
part 2 – suffering as παιδεία

Although Hebrews 12.1–13 as a whole has a certain unity, the new image in verses 4–13 deserves separate treatment.[121] This placement of the paragraph division could be disputed. In favor of a division beginning with verse 4 are the following considerations: (1) the main verbs in verses 1–3 were hortatory and imperatival; in verses 4–5 they are indicative;[122] (2) in conjunction with this change in mood,

---

[120] See section 2.5.

[121] The unity of the text is established by the motif of endurance in a struggle, the athletic imagery, and a number of link words. See n. 118 above.

[122] Attridge, *Hebrews*, 360, speaks of a somewhat abrupt shift from exhortation to alliterative description. Verse 5a might be construed as interrogative; so

the temporal reference of the verbs has shifted from the community's present needs to its past action (ἀντικατέστητε); (3) while there is no grammatical connection between verses 3 and 4, a καί links 4 and 5; and, perhaps most importantly, (4) the focus shifts from the contemplation of Jesus to the community's suffering and a theological rationale for it. On the other hand, the presence of agonistic language in verse 4 shows its connection with 12.1–3 and might be seen as favoring a paragraph division beginning with verse 5.[123] Verse 4 is thus a transition from the example of Jesus to the community's failure to understand the nature of "divine discipline." Although it is not a matter of critical importance, on balance this verse is better seen as part of what follows rather than what precedes.[124]

This new section, verses 4–13, is *theo*-logically, not christologically, oriented.[125] A backwards glance at the suffering of Christ may be implied in verse 4, but there is not a single, explicit reference to Jesus in verses 4–13. The rationale derives from a scriptural citation about the discipline of the Lord (παιδεία κυρίου). Κύριος here does *not* refer to Jesus; the author elaborates a Father/Child relationship in which κύριος is understood as θεός. The author's commentary nowhere suggests that Jesus is either ὁ παιδεύων or ὁ παιδευόμενος, this despite the description of Jesus earlier in the epistle as a son who learned obedience through suffering (5.8–9).[126]

It is sometimes suggested that the athletic imagery in verse 4 has changed from a footrace to boxing or wrestling.[127] If so, the image is not well developed; of the words ἀντικαθίστημι and ἀνταγωνίζομαι, only the latter is etymologically "agonistic," and neither word

---

Delitzsch, *Epistle to the Hebrews*, 310–11; Lünemann, *Commentary*, 704, n. 4; McCown, "Ο ΛΟΓΟΣ," 203–4; Peterson, *Perfection*, 300; Spicq, *Commentaire*, II, 392; RSV; and the Jerusalem Bible.

[123] The Jerusalem Bible begins a new paragraph with vs. 5.

[124] I see no merit in the division between vss. 2 and 3. See the RSV, NRSV, TEV, and NEB.

[125] Weiss, *Brief an die Hebräer*, 646, calls vss. 4–13 the rational argument which functions as a supplement to the specifically Christian argument of vss. 1–3.

[126] Ellingworth, *Hebrews*, 648, claims that the theme of discipline was applied to Christ in 5.8, but the key term, παιδεία, is not used there. Perhaps the reason for this is that the recipients of παιδεία are implicitly immature, an implication the author of Hebrews might not wish to make about Christ (cf. 4.15). The sensitivity of the ancients to the etymological link between παιδεία (discipline) and παιδία (childish play) is seen in Dio Chrysostom 4.30; Plato, *Laws* 656c; and Plutarch, *Mor.* 80c.

[127] Delitzsch, *Epistle to the Hebrews*, 309; Ellingworth, *Hebrews*, 646; Lane, *Hebrews*, 417; Lünemann, *Commentary*, 704; Montefiore, *Commentary*, 217.

has a strong athletic nuance. The blood language (μέχρις αἵματος) has its primary reference in the crucifixion of Jesus, not in the savagery of ancient sports.[128] Violence and death thus represent the supreme degree of opposition in a struggle against sin. The readers have not yet encountered such violent hostility. The persecution they have undergone consisted of reproaches, afflictions, imprisonment, and dispossession of goods (10.32–4; 13.3).

What is the "sin" against which the readers must struggle? It could be interpreted as "the subjective, inward struggle against sin" if interpreted in the light of verse 1.[129] In the context of verses 3–4 and given the community's experience described in 10.32–4, a more likely interpretation is that "sin" is here personified and is equivalent to "sinners" (cf. ὑπὸ τῶν ἁμαρτωλῶν, vs. 3).[130] What sense would it make to speak of struggling to the point of bloodshed against one's own inner desires?

This verse and the following one contain a mild rebuke. The readers have grown weary in a struggle that has not reached an extreme pitch, whereas Jesus, their supreme example of faith, endured the maximum without collapse or lassitude. Nevertheless, to say that "The sufferings of the community were insignificant in comparison with those endured by Jesus" seems a harsher judgment than the author intends.[131] The writer takes the sufferings of his addressees seriously; the tone is not severe, but pastoral.

A second aspect of the rebuke involves the community's failure to

---

[128] "Blood" here stands for "bloodshed." See M. Zerwick and M. Grosvenor, *A Grammatical Analysis of the Greek New Testament* (Rome: Biblical Institute, 1971) 684; BAGD, 74. Μέχρις αἵματος probably means "to the point of death" (Ellingworth, *Hebrews*, 645). Cf. 2 Macc. 13.14. For the possibility of a martial interpretation of μέχρις αἵματος, see *TDNT*, I, 173; and Bruce, *Epistle to the Hebrews*, 342, n. 64. On the word ἀντικαθίστημι in sports, see Spicq, *Lexicographie néotestamentaire*, I, 102–3. On the link between combat sports and blood, see Poliakoff, *Combat Sports in the Ancient World*, 85–8.

[129] Lane, *Hebrews*, 418. For an extreme example of the subjective interpretation, see Gambiza, "*Teleiosis* and *Paideia* as Interpretation of Sufferings": "It refers to the Christians struggling and fighting against their sinful desires" (62). Similarly, "Christians' sufferings are like a reform school wherein they are purged of the dross of self love and love for the world (12.2–7)" (81). Such interpretations do not arise from the text.

[130] See Carpzov, *Sacrae Exercitationes*, 582; Delitzsch, *Epistle to the Hebrews*, 310; Moffatt, *Hebrews*, 198; Westcott, *Epistle to the Hebrews*, 400. Windisch, *Hebräerbrief*, 110, agrees: "One should not seek the sin in the inner being ... but, as in the case of Jesus, with the persecutors."

[131] *Pace* Lane, *Hebrews*, 419.

remember.[132] The Jewish scriptures, which figured so prominently in the first ten chapters, are again the basis of the argument. The author laments that the readers have utterly forgotten the παρα-κλήσις, the encouraging admonition of scripture, even though it addresses them as "sons."[133] As he has done elsewhere in the epistle, the author makes a forceful application of the OT text to the readers, pluralizing the singular number (υἱέ μου – ὑμῖν ... υἱοῖς) and re-contextualizing the generic statement of the original for the very particular circumstances of the community.[134]

The qualifier ὡς is not to be taken simply as a comparative – addressing them as a parent might address a child – nor as "contrary to fact," *as if* they were sons, but rather as predicative – addressing them *as sons*, which in fact they are![135] The readers' relationship to God as sons (and daughters) is strategic not only for the exposition of verses 7–11, but for the entire epistle. Throughout the epistle (1.2, 5, 8; 3.6; 4.14; 5.5, 8; 6.6; 7.3, 28; 10.29), the author has highlighted the sonship of Jesus and, to a lesser extent, the analogous relationship of the readers to God (2.10–18). It is clear, especially from passages like 5.7–10, that sonship and suffering are not mutually exclusive, Jesus himself being the ultimate test case. Although Jesus was a son, he learned obedience through suffering. In 12.5–11 the readers are reminded that neither does their status as God's children exclude suffering. Indeed, it *entails* suffering, understood as παιδεία.

Some of the texts surveyed in chapter 3 made a similar connection between discipline and parent/child relationships. This was espe-

---

[132] On memory and forgetfulness in the epistle, see 2.6; 6.10; 8.12; 10.17, 32; 11.15, 22; 13.2, 3, 7, 16. Generally, the function of paraenesis is not to inform anew, but to remind. See Seneca, Epist. 94.11; and Malherbe, "Hellenistic Moralists," 281.

[133] The author uses the term παρακλήσις to describe the entire epistle in 13.22 (cf. 6.18). The intensive ἐκ- of ἐκλανθάνειν gives the sense of "utterly." See BAGD, 242. Zerwick and Grosvenor, *Grammatical Analysis*, 219, suggest the relative ἥτις is concessive, giving the sense of "*even though* [it addresses]."

[134] J. A. Sanders (*Torah and Canon*, Philadelphia: Fortress 1972, xiv) writes that "when one studies how an ancient tradition functions in relation to the needs of the community, [one] is studying midrash." By this definition, Hebrews is engaged in midrashic interpretation. The term "pesher" is misapplied. See Weiss, *Brief an die Hebräer*, 645, n. 4 and Attridge, *Hebrews*, 361, n. 40 on the genre of the exposition.

[135] So G. Bornkamm, "Sohnschaft und Leiden," in Walther Eltester, ed., *Judentum, Urchristentum, Kirche: Festschrift für Joachim Jeremias* (Berlin: Töpelmann, 1960) 197; also Weiss, *Brief an die Hebräer*, 648, and Ellingworth, *Hebrews*, 647.

cially common in Jewish wisdom literature, although most often
with reference to *human* family relationships.[136] The instances in
which wisdom literature speaks of *divine fatherly* discipline of persons are comparatively few.[137] This image is also developed in
certain Stoic authors. Seneca's *De Providentia* emphasized God's
paternal care for the sage. Like a stern parent, the deity was demanding and strict, yet divine discipline was grounded in love (1.6;
2.6; 4.11–12). Similarly, Epictetus speaks of God's providential care
as characteristic of "a good king and, in truth, of a father" (1.6.40).
Heracles, who was the son of Zeus, was not pampered by the deity,
but had to toil and perform exercises (3.26.31). This combination of
divine fatherly discipline, divine benevolence, and resulting human
benefit despite unpleasant hardship has strong affinities to Hebrews
12.5–11.

The author's citation follows the LXX text of Proverbs 3.11–12
except for the addition of μου. The passage contains two synonymous parallelisms. Verse 11 takes the form of a double prohibition:
"Do not despise ... neither grow weary." The grammatical object of
the first verb is παιδεία; the (logical) object of the second is "being
reproved." Verse 12, the second parallelism, substantiates the imperatives of the preceding verse. One should not despise God's discipline and reproof *because* they demonstrate not God's displeasure,
but rather God's fatherly love and acceptance.

The LXX contains one major variation from the MT. The second
stich of verse 12 begins with a Hebrew word which the Masoretic
pointing construes as meaning "and as a father." The LXX trans-
lator has read a hiphil form of a Hebrew verb meaning "afflict."
The resultant Greek text portrays God more severely than the
Hebrew.

The critical issue in the interpretation of this passage is the way
the author has used this text from Israel's wisdom tradition. In the
original context of Proverbs 3.11–12, παιδεία is unmistakably punitive in nature and corrective in aim. In the synonymous parallelism
of the passage, the noun is parallel to ἐλεγχόμενος, and the verb is
parallel to μαστιγοῖ, terms which are clearly punitive in that they

---

[136] I noted above (p. 90) that virtually the only text in Proverbs that explicitly speaks
    of *the Lord's* discipline is 3.11–12, the text that Hebrews appropriates. Sirach and
    Wisdom of Solomon occasionally portrayed God as one who administered dis-
    cipline, but not always with a familial image.
[137] Besides Prov. 3.11–12, God's fatherly discipline is found in Sir. 23.1–2 and Wis.
    11.10 and 12.20–2. See also Deut. 8.2–5.

presuppose wrongdoing on the part of those reproved or chastised.[138] Talbert calls attention to the parallelisms and concludes
that παιδεία is to be understood as "parental correction of youthful
misdirection."[139] Bertram is more blunt: "Since the reference in Hb.
12 is to sinful men, who are not willing to recognize their sin, παιδεία is accompanied by the more judicial function of conviction and
punishment."[140] But these opinions fail to take into account what
the author of Hebrews *does* with the appropriated text. Most importantly, is the author's understanding of divine παιδεία informed
exclusively from the text he has cited, or does he reconceptualize it
in such a way that Proverbs 3.11–12 becomes merely the carrier of
useful terminology?

Παιδεία is, without question, a polyvalent term. The history of
research in chapter 1 showed that, beginning in the early patristic
period, commentators were aware of several different nuances.
Chrysostom, appealing to Hebrews 12.11, saw παιδεία as a kind of
γυμνασία (training, exercise). This insight was echoed centuries later
by Theophylactus and Oecumenius, who both identified divine παιδεία with affliction, not with punishment. Scholars in the twelfth
to sixteenth centuries recognized an educative element in παιδεία,
but they usually related it to the sins of the one suffering. Luther,
Calvin, and Beza all conceived of divine discipline as fundamentally
punitive. Commentators from the seventeenth century to the present
have generally acknowledged two main options for παιδεία –
punishment/correction versus education/training – inclining toward
one or the other.

Semantically, any of these nuances is possible for παιδεία and its
cognates in Hebrews 12.5–11. Contextual factors, as always, must
determine the meaning. I suspect, however, that the first-century
usage of the word group *by pagan Greek speakers* was overwhelmingly *non*-punitive. The standard Classical Greek lexicon cites
only biblical texts for the meanings "chastisement" and "chastise,
punish" for the noun and verb respectively.[141] Philo and Josephus,

---

138 Μαστιγόω can refer, of course, to a literal flogging. In the present context
   Schneider (*TDNT*, IV, 518) suggests the meaning "to impart corrective punishment." For ἐλέγχω BAGD (249) suggests not simply "reprove, correct," but a
   heightened sense of "punish, discipline." Büchsel (*TDNT*, II, 474) is explicit
   about ἐλέγχομαι being the experience of a sinful person.
139 Talbert, *Learning Through Suffering*, 71.
140 *TDNT*, V, 609.
141 LSJ, 1286–7 cites Prov. 22.15 and Heb. 12.5 for παιδεία = "chastisement," and
   Hos. 7.12 and Luke 23.16 for παιδεύω = "chastise, punish."

despite their extensive familiarity with and commitment to the sacred texts of Judaism, were seen to use παιδεία in an almost exclusively non-punitive sense (see above, pp. 106–9). It is even possible that the difference in the meaning of παιδεία between 2 Maccabees (punitive) and 4 Maccabees (non-punitive; see above, p. 105) may have to do with the relative Hebraic versus Greco-Roman influences behind those texts.[142] In general, the punitive meaning of παιδεία tends to be found in translations of Hebrew texts or in works imbued with Hebraic thought.[143] Thoroughly Hellenized Jews working exclusively with Greek would be more likely to entertain a non-punitive idea of παιδεία. If this is so, a skillful, Greek-speaking author like the writer of Hebrews might employ a text from the LXX for the sake of this key word, but have a concept of παιδεία very different from that of the text. Only the author's exposition of the text would reveal this.

What, then, does the author *do* with the text and its key word? His exposition is substantial: ninety-eight words of commentary on twenty-two words of text. Yet the author's aim is not exegetical in the sense of explaining the original meaning of Proverbs 3.11–12. The use of the text is selective, with a view to serving paraenesis. The key word παιδεία is taken up and used both forcefully[144] and extensively. The noun occurs in verses 7, 8, and 11; the verb in 7 and 10. Another noun, παιδευτής, occurs in verse 9. In addition, the language of sonship, found twice in the citation, is exploited in the exposition, the words "father" and "son(s)" occurring three times each. What seems to be studiously avoided is the harsh, punitive language of ἐλέγχω and μαστιγόω. If these words had been used, they would imply culpable action on the part of the readers. But in 12.4–11 there is no suggestion that the readers are guilty of mis-behavior. Weiss seems to perceive this when he writes "It is ... not 'sin' that causes this suffering!"[145] Yet, he goes on to say that the

---

[142] 4 Macc. is thoroughly Greek in thought, form, and expression. 2 Macc, although clearly a work of Hellenistic historiography, may indirectly draw upon Palestinian sources. Jason of Cyrene, whose work is epitomized in 2 Macc., may very well have lived in Palestine and have known Aramaic or Hebrew. See M. Hengel, *Judaism and Hellenism* (Philadelphia: Fortress, 1981) I, 96; and II, 68, n. 328.

[143] See n. 162 below regarding παιδευτής.

[144] Note that this key word occurs immediately in the first phrase following the citation. It is thrust as far forward as possible, being preceded only by a preposition. The clause is terse and asyndetic, *"For the sake of παιδεία you must endure!"*

[145] Weiss, *Brief an die Hebräer*, 648.

passage is fully in line with the wisdom tradition and insists that παιδεία here means "correction" and "punishment."[146] Weiss might have appealed to the German distinction between *Zucht* (discipline) and *Zuchtigung* (punishment), nuances which are both contained in παιδεία. While it is true that the author of Hebrews appeals to a text in which παιδεία implies "punishment," his recontextualization exploits the nuances of "discipline" or "education." The more punitive nuances of παιδεία are not relevant to his rhetorical situation. God is not punishing the readers by their afflictions, but is educating them.[147]

The exposition makes the following points: (1) Παιδεία is a necessary component of the father/son relationship. Verse 7b affirms this with a rhetorical question; verse 8 restates it by showing that the contrary (a lack of παιδεία) implies the opposite condition (illegitimacy). (2) We should submit to God's παιδεία. Verse 9 makes this point by an *a minore ad maius* argument: we respected our human fathers when they disciplined us; all the more we should submit to divine discipline. An *a minore ad maius* argument depends on both some similarity between the two premises and some degree of difference. Verse 10 develops the difference. Although God's relationship to the readers is analogous to the relationship of human fathers to their sons, God is distinguished from human fathers by a providential knowledge and salvific purpose in divine discipline. (3) Lastly, the readers are assured in verse 11 that although discomfort is always associated with παιδεία, they can be assured of a positive outcome. Each of these points deserves a more detailed treatment.

The exposition begins with an imperative that reiterates the theme of the passage (and arguably, of the letter), "endurance." Endurance was the leitmotif of verses 1–3 and now, interpreted as God's παιδεία in 4–11, it provides one of several links between the two paragraphs. A few commentators take ὑπομένετε as an indicative.[148] The context, however, favors the imperative since the endurance of the readers is not assumed, but is precisely what is at stake. In 12.1 the author exhorts them to run "with endurance." If, in fact, the readers have completely forgotten the exhortation which addresses them as sons (vs. 5), it seems reasonable that 7a reissues the exhortation. The

---

[146] *Ibid.*
[147] Ellingworth, *Hebrews*, 649, observes that "the physical aspect of parental discipline conveyed by μαστιγοῖ is not mentioned in the exposition."
[148] Delitzsch, *Epistle to the Hebrews*, 314; Ellingworth, *Hebrews*, 650; Moffatt, *Hebrews*, 201.

commands of verses 12–13 also support the construal of ὑπομένετε as an imperative.

"For the purpose of παιδεία you must endure."[149] This first point of the exposition locates divine discipline and the suffering of the readers in the context of a salutary, familial relationship with God.[150] The experience of adversity, therefore, does not indicate God's rejection. Quite the contrary, according to the author of Hebrews, it reveals God's fatherly care.[151] The argument can be framed in a syllogism (reversing the order in the text).

General premise:	Every son receives discipline from his father (7c).
Specific premise:	God is dealing with you as sons (7b).
Conclusion:	Accept your situation (i.e. endure it) as discipline (7a).

In this way verse 7 restates the imperative of the citation (7a = vs. 5 = Prov. 3.11) and its rationale (7b = vs. 6 = Prov. 3.12), and further adds a general premise to substantiate (γάρ, 7c) the rationale. Thus 7c makes explicit the general premise, "fathers discipline sons," that Proverbs 3.11–12 only implies.

Verse 8 is a restatement of the general premise in the form of its contrapositive.[152] Verse 8 does, however, vary and extend the thought of 7c in three ways. First, it shifts back to the second person. It does not read "If a son is without discipline," but "If *you* are without discipline." Second, παιδεία is regarded as the common experience of all.[153] "Sharing" is an important theme in Hebrews.

---

[149] The textual variant εἰ παιδείαν is favored by Riggenbach (*Brief an die Hebräer*, 395), Bornkamm, "Sohnschaft und Leiden" (189, n. 3), and Bertram (*TDNT*, V, 622). This reading would produce parallel conditional clauses in vss. 7 and 8, but the textual evidence is "as ill supported as possible" (Delitzsch, *Epistle to the Hebrews*, 313).

[150] The collocation of παιδεία and being God's child is not restricted to Hebrews and the wisdom tradition. Plato observes how highly the heroic figure Minos is eulogized in that Homer says Minos "alone, being a son of Zeus, was educated by Zeus" (*Minos* 319d). Dio Chrysostom remarks that long ago persons received a good education (παιδεία) after the pattern of Heracles and were therefore called children of Zeus (*Disc.* 4.31). On Zeus as the athletic trainer of Heracles, see Epictetus 3.22.56–7.

[151] The benevolence and purposefulness of God in the sufferings of the sage are stressed by Epictetus, 3.24.112–14.

[152] The contrapositive of "If A, then B" is "If not B, then not A." The contrapositive of a true conditional statement is itself necessarily true.

[153] On sharing παιδεία, see Sir. 51.28, Josephus, *Apion* 1.73, and Dio Chrysostom 4.31.

Christ shares the experience of humanity; the saints have a share in
a heavenly calling, in Christ, and in the Spirit; they are partners in
the suffering of others; they receive a share in God's holiness; they
are reminded to practice sharing in their community.[154] "All" in
verse 8 probably includes the readers, the faithful enumerated in
chapter 11 and perhaps also Jesus, who shared fully in human nature
(μετέσχεν, 2.14–18) and its sufferings (5.8). Third, the result of a lack
of discipline is stated both negatively ("you are not sons") and positively ("you are illegitimate").[155] By not only denying those without discipline the status of sons, but by effectively branding them
as "bastards," the writer offers the readers a strong incentive to
reinterpret their suffering.

The second point[156] of the exposition develops the God/human
fathers analogy in a manner that hints at the dissimilarity of the two
elements. The argument is an example of the *a minore ad maius* or
qal va homer reasoning common in this epistle.[157] Human fathers,
who are worthy of respect,[158] are juxtaposed to the spiritual
Father,[159] who is deserving of even greater deference. No one in
antiquity would have questioned the right, indeed the obligation, of
a human father to provide discipline and education for his children.
The author asserts that God, as the Father of spirits, has a similar
role in the lives of God's children.

---

[154] See respectively 2.14, 3.1, 3.14, 6.4, 10.33, 12.10, 13.16.

[155] Ellingworth, *Hebrews*, 651, insists the condition in vs. 8 is contrary to fact even
though the form does not correspond to that class of condition. But the (complete?) list of unreal conditions in Hebrews given in BDF, section 360 (4) does not
mention Heb. 12.8, and Moffatt, *Hebrews*, 203, sees no reason to classify it as a
contrary-to-fact condition.

[156] The word εἶτα and a change in subject matter signal the transition. See BAGD,
234.

[157] Elsewhere in Hebrews see 2.1–4; 9.14; 10.28–9; and 12.25. See Aristotle, *Rhet.*
2.23.4. *Qal va homer* is Hebrew for "light and heavy."

[158] On the *patria potestas*, see the brief excursus in Moffatt, *Hebrews*, 203–4, and
Bonner, *Education in Ancient Rome*, 5–6 and 18–19.

[159] The expression "Father of spirits" is variously explained. See the excursus in
Weiss, *Brief an die Hebräer*, 652–3. Niederstrasser, *Kerygma und Paideia*, 403,
suggests a derivation from Christian liturgy. The LXX is a more likely source.
Expressions such as "God of spirits," "Lord of spirits," or "Sovereign of spirits"
are common in Jewish and Christian literature (Num. 16.22, 27.16; 2 Macc.
3.24; 1 Enoch 37.2; 1 Clement 59.3, and Rev. 22.6). See *TDNT*, V, 1014, and VII,
141. As far as I have been able to determine, the precise expression "Father of
spirits" does not occur in classical, Jewish, or Christian literature prior to the
Epistle to the Hebrews. Our author has probably altered the more traditional
wording to provide a contrast to earthly fathers. See Montefiore, *Commentary*,
221.

In Hellenistic writers παιδευτής is the standard term for "teacher." It is often used in educational contexts involving adults, and seldom has a punitive nuance.[160] It is sometimes juxtaposed with διδάσκαλος.[161] In the LXX both punitive and formative uses are found. God is the punisher of Israel in Hosea 5.2 and Psalms of Solomon 8.29.[162] But in 4 Maccabees 5.34, Eleazar, who has remained utterly faithful, addresses the Law "O teacher" (παιδευτά). Later the seven brothers refer to Eleazar as "our aged teacher" (ὁ παιδευτὴς ἡμῶν γέρων, 9.6). The numerous affinities already seen between Hebrews and the Maccabean literature (especially a highly rhetorical, native facility with Greek) suggest that the educative nuance of παιδευτής is more likely in Hebrews 12.9.

Elsewhere in the NT the word occurs only in Romans 2.20. This reference is instructive for it occurs in a series of parallel expressions. Paul critiques the integrity of some Jews' piety, asking "Εἰ δὲ σὺ Ἰουδαῖος ἐπονομάζῃ ... πέποιθάς τε σεαυτὸν ὁδηγὸν εἶναι τυφλῶν, φῶς τῶν ἐν σκότει, παιδευτὴν ἀφρόνων, διδάσκαλον νηπίων ... ὁ οὖν διδάσκων ἕτερον σεαυτὸν οὐ διδάσκεις;" The word παιδευτής stands parallel to ὁδηγός, φῶς, and διδάσκαλος. The word "foolish, ignorant" (ἄφρων) with παιδευτής indicates that the latter involves moral instruction, not simply the impartation of knowledge. This corresponds well to the word's usage in Hebrews 12.9. Human fathers are respected in their role as moral trainers and discipliners. The author of Hebrews conceives of God acting in a similar way through the hardships and persecution that the community is undergoing. Nothing in the context of Hebrews 12.7–11 requires the nuance of punisher or corrector for παιδευτής. "Moral instructor" is the primary nuance of the word in this context.[163]

The author speaks of "respect" for human fathers, but switches to another verb, "submit," for God. This change is doubtless an in-

---

[160] See Dio Cassius 41.33.3; Dio Chrysostom 4.132; Diodorus Siculus 9.1.2; 17.110.3; Diogenes Laertius 7.7; Dionysius of Halicarnassus 2.59.4; Epictetus 1.9.18; 2.19.29; Philo, *Prob.* 143; *Legatio* 53.

[161] Epictetus 1.9.12; Plutarch, *Camillus* 10.4; Polybius 31.31.2.

[162] It may be significant that in both instances where the meaning of παιδευτής is punitive, the text is a translation from Hebrew. In the case of Hosea this is evident (*musar*). The original language of the Pss. Sol. is widely thought to be Hebrew. (See Wright, "Psalms of Solomon," 640.) The same Hebrew word may have stood behind παιδευτής in that text as well.

[163] *Pace* BAGD, 603. A moral/educative meaning for παιδευτής in Heb. 12.9 finds support in the stated outcomes of "sharing in [God's] holiness" and "the fruit of righteousness" (vss. 10–11).

tensification. The author wishes "to contrast a limited subordination with a total one."[164] The result of submission to the "Father of spirits" is life. Life is an attribute of God (3.12, 9.14, 10.31, 12.22) and of that which issues from God (4.12, 10.20). It also characterizes the righteous person (10.38, citing Hab. 2.4). In the latter context (10.35–9) ζάω seems to refer to eschatological life. The endurance called for by the author promises great reward. Soon "the coming one" will arrive, and the righteous will live by faith. Ζάω in 12.9 may also be eschatological.[165] The readers' submission to God's discipline and their endurance in the contest culminates in eschatological life with God, just as it did in Jesus' case.[166]

Verse 9 implied a difference of degree between God and human fathers; verse 10 extends the contrast qualitatively. The contrast is neatly framed (οἱ μέν ... ὁ δέ) but not quite fully executed. The μέν clause contains two elements: the chronological duration of discipline and the standard or criterion of the discipliners. The δέ clause provides a contrastive element only for the latter.[167]

Human fathers administered discipline πρὸς ὀλίγας ἡμέρας, "for a few days." This expression might refer to the period of one's minority or to the brevity of the act of punishment itself, the former being more likely.[168] The standard of human paternal discipline is τὸ δοκοῦν αὐτοῖς (what seems right to them). It is implied that human discipline is fallible and, while well meant, may not always result in the betterment of the child.[169] Nothing is said about the temporal duration of divine discipline. Since the specific reality

---

[164] Braun, *An die Hebräer*, 415.

[165] "Because the future ζωή is the true one, it can simply be called ζωή without attribute ... The simple ζῆν can also be used in this sense." (*TDNT*, II, 864, and n. 271 for other references.)

[166] Zerwick and Grosvenor, *Grammatical Analysis*, section 455γ, refer to καί before "we shall live" as final. Cf. Bengel, *Gnomon*, 464; Grotius, *Critici Sacri*, vii, 1164; Francis S. Sampson, *A Critical Commentary on the Epistle of the Hebrews* (New York: Robert Carter & Brothers, 1856) 443; and Moulton, *et al.*, *Grammar*, III, 334.

[167] The phrase εἰς τὸ μεταλαβεῖν does not seem to serve as a contrastive element to πρὸς ὀλίγας ἡμέρας, *pace* Westcott, *Epistle to the Hebrews*, 405. But Lünemann, *Commentary*, 707, is probably right in seeing the former as an "epexegetical amplification" of ἐπὶ τὸ συμφέρον.

[168] Bruce, *Epistle to the Hebrews*, 343, and Windisch, *Hebräerbrief* 111, respectively. See references in Ellingworth, *Hebrews*, 654, especially 4 Macc. 15.27 and Wis. 3.5.

[169] See esp. Grotius, *Critici Sacri*, vii, 1164: "According to their own judgment, often from error, sometimes even instilling their own vices rather than virtues, such as greed and ambition."

interpreted here as παιδεία is religious persecution, the author would be unlikely to designate a duration of time for which it will occur. Just as in 12.1–3 the readers are enjoined to have endurance for a race of indeterminate length, so here they are called to endure discipline for an undesignated period of time. There are, however, a few intimations in the epistle that the end of sufferings may not be so remote (10.25, 36–7). In any case, the author no doubt conceived of *the benefits* of divine discipline as lasting, so that the idea is similar to the contrast in 1 Timothy 4.8 between bodily exercise and godliness, the latter having profit "for this life and the coming one."

The criterion of divine discipline is contrasted with that of human discipline. Whereas parental discipline was administered according to fallible human judgment (κατὰ τὸ δοκοῦν αὐτοῖς), the discipline imposed by God always works to the benefit of God's children. In the phrase ἐπὶ τὸ συμφέρον, "for (one's) benefit," Weiss notes that the author picks up an expression that played an important role in Stoic philosophy.[170]

It was seen in the history of research in chapter 1 that Greco-Roman comparative texts were largely neglected in scholarship on Hebrews prior to the middle of the twentieth century. J. J. Wettstein's normal meticulousness in amassing conceptual parallels for the NT was guilty of a serious omission in the case of Hebrews 12.5–11. Almost a century before Wettstein, Cornelius Lapide had cited two texts from Seneca's *De Providentia*. About the time Wettstein published his Greek NT, J. B. Carpzov briefly noted, somewhat derisively, that "those of the Portico" had a point of view quite different from that of Hebrews 12.11 (see section 1.2). From the mid-seventeenth century to the present, commentators have rarely discussed Stoic sources in their treatments of Hebrews 12.5–11.[171]

In ἐπὶ τὸ συμφέρον we have virtually a Stoic slogan. The sage sought to do what was beneficial or expedient (τὸ συμφέρον). This concept was closely associated with "the good" (τὸ ἀγαθόν).[172] The failure to distinguish what is expedient from what is inexpedient is the source of numerous ills to humankind.[173] And in one instance, Epictetus declares that one of the reasons we need παιδεία is to be

---

[170] Weiss, *Brief an die Hebräer*, 655.

[171] Moffatt, Spicq, and Windisch do make brief mention of Seneca's *De Prov.*

[172] Diogenes Laertius 7.98; Epictetus 1.22.1; 2.7.4; Marcus Aurelius 5.16.

[173] Epictetus 2.24.21–23.

able to distinguish between συμφέρον and ἀσύμφορον.[174] Thus certain Stoic writers and the Epistle to the Hebrews have this language in common.

Beyond just language, however, the concept and images of παιδεία have much in common. In both Seneca and Hebrews, the image according to which God allows persons to suffer hardship is the father/child relationship (*De Prov.* 1.6; 2.6; Heb. 12.9). In both, the fatherly love of God is affirmed despite the harshness of the experience of suffering (*De Prov.* 2.6; 4.7; Heb. 12.6, 11). In both, the intended effect of suffering is growth, maturation, and learning (*De Prov. passim*; Heb. 12.10–11). In both, the notion of learning through suffering is conjoined with athletic imagery (*De Prov.* 2.2–4, 7–9; Heb. 12.1–3, 11). In both, a list of exemplars of suffering is given (*De Prov.* 3.4–14; Heb. 11.1–12.3). In neither is there any suggestion that suffering is inflicted by deity as punishment for wrongdoing. One particular sentence in Seneca is remarkably similar in form to Hebrews 12.6: *Hos itaque deus quos probat, quos amat, indurat, recognoscit, exercet.* (Those, then, whom God approves, whom he loves, he hardens, reviews, and trains. *De Prov.* 4.7)[175] Such a high amount of correspondence suggests that the author of Hebrews was in tune with the pagan philosophical currents of his day, specifically Stoic ideas.

But our author has not absorbed his milieu indiscriminately. The goal of Stoic παιδεία is not the same as that of our author. Stoicism aims to produce a sage who is free and self-sufficient.[176] According to Hebrews, God's discipline has as its goal τὸ μεταλαβεῖν τῆς ἁγιότητος αὐτοῦ. Partaking of God's discipline (vs. 8) results in partaking of God's holiness.[177]

There are two possible construals of the clause "in order that [we] might partake of [God's] holiness." The reference might be to moral improvement in this life or to participation in the holiness of God

---

[174] *Ibid.*, 1.2.5–6.

[175] The next two sentences in *De Prov.* bear some resemblance to Heb. 12.7–8.

[176] Weiss, *Brief an die Hebräer*, 655: "Whereas at the end and goal of such παιδεία in Stoicism stands the 'sage' as a self-sufficient, free, and self-determining human being, the goal of the divine education in the Epistle to the Hebrews is described as 'participation in (divine) holiness.'" Similarly, Jentsch, *Urchristliches Erziehungsdenken*, 166. Ultimately, the Stoic sage was his or her own judge of success in the moral life. Cf. Seneca, Epist. 26.4.

[177] The word ἁγιότης occurs in the NT only here and in 2 Cor. 1.12. The root, however, is common in Hebrews and elsewhere. See especially 2.11, 10.14, 12.14, 13.12.

in eternity. "If a real alternative is seen here, we must opt for the latter."[178] But one need not regard the two construals as mutually exclusive; the dichotomy is a false one. The mention of righteousness in verse 11 and of bitterness, defilement, immorality, godlessness, and greed in 12.15–16 and 13.1–5 certainly establishes the author's interest in holy living in this life.[179] On the other hand, both righteousness and holiness can certainly designate "eternal blessedness."[180] The broader context may also lend support to this interpretation. The faithful forebears of chapter 11 and Jesus himself (12.1–3) attained fulfillment only after death.[181] Thus the argument of this second point of the exposition is that the readers should submit to the Father of spirits even more than to earthly fathers, since the former's discipline is always beneficent and is designed to enable them to share in God's holy character.

Verse 11 makes the final point of the exposition: at the time, παιδεία does not seem to be joyous, but grievous; yet its end result is the peaceful fruit of righteousness. This new point contrasts not human versus divine discipline, but the experience of discipline versus its aftermath, that is, a temporal contrast rather than a theological one. The benefit of discipline or education despite its unpleasantness is a topos of moral exhortation. Aristotle wrote that one does not educate the young for the sake of amusement "for learning involves distress" (μετὰ λύπης γὰρ ἡ μάθησις).[182] Seneca makes a similar statement, not about education *per se*, but about suffering in general: *Deinde quod acerbum fuit ferre, tulisse iucundum est; naturale est mali sui fine gaudere.* (Therefore, that which was bitter to bear is pleasant to have borne; it is natural to rejoice at the end of one's suffering: Epist. 78.14.)

The paradox of pain and profit was nowhere seen more vividly than in the terse formula ἔπαθον ... ἔμαθον (I suffered ... I learned),

[178] K. Weiss, "συμφέρω," *TDNT*, IX, 77.
[179] Note that ἁγιασμός in 12.14, cognate with ἁγιότης, is to be pursued. Indeed, "peace" (εἰρήνη) and "holiness" (ἁγιασμός) in 12.14 may be umbrella terms for many of the more specific injunctions in 12.15–17 and 13.1–5.
[180] Spicq, *Commentaire*, II, 396: Δικαιοσύνη "can designate the acquisition of virtue, moral rectitude, and union with God ... , but more certainly eternal blessedness."
[181] Weiss, *TDNT*, IX, 77–8, n. 18.
[182] Aristotle, *Pol.* 8.4.4 (1339a). See also Diogenes Laertius 5.1.18 (on Aristotle); also Wis. 3.5, Philo, *De Congr.* 160 and 175, *Quaest. in Gen.* 3.5; Jas. 1.2–4, and Clement of Alexandria, *Strom.* 6.24.10 (Epicurus). Aristotle makes the same point with an athletic image in *Eth. Nic.* 3.9.3. On the general idea of pleasure following pain, see Diogenes Laertius 10.129.

examined in chapter 3 (see pp. 139–41). Here, by a clever parono-
masia, the educative benefits of life's afflictions are affirmed. This
very juxtaposition of words is used in Hebrews 5.8 of Jesus. Despite
Jesus' status as God's Son, a status which the author has emphasized (1.2, 5, 8; 3.6; 4.14; 5.5), "he learned obedience from what he
suffered." Similarly in 12.5–11, those whom the scripture addresses
as sons (and daughters) must endure παιδεία that is invariably
grievous before it is joyous. As Aeschylus observed (*Agam.* 177–8),
Zeus has established by a fixed rule that learning comes by suffering.
The author of Hebrews, within his own theological framework,
affirms something very similar. No one evades suffering, not even
God's own Son, so certainly not God's human children.

The contrast in Hebrews 12.11 is nicely balanced (μὲν ... δέ) and
employs alliteration (πᾶσα ... παιδεία ... πρὸς ... παρὸν) and hyperbaton (δικαιοσύνης). The mention of joy as an implicit outcome
of endurance recalls the joy which Jesus attained beyond the cross
(vs. 2). This subtle echo again links the example of Christ and the
readers' experience. The admission that παιδεία is grievous (λύπης)
is contrary to the Stoic assertion that the sage is not touched by such
matters. To experience grief is to be swayed by a passion and is,
therefore, an error (ἁμάρτημα). The goal of the sage is to be free
from grief, sorrow, and envy.[183] The author of Hebrews, on the
other hand, frankly acknowledges the grief and suffering involved in
divine discipline without any attempt to minimize or dismiss it.[184]
Rather, our author appeals to the compensation that follows.

Only later, when discipline has done its work (cf. Jas. 1.2–4), does
it yield the peaceful fruit of righteousness, or perhaps, the fruit of
peace and righteousness,[185] to those who have been trained by it

---

[183] Epictetus 1.9.7; 4.4.32; Diogenes Laertius 7.110–12. See other references in
R. Bultmann, "λύπη," *TDNT*, IV, 315. Bultmann writes, "It seems that for
Stoicism ... there is no recognition of the positive meaning of pain. Even in later
Stoics we still find the same view that λύπη is a πάθος and hence a ἁμάρτημα
from which the sage must be free." This may be correct with strict regard to the
concept of λύπη, but as we saw in chapter 3, some Stoics, Seneca in particular,
saw positive benefits in suffering. Λύπη in Bultmann's remark is not to be understood as "suffering"; it is rather the emotional and irrational response to suffering. The Stoic sage sought to conquer all passions, but this did not preclude a
positive evaluation of suffering.

[184] Jesus himself is portrayed in the epistle as one acquainted with sorrow (5.7; 4.15).
In fact, Jesus' acquaintance with adversity is a significant part of his priestly
qualifications.

[185] Ellingworth, *Hebrews*, 656, and Lane, *Hebrews*, 425, prefer the latter translation,
taking the adjective "peaceful" as equivalent to a genitive. Δικαιοσύνης is clearly

(i.e. παιδεία). The word "trained" (γεγυμνασμένοις) evokes a final athletic image in the exposition.[186] This term supports a formative/educative function for παιδεία rather than a punitive one. This is παιδεία that trains and exercises rather than reproves and punishes. The collocation of παιδεία with γυμνάζω shows that the former can be viewed in athletic terms.[187] As the early fathers rightly saw, παιδεία is a kind of γυμνασία.[188]

When does the author envision "joy" being attained? The grief which afterwards changes to "joy" is usually interpreted eschatologically, but there is no need to restrict it to the distant future.[189] After all, joy *in* suffering was mentioned in 10.34. On the other hand, the joy that sustained Jesus on the cross was a proleptic vision of joy (12.2). So the experience of joy is apparently both immediate and ultimate. Unmitigated suffering need not persist till the eschaton; in this life as well, the readers can experience the triad of blessings mentioned in verse 11: joy, peace, and righteousness (cf. Rom. 14.17).[190]

The last two verses of the passage are not expository but paraenetic, as the imperatives show. They draw an inference from the foregoing (διό) and reintroduce imagery similar to that found in verses 1–3.[191] This imagery is not explicitly athletic, however. It might be termed somatic, or even medical. Hands and knees are

a genitive of apposition (BDF, section 167). The two terms are associated in Jas. 3.18. Weiss, *Brief an die Hebräer*, 657, sees an allusion to Prov. 3.9.

[186] The verb γυμνάζω, found only four times in the NT, also occurs in Heb. 5.14. There the author speaks of "mature Christians who through practice have their faculties trained (γεγυμνασμένα) for the discernment of good and evil."

[187] Ellingworth, *Hebrews*, 656. See also section 3.4 above.

[188] In section 1.2 see the remarks on Chrysostom, Oecumenius, and Theophylactus. Among modern commentators, see Jean Héring, *The Epistle to the Hebrews* (London: Epworth, 1970) 113: "the education which divine Providence gives is a gymnastic of the soul." Cf. Spicq, *Commentaire*, II, 395.

[189] Lane, *Hebrews*, 425. For an eschatological interpretation, see Michel, *Brief an die Hebräer*, 301; U. Wilckens, "ὕστερος," *TDNT*, VIII, 595. Weiss (*TDNT*, IX, 77–8, n. 18) seems willing to consider both, with the eschatological reference being dominant.

[190] In addition to 10.34, note χαρά in the task of community leadership (13.17). In 12.14 the community is urged to seek peace, a command that certainly pertains to the present. Seneca has his own triad of benefits that one gains after suffering, a triad that bears some resemblance to those mentioned by our author: *virtus, et firmitas animi et pax* (virtue, and a steadfast mind, and peace, Epist. 78.16); and note *gaudere* (rejoice) in 78.14.

[191] Weiss, *Brief an die Hebräer*, 658, says that the imagery of vs. 12 "quite obviously" recalls the athletic metaphor of vss. 1–3. So also Bruce, *Epistle to the Hebrews*, 347.

normally symbols of strength and activity, but in this case, the hands have gone slack and the knees have been weakened.[192] The image of an exhausted runner (or boxer?) is easy to detect here. So, the author issues a call to straighten or reinvigorate the hands and knees.[193] Having done that, the readers are then urged to "make straight paths for their feet." The thrust here is probably eschatological rather than ethical. Although the author is clearly concerned about holy living, the "straight" path in this context is not so much the path of moral behavior but the path by which one moves directly and successfully toward the goal.[194] The purpose of reinvigorating the limbs and striding carefully toward the goal is to avoid further disability and to achieve healing.[195]

The author's own rhetoric has shaped the imagery in verses 12–13, but the precise diction is deeply influenced by the LXX. The most obvious sources are Isaiah 35.3 (ἰσχύσατε, χεῖρες ἀνειμέναι καὶ γόνατα παραλελυμένα; Be strong, O slack hands and weak knees) and Proverbs 4.26 (ὀρθὰς τροχιὰς ποίει τοῖς ποσίν; Make straight paths for your feet).[196] Although references to hands are not particularly appropriate for the race imagery of verses 1–3, our author seems to prefer traditional language whenever possible. This preference was evident in the author's choice of Proverbs 3.11–12.

In a brief excursus prior to a summary, I would like to consider the author's selection of Proverbs 3.11–12 and compare his use of it to that of other authors. This question of selection arises because, given my non-punitive interpretation of the larger passage, it becomes clear that at least some aspects of Proverbs 3.11–12 were not suitable to the author's point of view. Why, for example, did he choose a passage that contained punitive terms? What features of the text made it useful in spite of this?

---

[192] The parallel forms (perfect passive participles) and alliteration in παρειμένας and παραλελυμένα are additional evidence of the author's rhetorical style.

[193] Ἀνορθώσατε with both hands and knees may involve a slight zeugma (Moffatt, *Hebrews*, 207).

[194] Lane, *Hebrews*, 427–8; H. Preisker, "ὀρθός," *TDNT*, V, 449–50.

[195] Ἐκτρέπω refers to dislocation of the limb, not deviation from the path. So Bruce, *Epistle to the Hebrews*, 348; Delitzsch, *Epistle to the Hebrews*, 327; Moffatt, *Hebrews*, 207; and Spicq, *Commentaire*, II, 396–7. Thus the warning is more likely against faltering and weak members of the community than against apostasy. See Lane, *Hebrews*, 428.

[196] Similar language is found in Sir. 2.13, 25.23, Philo, *Migr. Abr.* 24, and Odes of Solomon 6.16. For other references, see Moffatt, *Hebrews*, 207, and Weiss, *Brief an die Hebräer*, 658, n. 58.

4.5   Excursus: the use of Proverbs 3.11–12 in Hebrews and elsewhere

Why did the author of Hebrews cite Proverbs 3.11–12? It is quite possible that our author has employed a text that was not ideal in every respect, but was from a source regarded as authoritative by his readers, and was, in the main, suitable to his purposes. It must be the case that the LXX was authoritative for the recipients of the epistle. The author's argument clearly assumes this, and if on this point he was mistaken, the entire composition would lose most of its persuasiveness. Throughout the epistle the author assumes the speaker of the Greek scriptures to be God (1.5–13; 4.3; 5.5–6) or Jesus (2.12–13; 10.5–10) or the Holy Spirit (3.7–11; 10.15–17). The recipients must have shared this conviction. Second, the text of Proverbs 3.11–12 was, in the main, suitable to the writer's purposes. It is clear from the exposition in verses 7–11 that the author was primarily concerned with two things: the idea of παιδεία and the filial relationship with God that παιδεία implies. These terms – παιδεία, υἱός, πατήρ – dominate the exposition. The author wants his readers to view their afflictions as divine παιδεία and to be assured that, far from being a sign of God's displeasure, they are indications of God's love and beneficent, paternal care.

The second question is: How has the author recontextualized Proverbs 3.11–12 so as to shape its meaning for a new setting? In chapter 3 we saw that Jewish wisdom literature frequently, but by no means invariably, viewed suffering as the manifestation of God's punitive or corrective discipline. But this theological framework is not adequate to explain the author's exposition. The tendency to interpret Hebrews 12.5–11 wholly or even predominantly in the context of the wisdom tradition fails to appreciate *what the author does* with Proverbs 3.11–12.[197] The selective exposition interprets the readers' suffering as formative and educative rather than puni-

---

[197] An example of the punitive interpretation is Bertram, *TDNT*, V, 621–2; somewhat milder but tending in the same direction is Talbert, *Learning Through Suffering*, 71–2. Lane, *Hebrews*, 428–30, speaks of the maturing effects of divine discipline, but also calls sufferings "corrective in character." Weiss, *Brief an die Hebräer*, 648, likewise reads the text "entirely in line with biblical, Jewish wisdom." Jentsch, *Urchristliches Erziehungsdenken*, 163, n. 2, moves in the right direction when he insists that the OT concept of *paideia* does not exclude, but rather includes the positive Greek understanding of a "fruitful, beneficial process of education."

tive.[198] There is, then, tension between the conceptual milieu from which the citation is drawn and the "point" that the author wishes to make with the citation.

In order better to appreciate our author's use of Proverbs 3.11–12, I will briefly examine how this same text has been employed by other writers. These two short verses are cited or alluded to by several Jewish and Christian authors by the year 100 CE. The Jewish texts have already been cited above in chapter 3.[199] They are Job 5.17, Psalms of Solomon 3.4, and Philo, *De Congressu* 177.

As I mentioned earlier, Job 5.17 contains a likely echo of Proverbs 3.11–12. The texts share three key words: "reprove," "discipline," and "despise." The context is the first speech of Eliphaz. Divine discipline is Eliphaz's explanation of the sort of afflictions that befell Job. The following verses offer examples: famine, war, destruction. Eliphaz implies that God inflicts these woes as discipline. There is no explicit connection in this passage (vss. 17–27) to Job's alleged sin, but given the general perspective of Eliphaz (cf. 4.7, 17–18; 15.5–6), God's discipline is probably to be understood punitively. This is, of course, the perspective of a character within the story, not of the author.

The pseudepigraphical Psalms of Solomon also contain what may be a faint echo of Proverbs 3.11–12. The psalmist writes: οὐκ ὀλιγωρήσει δίκαιος παιδευόμενος ὑπὸ κυρίου. (The righteous person does not lightly regard being disciplined by the Lord: 3.4.) Two words in this line correlate with the LXX text of Proverbs 3.11: ὀλιγωρέω and παιδεύω. But this correlation is slight, and given the other minor grammatical differences, it is possible that this text is not a conscious echo of Proverbs 3.11 at all but only shares some of the thought world and vocabulary of wisdom literature. If, in any sense, it can be regarded as an interpretation of Proverbs 3.11, it should be categorized as punitive (cf. Pss. Sol. 3.5–8; 10.1–3).

The third Jewish author to be considered is Philo, who explicitly

---

[198] The author of Hebrews was not loath to portray God in punitive terms (see 6.4–6; 10.26–31), but these passages do not describe beneficent divine acts aimed at the betterment of persons struggling in their faith. They describe severe, eschatological judgment against persons who have utterly rejected faith. Furthermore, the author explicitly disavows this outcome in the case of his readers (6.9–12; 10.35–9). The harsh, monitory passages in Hebrews are directed toward apostates, not toward readers who are suffering persecution.

[199] Job 5.17, see p. 96 n. 40; Pss. Sol. 3.4, see p. 99; Philo, see p. 114.

cites Proverbs 3.11–12 in *De Congressu* 177. The treatise is an allegorical interpretation of Genesis 16.1–6. Philo interprets the last clause, "and Sarai afflicted her [Haggar]," as meaning that she "disciplined and admonished and chastened" her (172). Affliction is thus seen as a profitable experience. To establish this point further Philo refers to Genesis 27.40 where slavery, the most humiliating form of affliction, is imposed on Esau by his father, Isaac. Then comes the citation of Proverbs 3.11–12, the thrust of which is that Isaac's imposition of slavery on his son is an instance of God's discipline, indicative of love and paternal beneficence. But is this discipline, which takes the form of slavery in the case of Esau, construed punitively or educatively? Indeed, it may be both. Esau certainly is to learn from the experience, but Philo also characterizes him as "foolish" and "one who chooses war instead of peace."²⁰⁰

Among the early Christian writers who allude to Proverbs 3.11–12 are John, the author of Revelation, and Clement, bishop of Rome. In Revelation 3.19 the Christ of the Apocalypse addresses the church at Laodicea: ἐγὼ ὅσους ἐὰν φιλῶ ἐλέγχω καὶ παιδεύω· ζήλευε οὖν καὶ μετανόησον. If we regard φιλῶ as a synonym for ἀγαπῶ, three key words from Proverbs 3.11–12 occur in Revelation 3.19, and the structure of the clause is similar to 12a.²⁰¹ The four words following the allusion make it clear that the discipline of Christ is punitive and corrective. The church in Laodicea was "wretched" (vs. 17) and in need of repentance.

Lastly, Clement of Rome cites Proverbs 3.12 in the epistle traditionally attributed to him. Section 56 opens with an exhortation to intercede for persons who have fallen into some "transgression" (παραπτώματι). He continues, "Let us receive παιδεία, at which no one should take offense" (56.2). The mention of παιδεία prepares for a short catena of OT passages that feature the word prominently: Psalm 118.18, Proverbs 3.12, and Psalm 141.5. After a final and lengthy citation (from Job 5, beginning with vs. 17!), the conclusion again highlights παιδεία as the means by which one ultimately obtains mercy (56.16). The interpretation of discipline in this

---

²⁰⁰ A brief comparison between Philo's use of Proverbs 3.11–12 and that of Hebrews is given by R. Williamson, *Philo and the Epistle to the Hebrews* (Leiden: Brill, 1970) 573–5. Williamson notes that for Philo "discipline" means "reproaching and admonition," whereas for the author of Hebrews "discipline" refers to the persecution experienced by the community.

²⁰¹ Attempts to find great significance in the change to φιλῶ are misguided.

context is clearly corrective; the one being disciplined (ὁ παιδευόμε-νος) is assumed to have fallen into sin.

It appears, then, that Proverbs 3.11–12, both in its original expression and in the various Jewish and Christian authors who appropriated this text, referred to the loving, but punitive and corrective discipline of God. It was directed toward persons who in some sense had gone astray. Such was the thinking of Eliphaz toward Job, of Philo toward Esau, of the Apocalyptic Christ toward the Laodicean church, and of Clement toward some members of the church in Corinth. In this light, it is all the more remarkable that the author of Hebrews is *not* charging his readers with wrongdoing in saying that they are undergoing the παιδεία κυρίου. At least among the writers surveyed here, Hebrews seems to be unique in its non-punitive interpretation of discipline in Proverbs 3.11–12. Παιδεία in Hebrews 12.5–11 is a regimen, a period of training and testing, through which the readers will learn endurance, be assured that they are, in fact, God's sons and daughters, and enjoy the peaceful fruit of righteousness and God's holiness.

4.6 Summary: Hebrews 12.1–13 in context

A formative/educative interpretation of παιδεία is supported not only by the author's selective exposition of the text, but by at least three other considerations. One of these was discussed at the conclusion of chapter 3; the other two at the beginning of this chapter. First, the athletic imagery that suffuses the text favors a formative interpretation of παιδεία. Athletic language was concentrated in verses 1–3, but also appeared in 4, 11, 12 and 13. The view of suffering as an athletic contest that requires endurance contains no hint of culpability for the hardships endured. Indeed, such hardships are willingly assumed for the sake of participation in and completion of the agon. The collocation of παιδεία with such imagery suggests that "discipline" here refers to rigorous training, just as we would speak of athletes subjecting themselves to "discipline."

Secondly, the social context of the readers, as it is briefly described in the epistle (see section 4.1 above), was primarily one of persecution rather than moral failure. The need of the community was for endurance, confidence, and faith. Nowhere does the author suggest that the readers are guilty of sins for which they are being punished through persecution. We saw in chapter 3 that such a link between sin and persecution was precisely the assumption in 2

Maccabees (see pp. 100–3). The horrors of Antiochus' persecution would bring divine judgment down on his head, to be sure, but the persecution itself was already a sign of God's judgment and discipline of the Jews who had been unfaithful in various respects. The Epistle to the Hebrews has not a hint of this. Our author's theology of suffering has far more affinity to that of 4 Maccabees in which affliction and persecution serve as παιδεία toward the goal of virtue and piety.

Lastly, the literary context of Hebrews 12.1–13 favors a non-punitive interpretation of παιδεία. The immediately prior context extends from 10.19 to 11.40. In 10.19–39 we have the last major sequence of exhortation – warning – reassurance (cf. 5.11–6.12). Following the section on reassurance is the great litany of the faithful in chapter 11. If these luminaries from Israel's past are in any way models for the readers of the epistle, then the urgent need of the latter is not correction of wrongdoings, but perseverance in faith (cf. 10.35–6). Israel's forebears were not commended for enduring deserved punishment, but for remaining faithful in trying circumstances, deprivation, and abuse, particularly when the outlook was uncertain. The author surely intends at least a general analogy between these *exempla* and the situation of the readers. If so, then the παιδεία the latter are experiencing must be educative and non-punitive.

The paradigm of Jesus, needless to say, also fits this pattern. Whereas Jesus' death can be viewed from various angles, such as the cultic and salvific angle common to this epistle (cf. 1.3; 9.11–10.18) and to many early Christian writers, what is of importance to the author in 12.1–3 is Jesus as the model of endurance in extreme suffering. Jesus was not punished by God; he did not suffer for his own sins (4.15; 7.26–8). He was, however, "tested" (πειρασθείς, 2.18; πεπειρασμένον, 4.15) in every respect, and the author's chief pastoral inference from this fact is that Jesus therefore serves as a sympathetic and merciful high priest to others undergoing such testing. In suffering not condign punishment, but hostility at the hands of sinners (12.3; cf. 2.10; 5.7–8), Jesus learned obedience, was perfected, and became "the pioneer and perfecter" of faith for the readers of this epistle who similarly faced hostility.

5

SUMMARY, CONCLUSIONS, AND THESES

5.1 Summary and conclusions

The task that remains in this final chapter is to gather up the results of this study and to state them succinctly and with due force. Then, as a sort of epilogue, I will offer several theological theses on "Endurance in Suffering," touching on the relationship of suffering to sin and eschatology. These theses will incorporate the results of this study, but will intentionally push beyond its limits and broaden the discussion to include other biblical passages and to address modern concerns.

The impetus for this study was the suspicion that the primary frameworks in which Hebrews 12.1–13 was read were inadequate, especially with regard to the latter part of the passage. Martyrological influences on verses 1–3 are undeniable, but have sometimes been exaggerated. The athletic imagery in this passage was universally recognized, but had not been "pushed" to see if Jesus could be viewed chiefly as the model athlete, the champion of faith who had successfully reached the goal, as opposed to the supreme martyr who had laid aside joy to accept suffering. The athletic interpretation would capitalize on the imagery of the passage, both the explicit and the latent, and would bring together the agon motif so common in Hellenistic moralists and the rhetorical tradition of using exemplars to enjoin desired behavior.

Similarly, the influence of wisdom traditions is seen in verses 4–11, most obviously in the citation of Proverbs 3.11–12. But this tradition was not employed in a static fashion. The author had interpreted the text selectively, exploiting some of its facets while ignoring others. Moreover, the interpretation of the text revealed affinities to certain non-punitive views of suffering, many of them stemming from the Greco-Roman world.

In chapter 2 we saw that there was an ancient and rich tradition of using athletic imagery to describe the moral or philosophical life. The author of Hebrews stands in its stream. He issues a call to endurance in faith, depicting the life of faith as a race. In this race, runners must rid themselves of all hindrances and focus on the example of Jesus. The portrayal of Jesus was shaped in every way so as to make it paraenetically effective. The cross was mentioned, but not in its brutal and lethal aspects. The author used the Jesus tradition selectively so as to highlight endurance, shame, hostility, and joy, precisely those aspects of the tradition that pertained to the readers' situation. The much debated preposition ἀντί in 12.2 was seen to indicate the prospective joy of Jesus' exaltation to God's right hand, a joy for which he endured the cross. Lexical, contextual, structural, and rhetorical arguments converged to support this interpretation. Similarly, the readers could look forward to joy (vs. 11) if they persevered faithfully in their own race. Although martyrdom lurked in the peroration of chapter 11 (vss. 35–8), the author's immediate call was not to die, but to run with endurance as Jesus did.

In chapter 3 Charles Talbert's thesis about Jewish and Greco-Roman views of suffering was evaluated. Do, in fact, Jewish authors usually construe suffering as punitive correction for wrongdoing, and Greco-Roman authors as formative education? The survey showed that interpretations of suffering among both groups were diverse, and Talbert's thesis, while valuable *as a generalization*, does not apply without exception. In Jewish writers, non-punitive interpretations of suffering were found in wisdom literature, psalms, the Pentateuch, 4 Maccabees, Josephus, Philo, and the Babylonian Talmud. These interpretations took various forms: educative, formative, probative, and protest. Fourth Maccabees, in sharp contrast to 2 and 3 Maccabees, was especially noteworthy for the way it understood persecution as undeserved suffering that promoted piety and virtue. Punitive suffering, nevertheless, remained the "orthodox" view. This perspective was especially well represented in prophetic literature, Qumran, and early rabbinic literature. A significant subcategory of the punitive, or perhaps a type all its own, was expiatory suffering represented in Isaiah 53 and 4 Maccabees. Judaism thus showed evidence of serious engagement with, and diverse responses to, the problem(s) of human suffering. By no means was the Jewish interpretation monolithically punitive.

The second half of Talbert's thesis was also found to be in need of elaboration. Greco-Roman authors do, in fact, sometimes affirm the punitive nature of suffering. Popular piety especially inclined toward this view when acts of sacrilege and hubris seemed to be "punished" afterwards by calamitous events. If the perpetrators evaded punishment for their crimes, some thought that the penalty would be exacted from succeeding generations, a notion scholars have designated "inherited guilt." There was also more sophisticated philosophical recognition that human wrongdoing was at least sometimes responsible for personal suffering. Among the many instances in Greco-Roman writers where suffering was in some sense regarded as educative, a distinction must be made between cases in which sufferers were simply taught discretion by the brute force of their injuries and losses and those cases in which hardships and adversities were seen to be divine training in virtue and endurance. The most outstanding instances of the latter understanding were the axiom of Aeschylus (and others) that "One suffers and learns," and the extended reflections of certain Stoic philosophers, especially Seneca in *De Providentia*. Thus, whereas suffering was often viewed by Greeks and Romans without punitive connotations, the nature of the "education" that suffering effects was sometimes mundane, sometimes lofty; its operation was sometimes more or less mechanical, sometimes divinely purposeful.

Finally, I demonstrated that the images of athletic training and moral discipline were often combined. These two interpretations of suffering are mutually reinforcing, especially when the "discipline" (παιδεία) is understood in a non-punitive sense. The insight contributed by Chrysostom that παιδεία is γυμνασία is confirmed by this study. With specific regard to Proverbs 3.11–12, it was seen that our author's recontextualization of this passage differed from the way it had been appropriated by other writers. It was distinctive in that it was applied without any punitive connotation.

Returning to the central text of this study, Hebrews 12.1–13, it became clear that our author was astute and in tune with the rhetorical, religious, and philosophical currents of his day. He addressed a community whose primary needs were endurance in faith and fidelity to the confession that had originally constituted the group. Their endurance and fidelity were being tested by external forces that had subjected the community to hostility, abuse, imprisonment and dispossession of goods. The author addresses these needs of his readers in this passage by three means of encouragement: (1) a view of their ordeal as an ἀγών, a race or contest to be engaged successfully; (2) a litany of exemplars of faith, culminating in the supreme paradigm, Jesus, whose struggle was like theirs and whose successful completion of the course offered them the hope of victory; and (3) an interpretation of their sufferings as divine discipline, not in a punitive sense of retribution for sin, but along the lines of 4 Maccabees or Seneca's *De Providentia*, as education and training in virtue, or, in Hebrews' terms, holiness and righteousness. By these encouragements the author hoped to renew the community's faith.

I should clarify that in describing the author of Hebrews as astute and in tune with the intellectual currents of his day, I am not necessarily assuming that he had formal training, particularly with regard to philosophy. The rhetorical skill which he possesses certainly makes some amount of schooling in that discipline a reasonable conjecture. I would not, however, assume that he had received formal schooling in Hellenistic philosophy. Despite the many affinities between Hebrews and Stoic ideas, it would be unwarranted to assume that this biblical author had read or had any personal contact with Seneca or Epictetus, for example. The ideas and imagery found in Hebrews 12.1–13 had wide currency in the Mediterranean world of the first century CE. Such writings as 4 Maccabees and Paul's epistles clearly demonstrate that the "boundaries" between Jewish, Christian, and Greco-Roman ideas were permeable, if one should speak of "boundaries" at all. The comparisons made in chapters 2 and 3 were meant, in general, to show the "rootedness" of Hebrews in its milieu and its alignment with or divergence from other writings, not to suggest literary or even direct intellectual dependence on any person or writing other than the LXX.

Neither Hebrews 12.1–13 nor the epistle as a whole intends to be a theodicy, that is, a formal, comprehensive defense of the providence of God. Seneca's *De Providentia* and Philo's essay by the same title do attempt this, but Hebrews does not. It does not answer every question about the nature and causes of human suffering, in part because it addresses a particular type and a specific historical instance of suffering. The epistle is first and foremost pastoral. It begins with suffering as a "given" in the readers' experience and does not attempt to probe behind its existence with philosophical questions of causation or teleology. It does, however, *contribute to* a Christian theology of suffering, especially suffering related to religious persecution, and, with caution, more broadly, to the extent that suffering of other types may engender a similar response of weakened faith and commitment.

Negatively stated, the central contribution of this study toward a theology of suffering is the insight that Hebrews 12.1–13 does *not* support a punitive view of suffering. Such a view may be found in certain Biblical texts, but I am convinced that it is mistakenly read into the Epistle to the Hebrews. The παιδεία of which our author speaks is non-punitive; it is not the result of human wrongdoing. In light of this, the translation of the TEV is regrettable:

> My son, pay attention when the Lord punishes you, and do not be discouraged when he rebukes you. Because the Lord punishes everyone he loves, and chastises everyone he accepts as a son. Endure what you suffer as being a father's punishment; because your suffering shows that God is treating you as his sons. Was there ever a son who was not punished by his father?[1]

It goes beyond the message of Hebrews to say that *all* suffering is non-punitive and educative, but given the many voices that affirmed the "orthodox" view, and given that the very text appropriated by the author seems to affirm and was usually interpreted by others as affirming the "orthodox" position, it is significant that the author of Hebrews does *not* follow suit.

A non-punitive interpretation of human suffering, or, at the very least, of *some* instances of suffering, finds support elsewhere in Jewish and Christian scriptures. Several of these texts found in the Hebrew Bible and the LXX were treated in chapter 3. Here I need only call attention to a few NT passages. The well-known story of the man born blind is told in John 9. The scene begins with a miniature debate between Jesus and the disciples concerning the cause of the man's disability. The disciples' query, according to the evangelist, is not *whether* the man's blindness was the result of sin, but rather *whose* sin had caused it. They apparently did not entertain the possibility of such an event coming about innocently. Jesus, however, rejects *both* of the alternatives posed by the disciples, "Neither this man nor his parents sinned." The purpose of his blindness was that he might be the occasion of God's works being made manifest.[2]

Similarly in Luke 13.1–5, Jesus rejects a punitive view of suffering in the case of certain Galileans who were slain by Pilate's soldiers

---

[1] Heb. 12.5b–7; *Good News for Modern Man. The New Testament in Today's English Version* (3rd edn.; New York: American Bible Society, 1971).

[2] John 9.1–3. Raymond Brown (*The Gospel According to John I–XII* [New York: Doubleday, 1966] 371, n. 3) observes that "Jesus was asked about the cause of the man's blindness, but he answers in terms of its purpose."

and in the tragic collapse of a tower in which eighteen residents of Jerusalem were killed. Jesus does not exonerate the victims of these tragedies from all guilt; indeed, he uses the incidents to speak to the universal guilt of humankind. But his response does reject a rigid connection between the deaths of these persons and their alleged guilt.[3] Thus, the non-punitive stance of Hebrews 12.1–13 finds support in other NT texts.

But Hebrews 12.5–11 does not simply reject the punitive interpretation; it affirms positive benefit in suffering. As a result of divine παιδεία a person partakes of God's holiness and receives the peaceful fruit of righteousness. As we saw above (p. 205), there are several commonalities between Hebrews' positive construal of suffering and those found in Stoic writers, especially Seneca. Thus, for the author of Hebrews and some of his contemporaries, suffering not only was *not* an indication that a person had erred and incurred divine wrath, but was a positive indication of divine purpose and an occasion for advancement in moral or spiritual terms.

A particular emphasis of the Epistle to the Hebrews is the connection of divine discipline and sonship.[4] For our author, παιδεία is education *into sonship*. This connection is unmistakable in the case of the readers, but it is also true for Jesus. Although the author never uses the specific vocabulary of παιδεία/παιδεύω in reference to Jesus, or anywhere outside of Hebrews 12.5–11, it is clear that Jesus also had to learn the full significance of his sonship. This is most evident in his obedience and submission to death (5.7–9), but is implicit in every mention of his solidarity with humanity and pioneering role (2.10–18; 4.15; 12.2; 13.12–13). Jesus, like his brothers and sisters, endured the testing and the discipline that both presupposed and confirmed his sonship.

The idea of suffering's positive, educative potential finds support in other NT passages. In Romans 5.3–4, Paul writes, "We ... boast in our sufferings, knowing that suffering produces endurance, and endurance produces character, and character produces hope." According to Paul, the first quality produced by suffering is ὑπομονή, the very quality that is central to Hebrews 12.1–3. The prominence

---

[3] Whether this passage implies that Jesus rejected the *general* connection between suffering and sin might be debated. See Joseph A. Fitzmyer, *The Gospel According to Luke X–XXIV* (New York: Doubleday, 1985) 1007, n. 2; and Luke Timothy Johnson, *The Gospel of Luke* (Collegeville, MN: Liturgical Press, 1991) 211, n. 2.

[4] On this point in general, see Bornkamm, "Sohnschaft und Leiden," 188–98.

of "endurance" among Christian virtues is seen in other writers.[5] In a passage with striking similarities to Romans 5.3–4, James also connects endurance with the suffering of hardships: "My brothers and sisters, whenever you face trials of any kind, consider it nothing but joy, because you know that the testing of your faith produces endurance."[6] In both Paul and James, the connection between suffering and the development of endurance is mentioned casually, as something that is assumed.[7] It was apparently a common point of view among moral teachers, one which the author of Hebrews shared.

Another contribution of this study to a theology of suffering pertains to the athletic metaphor of Hebrews 12.1–3. The life of faith with its accompanying affliction may be construed as a contest or race. Chapter 2 showed that this image was popular with both Jewish and Greco-Roman moralists. Since the image of a race involves a goal and a prize or reward,[8] and since the exaltation of Christ is a recurring motif in Hebrews, this athletic metaphor should be understood as contributing to the eschatology of the epistle. It commends an eschatological perspective as a way of viewing and coping with suffering. Christ endured his agon and took his seat at God's right hand. The readers are likewise called to endure. The end to which they look is not death followed by exaltation, but the return of the one who is exalted (9.28; 10.36–9). In both cases, though, there is a reward, a prospective joy, which serves as an incentive to endurance.

The call to endurance in suffering could be misappropriated, however. A danger in "applying" this text simplistically would be to see it as demanding "endurance" in the sense of acquiescence to violence or injustice. The situation of the readers of Hebrews was certainly one of injustice: public ridicule, confiscation of goods, imprisonment, etc. Whether the community had any recourse or hope of earthly vindication is not addressed by the author. But it would clearly go against the implicit message of the text to suggest that

---

[5] See the references in Dunn, *Romans 1–8*, 251.

[6] Jas. 1.2–3 (NRSV). On the relation between Jas. 1.2–3 and Rom. 5.3–4, see the excursus in M. Dibelius and H. Greeven, *James* (Philadelphia: Fortress, 1975) 74–7.

[7] *Ibid.*, 72.

[8] See, for example, the passages cited in section 2.3 from Seneca, Plutarch, and 4 Macc. In Heb. 12, the reward of faithful endurance is "joy," "holiness," and "righteousness," all of which can be understood eschatologically as well as temporally.

the author condones the ongoing oppression of the readers, or of modern Christians, by calling them to endure.[9] On the one hand, we should affirm the value of Hebrews' message for Christians suffering today; on the other hand, we must recognize that it is by no means a *complete* program for how one is to confront situations of persecution or other types of suffering.

5.2   Theses: suffering, sin, and eschatology

The above are some theological reflections on the contribution of Hebrews to a theology of suffering. To conclude, I offer the following more general theses, most of them stated more fully and perhaps more eloquently elsewhere, in order to set the above reflections in the broader context of a Christian theodicy.

(1) Human suffering and its causes are exceedingly complex. No single explanation for suffering is fully adequate. Individual explanations usually pertain to certain types and circumstances of suffering and are ineffective in other relations. The suffering lying behind the Epistle to the Hebrews is religious persecution experienced in reproaches, scorn, imprisonment, and confiscation of property. A facile application of the author's arguments to other kinds of suffering could be theologically risky and pastorally disastrous.

(2) Much suffering is *not* caused by sin, nor is it inflicted by God. It is not clear that the author of Hebrews understood the persecution and the suffering of the persons to whom he wrote as sent by God. Nowadays most people of faith would make a distinction between God "using" suffering and "causing" it, but this distinction is rarely if ever expressed in ancient writers. The same ambiguity applies to the sufferings of Christ in Hebrews. There is no clear statement that God afflicted Jesus. Indeed, 12.3 is careful to speak

---

[9] Mary Rose D'Angelo ("Hebrews," in Carol A. Newsom and Sharon H. Ringe, eds., *The Women's Bible Commentary* [Louisville: Westminster/John Knox, 1992] 364–7) rightly warns against "the abusive connection of punishment and love" in patriarchal education and child rearing, but I think errs in saying that "Hebrews' counsel puts a divine sanction behind the abuse of women and abusive child rearing" (366). In a similar critique, Philip Greven (*Spare the Child. The Religious Roots of Punishment and the Psychological Impact of Physical Abuse* [New York: Alfred A. Knopf, 1990] 52) cites Heb. 12.5–11 as "the key text in the New Testament cited in favor of harsh physical discipline of children." D'Angelo and Greven may be justified in their criticism of *the effect* of this text, that is, its *history of interpretation*, but *the intent* of the text was never to address the issue of child-rearing or corporal punishment. Moreover, if my interpretation of Heb. 12.1–13 is correct, even the use of the text to support *divine* punitive discipline is misguided.

of Jesus enduring hostility "at the hands of sinners."[10] Even Hebrews 2.10 does not unambiguously affirm divine intentionality in Jesus' suffering. A sympathetic reading of the Epistle to the Hebrews suggests that both the readers' afflictions and those of Jesus had human causes.

(3) Not all suffering is the will of God. Many would regard this as a truism hardly in need of affirmation, but it must be affirmed because its opposite is sometimes implied. When a religious spokesperson attributes some new calamity to the will of God, often implying its punitive function, it probably reflects a rigid view of divine providence. This perspective was seen, for example, in 2 Maccabees. If God is all-powerful, nothing can thwart God. Hence, all that happens must be divinely caused. More nuanced versions of this view that distinguish between the "perfect" will of God and the "permissive" will of God are improvements, but still not fully adequate.[11] An adequate theodicy must grant a degree of irrationality in events that cause suffering. Things happen every day that God scarcely could will in *any* sense. Theists would do better to come to terms with chinks in the armor of God's omnipotence than with perverse lapses in God's goodness.[12]

(4) Most suffering is potentially formative, and this is perhaps the most significant insight of Hebrews 12.4–11. "So far as we value courage, endurance, patience, sympathy and a host of other virtues, we are bound to recognize that suffering, or the capacity for it, is their necessary condition."[13] This is an *ex post facto* human observation that few would deny. Suffering is often formative and maturing among those who are not embittered by it. But how, or whether, this is true in instances of extreme or disabling suffering, such as the holocaust or child abuse,[14] and whether God has formation as an *antecedent* purpose in suffering, are very difficult questions.

---

[10] Thus, Bertram distorts the meaning when he claims, "The experience of suffering *at the Father's hand* sets the Christian alongside Christ" (*TDNT*, V, 622, my emphasis).

[11] A classic example is Leslie D. Weatherhead, *The Will of God* (Nashville: Abingdon, 1983). Originally published in 1944, Weatherhead's little book has seen multiple printings and sales in excess of half a million copies. Despite the above criticism, it is worth reading.

[12] On the possibility of God being a source of human suffering, even in its extreme forms, see David R. Blumenthal, *Facing the Abusing God. A Theology of Protest* (Louisville: Westminster/John Knox, 1993).

[13] Robinson, *Suffering Human and Divine*, 22.

[14] These are the examples Blumenthal considers in *Facing the Abusing God*.

(5) God is with us in our suffering. This is a direct corollary of those passages in Hebrews that advance a "low" Christology. We do not have a High Priest who is unable to sympathize with our weaknesses, but one who has suffered and been tested (2.18; 4.15). We simply follow Jesus' example, bearing his abuse (13.12–13), assured of God's presence (13.5–6). In contrast to Stoicism, Jesus and those who follow him are allowed truly to experience suffering. There is nothing akin to the Stoic denial of its reality, no superhuman transcendence of its sorrow and grief. The author of Hebrews understands suffering as an essential aspect of human existence. If Jesus had not suffered, he would not have shared fully in our humanity and he would not have been able to serve as our High Priest. The Christology of Hebrews, which alternates between the High Priest who is like us and the Son who learned obedience through suffering, is a profound statement of God's presence with us.

(6) Endurance of suffering, especially of religious persecution, consists, in part, of holding to the confession, not abandoning the posture of faith and the communal life (3.6, 14; 4.14; 10.23–5). Even if suffering is not the will of God, it is certainly the will of God that one remain faithful amid suffering.

(7) Easing, alleviating, and ridding the world of suffering are part of God's calling for the church. Again, we must recognize that Hebrews does not provide a program for this. The author and his readers apparently had little recourse for putting an end to their persecution. (Abandoning the confession might have ended it, but this, of course, was unacceptable.) There are indications, however, of efforts to alleviate suffering within the community through hospitality and visitation (13.1–3), but there is nothing like a plan for societal reform. For the latter, we must look elsewhere in the canon, in our faith traditions, and to our own "cloud of witnesses."

(8) The complete conquest of suffering is eschatological. Such hope is a common source of strength for those who are suffering. In fact, the promise of a coming world has often fueled efforts at reforming this world. While engaging this world, Christians need not deprive themselves of eschatological hope. For many, the hope that animates and empowers the most is not the hope of utterly reforming this world, as eagerly as that goal is to be sought, but rather the hope of a new heaven and earth from which all suffering has been stripped away. This is the ultimate joy that lies before us, the peaceful fruit of righteousness on the other side of παιδεία.

BIBLIOGRAPHY

Primary sources

Aeschylus. *Agamemnon*, LCL, Cambridge, MA, Harvard University, 1926.

Aristotle. *The Art of Rhetoric*, LCL, Cambridge, MA, Harvard University, 1926.

Aucher, J. B. *Philonis Judaei Sermones Tres Hactenus Inediti*, 1822.

Aurelius, Marcus. *The Communings with Himself*, LCL, Cambridge, MA, Harvard University, 1987.

Baillet, M. *Discoveries in the Judaean Desert*, VII, Oxford, Clarendon, 1982.

Behr, Charles A. *P. Aelius Aristides, The Complete Works*, Leiden, Brill, 1986.

Bergson, L. (ed.), *Der Griechische Alexanderroman. Rezension β*, Stockholm, Almqvist and Wiksell, 1965.

Biblia Hebraica Stuttgartensia. K. Elliger and W. Rudolph (eds.), Stuttgart, Deutsche Bibelgesellschaft, 1983.

Blass, F. (ed.), *Aeschines Orationes*, Stuttgart, Teubner, 1978.

Brock, S. P. *Testamentum Iobi*, Leiden, Brill, 1967.

Charlesworth, James H. (ed.), *The Old Testament Pseudepigrapha*, 2 vols., Garden City, NY, Doubleday, 1983–5.

Danby, Herbert (ed.), *The Mishnah*, New York, Oxford University, 1933.

Diels, Hermann. *Die Fragmente der Vorsokratiker*, Berlin, Weidmansche, 1952.

Dindorf, W. (ed.), *Aristides*, Hildesheim, Georg Olms, 1964.

Dio Chrysostom. *Works*, LCL, Cambridge, MA, Harvard University, 1932.

Diogenes Laertius. *Lives of Eminent Philosophers*, LCL, Cambridge, MA, Harvard University, 1925.

Epictetus. *The Discourses, the Manual, and the Fragments*, LCL, Cambridge, MA, Harvard University, 1925–8.

Epstein, I. (ed.), *Hebrew–English Edition of the Babylonian Talmud*, London, Soncino, 1960–   .

Foerster, R. (ed.), *Libanii Opera*, Stuttgart, Teubner, 1915.

Freedman, H. and M. Simon (eds.), *Midrash Rabbah*, London, Soncino, 1939.

Greek New Testament. K. Aland, *et al.* (eds.), 3rd edn., New York, UBS, 1975.

Hammer, Reuven. *Sifre: A Tannaitic Commentary on the Book of Deuteronomy*, New Haven and London, Yale University, 1986.

Hausrath, A. (ed.), *Corpus Fabularum Aesopicarum*, Leipzig, Teubner, 1959.

Hense, O. C. *Musonii Rufi Reliquiae*, Leipzig, Teubner, 1905.

Herodotus. *The Histories*, LCL, Cambridge, MA, Harvard University, 1920.

Isocrates. *Evagoras*, LCL, Cambridge, MA, Harvard University, 1945.

Jaekel, Siegfried (ed.), *Menandri Sententiae*, Leipzig, Teubner, 1964.

Josephus. *The Jewish War*, LCL, Cambridge, MA, Harvard University, 1927–8.

    The Works of Josephus. Complete and Unabridged, Peabody, MA, Hendrickson, 1987.

Koetschau, Paul. *Die griechischen christlichen Schriftsteller der ersten drei Jahrhunderte, Origenes, erster Band*, Leipzig, J. C. Hinrichs'sche, 1899.

Lauterbach, J. Z. (ed.), *Mekilta De-Rabbi Ishmael*, Philadelphia, Jewish Publication Society of America, 1933–5.

Lucian. *De Peregrini Morte*, LCL, Cambridge, MA, Harvard University, 1936.

Malherbe, A. *Moral Exhortation: A Greco-Roman Sourcebook*, Philadelphia, Westminster, 1986.

Moffatt, James. *The New Testament: A New Translation*, London, Hodder & Stoughton, 1913.

Musurillo, H. *The Acts of the Christian Martyrs*, Oxford, Clarendon, 1972.

Novum Testamentum Graece. E. Nestlé and K. Aland (eds.), 26th edn., Stuttgart, Deutsche Bibelgesellschaft, 1979.

Novum Testamentum Graece. Constantinus de Tischendorf (ed.), Leipzig, B. Tauchnitz, 1904.

Pearson, A. C. (ed.), *The Fragments of Sophocles*, Amsterdam, Adolf M. Hakkert, 1963.

Phillips, J. B. *The New Testament in Modern English*, New York, Macmillan, 1976.

Philo. *Works*, LCL, Cambridge, MA, Harvard University, 1927–62.

Plato. *Phaedrus*, LCL, Cambridge, MA, Harvard University, 1914.

    Gorgias, LCL, Cambridge, MA, Harvard University, 1925.

    Republic, LCL, Cambridge, MA, Harvard University, 1930.

Plutarch. *Lives*, LCL, Cambridge, MA, Harvard University, 1914–26.

    Moralia, LCL, Cambridge, MA, Harvard University, 1927–76.

Seneca, *Tragedies*, LCL, Cambridge, MA, Harvard University, 1917.

    Epistulae Morales, LCL, Cambridge, MA, Harvard University, 1917–25.

    Moral Essays, LCL, Cambridge, MA, Harvard University, 1928–35.

Septuaginta. Alfred Rahlfs (ed.), Stuttgart, Deutsche Bibelgesellschaft, 1979.

Sophocles. *Oedipus at Colonus*, LCL, Cambridge, MA, Harvard University, 1912.

Vermes, G. *The Dead Sea Scrolls in English*, 3rd edn., New York, Penguin, 1987.

von Arnim, Hans F. A. *Hierokles ethische Elementarlehre*, Berlin, 1906.

Wachsmuth, C. and O. Hense (eds.), *Ioannis Stobaei Anthologium*, 5 vols., Berlin, Weidmann, 1974.

West, M. L. (ed.), *Iambi et Elegi Graeci*, New York, Oxford University, 1972.

Secondary literature

Abel, P. F.-M. *Les Livres des Maccabées*, Paris, Gabalda, 1949.

Adam, James. "Ancient Greek Views of Suffering and Evil," in A. M. Adams (ed.), *The Vitality of Platonism*, Cambridge, Cambridge University, 1911, 190–212.

Alewell, K. "Über das rhetorische ΠΑΡΑΔΕΙΓΜΑ: Theorie, Beispielsammlungen, Verwendung in der römischen Literatur der Kaiserzeit," Dissertation, Leipzig, 1913.

Anderson, H. "3 Maccabees," in J. H. Charlesworth (ed.), *OTP*, 2 vols., Garden City, NY, Doubleday, 1985, II, 509–29.

"4 Maccabees," in J. H. Charlesworth (ed.), *OTP*, 2 vols., Garden City, NY, Doubleday, 1985, II, 531–64.

Andriessen, P. "Renonçant à la joie qui lui revenait," *Nouvelle Revue Théologique*, 97 (1975), 424–38.

Andriessen P. and A. Lenglet. "Quelques passages difficiles de l'Epître aux Hébreux (5,7.11; 10,20; 12,2)," *Biblica*, 51 (1970), 207–20.

Aquinas, Thomas. *Super Epistolas S. Pauli Lectura*, Raphael Cai (ed.), 8th edn., Rome, Marietti, 1953.

Attridge, Harold W. *The Epistle to the Hebrews*, Philadelphia, Fortress, 1989.

Aune, David E. "De Esu Carnium Orationes I and II," in H. D. Betz (ed.), *Plutarch's Theological Writings and Early Christian Literature*, Leiden, Brill, 1975.

Balla, E. "Das Problem des Leides in dem israelitisch-jüdischen Religion," in Hans Schmidt (ed.), ΕΥΧΑΡΙΣΤΗΡΙΟΝ: *Studien zur Religion und Literatur des Alten und Neuen Testaments*, Göttingen, Vandenhoeck and Ruprecht, 1923, 214–60.

Balz, H. and G. Schneider (eds.), *Exegetical Dictionary of the New Testament*, Grand Rapids, Eerdmans, 1993.

Barr, James. *Semantics of Biblical Language*, Oxford, Oxford University, 1961.

Bartlett, J. R. *The First and Second Books of the Maccabees*, Cambridge, Cambridge University, 1973.

Batley, J. Y. *The Problem of Suffering in the Old Testament*, Cambridge, Cambridge University, 1916.

Bauer, W. *A Greek–English Lexicon of the New Testament and Other Early Christian Literature*, W. F. Arndt, F. W. Gingrich, F. W. Danker (eds.), 2nd edn., Chicago, University of Chicago, 1979.

Bauerfeind, Otto. "τρέχω," *TDNT*, VIII, 226–35.

Bengel, Johannes A. *Gnomon Novi Testamenti*, 3rd edn., Tübingen, sumtibus Ludov. Frid. Fues, 1855.

New Testament Commentary, 2 vols., Grand Rapids, Kregel, 1982.

Bertram, Georg. "Der Begriff der Erziehung in der griechischen Bibel," in *Imago Dei. Festschrift for G. Krüger*, Leipzig, Hinrichs, 1932, 33–51.

"παιδεύω," *TDNT*, V, 596–625.

Bèze, Théodore de. *Cours sur les Epîtres aux Romains et aux Hébreux*

(1564–66) d'après les notes de Marcus Widler, P. Fraenkel and L. Perrotet (eds.), Geneva, Droz, 1988.

Blass, F. and A. Debrunner. *A Greek Grammar of the New Testament and Other Early Christian Literature,* trans. and ed. by Robert W. Funk, Chicago, University of Chicago, 1961.

Blumenthal, David R. *Facing the Abusing God. A Theology of Protest,* Louisville, Westminster/John Knox, 1993.

Bonnard, P.-E. "La Traduction de Hébreux 12:2: 'C'est en vue de la joie que Jésus endura la croix,'" *Nouvelle Revue Théologique,* 97 (1975), 415–23.

Bonner, Stanley R. *Education in Ancient Rome,* Berkeley and Los Angeles, University of California, 1977.

Bornkamm, G. "Sohnschaft und Leiden," in Walther Eltester (ed.), *Judentum, Urchristentum, Kirche: Festschrift für Joachim Jeremias,* Berlin, Töpelmann, 1960, 188–98.

Braun, Herbert. *An die Hebräer,* Tübingen, Mohr-Siebeck, 1984.

Bright, John. *Jeremiah,* Garden City, NY, Doubleday, 1965.

Brown, R. E. *The Gospel According to John I–XII,* New York, Doubleday, 1966.

Brown, Schuyler. "Philology," in Eldon Jay Epp and George W. MacRae (eds.), *The New Testament and its Modern Interpreters,* Atlanta, Scholars Press, 1989, 127–47.

Bruce, F. F. *The Epistle to the Hebrews,* Grand Rapids, Eerdmans, 1964.

The Acts of the Apostles, The Greek Text with Introduction and Commentary, Grand Rapids, Eerdmans, 1990.

Buchanan, George W. *To the Hebrews,* Garden City, NY, Doubleday, 1972.

Büchler, A. *Studies in Sin and Atonement in the Rabbinic Literature of the First Century,* New York, Ktav, 1939.

Büchsel, F. "ἐλέγχω," *TDNT,* II, 473–6.

Bultmann, R. "λύπη," *TDNT,* IV, 313–24.

Burkert, Walter. *Greek Religion,* Cambridge, MA, Harvard University, 1985.

Butcher, S. H. "The Melancholy of the Greeks," in his *Some Aspects of the Greek Genius,* Port Washington, NY, Kennikat, 1969.

Calvin, John. *Calvin's Commentary on the Epistle to the Hebrews,* London, Cornish, 1824.

Ioannis Calvini in Novi Testamenti Epistolas Commentarii, Berlin, Eichler, 1834.

Carmignac, J. "La Théologie de la souffrance dans les Hymnes de Qumran," *Revue de Qumran,* 3 (1961–2) 365–86.

Carpzov, J. B. *Sacrae Exercitationes in S. Pauli Epistolam ad Hebraeos ex Philone Alexandrino,* Helmstedt, 1750.

Cosby, Michael R. *The Rhetorical Composition and Function of Hebrews 11 in the Light of Example Lists in Antiquity,* Macon, GA, Mercer University, 1988.

Costé, J. "Notion grecque et notion biblique de la 'souffrance éducatrice,'" *Recherches de Science Religieuse,* 43 (1955), 481–523.

Coxon, Allan H. "Xenophanes," *OCD*, New York, Oxford University, 1970, 1141.

Craddock, Fred B. *The Pre-Existence of Christ in the New Testament*, Nashville, Abingdon, 1968.

Critici Sacri, sive, Annotata Doctissimorum Virorum in Vetus ac Novum Testamentum, John Pearson *et al.* (eds.), Amsterdam, Boom, 1698. (Originally London, 1660.)

Cross, F. L. and E. A. Livingston (eds.), *The Oxford Dictionary of the Christian Church*, 2nd edn., Oxford, Oxford University 1974.

Croy, N. Clayton. "A Note on Hebrews 12:2," *JBL*, 114 (1995), 117–19.

Dana, H. E. and J. R. Mantey. *A Manual Grammar of the Greek New Testament*, Toronto, Macmillan, 1957.

D'Angelo, Mary Rose. "Hebrews," in Carol A. Newsom and Sharon H. Ringe (eds.), *The Women's Bible Commentary*, Louisville, Westminster/ John Knox, 1992.

Delarue, Earl George. "Lucii Annaei Senecae *De Providentia*: A Commentary," Dissertation, Cornell University, 1974.

Delitzsch, F. *Commentary on the Epistle to the Hebrews*, 2 vols., 3rd edn., Edinburgh, T. & T. Clark, 1883.

DeSilva, David A. "Despising Shame: A Cultural–Anthropological Investigation of the Epistle to the Hebrews," *JBL*, 113 (1994), 439–61.

Despising Shame. Honor Discourse and Community Maintenance in the Epistle to the Hebrews, SBLDS 152, Atlanta, Scholars Press, 1995.

Dibelius, M. and H. Greeven. *James*, Philadelphia, Fortress, 1975.

Dodds, E. R. *The Greeks and the Irrational*, Berkeley, University of California, 1966.

Doran, Robert. *Temple Propaganda: The Purpose and Character of 2 Maccabees*, Washington, DC, Catholic Biblical Association of America, 1980.

Dörrie, Heinrich. "Leid und Erfahrung. Die Wort- und Sinn-Verbindung παθεῖν – μαθεῖν im griechischen Denken," *Akademie der Wissenschaften und der Literatur*, 5 (1956), 303–44.

Downing, John. "Jesus and Martyrdom," *JTS*, 14, 2 (1963), 279–93.

Dunn, James D. G. *Romans 1–8*, Dallas, Word, 1988.

Dyck, T. L. "Jesus our Pioneer: ΑΡΧΗΓΟΣ in Heb. 2:5–18; 12:1–3," Dissertation, Northwest Baptist Theological Seminary, 1980.

Ellingworth, Paul. "New Testament Text and Old Testament Context in Heb. 12:3," in E. A. Livingstone (ed.), *Studia Biblica 1978*, JSNT, Suppl. 3, 1980, 89–96.

Commentary on Hebrews, Grand Rapids, Eerdmans, 1993.

Ellsworth, James D. "Agon: Studies in the Use of a Word," Dissertation, University of California, Berkeley, 1971.

Elman, Y. "The Suffering of the Righteous in Palestinian and Babylonian Sources," *Jewish Quarterly Review*, 80, no. 3–4 (January–April 1990), 315–39.

Falkenroth, Ulrich and Colin Brown. "ὑπομένω," in Colin Brown (ed.), *The New International Dictionary of New Testament Theology*, Grand Rapids, Eerdmans, 1981, II, 772–6.

Farquharson, A. S. L. *The Meditations of the Emperor Marcus Antoninus*, Oxford, Clarendon, 1944.

Festugière, A. M. "ὑπομονή dans la Tradition Grecque," *Recherches de Science Religieuse*, 30 (1931), 477–86.

Fiore, Benjamin. *The Function of Personal Example in the Socratic and Pastoral Epistles*, Rome, Biblical Institute, 1986.

Fitzmyer, Joseph A. *The Gospel According to Luke X–XXIV*, New York, Doubleday, 1985.

Ford, J. M. "The Mother of Jesus and the Authorship of the Epistle to the Hebrews," *Bible Today*, 82 (1975) 683–94.

Fraenkel, E. *Aeschylus' Agamemnon*, Oxford, Clarendon, 1950.

Frey, H. "Zur Sinndeutung des Leidens im Alten Testament," *Wort und Dienst*, 6 (1959), 45–61.

Gambiza, F. K. M. *"Teleiosis* and *Paideia* as Interpretation of Sufferings: The Perfecting of Jesus and the Disciplining of Christians in the Letter to the Hebrews," Th.D. Dissertation, Christ Seminary-Seminex, 1981.

Gärtner, Burkhard. "πάσχω, Suffer," in Colin Brown (ed.), *The New International Dictionary of New Testament Theology*, Grand Rapids, Eerdmans, 1981, III, 719–26.

Gaster, T. H. *The Dead Sea Scriptures*, New York, Doubleday, 1956.

Gerstenberger, E. S. and W. Schrage. *Suffering*, Nashville, Abingdon, 1980.

Gesenius' Hebrew Grammar. E. Kautzsch and A. E. Cowley (eds.), Oxford, Clarendon, 1910.

Gouge, William. *Commentary on the Whole Epistle to the Hebrews*, Grand Rapids, Kregel, 1980.

Grässer, Erich. *Der Glaube im Hebräerbrief*, Marburg, Elwert, 1965.

Aufbruch und Verheissung: Gesammelte Aufsätze zum Hebräerbrief, Berlin, Walter de Gruyter, 1992.

Greer, Rowan A. *The Captain of our Salvation. A Study in the Patristic Exegesis of Hebrews*, Tübingen, Mohr, 1973.

Greven, Philip. *Spare the Child. The Religious Roots of Punishment and the Psychological Impact of Physical Abuse*, New York, Knopf, 1990.

Guthrie, George H. *The Structure of Hebrews, A Text-Linguistic Analysis*, Leiden, Brill, 1994.

Guthrie, W. K. C. *The Greeks and their Gods*, London, Methuen, 1950.

Hadas, Moses. *The Third and Fourth Books of Maccabees*, New York, Harper, 1953.

Humanism. The Greek Ideal and its Survival, Gloucester, MA, Peter Smith, 1972.

Hagen, K. *A Theology of Testament in the Young Luther: The Lectures on Hebrews*, Leiden, Brill, 1974.

Hebrews Commenting from Erasmus to Bèze, Tübingen, Mohr, 1981.

Hamm, D. "Faith in the Epistle to the Hebrews: The Jesus Factor," *CBQ*, 52 (1990), 270–91.

Harris, H. A. *Greek Athletics and the Jews*, Cardiff, University of Wales, 1976.

Hartley, John E. *The Book of Job*, Grand Rapids, Eerdmans, 1988.

Hauck, F. "ὑπομένω," *TDNT*, IV, 581–8.

Hengel, M. *Crucifixion in the Ancient World and the Folly of the Message of the Cross*, Philadelphia, Fortress, 1977.

Judaism and Hellenism, Philadelphia, Fortress, 1981.

Héring, Jean. *The Epistle to the Hebrews*, London, Epworth, 1970.

Holladay, Carl R. *Fragments from Jewish Hellenistic Authors*. Vol. IV: *Pseudo Orpheus*, SBL Texts and Translations, Pseudepigrapha, Atlanta, Scholars Press, 1996.

Holladay, William L. *Jeremiah 1*, Philadelphia, Fortress, 1986.

Hoppin, R. *Priscilla, Author of the Epistle to the Hebrews and Other Essays*, New York, Exposition, 1969.

Horning, E. B. "Chiasmus, Creedal Structure, and Christology in Hebrews 12:1–2," *Biblical Research*, 23 (1978) 37–48.

Howland, R. L., "Athletics," *OCD*, New York, Oxford University, 1970, 142–3.

Hughes, Philip E. "The Epistle to the Hebrews," in Eldon Jay Epp and George W. MacRae, (eds.), *The New Testament and its Modern Interpreters*, Atlanta, Scholars Press, 1989, 351–70.

Hurst, L. D. *The Epistle to the Hebrews: Its Background of Thought*, SNTSMS 65, Cambridge, Cambridge University, 1990.

Jaeger, W. *Paideia: The Ideals of Greek Culture*, 3 vols.; Oxford, Oxford University, 1946.

Jentsch, W. *Urchristliches Erziehungsdenken. Die Paideia Kyriu im Rahmen der hellenistisch-Jüdischen Umwelt*, Beiträge zur Förderung Christlicher Theologie 45,3, Gütersloh, Bertelsmann, 1951.

Jewett, R. *Letter to Pilgrims: A Commentary on the Epistle to the Hebrews*, New York, Pilgrim, 1981.

Johnson, Luke T. *The Writings of the New Testament, An Interpretation*, Philadelphia, Fortress, 1986.

The Gospel of Luke, Collegeville, MN, Liturgical Press, 1991.

Kamerbeek, J. C. *The Plays of Sophocles, Part III, Antigone*, Leiden, Brill, 1978.

Käsemann, E. *Jesus Means Freedom*, Philadelphia, Fortress, 1969.

The Wandering People of God: An Investigation of the Letter to the Hebrews, Minneapolis, Augsburg, 1984.

Kirkwood, G. *Selections from Pindar, Edited with an Introduction and Commentary*, Chico, CA, Scholars Press, 1982.

Kohler, Kaufmann. *Jewish Theology*, New York, Macmillan 1918.

Kraemer, David. *Responses to Suffering in Classical Rabbinic Literature*, New York, Oxford University, 1995.

Kraft, Robert A. and George W. E. Nickelsburg (eds.). *Early Judaism and its Modern Interpreters*, Atlanta, Scholars Press, 1986.

Lane, W. L. *Hebrews 1–8, Hebrews 9–13*, Dallas, Word, 1991.

Lapide, C. *Commentaria in Omnes Divi Pauli Epistolas*, Antwerp, Meursium, 1665.

Leaf, W. *The Iliad*, Amsterdam, Adolf M. Hakkert, 1960.

Leaney, A. R. C. "The Eschatological Significance of Human Suffering in the Old Testament and in the Dead Sea Scrolls," *Scottish Journal of Theology*, 16 (1963), 286–96.

The Rule of Qumran and its Meaning, London, SCM Press, 1966.

Lenglet, A. "A la suite de l'initiateur (He 12,1–4)," *Assemblées du Seigneur*, 51 (1972), 56–61.

Liddell, H. G. and R. Scott. *A Greek–English Lexicon*, 9th edn., H. Stuart Jones and R. McKenzie (eds.), New York, Oxford University, 1940.

Lindars, Barnabas. *The Theology of the Letter to the Hebrews*, Cambridge, Cambridge University, 1971.

Lindström, Fredrik. *God and the Origin of Evil. A Contextual Analysis of Alleged Monistic Evidence in the Old Testament*, Lund, Gleerup, 1983.

Suffering and Sin. Interpretations of Illness in the Individual Complaint Psalms, Stockholm, Almqvist and Wiksell, 1994.

Loader, W. R. G. "Christ at the Right Hand. Ps cx.1 in the New Testament," *New Testament Studies*, 24 (1977–8), 199–217.

Logan, S. P. "The Background of Paideia in Hebrews," Dissertation, Southern Baptist Theological Seminary, 1986.

Long, A. A. and D. N. Sedley. *The Hellenistic Philosophers*, 2 vols., Cambridge, Cambridge University, 1987.

Lünemann, G. *Commentary on the Epistle to the Hebrews*, New York, Funk & Wagnalls, 1890.

Luther, Martin. *Luthers Vorlesung über den Hebräerbrief nach der Vatikanischen Handschrift*, E. Hirsch and H. Rückert (eds.), Berlin and Leipzig, Walter de Gruyter, 1929.

Lutz, Cora E. "Musonius Rufus, The Roman Socrates," *Yale Classical Studies*, 10 (1947), 3–147.

McCown, Wayne G. "Ὁ ΛΟΓΟΣ ΤΗΣ ΠΑΡΑΚΛΗΣΕΩΣ: The Nature and Function of the Hortatory Sections in the Epistle to the Hebrews," Dissertation, Union Theological Seminary, Richmond, VA, 1970.

McKenzie, John L. *Second Isaiah*, Garden City, NY, Doubleday, 1968.

Mackenzie, Mary M. *Plato on Punishment*, Berkeley, University of California, 1981.

Macleod, C. W. *Iliad, Book XXIV*, Cambridge, Cambridge University, 1982.

Malherbe, Abraham J. "Pseudo Heraclitus, Epistle 4: The Divinization of the Wise Man," *Jahrbuch für Antike und Christentum*, 21 (1976), 42–64.

"Greco-Roman Religion and Philosophy and the New Testament," in Eldon J. Epp and George W. MacRae (eds.), *The New Testament and its Modern Interpreters*, Atlanta, Scholars Press, 1989.

"Hellenistic Moralists and the New Testament," *ANRW*, II.26.1, New York, Walter de Gruyter, 1992, 267–333.

Mansoor, Menahem. *The Thanksgiving Hymns, Translated and Annotated with an Introduction*, Grand Rapids, Eerdmans, 1961.

Mende, T. "'Wen der Herr liebhat, den züchtigt er' (Hebr 12,6). Der alttestamentliche Hintergrund von Hebr 12,1–11; 1,1–4; 2,6–10," *Trierer Theologische Zeitschrift*, 100, no. 1 (1991), 23–38.

Metzger, Bruce M. *A Textual Commentary on the Greek New Testament*, 2nd edn., New York, UBS, 1975.

Michaelis, Wilhelm. "πάσχω," *TDNT*, V, 904–39.

Michel, Otto. *Der Brief an die Hebräer*, 11th edn., Göttingen, Vandenhoeck & Ruprecht, 1960.

Moffatt, J. *Hebrews*, Edinburgh, T. & T. Clark, 1979.

Montefiore, Hugh. *A Commentary on the Epistle to the Hebrews*, New York, Harper, 1964.

Moore, Carey A. *Judith*, Garden City, NY, Doubleday, 1985.

Moore, George F. *Judaism in the First Centuries of the Christian Era*, Cambridge, MA, Harvard University, 1927.

Mora, G. *La Carta a los Hebreos como escrito pastoral*, Barcelona, Herder, 1974.

Motto, Anna L. *Seneca Sourcebook: Guide to the Thought of Lucius Annaeus Seneca*, Amsterdam, Adolf M. Hakkert, 1970.

Moulton, J. H., W. F. Howard, and Nigel Turner. *A Grammar of New Testament Greek*, Edinburgh, T. & T. Clark, II, 1919; III, 1963.

Moulton, J. H. and George Milligan. *The Vocabulary of the Greek Testament*, Grand Rapids, Eerdmans, 1980.

Murphy-O'Connor, Jerome. "The Judean Desert," in *EJMI*, 119–56.

Nauck, W. "Freude im Leiden: Zum Problem der urchristlichen Verfolgungstradition," *Zeitschrift für die neutestamentliche Wissenschaft*, 46 (1955), 68–80.

Niederstrasser, H. *Kerygma und Paideia: Zum Problem der erziehenden Gnade*, Stuttgart, Evangelisches Verlagswerk, 1967.

Nisius, J. B. "Zur Erklärung von Hebr. 12,2," *Biblische Zeitschrift*, 14 (1917), 44–61.

North, Christopher R. *The Suffering Servant in Deutero-Isaiah*, London, Oxford University, 1956.

Owen, John. *An Exposition of the Epistle to the Hebrews*, New York, Robert Carter, 1855.

Paton, L. B. "The Problem of Suffering in the Pre-Exilic Prophets," *JBL*, 46 (1927), 111–31.

Peake, Arthur S. *The Problem of Suffering in the Old Testament*, London, Epworth, 1947, (1st edn., Robert Bryant, 1904).

Peters, Norbert. *Die Leidensfrage im alten Testament*, Biblische Zeitfragen, Münster Aschendorff, 1923.

Peterson, David. *Hebrews and Perfection. An Examination of the Concept of Perfection in the Epistle to the Hebrews*, Cambridge, Cambridge University, 1982.

Peterson, W. *M. Fabi Quintiliani Institutionis Oratoriae. Liber Decimus*, Hildesheim, Georg Olms, 1891.

Pfitzner, Victor C. *Paul and the Agon Motif*, Leiden, Brill, 1967.

Pleket, H. W. "Games, Prizes, Athletes and Ideology," *Stadion*, 1, 1 (1975), 49–89.

Pobee, John S. *Persecution and Martyrdom in the Theology of Paul*, Sheffield, JSOT, 1985.

Poliakoff, Michael B. "Jacob, Job, and Other Wrestlers: Reception of Greek Athletics by Jews and Christians in Antiquity," *Journal of Sport History*, 11.2 (1984), 48–65.

Studies in the Terminology of the Greek Combat Sports, 2nd edn., Beiträge zur Klassischen Philologie 146, Frankfurt, Hain, 1986.

Combat Sports in the Ancient World, New Haven, Yale University, 1987.

Pope, M. H. "Book of Job," *Interpreter's Dictionary of the Bible*, Nashville, Abingdon, 1962, II, 911–25.

Porton, Gary G. "Talmud," *ABD*, VI, 310–15.

Preisker, H. "ὀρθός," *TDNT*, V, 449–51.

Price, Bennett J. "'Paradeigma' and 'Exempla' in Ancient Rhetorical Theory," Dissertation, University of California, Berkeley, 1975.

Quasten, Johannes. *Patrology*, Westminster, MD, Christian Classics, 1986.

Rad, Gerhard von. *Old Testament Theology*, New York, Harper, 1962.

Reddish, Mitchell G. "The Theme of Martyrdom in the Book of Revelation," Dissertation, Southern Baptist Theological Seminary, 1982.

Renehan, Robert. "The Greek Philosophic Background of Fourth Maccabees," *Rheinisches Museum für Philologie*, 115 (1972), 223–38.

Rengstorf, Karl H. *A Complete Concordance to Flavius Josephus*, Leiden, Brill, 1973–83.

Riggenbach, Eduard. *Historische Studien zum Hebräerbrief: Die ältesten lateinischen Kommentare zum Hebräerbrief*, Leipzig, A. Deichert, 1907.

Der Brief an die Hebräer, Wuppertal, Brockhaus, 1987.

Roberts, J. J. M. *Nahum, Habakkuk, and Zephaniah. A Commentary*, Louisville, Westminster/John Knox, 1991.

Robertson, A. T. *A Grammar of the Greek New Testament in the Light of Historical Research*, Nashville, Broadman, 1934.

Robinson, H. Wheeler. *The Religious Ideas of the Old Testament*, New York, Scribner, 1919.

Suffering Human and Divine New York, Macmillan, 1939.

Robinson, Theodore H. *The Epistle to the Hebrews*, New York, Harper, 1933.

Saldarini, Anthony J. "Reconstructions of Rabbinic Judaism," in *EJMI*, 437–77.

Sampson, Francis S. *A Critical Commentary on the Epistle to the Hebrews*, New York, Robert Carter & Brothers, 1856.

Sanders, E. P. "Rabbi Akiba's View of Suffering," *Jewish Quarterly Review*, 63 (1972–3), 332–51.

Paul and Palestinian Judaism: A Comparison of Patterns of Religion, Philadelphia, Fortress, 1977.

Sanders, J. A. *Suffering as Divine Discipline in the Old Testament and Post-Biblical Judaism*, Rochester, NY, Colgate Rochester Divinity School, 1955.

Torah and Canon, Philadelphia, Fortress, 1972.

Sandmel, Samuel. "Parallelomania," *JBL*, 81 (1962) 1–13.

Scharbert, Josef. *Der Schmerz im Alten Testament*, Bonn, Hanstein, 1955.

Schechter, Solomon. "The Doctrine of Divine Retribution in Rabbinical Literature," *Studies in Judaism*, 1st Series, Philadelphia, Jewish Publication Society of America, 1896, 213–55.

Schmidt, H. *Gott und das Leid im alten Testament*, Giessen, Topelmann, 1926.

Schneider, Carl. "μαστιγόω," *TDNT*, IV, 515–19.

Schneider, J. "σταυρός," *TDNT*, VII, 572–84.

Schürer, Emil. *The History of the Jewish People in the Age of Jesus Christ*, rev. and ed. by G. Vermes, F. Millar and M. Goodman, Edinburgh, T. & T. Clark, 1987.

Scott, J. J. "Archegos in the Salvation History of the Epistle to the Hebrews," *Journal of the Evangelical Theological Society*, 29, no. 1 (1986) 47–54.

Seaton, R. C. "The Aristotelian Enthymeme," *Classical Review* (June, 1914) 113–19.

Seesemann, Heinrich. "ὄγκος," *TDNT*, V, 41.

Simundson, Daniel J. *Faith Under Fire – Biblical Interpretations of Suffering*, Minneapolis, Augsburg, 1980.

Skehan, Patrick W. *The Wisdom of Ben Sira*, New York, Doubleday, 1987.

Smith, R. H. *Hebrews*, Minneapolis, Augsburg, 1984.

Smyth, H. W. *Greek Grammar*, Cambridge, MA, Harvard University, 1956.

Spicq, C. *L'Epître aux Hébreux. Traduction, notes critiques, commentaire*, 2 vols., Paris, Gabalda, 1977.

Notes de Lexicographie néotestamentaire, Göttingen, Vandenhoeck & Ruprecht, 1978, I.

Staab, Karl. *Pauluskommentare aus der griechischen Kirche*, Münster, Aschendorff, 1933.

Stamm, Johann J. *Das Leiden des Unschuldigen in Babylon und Israel*, Zürich, Zwingli, 1946.

Stauffer, E. "ἀγών," *TDNT*, I, 134–40.

Stoike, Donald A. "De Genio Socrates," in H. D. Betz (ed.), *Plutarch's Theological Writings and Early Christian Literature*, Leiden, Brill, 1975.

Strathmann, H. *Der Brief an die Hebräer, übersetzt und erklärt*, 7th edn., Göttingen, Vandenhoeck & Ruprecht, 1963.

"μάρτυς," *TDNT*, IV, 474–514.

Strobel, A. *Der Brief an die Hebräer*, Göttingen, Vandenhoeck & Ruprecht, 1975.

Sutcliffe, E. R. *Providence and Suffering in the Old and New Testament*, London, Thomas Nelson, 1953.

Talbert, Charles H. *Learning Through Suffering. The Educational Value of Suffering in the New Testament and in Its Milieu*, Collegeville, MN, Liturgical Press, 1991.

Thayer, Joseph H. (ed.), *A Greek–English Lexicon of the New Testament*, New York, 1889.

Theron, L. "Progression of Thought in Seneca's 'De Providentia,'" *Acta Classica*, 13 (1971), 61–72.

Thiering, Barbara. "Suffering and Asceticism at Qumran as Illustrated in the Hodayot," *Revue de Qumran*, 31 (March 1974), 393–405.

Tholuck, A. *A Commentary on the Epistle to the Hebrews*, Edinburgh, Clark, 1842.

Thompson, J. W. *The Beginnings of Christian Philosophy: The Epistle to the Hebrews*, Washington, DC, Catholic Biblical Association, 1982.

Trilling, W. "Jesus der Urheber und Vollender des Glaubens (Hebr. 12,2)," in O. Knoch (ed.), *Das Evangelium auf dem Weg zum Menschen*, Frankfurt, Knecht, 1973, 3–23.

Turner, H. "To Purchase Joy? (Heb, 12:2)," in *Grammatical Insights into the New Testament*, Edinburgh, Clark, 1965, 172–3.

van der Horst, P. W. "Corpus Hellenisticum Novi Testamenti," *ABD*, New York, Doubleday, 1992, I, 1158.

Vanhoye, A. "La souffrance éducatrice. Heb. 12,5–7. 11–13," *Assemblées du Seigneur*, II, 52 (1974), 61–6.
Structure and Message of the Epistle to the Hebrews, Rome, Pontifical Biblical Institute 1989.

Vermes, Geza. *The Dead Sea Scrolls in English*, 3rd edn., London, Penguin, 1987.

Watts, John D. W. *Isaiah 34–66*, Waco, TX, Word, 1982.

Weatherhead, Leslie D. *The Will of God*, Nashville, Abingdon, 1983.

Weiss, Hans-Friedrich. *Der Brief an die Hebräer*, Göttingen, Vandenhoeck & Ruprecht, 1991.

Weiss, K. "συμφέρω," *TDNT*, IX, 69–78.

Westcott, B. F. *The Epistle to the Hebrews*, London, Macmillan, 1889; 3rd edn., 1920.

Westcott, B. F. and F. J. A. Hort. *The New Testament in the Original Greek*, New York, Harper, 1895.

Westermann, Claus. *Isaiah 40–66*, Philadelphia, Westminster, 1969.

Wettstein, J. J. *Novum Testamentum Graecum*. Graz, Akademische Druck, 1962.

Wichmann, Wolfgang. *Die Leidenstheologie. Eine Form der Leidensdeutung im Spätjudentum*, Beiträge zur Wissenschaft vom Alten und Neuen Testament, Folge 4, Heft 2, Stuttgart, Kohlhammer, 1930.

Wilckens, U. "ὕστερος," *TDNT*, VIII, 592–601.

Williams, Sam K. *Jesus' Death as Saving Event: The Background and Origin of a Concept*, Missoula, MT, Scholars Press, 1975.

Williamson, Ronald. *The Epistle to the Hebrews*, London, Epworth, 1965.
Philo and the Epistle to the Hebrews, Leiden, Brill, 1970.

Windisch, Hans. *Der Hebräerbrief*, Tübingen, Mohr, 1931.

Winston, David. *The Wisdom of Solomon*, Garden City, NY, Doubleday, 1979.

Wright, F. A. "Olympian Games," *OCD*, New York, Oxford University, 1970, 750–1.

Wright, J. R. G. "Form and Content in the 'Moral Essays,'" in C. D. N. Costa (ed.), *Seneca*, London, Routledge and Kegan Paul, 1974.

Wright, R. B. "Psalms of Solomon," in James H. Charlesworth (ed.), *OTP*, Garden City, NY, Doubleday, 1985, II, 639–70.

Yadin, Yigael. *The Scroll of the War of the Sons of Light against the Sons of Darkness*, London, Oxford University, 1962.

Young, David C. *Three Odes of Pindar*, Leiden, Brill, 1968.

Young, Douglas. *Theognis*, Leipzig, Teubner, 1961.

Zeitlin, Solomon. *The Second Book of Maccabees*, New York, Harper, 1954.

Zerwick, M. and M. Grosvenor. *A Grammatical Analysis of the Greek New Testament*, Rome, Biblical Institute, 1971.

Zuntz, G. *The Text of the Epistles*, London, Oxford University, 1953.

INDEX OF ANCIENT TEXTS

Selected texts up to about the fifth century CE are indexed.

Hebrew Bible

Genesis

3.1, 54
16.1–6, 212
16.6, 113
27.40, 212
32.24–30, 54

Exodus

15.9, 112
15.25, 113
15.26, 111
16.4, 94
20.5–6, 87n25
22.22, 114
34.7, 87n25

Numbers

16.1–11, 110
17.3, 189n112
33.8, 6

Deuteronomy

8.2, 113
8.2–5, 94, 95
8.5, 94
24.16, 87n25

2 Samuel

7.14–15, 89n30

1 Kings

12.11, 107n64

2 Kings

21.16, 85

Job

1.1, 96
1.22, 96
2.10, 96
5.17, 96n40, 211, 212
23.10, 96, 97n41
23.10–12, 81n10
33.9–12, 96
38.4, 96
40.2, 96
42.1–6, 96

Psalms

6.1–2, 97–8 and n44
8.5–7, 42n11
17.3, 81n10, 120
26.1–3, 81n10, 120
38.2–3, 98
39.8–11, 98
66.8–12, 81n10, 98, 120
105.16–19, 98, 120
110, 5, 192
110.1, 187, 188n100
118.18, 212
141.5, 212

Proverbs

3.11, 6, 88, 99, 196, 200, 211
3.11–12, 2, 6, 9, 21, 23, 25, 27, 28, 36,
    78, 88, 89, 90, 96n40, 99, 114, 122,
    157, 166, 190, 196 and n136, 197, 198,
    200, 209, 210, 211, 212 and n200, 213,
    215, 217
3.12, 5, 88, 89, 196, 200, 212
3.12a, 212
4.26, 209
5.13, 90
8.36, 189n112
9.7, 90
13.23, 129
13.24, 15, 89
17.3, 81n10, 120
22.15, 15, 89, 197n141
23.13–14, 89
24.30–2, 90
25.1, 90

Ecclesiastes

1.2, 96
2.14–15, 95
7.15, 95
9.2, 95
12.8, 96

Isaiah

1.5–9, 87
1.25, 81n10
35.3, 209
48.10, 81n10
52.13–53.12, 86
53.5–6, 86
53.7, 112n79

Jeremiah

2.1–37, 84
6.27–30, 81n10
7.28, 85
9.6–9, 81n10
26.20–3, 85
30.14, 85
31.18–20, 85
31.29–30, 87n25

Ezekiel

5.6, 85
5.11, 85

5.12, 85
5.15, 85
18.20, 87n25
23.46–7, 85
23.48, 85

Hosea

5.2, 55, 202
7.12, 197n141

Joel

1.2–2.27, 88

Amos

3.6, 130n127
4.6–12, 88

Habakkuk

2.4, 81

Zephaniah

3.1–8, 84

Zechariah

13.8–9, 81n10

Malachi

3.2–4, 81n10

Apocrypha

Judith

8.25–7, 95n39

1 Maccabees

2.37, 102

2 Maccabees

5.15–16, 102
5.17, 101
5.17–20, 101n51, 102
6.3–6, 101
6.7–11, 101, 102
6.12–16, 101–2, 105

6.18–7.42, 102, 103
6.19, 38
6.21–3, 38
6.28, 38
7.1, 38
7.7–8, 38
7.9, 38
7.11, 38
7.14, 38
7.18, 102n52
7.23, 38
7.24–30, 38
7.29, 38
7.30–8, 103
7.31–3, 102
7.32–3, 105
7.38, 102 and n53
10.1–3, 103
10.4, 102, 103

3 Maccabees

1.9–21, 103
2.13, 104
2.17, 104
2.19, 104
6.10, 104

4 Maccabees

1.11, 65
1.17, 105
5.23, 65
5.24, 105n61
5.34, 202
6.9, 65, 187
6.9–10, 56
6.28–9, 105
7.9, 65
7.22, 65
8.28, 39
9.6, 65, 202
9.8, 56, 65
9.22, 65
9.30, 65
10.10, 105
11.6, 105
11.12, 105
11.20, 56n47, 105n61
12.14, 56n47, 105
13.1, 187
13.9, 187
13.22, 105

14.1, 187
14.5, 65n81
14.11, 187
15.2–3, 37n2
16.1, 65
16.2, 187
16.8, 65
16.16, 56n47, 105
16.17, 65
16.19, 65
17.7, 65
17.10, 39, 65, 174
17.11–16, 56–7, 65
17.12, 39
17.12–13, 65
17.13, 57n49
17.14, 62
17.17, 39
17.17–18, 65
17.21–2, 106

Sirach

2.1–6, 93, 95
4.17, 91, 93, 94n38, 95
7.23, 91
8.8, 91
16.25, 90
18.13, 91n34
18.14, 90
22.27–23.3, 91
24.31–2, 90
30.1, 91
33.25, 91
50.27, 90, 91

Tobit

13.2, 99n48
13.5, 99n48
13.10, 99n48

Wisdom of Solomon

1.6, 59
3.1–12, 91, 95
4.2, 55
10.12, 55
11.1–14, 92, 95
11.9–10, 92
12.8, 41n10
12.19–22, 93, 95
12.22, 93n36

New Testament

Matthew

2.22, 178
7.14, 9 and n21
17.24–7, 179
20.28, 179

Mark

10.45, 179

Luke

13.1–5, 219
23.16, 197n141
24.26, 184

John

6.15, 177
9.1–3, 219 and n2
9.2, 87n25
10.18, 9, 177

Acts

8.26–35, 87n26
8.32, 112

Romans

2.20, 202
5.3–4, 34, 220, 221 and n6
12.17, 179
14.17, 208

1 Corinthians

4.9, 62
9.24–7, 173 and n52
11.1, 75n111

Galations

2.2, 173

Philippians

2.6–8, 26
2.6–11, 186
2.16, 173

1 Thessalonians

1.6, 75n111
4.8, 168

1 Timothy

4.8, 204

Hebrews

1.2, 175n56, 183, 207
1.3, 184, 186n91, 188
1.5, 207
1.8, 207
1.13, 184
1.14, 31, 67n90
2.7, 42n10
2.7–9, 183, 184
2.9, 42n10
2.9–10, 163
2.10, 42, 175, 176n67, 177, 214, 223
2.10–18, 195, 220
2.14–18, 201
2.18, 163, 214, 224
3.6, 74, 207, 224
3.14, 74, 224
4.1, 167n18
4.13, 42n12
4.14, 207, 224
4.14–16, 168, 170n29
4.15, 207n184, 214, 220, 224
5.5, 207
5.7, 207n184
5.7–8, 187, 214
5.7–9, 220
5.7–10, 195
5.8, 41n10, 151, 163, 193n126, 201, 207
5.8–9, 42, 193
5.9, 177
5.11–6.12, 214
5.13–14, 134n136
5.14, 42, 70, 208n186
6.4–6, 211n198
6.6, 189n111
6.9–12, 172, 211n198
6.12, 67n90, 167n18
6.15, 167n18
6.19–20, 41n10
6.20, 41 and n10
7.6, 167n18
7.26–8, 214
7.28, 177
8.1, 184, 188

9.14, 185
9.15, 67n90, 167n18, 168
9.28, 221
10.12, 184, 188
10.14, 168, 177, 185
10.19, 214
10.19–24, 170n29
10.19–25, 168
10.19–39, 214
10.20, 176
10.23–5, 224
10.25, 204
10.26–31, 162, 211n198
10.28, 39, 169
10.32, 42, 162, 163, 187
10.32–4, 2, 70, 164, 194
10.32–5, 34, 73
10.32–6, 162, 180, 189
10.33, 73
10.33–4, 163
10.34, 182, 208 and n190
10.35, 68n92, 74, 182
10.35–6, 73, 214
10.35–9, 172, 203, 211n198
10.36, 39, 58, 73, 74, 162, 167n18
10.36–7, 204
10.36–9, 221
11.1, 181
11.1–12.3, 34, 205
11.4, 72
11.4–7, 167
11.4–31, 37
11.4–12.3, 72
11.6, 68n92, 74, 170, 181
11.7, 181
11.8, 181
11.8–22, 167
11.10, 181
11.13, 58, 167n18, 175n56, 181
11.17, 167n18
11.23–31, 167
11.24–26a, 182
11.26, 68n92, 73, 170, 182, 187
11.26b, 182
11.27, 183
11.32, 1n1, 38
11.32–8, 167
11.33, 167n18
11.33–8, 38
11.34, 38
11.35–7, 38
11.35–8, 3, 170, 216
11.36–8, 170n29
11.39, 38, 58, 167n18, 168, 175n56

11.39–40, 74, 168, 170
11.40, 165, 168, 214
12.1, 5, 22, 38, 39, 59, 61, 62, 63, 73, 163, 165, 166, 167, 169, 172, 173, 186, 191, 199
12.1–2, 57, 67, 68 and n94, 166, 173, 207
12.1–3, 1, 2, 3, 11, 26, 35, 38, 39, 40, 41, 42, 57, 58, 68 and n93, 69, 70, 71, 73, 76, 162, 163, 166, 167, 168, 170n29, 171, 190, 192, 193n125, 199, 204, 205, 206, 208 and n191, 209, 213, 214, 215, 221
12.1–13, 1, 2, 3, 4, 5, 9, 12, 17, 21, 24, 29, 30, 31, 34, 35, 36, 37, 42, 58, 68, 70, 76, 78, 83, 157, 158, 159, 162, 163, 165, 166, 167, 192, 214, 215, 217, 218, 219, 220, 222n9
12.2, 4, 6, 8, 11, 12, 13, 15, 16, 17, 18, 25, 37, 65, 66, 73, 74, 76, 163, 167, 174 and n54, 176 and n67, 177, 178, 179 and n71, 180, 181, 182, 183, 184 and n86, 185, 186, 187, 188, 192, 208, 216, 220
12.2–3, 34, 35, 73, 75, 167n16, 187
12.3, 31n94, 68, 70, 73, 163, 165, 167, 186, 188, 189n112, 190, 193, 214, 222
12.4, 15, 18, 31n94, 32n96, 42, 69, 70, 163n4, 167, 186, 187, 192, 193, 213
12.4–11, 11, 21, 27, 28, 29, 107, 122, 151, 162, 166, 167 and n16, 190, 198, 199, 215, 223
12.4–13, 1, 2, 30, 192, 193 and n125
12.5, 167, 193, 197n141, 199
12.5a, 192n122
12.5–6, 2, 5, 35, 78, 89
12.5–10, 9, 10
12.5–11, 13, 28, 34, 77, 78, 84, 166, 195, 196, 197, 204, 207, 210, 213, 220, 222
12.6, 9, 18, 205
12.7, 22, 39, 163, 167, 186, 198, 199, 200 and n149
12.7–11, 195, 210
12.7b, 199
12.8, 10, 198, 199, 200 and n149, 201 and n155, 205
12.9, 14, 198, 199, 202 and n163, 203, 205
12.10, 10, 31, 198, 199, 203
12.10–11, 202n163, 205
12.11, 6, 7, 8, 10, 11, 13, 15, 21, 22, 24, 25, 31, 42, 70, 166 and n14, 167, 181, 197, 198, 204, 205, 206, 207, 208, 213, 216
12.12, 69n96, 208n191, 213
12.12–13, 58, 69, 166, 200, 209

Hebrews (cont.)

12.13, 166, 213
12.14, 206n179, 208n190
12.15–16, 206
12.16, 19, 25, 178, 180, 184 and n86
12.18–24, 165n9
13.1–2, 164
13.1–3, 224
13.1–5, 206
13.3, 163n5, 194
13.4, 164
13.5–6, 224
13.7, 182
13.10–14, 165
13.12, 163
13.12–13, 220, 224
13.13, 73, 187
13.17, 208n190
13.22, 165, 195n133

James

1.2–3, 221n6
1.2–4, 207
5.15, 69n95

1 Peter

1.8, 184
3.9, 179

Revelation

3.19, 23, 212
13.8, 9n20

Other sources

(Pseudo-) Aeschines

Epistle 5.4, 145n172

Aeschylus

Agamemnon 177–8, 142, 207
Agamemnon 250–1, 142
Eumenides 520–1, 142n162
Persians 813–15, 135

Aesop

Fable 134, 145n173
Fable 223, 145n173

Appian

4.7, 63, 171n37
11.60.314, 179
12.13.87, 141

Aristides

15.231, 60n58
52.435, 60n58

Aristotle

Nicomachean Ethics 1.8.9, 48
Nicomachean Ethics 2.2.6–7, 48
Nicomachean Ethics 3.1.7, 179
Nicomachean Ethics 3.9.3–4, 48–9
Politics 7.4.4, 144n167
Politics 8.4.4, 206n182
Rhetoric 1.2.8, 71
Rhetoric 2.20.9, 71, 165n8
Rhetoric 3.9.2, 69
Rhetoric 3.9.2–3, 190

Aurelius, Marcus

2.11, 155
3.4.3, 52
6.36, 155
7.33, 156

2 Baruch

13.1–10, 99n45
79.1–4, 99n45

Caesar

Bellum Civile 3.10, 145

Cicero

In Verrem 2.5.62, 186
In Verrem 2.5.165, 186
Pro Rabirio 5.16, 186

Democritus

Fragment 182, 144n167

Demosthenes

25.97, 47n25

Dio Cassius

41.10.1, 67

Dio Chrysostom

3.11, 60n59
4.31, 200n150
8.11–15, 49
8.20ff, 50

Diodorus Siculus

4.20.1, 63, 171n37
9.2.1, 159n204
9.2.5, 46
13.17.1, 62
14.42.1, 67n87
15.48–9, 136
16.56.3–8, 136

Diogenes Laertius

5.1.18, 144n167

Dionysius of Halicarnassus

8.33.3, 141
14.8.1, 63n70

Epictetus

1.2.5–6, 205n174
1.6.32–6, 50n32
1.6.40, 151
1.9.12, 159
1.18.20–3, 51
1.24.1, 51, 151
1.29.33, 151
1.29.33–5, 159
2.18.22, 50
2.19.24–6, 76
2.19.25, 62n66
3.15.1–7, 51
3.22.51, 51
3.22.56–7, 200n151
3.22.57, 50, 151
3.22.58, 50
3.22.58–9, 62n66
3.24.16, 174n55
3.24.113, 51, 151
3.25.2–3, 66
3.26.28, 151n187
3.26.31, 50n32, 151

4.1.151, 76
4.4.30, 51
4.4.30–2, 159
4.8.43, 76

Encheiridion

29.2, 51
Fragment 10 (179), 65n77

Heliodorus

Ethiopian Story 7.5.5, 66

Herodotus

1.207, 140
8.109, 169
9.60, 66

Hesiod

Works and Days 89, 140
Works and Days 218, 140

Hierocles

1.3.54, 153–4 and n196
2.9.7, 154 and n196

Homer

Iliad 17.1–32, 140
Iliad 20.198, 140
Iliad 24.527–33, 134, 139n149
Odyssey 1.32–4, 135

Josephus

Antiquities 2.293–314, 107
Antiquities 3.11–12, 107
Antiquities 3.13–16, 107, 112
Antiquities 8.208, 67
Antiquities 8.217, 107n64
Antiquities 8.302, 67n90
Antiquities 10.262, 108n65
Antiquities 12.431, 174
Antiquities 15.269, 67
Antiquities 18.299, 59
Antiquities 20.263, 106
Vita, 8, 106
War 1.648–50, 108
War 1.656, 108
War 4.134, 59

Josephus (cont.)

War 5.378, 108
War 5.401–3, 108
War 5.411–14, 108
War 6.110, 108
War 7.328, 108
War 7.331, 109
War 7.333, 109
War 7.359–60, 109

Julius Pollux, see *Pollux*

Libanius

Progymnasmata X.α.13, 145n174
Progymnasmata XI.δ.1, 145n174

(Pseudo-) Longinus

On the Sublime 14.2, 59

Lucian

Anacharsis 10, 44n19
Anacharsis 11, 61n63
Anacharsis 25, 63n70

Manual of Discipline (Qumran)

8.2–4, 121

Marcus Aurelius, see *Aurelius*

Musonius Rufus

Essay 6, 152, 153, 159n204
Essay 7, 152–3

Pausanias

7.24.5–25.4, 136n144
9.2.6, 66

Philo

De Abrahamo 35, 55
De Abrahamo 48, 55
De Abrahamo 256, 55n41
De Agricultura 111–21, 53
De Cherubim 77–82, 112–13
De Congressu 157–80, 113
De Congressu 177, 211, 212
De Ebrietate 79, 114n80
De Ebrietate 80–1, 109n73

De Exsecrationibus 126–62, 110
De Exsecrationibus 163, 110
De Migratione Abrahami 27, 55n41
De Praemiis 3, 110
De Praemiis 4–5, 54n39
De Praemiis 13, 67
De Praemiis 27, 68n92
De Praemiis 31, 68n92
De Praemiis 50, 68n92
De Praemiis 68–73, 110
De Praemiis 119, 111
De Providentia 34, 115
De Providentia 39, 115
De Providentia 41, 114n80, 115
De Providentia 53, 114n80, 115
De Providentia 55, 115
De Vita Mosis 1.48, 54n39
De Vita Mosis 1.90–5, 111
De Vita Mosis 1.96–146, 111
De Vita Mosis 1.110, 114n80
De Vita Mosis 1.191–2, 111
De Vita Mosis 1.193–7, 111
De Vita Mosis 1.199, 112
De Vita Mosis 1.222, 67n90
De Vita Mosis 2.53–7, 111
Legum Allegoriae 2.90, 109n73
Legum Allegoriae 2.108, 54
Legum Allegoriae 3.48, 54n39
Legum Allegoriae 3.190, 54n40
Quod Deterius Potiori Insidiari Soleat 52, 189n114
Quod Omnis Probus Liber Sit 26, 64
Special Laws 2.91, 63n70

Pindar

Isthmian 1.40, 140n154

Plato

Gorgias 526e, 47, 53
Minos 319d, 200n150
Phaedrus 274b, 66
Republic 379a–380d, 139n149
Republic 379e, 134n137
Republic 380a–b, 139 and n150
Republic 403c–e, 47
Republic 608c, 67
Symposium 222b, 140n153

Plutarch

Comparatio Aristidis et Catonis Maioris 2, 52n36

Lycurgus 26.1, 52
Moralia 8d, 66n86
Moralia 71a, 60n61
Moralia 165e–171, 137
Moralia 192d, 63n70
Moralia 467e, 174n55
Moralia 467e–f, 74
Moralia 561a, 53
Moralia 675c, 43n13
Moralia 679b, 60n60
Moralia 724–5, 64
Moralia 764c, 158n201
Moralia 793–4, 52
Moralia 1105c, 52

Polybius

1.1.2, 158
3.62, 66
29.17.4, 64

Pollux, Julius

Onomasticon 3.30.148, 41n10

Psalms of Solomon

2.3–7, 99
3.4, 99, 211
3.5–8, 211
7.9, 99
8.26–9, 99
8.29, 202
10.1–3, 99–100, 211
13.9, 100
18.4, 100
18.7, 99

Quintilian

5.11.6, 73
10.1.33, 45n21

Rabbinic literature – Mishnah and Talmud

m. Abot 5.8–9, 125 and n106
m. Šabb. 2.6, 125 and n107
y. Yoma 38c, 126 and n109
b. Ber. 5a, 128 and n122
b. Ber. 5b, 126 and n112
b. Hagiga 4b–5a, 129 and n124
b. Šabb. 32b, 126 and n111
b. Šabb. 33a, 126 and n112
b. Šabb. 55a, 127 and n113

b. Šabb. 55b, 128 and n121
b. Sanh. 101a, 127 and n115

Rabbinic literature – other

Genesis Rabbah 33.1, 127 and n114
Mekilta De-Rabbi Ishmael, Bahodesh 10, 127 and n116, n117, n118, 128n119
Mekilta De-Rabbi Ishmael, Nezikin 18, 127n113
Sifre, Piska 32, 128 and n119

Rhetorica ad Alexandrum

1439a, 72

Rhetorica ad Herennium

4.3.5, 72 and n105, 165n8
4.49.59, 72n105
4.49.62, 72n105

Seneca

Ad Helviam 2.3, 146
Ad Marciam 5.5, 146
Ad Polybium de Consolatione 17.2, 146n176
De Providentia 1.1, 147
De Providentia 1.5, 21n57, 148, 158
De Providentia 1.6, 149, 196, 205
De Providentia 2.1, 147
De Providentia 2.2, 52, 149
De Providentia 2.2–4, 149, 158, 205
De Providentia 2.3–4, 52
De Providentia 2.5, 149
De Providentia 2.5–6, 149
De Providentia 2.6, 31n92, 149, 196, 205
De Providentia 2.7–9, 149, 205
De Providentia 2.9, 62, 149
De Providentia 3.2, 147, 150
De Providentia 3.4–14, 205
De Providentia 4.1–3, 149
De Providentia 4.4, 150
De Providentia 4.7, 31n92, 150, 205
De Providentia 4.11–12, 149, 196
De Providentia 4.12, 149
De Providentia 5.1, 148n183
De Providentia 5.10, 150
De Providentia 6.1, 148
Epistle 6.5–6, 74n107
Epistle 11.8–10, 74n108
Epistle 13.2, 69
Epistle 15.4–5, 51
Epistle 17.1, 51

Seneca (cont.)

Epistle 34.2, 51
Epistle 42.1, 76
Epistle 52.7, 74n107
Epistle 66.19, 146
Epistle 66.21, 146
Epistle 66.38, 146
Epistle 67.10, 64
Epistle 74.10, 146n177
Epistle 78.14, 206, 208n190
Epistle 78.16, 52, 208n190
Epistle 80.2–3, 51
Epistle 88.18–19, 51
Epistle 94.40, 74
Epistle 94.74, 146
Epistle 109.6, 51
Epistle 110.3, 146
Epistle 110.10, 150n186
Quaestiones Naturales 3. Pref. 12, 146, 147

Solon

13.29–31, 137n145
Fragment 14, 134n138
Fragment 15, 138 and n147

Sophocles

Ajax 278–9, 143n164
Antigone 1350–3, 142
Fragment 680, 143 and n164
Fragment 961, 143n164
Oedipus Coloneus 7–8, 142
Philoctetes 534–8, 142

Tacitus

Annales 15.44, 163n4

Testament of Moses

12.10–13, 99n45

Thanksgiving Hymns (Qumran)

1.31–3, 118
3.7–12, 121n94
4.18–19, 117
4.33–7, 119
5.15–16, 119
6.29–30, 117
9.6–7, 119
9.9–11, 119

9.24–6, 119
11.8, 120n92
11.8–9, 118
14.16, 117
14.23–5, 118
15.17, 117
15.19, 117
17.21–2, 119

Theognis

377–8, 138 and n148
383–5, 138 and n148
731–52, 137 and n145

Thucydides

1.128.1, 136n143

Tyrtaeus

12.1–14, 44–5 and n20

Words of the Heavenly Lights (Qumran)

3, 121

Xenophanes

2.1–14, 45–6 and n23
2.17–18, 43n13

Xenophon

Hellenica 1.7.19, 189n113
Memorabilia 3.12.1–4, 45n20

Other early Christian literature

Chrysostom

Homily 30, 7

Clement of Rome

1 Clement 19.2, 5
1 Clement 56.2, 212
1 Clement 56.4, 5
1 Clement 56.16, 212
1 Clement 63.1, 5n7

Eusebius

Historia Ecclesiastica 6.25.11, 162n1

Origen

De Principiis, 6n11
Exhortatio ad Martyrium 37, 6
Homily 27, 6
Selecta in Exodum, 6

Tertullian

De Patientia 11, 5n8

Theodoret

Commentary on Hebrews, 8

INDEX OF TOPICS

*Page numbers in **bold** type indicate the more important references.*

a minore ad maius argument, 199, 201 and n157

Abraham, 54, 58, 179, 181

adversity (*see* hardships)

affliction, 86, 92, 93, 97, 99n48, 113–14, 118–21, 123, 137, 146n176

agon, 43 and n16, 49, 50, 52–3, 55, 57–8, 61–2, 66, 68, 76

alliteration, 207, 209n192

anachronism, 124

anaphora, 167n17

anointing, 10 and n23, 54

apostasy, 18, 84–5, 172, 209n195

atheism, 137, 153n194

athletic imagery, 2–3, 7, 10, 21, 35, **40–70**, 149, 158–9, 163, 166, 170, 173, 181, 190, 193, 208 and n186, n188, 213, 215, 221

athletics, 43, 51

authorship of Hebrews, 1n1

blood, 39, 69 and n99, 105, 125, 126, 150, 194 and n128

body, 49, 50n30

boxing, 43, 46, 51, 69, 173, 174n53, 193

chastisements of love, 18, 128, 129, 130

chiasmus, 191

Christology, 224

comedy, Greek, 143 and n166

comparative texts, 4n3, 19, 22–3 and n59, 26, 28–9

cross, 68, 177, 181, 183, 184, 185, **186**, 208, 216

Cynics, 49, 76n117

date of Hebrews, 162

diatribe, 43

discipline (*see also paideia*), 3, 11–12, 13, 17–18, 20, 85, **88–95**, 99, 101, 193, 196 and n137, 199, 200, **203–7**, 213–14, 217, 218, 220

disease, **97–100**, 108, 110, 111, 122, 135, 137

earthquake, 115, 136, 137, 154

education, 32–3, 51, 197, 220

encomium, 167

endurance, 40, 63–4, 73–4, 116, 142, 146, 152, 153, 162–3, 166, 168, 170, **174**, 180–1, 182, 186, 188, 191, 192, 199, 200, 203, 213, 214, 217, 220–1

enthymeme, 71

eschatology, 83, 117, 118, 127, 221, 224

exaltation, 177, 181, 184, 185, 188, 216, 221

exemplars, 3, 35, **70–6**, 168, 175n56, 192, 205

expiation, 121 and n96, 126n110

faith, 73, 75, 165, 167, **176** and n67, 181, 183, 194, 216, 217, 218, 221, 224

famine, 88, 113, 114n80, 115, 122, 125, 126

Father/Son imagery, 2, 89, 149, 151, 193, 195–6, 199, 200 and n50, 203–4, 206, 220

folly, 89, 108, 109, 116, **135–8**, 156, 179

forerunner, 41 and n10

gymnasia, 44

hardships, 50 and n30, 107, 130, 134, 142, 146–9, 150, 151–3, 156, 158

Heracles, 50, 55, 196

holiness, 201, 205 and n177, 206n179

hostility, 73, 164, 186, **188–9**, 194

hyperbaton, 169n23, 188n105, 207

ideal person, 75–6 and n116, n117
imperturbability, 50, 58
inclusio, 1n2, 165, 166
inheritance, 67n90
inherited guilt, 87n25, 137 and n145, 138n146, 203, 217

Jacob, 54 and n40, 55n43, 58, 95n39
Jesus, 39, 73–6, 174–5 and n56, 176, 177, 181, 185, 193, 207, 214, 216
joy, 11, 12, 13, 15–16, 19, 24, 68n92, 73, 119, 121, 123, 146, 177, 181, 182, 183, 184, 185, 207

martyr, martyrdom, 2, 38 and n3, 39 and n6, 56, 62, 65, 169, 187, 215–16
memory, 195n132
Midrash, 195n134
military imagery, 50n29, 158
Moses, 54, 94, 107, 111, 181, 182–3, 187
Musar, 84, 85, 86, 88, 89

Neo-platonism, 52
Noah, 55, 73n106, 181

paideia (*see also* discipline), 3, 14, 15, 16, 23, 25–6, 28, 34, 77–8, 84, 90, 91, 98, 99, 101, 105–6, 109, 114, 158–9, 195, **196–200**, 204–5, 208, 210, 213–14, 217, 219, 220
paraenesis, 164, 198
parallels (*see* comparative texts)
patience (*see* endurance)
pedagogy (*see* education)
perfecter, perfection, 176, 177
permissive will of God, 21, 223 and n11
persecution, 100, 222, 224
plague, 107, 111 and n76, 116, 122, 143
pleasure, 50n30, 58
possession, 163, 168, 170
prize (*see* reward)
punishment, 14 and n39, 92, 95, 97, 100, 101, 103–4, 110, 123, 124, 126, 136–7, 139, 153, 156
punitive/non-punitive categories, 3, 14, 15, 20, 34, **77–158**, 196–8, 208, 209, **210–14**, 216–17, 219, 222n9

Qumran, 116–23

redaction criticism, 97n43
refining, 81 and n10, 82, 92, 95n39, 97n41, 98, 120, 150
reward, 65, 68, 221 and n8
rhetoric, 70–3 and n102
running, 53 and n38, 58, 173, 174

sacrilege, 103, 136, 156, 217
salvation, 31
shame, 73, 186, 187 and n96
sharing, 201 and n154
sin, 31 and n94, 194, 197, 213, 219, 222
Son (*see* Father/Son imagery)
soul, 47, 50n30, 52
spectators, 58–61, 169–70
Stoics, Stoicism, 21, 24, 29, 31, 34, **50–5**, 65n80, 75–6, 144 and n170, **145–56**, 174, 196, 204–5, 207 and n183, 217, 218, 220, 224
structure of Hebrews 12.1–13, 1n2, 164–7, 167n16, **191–3**
suffering, 1, 30, 34, **78–158**, 163, 195, 206–7, 215–24
superstition, 137, 156

teacher, 202
theme of Hebrews 12.1–13, 166
theodicy, 218, 222, 223
torture, 39–40
tragedy, Greek, 141–4

unity of Hebrews 12.1–13, 190n118, 192n121

vicarious suffering, 80, 86, 105–6
virtues, four cardinal, 64

weight, 62–3
will of God, 223 and n11, 224
wisdom tradition, 2, 28, 35, 88–95, 210, 215
    protest voices in, 95–7
witness, 38–9, 59–61, 169

Society for New Testament Studies
MONOGRAPH SERIES

Recent titles in the series

75. Covenant and sacrifice in the Letter to the Hebrews
    JOHN DUNNILL
76. The plan of God in Luke–Acts
    JOHN T. SQUIRES
77. Luke's portrait of Paul
    JOHN C. LENTZ, JR
78. The preface to Luke's gospel
    LOVEDAY ALEXANDER
79. St Paul's theology of proclamation: 1 Corinthians 1–4 and Greco-Roman rhetoric
    DUANE LITFIN
80. Discipleship and family ties in Mark and Matthew
    STEPHEN C. BARTON
81. Romans and the apologetic tradition
    ANTHONY J. GUERRA
82. Wrestling with rationality in Paul: Romans 1–8 in a new perspective
    JOHN D. MOORES
83. Paul on marriage and celibacy
    WILL DEMING
84. The faith of Jesus Christ in early Christian traditions
    IAN G. WALLIS
85. Feasting and social rhetoric in Luke 14
    WILLI BRAUN
86. Power through weakness
    TIMOTHY B. SAVAGE
87. The paradox of salvation: Luke's theology of the cross
    PETER DOBLE
88. Apocalyptic eschatology in the gospel of Matthew
    DAVID C. SIM
89. The character and purpose of Luke's christology
    H. DOUGLAS BUCKWALTER
90. Matthew's Emmanuel: divine presence and God's people in the first gospel
    DAVID KUPP
91. The Zion traditions and the aims of Jesus
    KIM HUAT TAN
92. Paul's gift from Philippi: conventions of gift-exchange and Christian giving
    GERALD PETERMAN
93. The pastoral letters as composite documents
    JAMES D. MILLER
94. Christology and the synoptic problem: an argument for Markan priority
    PETER M. HEAD
95. Jesus and the angels: angelology and the christology of the apocalypse of John
    PETER R. CARRELL
96. Philo and Paul among the Sophists
    BRUCE W. WINTER
97. Eschatology in the making: Mark, Matthew and Didache
    VICKY BALABANSKI
98. Endurance in suffering: Hebrews 12: 1–13 in its rhetorical, religious and philosophical context
    N. CLAYTON CROY
99. Jesus und der Täufer: Schlüssel zur Theologie und Ethik des Lukas
    PETER BÖHLEMANN

250